NEW WINE IN OLD WINESKINS

NEW WINE IN OLD WINESKINS

Evangelicals and Liberals
in a Small-Town Church

R. Stephen Warner

UNIVERSITY OF CALIFORNIA PRESS

Berkeley   Los Angeles   London

Material from the following publications appears with the permission of the copyright holders:

The Sneetches and Other Stories by Dr. Seuss (Theodor Seuss Geisel), copyright © 1961 by Random House, Inc.

The Problem of Wine Skins: Church Structure in a Technological Age by Howard A. Snyder, copyright © 1975 by InterVarsity Press

Movement and Institution by Francesco Alberoni, translated by Patricia C. Arden Delmoro, copyright © 1984 by Columbia University Press

New American Standard Bible, copyright © 1960, 1962, 1963, 1968, 1971, 1972, 1973, 1975, 1977 by The Lockman Foundation

Excerpts from *The Jerusalem Bible,* copyright © 1966 by Darton, Longman & Todd, Ltd., and Doubleday & Company, Inc. Reprinted by permission of the publisher.

University of California Press
Berkeley and Los Angeles, California

University of California Press, Ltd.
Oxford, England

Copyright © 1988
by The Regents of the University of California

First Paperback Printing 1990

Library of Congress Cataloging-in-Publication Data

Warner, R. Stephen
  New Wine in Old Wineskins

  Bibliography: p.
  Includes index.
  1. Mendocino Presbyterian Church (Mendocino, Calif.)
2. Sociology, Christian—California—Mendocino.
3. Mendocino (Calif.)—Church history. I. Title.
BX9211.M4145W37   1987   285′.179415   87-13790
ISBN 0-520-07204-9 (alk. paper)

Printed in the United States of America

1 2 3 4 5 6 7 8 9

And nobody puts new wine into old wineskins.
                                    —Mark 2:22

Men make their own history, but they do not make it just as they please.
                                    —Karl Marx,
                The Eighteenth Brumaire of Louis Bonaparte

The real effects of moral causes are not always immediate.
                                    —Edmund Burke,
                Reflections on the Revolution in France

Contents

Preface

Twenty years ago, the most newsworthy figures in American Protestantism were men of the left, Martin Luther King, Jr., and William Sloane Coffin. Today, their place in the headlines has been taken by men of the right, like Jerry Falwell and Pat Robertson. Prophetic liberalism has given way to ardent evangelicalism. Thirty-five years ago, Dwight Eisenhower expressed his sincere conviction that "our government makes no sense unless it is founded on a deeply felt religious faith—and I don't care what it is." But Ronald Reagan is the third president in a row to have trumpeted evangelicalism as a key to his political identity. Indiscriminate universalism has ceded to assertive particularism. *New Wine in Old Wineskins* explores the meaning of these changes in the trajectory of one religious institution, the Presbyterian Church of Mendocino, California.

The church in Mendocino is a mirror for American Protestantism from the fifties to the eighties. At the end of the fifties, the congregation was the sort of Protestant social club portrayed by Will Herberg in his contemporaneous study, *Protestant, Catholic, Jew.* Then in 1962, an energetic Chinese-American pastor came to the pulpit in Mendocino, bringing the same messages of social justice and world peace that King and Coffin brought to the nation at large. But his regime (and that of his liberal successor, who served until 1972) earned a mixed response from the congregation, and the resources of the church were strained. This was the experience of mainline churches across the country, as Jeffrey Hadden found in his study, *The Gathering Storm in the Churches* (1969), and the historic denominations—the Presbyterians, Methodists, and Episcopalians—went into a period of decline from which they have still not recovered. But other churches were prospering, as Dean Kelley argued in his controversial book, *Why Conservative Churches Are Growing* (1972), and the Mendocino church soon joined them. For in Mendocino, evangelical insurgents called to the pulpit a man to their own liking in 1973, and he capitalized on the influx of exurbanites being drawn by the charm of Mendocino itself. The book recounts the story of the men and women and the social forces that wrought these changes.

In its close fit with historical trends, the Mendocino church is atypical as a congregation yet a microcosm of the United States. The factors causing change in this church—demographics, economics, denominational policies, and cultural currents—were in other combinations the factors shaping American religion at large. The particular focus of the book, though, is on movements of the religious left and right. There were beatniks and hippies and the "new breed" of prophetic clergy of the 1960s. There were itinerant evangelists bent on converting the hippies and graduates of evangelical seminaries who became "leaven" in the church. Their energies are the new wine of the title.

Mendocino Presbyterian Church, founded in 1859, is the old wineskin. Its traditions—preaching, hymn singing, and the Bible; lay governance and gothic architecture—provided the grounds on which the battle of the movements was fought. It felt their impact, and it absorbed their energies. Organized religion is more salient to the people of the United States than is any other public activity. Americans express their ideals and their highest aspirations in their churches, and they are used to having their way. Churches are settled institutions because they enlist the quotidian commitments of ordinary people. In that sense, churches are naturally conservative, and they tend to temper radical aspirations, whether of the left or the right. Movements are evanescent; the church abides.

A plan of the book is to be found at the end of chapter one. The book opens with a view of the church in the throes of its evangelical enthusiasm, as I encountered it in the summer of 1976.

RSW

Evanston, Illinois
June 10, 1987

Prologue: Bicentennial Sunday in Mendocino

O beautiful for pilgrim feet,
Whose stern impassioned stress
A thoroughfare for freedom beat
Across the wilderness!
America! America!
God mend thine every flaw,
Confirm thy soul in self-control,
Thy liberty in law!
　　　　—Katherine Lee Bates,
　　　　　America the Beautiful

The fog had lifted early on the morning of July 4, 1976, so the village was visible as I crested the hill on the highway coming in from the south. The view struck me as spectacular but incongruous. The town—false storefronts, high-pitched roofs, rickety water towers, and especially the tall church steeple—was a transplant from New England. But the setting—the crisp air, the browned hillsides, the blooming wildflowers, the brilliant light, and the deep blue of the ocean—was Mediterranean. It was, in fact, California, where I was lucky to be doing a half year of sociological research.

Main Street

There were many other temporary residents. Along the street were parked the cars of weekenders and summer vacationers. There were station wagons from Washington and Arizona, sporty cars from Nevada, a smattering of sedans from points east, and California Winnebagos, Peugeots, and BMWs. Bumper stickers on some cars announced that the occupants were for Ford or Carter or would rather be skiing. These tourist vehicles competed for streetside space with beat-up vans, buses, pickups, and VW bugs that bore the dust of country roads and implored onlookers to save the whales or honk if they loved Jesus. In the driveways of the white-painted houses, or under the flowered trellises of their carports, were the Chevrolets and Toyotas of those who lived in town.

People were out walking and wandering into galleries and boutiques. Some stopped by the displays of the jewelry and pottery vendors who set up their tables on the wooden sidewalk. A dark-haired woman in a richly colored poncho presided over a mobile burrito stand. Garlicky smells came out of a store that called itself the Deli, and people paused to read the announcements on the bulletin board outside. The World's Largest Salmon Barbeque had been held on July 3 in Fort Bragg. The Mendocino Bicentennial Parade and Birthday Celebration, featuring floats, a marching band, songs, and a recitation of the Declaration of Independence, was to begin at noon. Someone had puppies to give away, and a young family needed a house to rent. A handyman offered honest work at low rates, and a Tai-Chi class was forming. Next to the Deli, other strollers stopped to look down on the ducks swimming in the remnant of a drought-stricken pond.

The busiest place in town that morning, though, was not the street, the galleries, the shops, or the brushy path above the ocean cliffs. It was the parking lot beneath that tall steeple, the parking lot of Mendocino Presbyterian Church.

E Pluribus Unum

Inside the white wooden church, a large congregation was gathering in the quarter hour before eleven that morning. The organist played a medley of American hymns as the worshippers filed in. To each person entering, the ushers handed a mimeographed bulletin containing the order of worship and announcements for the week. A rack on the back of each pew held sufficient hymnals for every other worshipper. Friends greeted each other, settled in, and waited for the peal of the great bell to signal the start of the service.

The interior of the church would be familiar to anyone with a reformed, or New England Congregational, church background. In a word, it was plain. Rows of pews fixed to the floor of the sanctuary faced a raised platform (here called the chancel) on which stood a lectern on the left and the pulpit on the right. Next to the lectern stood the American flag; by the pulpit, a church flag. A piano stood below the lectern, and across the front of the sanctuary to the right was an organ console. At the far end of the chancel was a narrow, wooden table that held a candelabrum. Under it was a vase of flowers, and above it was a large, ungainly cross made of driftwood. Hanging on the walls to each side of the chancel were two quilted soft sculptures picturing descending doves. The cross, the flags, the flowers, the candles, the quilts—these were the only decorations in the sanctuary. The ceiling was pitched and open, and the lighting fixtures were a single chandelier in the center and electrified kerosene lanterns along the sides. The windows were of unadorned, amber-colored glass. The two aisles leading from back to front were covered with resilient, sound-absorbent carpet, but the effect was less of ornament than of utility.

The organ moved through *God of Our Fathers* and *Rock of Ages* to *Nobody Knows the Trouble I Seen* and *Amazing Grace* while the congregation assembled. The bulletin proclaimed that "this worship service is dedicated to the glory of almighty God in thankfulness to him for our nation." Prayers, responsive readings, hymns, anthems, an offering, and some special readings and a psalm lining were scheduled along with the sermon. The hymns were to include *The Battle Hymn of the Republic* and *America the Beautiful*. Plans for the parade, a box-lunch auction, and an afternoon picnic were announced in the bulletin. A poem on some personal implications of "independence," written by a member of the congregation, was included. Inspirational quotations from Abraham Lincoln and John F. Kennedy were printed. Much of the verbal content of the service to come, but not the sermon, was thus available for perusal prior to its start.

Shortly before eleven, the fifteen rows of pews were packed, a dozen or more from side to side, across the two aisles. In this rural California setting, the worshippers were all white, but they were otherwise a mixed lot. About one in five were elderly women, many sitting together, several toward the front where the pews were fitted with hearing aids. Another two-fifths were couples in various stages of middle age, from forties to late sixties, some of them sitting with their college-age children, home for the summer. In their dresses, slacks, and sport coats, these women and men would not surprise a visitor to any Presbyterian church, though ties among the men and hats among the women were few. But another third were much younger couples, in their twenties and thirties, many of the women dressed in gingham and the men in plaid shirts and jeans. Some of these couples were accompanied by their school-age children, wearing T-shirts carrying the insignia of the Good Shepherd School. Most of these women had long hair; some of their husbands wore mustaches and a few were bearded. A scattering of single men and women, of similar age and dress, sat among them, close under the pulpit on the right-hand side.

At the rear of the church, attired in maroon robes, the adult choir began to line up. Next to the choir, carrying Bibles, stood the minister, a man of about forty wearing a business suit and a turtleneck, and a lay reader, wearing dungarees and a leather jacket, and they waited while the head usher, an ancient, stooped man, began to pull on the rope at the base of the steeple to ring the two-minute peal mandated for the occasion by President Ford's proclamation. As the sound of the bell died away, the usher moved across the back of the church to a ledger fixed to the wall and inscribed "223" for the day's attendance. The minister and the lay reader went forward to the chancel.

"Happy Fourth of July," the minister began. "HAPPY FOURTH OF JULY!" shouted the people back to him, and the assembly became a gathered congregation. The minister asked the people to greet those around them, and having allowed a minute for the ensuing hubbub, he repeated some of the announcements from the bulletin, drawing attention to the participation of the church choir in the afternoon parade. After a few other announcements, he paused and then said, rather gravely, "Now let us worship the living God."

The congregation responded with enthusiasm and intelligence to the scheduled order of worship. Four unison readings—a call to worship, a prayer of confession, a prayer of petition, and an Old Testament reading—were recited with energy. Three hymns and a psalm lining (the latter introduced and led by the choir director as a responsive chant on a melody freely improvised by her) were sung loudly and in tune. Everyone seemed eager to take part. About a fifth of the congregation, too, all volunteers, had designated roles to play in the service. There were four ushers, three lay readers, and over thirty musicians, including the members of the adult and children's choirs, their directors and accompanists, and the high-school boy who played a snare drum to accompany *The Battle Hymn of the Republic*. A half dozen had helped with the decorations for the service.

So this was not a religious event that was remote from or alien to those who experienced it. The congregation took an active part, and they did so on what appeared to be their own terms. Their voices were exercised and their laughter encouraged. Their everyday dress was welcomed; even the minister wore street clothes and no visible symbol of office. They addressed God in the vernacular as "you" and not as an archaic "thou." They pronounced "Amen" to rhyme with "say men."

The size and enthusiasm of this congregation suggest that the messages purveyed in the service were conformable to their attitudes.
Although few of them could have had the learning and imagination to
have anticipated everything that was to be said that day, it must be
true that it pleased them in many ways. Let us then turn to the
message.

In God We Trust

Certainly patriotism was an obvious theme for the day. Great
national events were commemorated, not only July Fourth and the
Declaration of Independence but also the Civil War and Abraham
Lincoln and the establishment of a godly commonwealth in the New
World by the Puritans. A lay reader presented an excerpt from William Bradford's *Of Plimouth Plantation,* on the signing of the Mayflower Compact, and the choir director introduced psalm lining as a
practice of colonial American churches. The minister expressed his
own patriotism in the opening words of his sermon:

> I love America. It's very positive that I can use the pulpit to say that. I
> think I can do it today without too many people throwing things at me.
> The 1960s may not have allowed me to do that. I wasn't very brave
> then.
> To live in this land of the free is a priceless gift. I believe it to be a
> gracious gift from God, something not to be taken lightly but to be
> cherished, treasured, and sacrificed for. I believe that we live in the best
> of nations, in a political system that holds a very sane estimate of the
> nature of man. I say this in complete awareness of our faults and our
> cracks and our injustices. I know that America can and must improve,
> but I am convinced that she is the best of all possible nations today.

To a considerable extent, this church service was a palpable celebration of American nationhood. One needed no unusual perception to
see that.

God was not, however, reduced to a tribal deity. His transcendence was also repeatedly affirmed. The choir sang a familiar paraphrase of Psalm 100 proclaiming God's international dominion. "All
people that on earth do dwell, sing to the Lord with cheerful voice."
The congregation sang a hymn based on St. Paul's universalism: "In
Christ there is no East or West, in Him no South or North, but one
great fellowship of love throughout the whole wide earth." The nation was celebrated but not idolized. "Righteousness exalts a nation,"
began the Old Testament reading, "but sin is a reproach to any peo-

ple" (Prov. 14:34). A litany petitioned God for deliverance from ethnocentrism:

LEADER: From brassy patriotism and a blind trust in power;

PEOPLE: Deliver us, O God.

LEADER: From divisions among us of class or race; from wealth that will not share, and poverty that feeds on food of bitterness;

PEOPLE: Deliver us, O God.

LEADER: From a lack of concern for other lands and peoples; from narrowness of national purpose; from failure to welcome the peace you promise on earth;

PEOPLE: Deliver us, O God.

The minister in his sermon spoke of God alone as the true object of man's devotion; God, he said, is the divine author and giver of the liberty, peace, and happiness that America has enjoyed.

The freedom and worth of the individual person were extolled, and they were also claimed to be the product of God and of religiously motivated men. Said the local poet, in her contribution to the service,

> Independence doesn't come
>   like a feather
> Floating gently on the breeze,
>   carried by another's will
> To be seized
>   by any local opportunist.
> It comes violently,
>   like the Kingdom of God
> Who invades Neanderthalian primitive ego
>   with love explosive,
> Catapulting mind and soul and body
>   into a thousand jagged pieces
> To be put together in a new shape
>   by the glue of Him
> Who speaks words of dynamite.

The choir sang an American folk hymn, which spoke of the personal relationship between the believer and the savior. "What wondrous love is this that caused the Lord of bliss to bear the dreadful curse for my soul!" The sermon traced the principle of the inestimable value of the individual person to roots in the teachings of Socrates and Moses and through its elaboration by Thomas Jefferson.

The minister tried to explicate the meaning of personal freedom for the members of his congregation by using their names and their idiosyncrasies in a format he said he had borrowed from a 1930s essayist:

Freedom is living in Mendocino. [pause.] Amen. [laughter.]

It's a walk along the headlands at dusk to watch the bobbing boat lights in Big River Bay.

It's the right to assemble here this morning to worship God without fear of reprisal. And it's also the right to go up the hill and worship at the Southern Baptist Church or the Roman Catholic Church or any other church that you desire to worship in.

Freedom is our local Citizens' Advisory Planning Board endlessly meeting to develop an orderly plan for our community growth. . . .

Freedom is Baird Ingram and his salty sailors sailing off to save God's whales with love. [laughter.]

It's Mariel Grant and Ezekiel Trout being able to walk barefoot whenever they please.

It's being able to choose between the Good Shepherd School and the Mendocino Elementary School for your children.

It's Larry Redford and Phillippe Ericson arguing creationism versus evolutionary hypotheses in the *Beacon* and the rest of us reading on. . . .

It's Ed and Eleanor Kearney going for a visit to Russia when they want to and it's us staying at home. . . .

It's many things but it's freedom for us and it is God-given and it's good.

Above all, the explicit message of the service was that freedom is one of a host of blessings that have been visited upon Americans in a covenant with God. The conditions of this covenant were declared to be those that Moses had laid down for the children of Israel prior to their entry into Canaan. The Old Testament responsive reading was based on the eighth chapter of Deuteronomy.

So you shall keep the commandments of the Lord your God, by walking in his ways and fearing him.

For the Lord your God is bringing you into a good land, a land of brooks of water, of fountains and springs, flowing forth in valleys and hills. . . .

And you shall eat and be full, and you shall bless the Lord your God for the good land He has given you. . . .

Beware lest you say in your heart, "My power and the might of my hand have gotten me this wealth."

You shall remember the Lord your God, for it is he who gives you power to get wealth;

And if you forget the Lord your God and go after other Gods and worship them, I solemnly warn you this day that you shall surely perish.

Like the nations that the Lord makes to perish before you, so shall you perish, because you would not obey the voice of the Lord your God.

Time and again throughout the hour-long service, this concept of a fateful contract of the people with God was recalled.

Indeed, if the scriptural text for the day was Moses' farewell speech, the secular text was not the Declaration of Independence but the Mayflower Compact. It was less the achievements of the Founding Fathers than those of the Puritans that were commemorated, and imagery more appropriate to Thanksgiving than to the Fourth of July was repeatedly invoked. The Mayflower Compact was read in its entirety by one of the lay readers, and its phrases were invoked in the sermon: America was settled "for the glory of God and the advancement of the Christian faith"; the commonwealth was founded "for our better ordering and preservation"; to this commonwealth the subscribers pledged "all due submission and obedience." The role of religion in the preservation of the conditions for a free society was the theme of the day.

It was to the conditional nature of American freedom that the minister devoted the closing minutes of his sermon. He spoke of the one great visible symbol of American freedom, the Statue of Liberty. "But," he went on, "she only tells half of the story of our freedom."

> Someone has suggested, wisely, I believe, that she needs a sister, who will sit on the west coast in the harbor of San Francisco Bay and proclaim the other half of her message. That other half would be a statue of responsibility, one that would proclaim that freedom always demands personal responsibility and restraint. . . .

This brought the minister back to his theology:

> The great problem of human liberty is the problem of inward and voluntary control. . . . I believe that the surest guarantee against further government control and outward hindrances upon our way of life is a greater measure of self-imposed restraint.

> Listen to these words of Edmund Burke. "The less control there is within, the more there must be from without." Man needs a master— you and I do—if he is not to have a fellow man for a master, with all the harm that comes both to the tyrant and the slave in such a relation. . . . Nothing else in this world is powerful enough to withstand the human ego but God.

Then the minister spoke directly to each individual:

If you wish to be a good American on this day, on this bicentennial Sunday, a good citizen, then you can serve her in no better way than by serving the Lord our God, the Lord of nations, who brought her into being as an answer to the prayers of our pilgrim ancestors.

Our Christianity needs to be very personal at this point. It needs to be lived out within the limited democracy of the church first. But it must also be aware of its responsibility for the nation as well. For we are leaven and light and salt in this nation. . . .

He concluded with a local reference:

Visitors to our little village often remark at how beautiful the skyline is from Chapman Point on Highway One. And the crowning and highest point on that skyline is the steeple of this church. It stands as a symbol of voluntary order in a sometimes very chaotic village. And so must the church be an island of order and sanity and faith from which our community takes its pattern. Let us as Christians strive and work and pray that this church and all churches may be the true leaven of this nation.

Blessed is the nation whose God is the Lord.

Amen.

No other Sunday service at the church that year had such a patriotic theme, and the scriptural text was much more often New than Old Testament. Yet the service and its centerpiece, the sermon, were representative of the religious message promulgated at Mendocino Presbyterian in the mid-1970s. God was thanked and his providence extolled for traditional institutions, above all the family and the church. This conservative message was always presented in an informal, even folksy style, without heavy trappings of churchliness and with manifest attention paid to the diverse lifestyles within the congregation. Repeatedly, man's need for God was preached by the pastor and confessed by members of his congregation. The living God is the maker of our lives, said the pastor, and one often heard testimonies from his flock about what the Lord was doing in their lives.

A wide range of persons in the congregation had developed what they called a personal relationship with the Lord, and they were far less interested in the visitor's denominational background than in whether you "knew the Lord." This church had become a focal point of enthusiastic new Christians of many religious backgrounds—not only Presbyterian but also Lutheran, Anglican, and Baptist; not only Protestant but also Catholic and Orthodox; not only Christian but also Jewish. Their dwelling places ranged from the humble to the opulent:

a spotless loft in what had been a barn; a converted chicken coop fitted with stained-glass windows and overgrown with nasturtiums; tiny cabins hidden among the redwoods; Victorian farm houses and graceful bungalows on the village streets; and split-level palaces on the ocean cliffs. Yet their church was also one of the oldest Presbyterian churches in California, one with a long and proud history.

It is the vitality of this old, small-town church that is the focus of my book. What was the source and the nature of the enthusiastic participation of a heterogeneous group in the affairs of a rather conservative church? What does the answer to that question tell us about American Protestantism? I already knew, when I went to church that morning, that the congregation had grown significantly in recent years. Five years earlier, the last time the Fourth of July had fallen on a Sunday, there were only one-third as many persons in attendance (seventy-eight, to be exact, the number inscribed by the same head usher) as there were this year, and the worshippers represented only sixty per-cent of the membership at that time. Today, there were two hundred and twenty-three, which was a number equal to 110% of a much-increased membership roll. The membership had grown by half and the attendance rate had almost doubled. What had happened?

Perhaps a score of the day's worshippers had turned out solely for the bicentennial celebration. But two hundred was not an unusual entry on the usher's ledger for 1976. More important was that the bitter war in Vietnam was by 1976 a matter of collective amnesia. Still more significant were the Jesus people who had followed the hippies into rural California. And much of the growth could be attributed to the arrival in town of new permanent residents, drawn by the lure of a small and quaint but cosmopolitan town to live off the rewards of lives of work spent elsewhere. Those I spoke to in the congregation believed that the primary reason for the church's rapid growth was the new pastor, Eric Underwood, who had come to Mendocino in 1973. One hundred of the 203 adult members of the congregation on bicentennial Sunday had joined the church in the three years since his arrival. By 1976, his church had become the fastest-growing Presbyterian church in northern California. How this happened and what it means is the story I plan to tell.

1.

A Quarter Century Distilled

... The anthropologist characteristically approaches ... broader interpretations and ... abstract analyses from the direction of exceedingly extended acquaintances with extremely small matters.

—Clifford Geertz, *The Interpretation of Cultures*

We have just had a glimpse of a special day in the life of an extraordinarily vital institution: Bicentennial Day at Mendocino Presbyterian Church. Such an event is thrilling for the participants and a choice opportunity for the observer. There are no doubt other ancient but bustling rural churches to be found in America today. Yet the intersection of rare qualities that this congregation represents—old, fast-growing, heterogeneous, evangelical—all brought together in one day of celebration, makes it most unusual among Presbyterian churches. Paradoxically, though, this uniqueness makes Mendocino Presbyterian typical of the American Protestant experience in the last quarter century. Since the 1950s, this church has mirrored the trajectory of American Protestantism as a whole, from self-congratulatory complacency through controversial social activism to resurgent evangelicalism. And the engines of these changes—demographic shifts, cultural styles, bureaucratic imperatives, and passionate commitment—are those that have impinged upon American churches in general.

The Complacent Fifties

The 1950s were boom years for American religion. Whether measured by church membership, weekly attendance, monetary contributions, public opinion, or new church construction, the fifties were a period of unparalleled prosperity for organized religion in America.

Figure 1 depicts membership trends for three major American Protestant denominations for 1947 through 1960 and superimposes them on the contemporaneous record of Mendocino Presbyterian. (For a brief discussion of Presbyterian terminology, see "Presbyterian church" in the glossary.)

The three denominations are the United Methodist Church, which grew from 9.1 to 10.6 million members during those thirteen years, the United (northern) Presbyterians, who went from 2.4 to 3.3 million, and the Episcopalians, from 2.2 to 3.3 million.[1] The tiny Mendocino church had 69 members in 1947 and 152 in 1960.

Clearly, Mendocino Presbyterian, though its fortunes changed more rapidly than those of the national denominations, shared in the era of religious good feeling.

All the major religious bodies in the United States reported gains; the boom was indifferent to theological divisions. President Eisenhower may have best expressed the indiscriminately proreligious attitude of the time when he said, "Our government makes no sense unless it is founded in a deeply felt religious faith—and I don't care what it is."[2]

But while the boom emboldened church officers to make expensive commitments, many theologians questioned its profundity. The religious bestseller of the decade was Norman Vincent Peale's *The Power of Positive Thinking*, and Peale's ideas, distributed to their employees by executives of US Steel and to his guests by hotelier Conrad Hilton, seemed only too comfortably in tune with the self-congratulatory air of the period. The religious revival, it seemed, might be little more than a shallow reflection of American triumphalism.

Will Herberg, Jewish theologian and sociologist, confronted head-on the paradox of 1950s religiosity in his influential book *Protestant-Catholic-Jew*, first published in 1955. "America," he wrote, "seems to be at once the most religious and secular of nations." Americans were far more likely than citizens of other industrial nations to attend and belong to churches, yet they knew abysmally little about their purported faiths. A majority of Christians, for example, could not name even one of the first four books of the New Testament, the gospels. And Americans, unlike even passionate European anticlericalists, acknowledged in polls that their religion had little bearing on their political or business lives.

Herberg concluded that the postwar religious revival was a celebration of the American way of life, the value system of the United

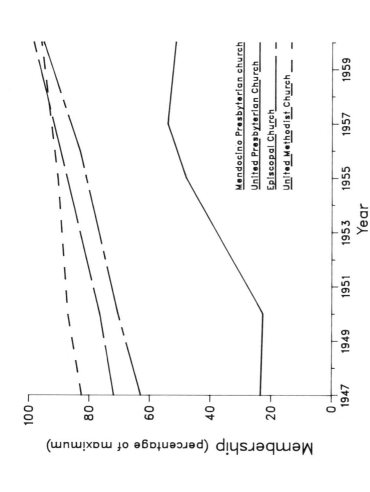

Figure 1   Memberships in Four Protestant Churches from 1947 to 1960 Mainline Churches and Mendocino Presbyterian Church Measured in Percentage of Maximum Membership

States. To "belong to" the Catholic church, to one of the many main-line Protestant denominations, or to one's local synagogue was in effect to exercise one of three equally acceptable options of being religious in America, which in turn was the best way of showing that one was, no matter of what ethnic background, in fact an American. Herberg's thesis was that

> the religious revival underway in this country today—the notable in-crease in religious identification, affiliation, and membership—is a re-flection of the social necessity of "belonging" and today the context of "belonging" is increasingly the religious community.[3]

No religion is exempt from the influence of its social context, but Herberg's point was that American religion in the 1950s was unusu-ally dependent on its cultural environment.

True to this picture, Mendocino Presbyterian grew rapidly in mem-bership in the 1950s, and it did so, in large measure, as a social and civic club, as we shall see in chapter four. To be a "Presbyterian" in Mendocino in those days was less a matter of affirming the teachings of John Calvin and John Knox than of testifying that one was decent, churched, and not Portuguese. The Portuguese, who were also de-cent people, lived in the flats and attended the Catholic church.[4]

But if religious participation was directly supported by the culture, it follows that organized religion would be particularly vulnerable to cultural change. Just beneath the surface of such scholarly inquiries as Herberg's—and a host of more overtly hortatory writings—was an urgent warning: this religious boom is superficial. The warning had both a practical, strictly business aspect and an Old Testament, pro-phetic aspect. Don't make commitments—job security, mortgages—you may not be able to keep. Don't go whoring after Babylon. Yah-weh is a God of judgment.

The Sixties: Numerical Decline and Organized Activism

Indeed, the fortunes of the churches soon changed for the worse, as we see in figure 2. Membership in the United Presbyterian Church and the United Methodist Church peaked in 1965 and began to decline. One year later, the Episcopal Church followed suit. The decline became severe in all three churches and, by 1984, had cost the Presbyterians over one million members nationally. In Mendocino, the period of decline set in sooner, in 1958, and it was seemingly interrupted by an occasional year of renewed growth. Yet, as we shall see in chapters four and twelve, its numerical decline in the 1960s was more serious than our graph shows: attendance and contributions suffered greatly. The declines were not precipitous, and it would be misleading to say that a bubble had burst. Yet the cultural wind did seem to have gone out of the ecclesiastical sails.

At the same time, neither as a cause nor as a consequence of numerical decline, but as a complex response to the same inner weakness that Herberg had described, another, more immediately newsworthy, change took place in American Protestantism. Its clergymen became political activists. There was James A. Pike, Episcopal Bishop of California (1958–1966), iconoclast and champion of civil liberties, celebrated by San Francisco activists with "I Like Pike" buttons. There was Eugene Carson Blake, Stated Clerk (chief administrative officer) of the United Presbyterian Church (1951–1966), later General Secretary of the World Council of Churches (1966–1972), prophet of church union and social justice, arrested in a Maryland civil-rights demonstration in 1963. There was William Sloane Coffin, ordained Presbyterian, chaplain of Yale University (1958–1975), and outspoken critic of the American role in Vietnam. Above all, there was Martin Luther King, Jr., and his Southern Christian Leadership Conference, waging a historic battle for equal rights first in the south and then in the cities of the north. As an inactive member of the Presbyterian Church while away at college, I was proud of the role of my church in the very movements that were important to us in Berkeley.

Not only ministerial superstars were involved. All over the United States, unsung Protestant clergy joined the civil-rights, farm-workers', antiwar and other movements, in cities, suburbs, and the countryside. In Mendocino, there was Peter Hsu (1962–1966), a Chinese-American deeply committed to the struggle for racial justice, and an early critic of the Vietnam War.

American Protestantism seemed to have switched virtually overnight from positive thinking to prophetic outcry. The best single analysis of what had happened was presented in Jeffrey Hadden's *The Gathering Storm in the Churches*,[5] published in 1969 (mostly on the basis of data from 1965). Hadden documented the confusion felt by Protestant laity about the presumed historic essentials of their several faiths: Biblical authority, virgin birth, resurrection. So much Herberg had already told us. Hadden also showed that in the face of lay confusion over theology, younger Protestant clergy were moving as a body in a more liberal theological direction (even though they continued to be distinguishable by their denominational identifications, Methodists being more liberal than Episcopalians). Young clergy were especially united by their political and social views—their support of the civil-rights move-

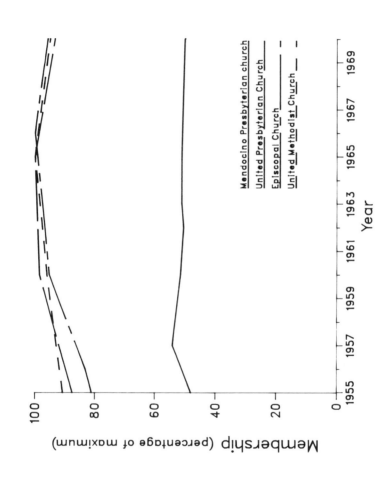

Figure 2 Memberships in Four Protestant Churches from 1955 to 1970 Mainline Churches and Mendocino Presbyterian Church Measured in Percentage of Maximum Membership

ment, above all—despite the formal denominational boundaries that separated them.

Hadden's "gathering storm" was the ideological tension between this "new breed" of liberal, activist clergy and the predominantly conservative laity they served. The laity did not know quite what they believed religiously, and they only paid lip service to ideals of social justice. They were, for the most part, opposed to their churches' and their ministers' involvement in overt protest activities. But the young clergy were deeply convinced of the morality of social-justice causes, and many of them chafed at the restraints they felt their parishioners placed on them. Those who found it least difficult to engage in political action had seminary, administrative, and campus-ministry jobs. "One of the most important observations of my studies," Hadden wrote, "is that the churches have been systematically isolating radicals from the parish, and hence from potential conflict with laity, for many years. Today the radicals have saturated virtually every non-parish structure within the church."[6] Such social concentration produced what sociologists call a reference group of liberal clergy, persons who were more accustomed to taking into account each other's views than the views of laity. The result was a dangerous polarization in the churches.

In Mendocino, Peter Hsu and his successor, Mark Kimmerly (1967–1972), were part of the new breed. Hsu later became a seminary professor and church executive. Kimmerly had just completed a master's degree in seminary after an earlier period as a small-town pastor. It was as true in Mendocino as it was nationally that the years of activism (1962–1972 in the small town) broadly coincided with years of numerical decline, but neither locally nor nationally did activism simply "cause" decline. Later on in this book we will consider explanations of church growth and decline, but even now it is clear that the peak years of activism—both in our small town and the nation at large—came after, not before, the onset of numerical decline. Both decline and activism were responses to the flaccidity of fifties religion. The laity were bored, the clergy disgusted. The former drifted away, the latter fought to make the church worthy of itself, trying to raise the political consciousness of the laity that remained.[7] This is certainly what happened in Mendocino.

Conservative and Mainline Paths Diverge

Some observers in the late 1960s said flatly that the decline of the mainline churches meant that religion in America was dying. But certain churches continued to grow through the 1960s. Figure 3 compares their record to those of the Methodist, Episcopal, and Presbyterian churches.

Our three new cases are the Southern Baptist Convention, the Church of Jesus Christ of Latter-Day Saints (the Mormons), and the Assemblies of God. The Southern Baptists include many Biblical fundamentalists among their members, and the "born again" experience of conversion is a norm among them. The Mormon church is now a worldwide communion, the first world religion to be founded in the United States. Though Mormonism is officially considered a heresy by many Christian bodies, it is increasingly accepted socially as merely another Christian denomination, albeit one with a particularly traditional family-centered value system. The Assemblies of God are a relatively new denomination, stemming from the American revival of pentecostalism early in the twentieth century. Their most distinctive practice is ritual speaking in tongues.

These groups differ greatly, and they tend to regard each other as misguided. Yet they have "theological conservatism" in common. That is, they tend toward literal interpretation of scriptures, a belief in supernatural intervention, and an insistence that traditional religion must stand aloof from the secular culture rather than accommodate it. They are not affiliated with the National Council of Churches, membership in which is a defining characteristic of "mainline" churches. The conservative churches tend not to be involved on the liberal side of social action issues. And they—particularly the Southern Baptists and the Mormons—grew apace in the 1960s.

The numbers reported in figure 3 represent my own research, but the observation about recent conservative church growth is not original. It was, in fact, the empirical centerpiece of the sociology of religion's most notorious book of the 1970s, *Why Conservative Churches Are Growing*, by Dean Kelley,[8] first published in 1972. Kelley argued that the contrasting membership trends—growth versus decline—meant that the conservative churches were doing something right, something the mainline churches were not doing. They were evidently providing "ultimate meaning," which is, said Kelly, what people go to church for. The mainline churches evidently were not, and they were dying because of that failure.

Kelley's book stirred up a hornet's nest of controversy. Scholars tried to refute him, and we will examine some of the resulting (inconclusive) literature in chapter eight. Churchmen reviled Kelley, since he was a longtime employee of the National Council of Churches, whose constituent denominations he seemed to be attacking. Many of his critics were offended by what they supposed was the real message

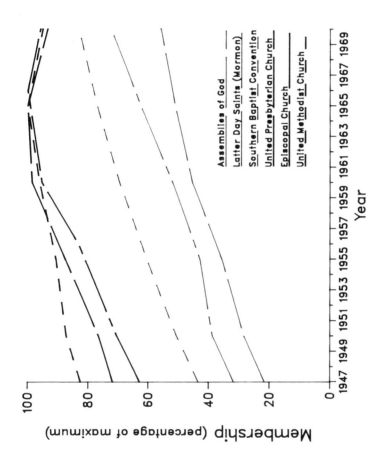

Figure 3   Memberships in Six Protestant Churches from 1947 to 1970 Conservative Churches and Mainline Churches Measured in Percentage of Maximum Membership

of his book. Kelley was insinuating, they said, that the liberal churches were guilty of sins not just of omission (their alleged failure to provide ultimate meaning) but of commission (their dabbling in politics). That plenty of other people—conservative politicians, columnists, and some outspoken church laypersons—were saying similar things outright only made Kelley's veiled attack seem more like an act of betrayal.

Kelley counterattacked with vigorous polemics and stinging epithets. He accused his critics of insulting church laity. He attacked the "fatuousness" of mainline church policies. But he acknowledged an ambiguity in his argument. The word "conservative" in the book's title implied that churches might have to be on the political right wing to be successful as churches. But, said Kelley, that was not what he meant to say. He meant to say that churches have to be "strict," to adhere to their principles, to mean what they say, if they are to be the providers of ultimate meaning. The trouble was that all of Kelley's examples of "strictness" were also examples of conservatism. And his favorite examples of "leniency," groups that don't really mean what they say, were liberal.

Further research has cast doubt on the notion that "strictness" alone produces growth and other signs of vitality. (We shall have more to say about this in chapter ten.) But Kelley's original observation remains valid. Conservative churches have continued to grow while mainline churches have declined.

The Seventies: Mainline Decline and Conservative Growth

The pattern persisted throughout the 1970s. Indeed, from the point of view of the Episcopal church, the Methodist church, and especially the Presbyterian church, the loss of membership approached critical proportions in that decade. Membership figures are not matters of mere statistical curiosity or blind bureaucratic priorities. Other things being equal, a decrease in membership means decreased contributions, which means scaled-back missionary, educational, and social-action programs. To church leaders it meant loss of their jobs. Individual Presbyterians gave increasingly generously as the seventies wore on, but their accumulated dollars bought less in the face of declining numbers and rapid inflation. The result was that the United Presbyterian Church till was, in real-dollar terms, twelve percent poorer in 1980 than in 1965. And the Presbyterians had lost more than a quarter of their membership.[9]

While mainline religious leaders were demoralized, conservatives were emboldened. Little was heard from Blake and Coffin, and Pike and King were dead. The clergymen for the seventies were Billy Graham, Southern Baptist evangelist; Oral Roberts, pentecostal faith healer; and Robert Schuller, updated version of Norman Vincent Peale. By the end of the decade, television evangelists were commanding attention, particulary the strident Jerry Falwell and the genial Pat Robertson. Roberts and Graham could be ignored by most secular Americans, but everyone had to take notice of conservative religion when a born-again Georgia farmer became the Democratic candidate for President in 1976 and induced the Republican incumbent to trumpet his own evangelical credentials. The evangelicals were on a roll in the seventies.

In figure 4 and table 1 we see that the Southern Baptist Convention consolidated its position as the largest Protestant denomination and continued to grow in the 1970s. (The larger a changing number, the more likely its percentage increase will be small, because the large denominator tends to pull it down. Therefore, the SBC rate of increase is modest.) But the Latter-Day Saints and Assemblies of God positively leaped upward in membership in the seventies, the Mormons outstripping the Presbyterians and Episcopalians in total American membership for the first time. Evidently, many Americans were being touched by the Southern Baptists' message of Bible and salvation, the Mormons' exaltation of family life, and the Assemblies' pentecostal practice of spiritual gifts.

What is most startling is the explosive growth of Mendocino Presbyterian Church, which more than doubled its membership in the 1970s after bottoming out early in 1971. The fitful period of numerical decline (1957–1970) came to an abrupt end, and a period of rapid and sustained growth set in, making this congregation the fastest-growing church in the Presbyterian Synod of the Pacific. (See glossary entry "Presbyterian church.") While the United Presbyterian Church as a denomination was declining, the experience of this one congregation was countercyclical.

Figure 5 shows that although the decline of Mendocino Presbyterian in the 1960s mirrored that of its parent denomination and other mainline churches, its growth in the 1970s paralleled that of the Assemblies of God. It is as if this local congregation suddenly started acting more pentecostal than Presbyterian. There is some truth in that impression, for there was a dramatic ideological shift in the clerical leadership of the church early in the decade. A liberal clergyman left, and a conservative arrived. Chapters seven and nine in this book chronicle that shift.

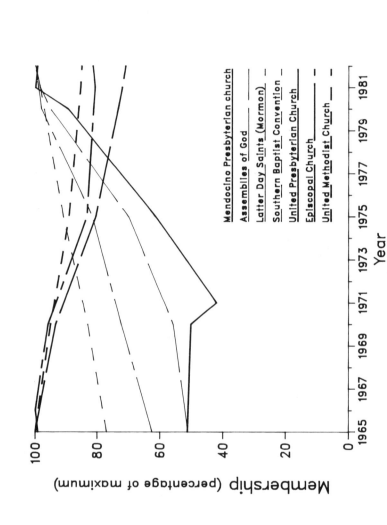

*Figure 4   Memberships in Seven Protestant Churches from 1965 to 1982
Measured in Percentage of Maximum Membership*

I do not want to suggest that only clerical leadership makes a difference to the growth of churches. We will see, for example, in chapter seven that an influx of new residents to Mendocino began to swell the rolls of the Presbyterian church in 1971, two years before the advent of Eric Underwood, the popular evangelical preacher of the 1970s. We will also see in chapter twelve that a new generation of teenagers, the children of those who joined in the early 1970s, began to sign up with the church toward the end of the decade. Migration and birth rates are only two of the factors that are outside the control of any minister, no matter how magnetic. The influence of external, contextual factors on church growth will be assessed in chapter eight.

Yet it remains true that Mendocino Presbyterian grew rapidly under theologically conservative leadership in the 1970s, just as it had declined slowly under politically liberal leadership in the 1960s. This single church exemplified the patterns that Will Herberg, Jeffrey Hadden, and Dean Kelley had identified in American Protestantism as a whole. It was not the typical Presbyterian church. Nor was the particular combination of factors that caused its ups and downs replicated in other churches. But in its overall pattern of liberalism and decline followed by conservatism and growth, it was a microcosm of social history.

Religious Institutions and Religious Movements

The focus of our story is the Presbyterian church of Mendocino, an old wineskin. We shall see its fortunes change as it is filled, emptied, and filled again. Yet throughout these changes it is still recognized by the people of its community as "the Presbyterian church." In a word, this church is a religious institution.

Laypersons and sociologists alike use the term "institution" to refer both to customary practices (such as "the institution of marriage") and to particular organizations (Mendocino Presbyterian Church). What these usages have in common is that the practices and associations so characterized are endowed with value; there is an element of normative obligation, more than mere convenience, associated with them. One influential sociology textbook defines an institution as "a complex normative pattern that is widely accepted as binding in a particular society or part of a society." While that definition reflects the cultural aspect of the concept, another text taking the organizational perspective uses similar language: "When an association serves broad rather than narrow interests, and does so in an accepted, orderly, and enduring way, it may be called an institution."[10]

Table 1 Membership Change in Mendocino Presbyterian Church, Three Mainline Denominations, and Three Conservative Denominations, 1939–1982 (Data Base for Figures 1–5)

Year	MPC	United Presbyterian Church	Episcopal Church	United Methodist Church	Assemblies of God	Latter-Day Saints	Southern Baptist Convention
1939	84					724,401	
1940	89	2,158,834	1,996,434	8,043,545	198,834		4,949,174
1941	89						
1942	83						
1943	87						
1944	92						
1945	103						
1946	100						
1947	69	2,373,345	2,155,514	9,135,248	241,782	911,279	6,079,305
1948	72						
1949	78						
1950	69	2,532,429	2,417,464	9,653,178	318,478	1,111,314	7,079,889
1951	80						
1952	83						
1953	113						
1954	134						
1955	142	2,890,718		10,029,535	400,047	1,230,021	8,467,439
1956	154		2,852,965				
1957	160						

Year						
1958	154					
1959	152					
1960	146	3,259,011	3,269,325	10,641,310	508,602	1,486,887	9,731,591
1961	143					
1962	149					
1963	151					
1964	151					
1965	152	3,304,321		11,067,497	572,123	1,789,175	10,770,573
1966	154		3,429,153				
1967	142					
1968	148					
1969	148					
1970	124	3,087,213	3,285,826	10,509,198	625,027	2,073,146	11,682,032
1971	136					
1972	138					
1973	154					
1974	181					
1975	186	2,657,699	2,857,513	9,861,028	785,348	2,336,715	12,733,124
1976	223					
1977	228					
1978	256					
1979	264					
1980	295	2,423,601	2,786,004	9,519,407	1,064,490	2,811,000	13,600,126
1981	293	2,379,249	2,767,440	9,457,012	1,103,134	2,840,000	13,782,644
1982	297	2,342,441	2,794,139		1,119,686	2,864,000	13,991,709

Source: *Yearbooks* (1961–1984) and Mendocino Presbyterian Church Minutes of Sessions.

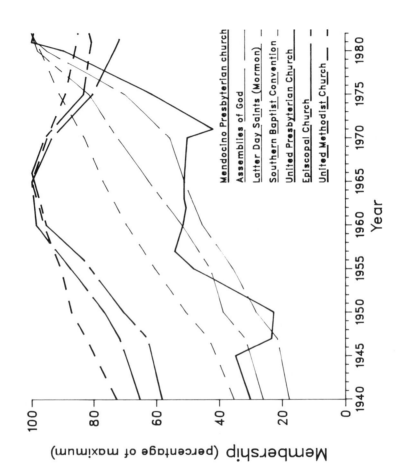

Figure 5   Memberships in Seven Protestant Churches from 1940 to 1982 Measured in Percentage of Maximum Membership

As an institution in American society, both as a set of practices and a system of associations, religion has an accepted place among other institutions, such as the home, the school, and the state. In other words, as a general rule, religious institutions occupy a specialized sphere in our society. They have a place, however vaguely defined, in many people's lives and in the structure of the community. This place is often located temporally and spatially, so that parking in some parts of town is scarce on Sunday morning. The differentiation of religious from secular activities is both a concession of religion to the society (as the price of institutionalization) and a particular triumph of religion in America. Freedom for, as well as freedom from, religion is guaranteed in our system.

The particular form of religious institutionalization in mainline American Protestantism is the "denomination," such as Methodism, Episcopalianism, or Presbyterianism.[11] Over the past century, the various mainline Protestant bodies have reached a series of implicit understandings with the surrounding society, with each other, and with their members. The denominations build edifices within, rather than removing themselves from, the community. They readily accept into their membership newcomers to the community who were formerly attached to another, historically suspect, Protestant body. And they make "no great demands" on the individual member "for high levels of religious commitment."[12] The denomination is the form of religious institution best suited to a pluralist society. The unwritten rules of denominationalism allow differing groups to live in harmony and their members to pursue their diverse lives, while allowing religious organizations to pursue their special goals without hindrance.

There is every indication that this institutional pattern suits most Americans. The more than eighty-five percent of those polled by Gallup who regularly claim that religion is very important or fairly important in their lives; the more than two-thirds who claim church or synagogue membership; the forty percent who attend church weekly—for most of them, religion is properly circumscribed.[13] Even in this highly religious modern society, only a few need a deeper commitment than is suited to the attenuated aspirations of the denominations.

Intermittent commitment to a taken-for-granted religious institution is not, however, sufficient for a significant minority of Americans. The accommodation of American religion to a specialized and protected social niche inspires them with a mixture of sadness and disgust. They continually try to up the ante of religious commitment, cajoling their fellow parishioners into higher levels of involvement and their ministers into more forceful witness. Some of them are ministers themselves, refusing to be sunk in the despondency of compromised faith. Others reject the established churches outright as hopelessly corrupt, committing themselves to more radical movements. A few even start their own religious groups.

As a highly churched, historically moralistic, Judeo-Christian society, the United States is particularly susceptible to such spiritual discontents. Indeed, the impulse to sectarian protest is built into the very structure of our religious institutions. Seldom able to compensate their adherents with tangible rewards commensurate with a high level of commitment, churches instead induce them to take their official ideals with utter seriousness. A few of them go for it. So it is that those who are most deeply involved with compromised religious institutions are also likely to be those most aflame with some passion for purity. An impulse toward sectarian protest is thus an inherent component of even the most settled religious organization.[14] And America has more different religious organizations than any other society on earth. Religious institutions, which are by their very nature conservative, are therefore also an inexhaustible wellspring of social movements, a source of new wine.

Those who demand deeper involvement, spiritual renewal, purity, and prophecy effectively reject the accommodation that religion and society have made with each other. Whatever the particular sectarian impulse—whether moral reawakening or social transformation is its immediate goal—religious radicals always try to break out of religion's accepted niche. They refuse to accept the differentiation of society into special spheres. They want people to stop following a routine course through life and history, to start being one-hundred-percent involved with their destinies.

When people's religious lives are oriented toward institutionalized norms, we can safely pay relatively little attention to their personal views if our intention is to understand the institution itself. To be sure, only the people's involvement keeps the institution going. But institutional behavior is channeled by interpersonal norms, as explained by sociologist John Wilson.

> People in their routine, day-to-day behavior ordinarily sustain interaction with one another by interpreting each other's behavior according to prevailing social norms and responding on the basis of this interpretation. In this sense social behavior is both spontaneous and normatively structured.[15]

When the normative structure breaks down, however, when the old expectations are no longer convincing as a medium of interpersonal coordination, individuals improvise. Social movements, both causes and consequences of normative disorientation, attempt to structure a new interpersonal consensus. Under these circumstances, idiosyncratic motivations of individuals, including movement leaders, require greater scrutiny from the student of social change. For some of those idiosyncrasies may shape the institutions of tomorrow. Wilson insists that we must recognize that

> social movements nuture both heroes and clowns, martyrs and cowards, fanatics and fools. They function to move people beyond their mundane selves to acts of bravery, savagery, and selfless charity. Animated by the injustices, sufferings, and anxieties they see around them, men and women in social movements reach beyond the customary resources of the social order to launch their own crusade against the evils of society. In so doing they reach beyond themselves and become new men and women.[16]

Yet it is the sociological effects more than the psychological roots of religious movements that will interest us, even as we follow the lives of a number of individuals over several years. Our setting is an institution, and in Mendocino the new wine of religious enthusiasm was indeed eventually poured into the old wineskin of the Presbyterian church.

As an institution moves through time, it seldom remains the same, though we in our longing for continuity may imagine "the local church," "the traditional family," and the "little red schoolhouse" to be entities that were at one time settled anchors of social life. Small-town churches change continuously as people of differing kinds come and go and expect more or less of their organized religious life. But the Mendocino church was subject to two especially sudden changes in the 1960s and 1970s. Both of these changes were the result of a new minister being called, and each was accomplished with scrupulous adherence to the laws of the Presbyterian church. From the point of view of the congregation, however, these were unexpected turns that did not accord with informal institutional expectations.

One of these shifts was the call in 1962 to Peter Hsu, who thus became the first nonwhite pastor to a white Presbyterian church in California. The second was the call in 1973 to Eric Underwood, a product of the independent evangelical seminary, Fuller, rather than of the denomination's own seminary system. The first man led the church in the direction of witness for social justice, and the church was never the same afterward. The second man brought a radically different message—a sustained course of Bible study and an ethical concentration on family life—that drew scores of recruits.

These two points of inflection in the trajectory of Mendocino Presbyterian, 1962 and 1973, were not merely the result of the powerful personalities of two men. Each represented a point of collision between the old church and a newer religious social movement. Peter Hsu and Mark Kimmerly were part of the 1960s new breed of clergy about which Jeffrey Hadden wrote. For these young prophets, the churches' comfortable accommodation with society had to be challenged. For Peter Hsu, the church could no longer nestle in a corner of society but instead had to serve its community, particularly the socially despised among them.

Eric Underwood was one of the "young evangelicals" of the 1970s,[17] whose coming to Mendocino represented another turn for the church. In his case, rather than the new minister's call being a collision of seminarians' priorities with local customs, a social movement at the grass-roots level prepared the way for his pastorate. For in Mendocino itself, fostered by the Presbyterian church as an outgrowth of Hsu's and his successor's overtures to the community, a radical evangelical movement grew from 1969 onward. Led by a man named Larry Redford, this group too was dedicated to breaking the church out of its niche, but its radical goal was to make the church itself into the community to be served. By 1972, Redford was bold enough to pull off a coup and bring in his own man as minister. Redford's efforts gave new vitality to the old wineskin itself.

Our story, then, describes the intersection of institution and movement in the life of one church. The ministers, the members, and the sectarian radicals are real people. They act with a mixture of motives and more or less forethought. None of them, however, is gifted with perfect foresight, and what they accomplish is not always what they intend. Only in hindsight can we see how they were partners, competitors, and antagonists in the shaping of the church's history. Hsu, Kimmerly, Redford, and Underwood have left Mendocino, but the church abides.

Plan of the Book

To gain the necessary perspective on the Mendocino church, I will do a bit of theorizing in chapter two. I will elaborate the concepts of liberal and conservative Protestantism and of religious institutions and movements that have just been introduced. Then I will develop some propositions that inform the rest of the book. Foremost among these are the claims that (1) grass-roots Protestantism is likely to be conservative and (2) conservative (or evangelical) Christianity can be surprisingly worldly.

Yet the research for this book did not begin as a test of this or any other theory in the sociology of religion. The theory emerged from an intensive field study of the Mendocino church in 1976. Chapter three, the methods chapter, tells the story of the research itself and how it led to the book's findings. It also introduces another concept, "elective parochialism," which I found necessary in order to understand the orientation of Mendocinoites.

Chapter four goes back to 1959 to take up the history of Mendocino Presbyterian Church on the occasion of the centennial of its founding. We will see an evidently successful religious institution brought suddenly from Will Herberg's 1950s to Jeffrey Hadden's 1960s with the advent of a progressive pastor, Peter Hsu. The gathering storm, though, breaks not over him, but over his successor, Mark Kimmerly.

Chapters five and six trace the growth in Mendocino of an evangelical movement under the leadership of Larry Redford, who joined the Presbyterian church under Peter Hsu and was mobilized by Mark Kimmerly to channel his religious enthusiasm into a rescue mission to hippies. Just as Redford was struggling to keep his mission afloat, a massive Jesus-movement revival swept Mendocino, converting all but a handful of the residents of a local hippie commune. The power of that revival created a new pool of recruits for Redford's mission, and he found himself the pastor of a growing charismatic fellowship.

In chapter seven, we return to the old church to find Mark Kimmerly sprucing and pruning but finally leaving in discouragement, while Redford and his evangelical allies come to dominate the search committee that chooses Kimmerly's successor, Eric Underwood.

Chapter eight does test and give evidence for a theory: that Underwood's leadership was the direct cause of the church's unprecedented membership growth from 1973 onward. To that end, the chapter steps back from Mendocino to look at data from other churches and the specialized literature on church growth and decline. Chapter nine analyzes Underwood's ideology—a combination of worldly evangelicalism and elective parochialism—and explains its appeal to the people of Mendocino.

Chapters ten and eleven look at the protracted tension that immediately set in between Redford's movement and Underwood's institution, despite their ideological compatibility. They fought over the education of the young, treated deviants, or "backsliders," differently, and competed for members' commitments. Slowly but persistently, Redford developed an organizational identity independent of the church.

Chapter twelve details the qualitative development of the church under the regime of Underwood. Paradoxically, its ideologically inward turn allowed the church to provide more support for the parent denomination and its cosmopolitan concerns than it had under liberal auspices. Our history of Mendocino church ends with the church's call to an associate pastor for youth, a sign of the congregation's concern for the children of the counterculture converts and of its renewed sense of responsibility to its surrounding community.

The book's conclusion speculates, on the basis of the history told and the literature discussed, about why it is that conservative religion was so popular in the 1970s and whether that conservative resurgence represents a threat to American institutions. I argue that partisans of the theological and political left must reevaluate the disdain they have shown for the values of personalism and particularism. An epilogue presents what to my knowledge has happened to the people of Mendocino, who taught me this lesson. A glossary explains terms that may be unfamiliar to the non-Protestant reader.

The arguments of the present chapter, the theoretical chapter, the chapter on church growth and decline, and the conclusion are relatively abstract, and they contain a large percentage of my own interpretation. I have written them for the general reader, but they do nonetheless constitute a sociological treatise. However, the prologue, the methods chapter, the history in chapters four through twelve, and the epilogue tell the story of ordinary human beings living their daily lives and intermittently struggling to give them meaning and purpose. They happened to have a sociologist looking in on them for eight years, living among them for the better part of one year, and developing affection and respect for them, while becoming increasingly convinced that they were playing parts in a drama that was bigger than any one of them. I hope they will forgive the intellectual arrogance of that conviction, but I believe that they will nonetheless find here a faithful account of what they did. I hope they will also understand that space does not allow me to chronicle all their efforts. I have changed personal names and scrambled a few facts, but the ultimate justification for this book is that it contains their true story.

2.

The Action in American Protestantism

The first requirement for a concept is that it accurately reflect the forces actually operating in the world. That is, the definition of a concept is a hypothesis that a certain sort of thing causes other things of interest to us.
—Arthur L. Stinchcombe,
Constructing Social Theories

To follow the course of American Protestantism over the past few decades—its pendulum swings from liberal to conservative, and its alternation of routine and fervor—we will need a cultural map. Drawing one will be the first task of this chapter.

On the horizontal dimension of the map, we will place what church historian Martin Marty calls the two-party system in American Protestantism.[1] The two parties are liberalism, on the left, and evangelicalism, on the right. The liberal party and its platform of social justice were dominant in the 1960s, nationally and in Mendocino. But the evangelical party, preaching a message of personal salvation, came to the fore in the 1970s. While one party enjoys a temporary ascendancy, constituents of the other party (individuals, congregations, schools, denominations, federations) do not disappear but instead dig in to hold on to what they can until their day returns. Figure 6 compares several aspects of the two parties' ideologies, as they appear in the United States today.

The root of the liberal position is the interpretation of Christ as a moral teacher who told his disciples that they could best honor him by helping those in need:

	Liberal	Evangelical
Party platform	Social Justice	Personal Salvation
Christology	Principle or Prophet	Personal Savior
Religious Duty	Do the Deed	Name the Name
Admired trait	Altruism	Humility
Grievous sin	Selfishness	Pride
Societal Ethic	Universalistic	Particularistic
Unit of confession	Community	Individual
Recruitment	Ascribed	Achieved
Interpretation of Bible	Symbolic/Liberal	Prosaic/Literal

Figure 6   Ideological Content

> Verily I say unto you, inasmuch as ye have done it unto one of the least
> of these my brethren, ye have done it unto me (Matthew 25:40, KJV).*

The evangelical position sees Jesus (as they prefer to call him) as one
who offers salvation to anyone who confesses his name.

> Whosoever therefore shall confess me before men, him will I confess
> also before my Father which is in heaven (Matthew 10:32, KJV).

Liberals are told that their needs have been met. They are therefore
obligated to share their abundance with whomever is in need, regardless of race, color, or creed. Evangelicals, by contrast, are obligated
above all to share their creed. They care, and they are supposed to
care, whether someone acknowledges Jesus as savior. Because the
Bible is the source of revelation about Jesus, evangelicals treasure it
and credit even its implausible stories. Liberals, however, argue that
those stories are timebound, and they seek the deeper truths that are
obscured by myth and use the Bible alongside other texts as a source
of wisdom.

Both parties have deep roots in the Christian tradition, and many
theologians convincingly argue that a Christian church without an
admixture of both is spiritually impoverished. The Roman Catholic
church still successfully incorporates both positions. Yet groups in
American Protestantism have long been polarized between them, for
reasons that we will explore later in this chapter.

The other dimension of our map, the vertical one, is more abstract,
depicting a contrast that pertains not only to American Protestantism
but to religion in general. Religious life has two forms: a ritualistic,
differentiated, or institutional form; and an effervescent, holistic, or

*[For an explanation of Bible translations and their abbreviations, see the glossary.]

	Institutional	Nascent
Concept of religion/world nexus	Differentiated	Holistic
Artifacts used in worship	Extraordinary	Quotidian
Image of God/the Sacred	Remote	Familiar
Address to God/the Sacred	Formal/Archaic	Colloquial
Intervention of God/the Sacred	Past or Future	Imminent
Mode of participation	Concentrated	Dispersed
Mode of ritual	Acknowledged	Self-Styled
	Stereotypy	Spontaneity
Organizational form	Institution	Movement

Figure 7   Religious Form

nascent form. The first form, the institutional, is the "religion" with which most of us are familiar. We encounter it in the large, ornate buildings that attract scores of well-dressed people on Sunday mornings. The other form I shall call the "nascent state," after the Italian sociologist Francesco Alberoni.[2] It is less familiar and is found in out-of-the-way places like storefronts and weekday home prayer meetings. It is the religiosity of the radical movement and is inherently unstable and sporadic, but many individuals and churches were swept up in it during the 1960s and 1970s. Its heyday in Mendocino was from 1969 through 1976.

Figure 7 compares the two forms. Consider the typical downtown Protestant church. People wear their Sunday best to attend services on a holy day in a sacred place. Within the sacred place, some spaces are more sacred than others, the altar, for example. Leadership in worship is monopolized by religious professionals, whose supramundane attire is a badge of their status. They speak with an intonation that would sound strange outside the sacred walls, and they follow a formal and explicit order of worship. They treat the religious artifacts—the pulpit Bible, the cross, the communion elements, the offering plate—with solemn respect. Aside from any words that are uttered in such an hour of worship, the entire ritual itself expresses the idea of the persistence and majesty of an extraordinary realm, the sacred world, which is set off from the business of this world, the secular world.

Those in the nascent state, however, refuse to acknowledge a special place for religion, for their claims are more radical than those of the institutional church. They adopt symbols that fuse sacred and secular, where guitars are as godly as organs, Ritz crackers suffice for communion, and everyday speech is used to address God. Their meetings seem to be less orderly than the services in the institutional

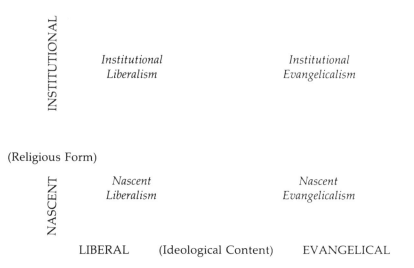

Figure 8   *Cultural Map: Varieties of Contemporary American Protestantism*

church, and that is partly due to the much greater proportion of their members who take a leading role in the proceedings. The experience itself proclaims the continuity of sacred and secular life: nothing is innocent of religion.

When we cross the two dimensions of religious form and theological content, we derive our map, or matrix, of tendencies in American Protestantism today (see fig. 8). This matrix may be used to characterize the religious leanings of individuals, and in this book we will encounter "institutional liberals" and "nascent evangelicals" as protagonists. The map may also pertain to religious events, and my students and I use it in our sociology of religion class to describe the worship services we observe on field trips. Furthermore, if we are careful to acknowledge that the two dimensions are continua rather than dichotomies and that religious organizations are frequently internally diverse, we can use the map to describe whole churches. Finally, we can use the map to outline a cultural trajectory of American Protestantism since the Eisenhower years. In that sense, the cultural action in American Protestantism moved from near the center at the top of the map in the late 1950s, counterclockwise down to and across the bottom in the 1960s and 1970s, to right of center again near the top in the 1980s. With some qualifications that will occupy us in chapters to come, this was also the trajectory of Mendocino Presbyterian.

This book will show how conservatives came to prominence in Mendocino by successfully preempting the symbols of religious vitality. With the malaise of liberal culture in the United States today, similar stories could probably be told of resurgent conservatism in other places and other institutions—school boards, town councils, and colleges—across the land.

Evangelicalism Nascent in Mendocino, 1976

The religious action in Mendocino in the mid-1970s was evangelicalism in the nascent state. Since that type of religion will play a central role in the story to follow, I will flesh out the foregoing sketches of religious content and religious form with a description of the regular meetings of Antioch Fellowship, the group of charismatics who met at the Presbyterian church in Mendocino.[3] The time is early summer, 1976.

Antioch Fellowship's "body meetings," as they were called, took place every Friday night (not Sunday morning) in the Presbyterian church social hall (not the sanctuary). Folding chairs (not pews) were arranged in semicircular rows to define the front of the room as the long, windowed south wall, not the end with a stage. There was no altar, but instead a blackboard had been wheeled over to face the rows of chairs. The lights were always brightly lit.

Those attending numbered between forty and sixty, when all finally drifted in. They were mostly young adults, in their late 20s through mid-30s, though a few teenagers and middle-aged persons were regulars as well. Those with young children brought them along to be looked after by a rotating corps of mothers and fathers. The school-age children would play outside until dark, at which time they would be brought to basement classrooms while the body meeting proceeded upstairs. There were usually a few infants, and it was common to see one or two mothers nursing their babies during the meeting.

The mode of dress was cleaned-up everyday, not Sunday best: wool or flannel shirts and jeans for the men; shirtwaist dresses or sweaters and skirts for the women. Genders were distinct. Some women brought knitting or embroidery to work on, and a couple of the men brought guitars and tambourines. There were no hymnals on the chairs and no one handed out bulletins as you entered the room, so the only way you could know that this was to be a religious event, rather than a meeting of the Grange, was that most people carried Bibles and the literature table featured titles such as *Mere Christianity*, *The Holy Spirit and You*, *The Cross and the Switchblade*, *The Total Woman*, and *Dare to Discipline.* The religiousness of the event had to be announced explicitly, since it was not implicit in the form, which was purely nascent.

It seemed, though no one ever said so, that the informality and air of spontaneity were deliberate, essentially transparent symbols of stylistic continuity with the sixties counterculture out of which many of the group's members had come. They seemed to want life to be fluid, not rigid, to have continuity, not compartments. So the meeting always started up casually and late, often with someone strumming the guitar to announce that he (it was always a he) was ready to lead into song. When he began to play, attention was focused away from the book table and conversational circles and toward the music.

Yet there was a structure, the role of worshiptime leader being a designated and regularly rotated one, and the meeting, as we shall see, having a fairly regular sequence. Structure was unacknowledged but not absent. One evening, after a particularly joyful session of song, I complimented the song leader on his "liturgy." We had become friendly by that time, so I took it with a smile when he said, "I could punch you in the nose for that word."

The leader did not call all the tunes. Many song requests came from the body, and a couple of the women could be counted on to ask for old favorites. Everyone seemed to know the songs, and, in truth, they were simple enough that I learned several within a few weeks. I found out that some of the most popular songs were settings of words straight out of the King James Bible, such as this excerpt from Psalm 48:[4]

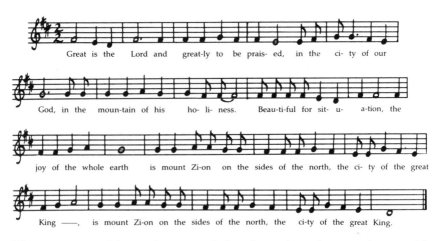

The group would not always wait for the guitar player, who would then have to find the key that they had already chosen. Some songs called for the tambourine, others for sweet harmony. The fellowship was a musically skilled group. Sometimes I referred to them in my notes as the "Antioch Chorale."

After a few songs, the leader would call for a round of prayer. Like the songs, the prayers were participatory, but the language was that of everyday speech, not of King James. A period of announcements and introductions usually followed the prayer. Work parties were announced. The child-care sign-up sheet was circulated. Letters were read. One letter from a member sojourning in England began, in self-conscious reference to the epistles of Paul, "To Larry and Sue and All the Saints of Mendocino." News from other evangelical fellowships was shared.

Every week, there were "sharings" from people about "what the Lord has been doing in my life." Here is a story told one night by Sol Bloom, a "fulfilled Jew," who had joined the fellowship in 1974. Sol was planning a trip to New York to visit his family. He wrote to an old buddy, whose last known address was in Ithaca, to see if they could get together while Sol was in the East. Well, the address on the envelope was no good, but Sol's friend had a job in the Ithaca post office and saw the letter on the sorting table. Praise God! But the friend, still a plain Jew, was dismayed to learn that Sol, like one of his coworkers in the post office, had become a born-again Christian. Oy veh! Pray for this man, said Sol. The Lord has him surrounded. Hallelujah!

On the Friday after the group had returned from a weekend campout, Jane Bloom, Sol's gentile wife, told a miracle story. Her four-year-old, Jonah, had lost his shoes, and he enlisted his mother's help in the search. The two of them wandered to the end of the campground, well beyond the area the children had played in. They found no shoes but did meet a forlorn black woman, alone in a campsite. She was from San Francisco and said she had never been in the country before in her life. Jane did not say why the woman was alone in a state park on a summer Saturday, but one could guess that a weekend date had gone awry. So Jane invited her to join the Bloom family for dinner, and—Praise God!—four hours later she did show up for dinner and then for communion at the evening fellowship campfire. Just think, Jane said. This woman may be standing up to receive the Lord with another fellowship this very night! The Lord is clearly chasing her, even using little Jonah as His instrument.

And the shoes? Having all but forgotten them during the afternoon, Jane went over to the creek for a moment of quiet. As she sat, she felt something under her legs. Jonah's shoes! The Lord works in the smallest details of our lives, Sol concluded.

Sue Redford, wife of Larry, the fellowship's leader, always had something to share, though I often found myself baffled by her poetic imagery. One night, thought, she was charmingly pointed. She reported that she had recently emerged from a bout of depression. "I felt lonely and worthless. Do you ever feel that way?" "Oh, yes," many replied. Well, Sue said, a conversation with the Lord had helped her put her moods into perspective. She had complained to the Lord about being emotionally overwrought. "But he said to me, with this little smirk on his face, that my intensity is necessary for my poetry. I couldn't write without it." Everyone laughed with her.

In their prayers and testimonies, fellowship members asserted that God is approachable, familiar, and involved in their daily lives. Prayers were always addressed in sweet, colloquial tones to "Lord," or "Jesus," or "Father." Sometimes all three names were used, in an ingenuous trinitarianism. Stories about the Lord's presence could be shared with others without diminishing the intimacy of the relationship. In the sense that everyone was thereby in direct contact with God, the Antioch group was charismatic.

The fellowship was charismatic in a more restricted sense, too, since most members had experienced the "second baptism" or "spirit baptism" associated with Pentecost (Acts 2). Some had, they said, the gift of healing. Others were known for their gift of prophecy. Almost everyone seemed to have the the gift of tongues, but on most nights you had to listen closely for its manifestation. Only once in seven months of regular attendance at fellowship meetings did I hear anyone speak distinctly and individually in tongues.

The way "the gift" was usually exercised was in a free-praise chant. This would occur when a particularly stirring song came to an end, the final notes being held in a major chord. People would begin chanting on a monotone or a simple pattern such as *do do mi do, do do do mi do*, while others, women, embroidered the harmony up and down with, for example, *do sol MI DO sol*. Some said, "Oh, Lord Jesus, Jesus we praise you," while others merely chanted "Jesus," barely audibly. Still others spoke in their "private prayer language," their tongue-speech, also chanting in harmony with the others. Some individuals' tongue-speech is highly percussive and consonantal; others' speech is as full of vowels as Hawaiian. During such a chant, many members raised their arms in the charismatic gesture that means "fill me, Lord." Some couples, arms around each other, made the gesture with their free arms, his right, her left.

The blend of sound at Antioch Fellowship was euphonious, and it was typical of contemporary charismatic worship. Beautiful and moving to the participants, the whole room ringing with sound, it was, nonetheless, emotionally measured. Never, in my experience or that of other students of the charismatic movement that I know, did it lead to shakes or fainting. "We're not weirdo Pentecostals," an Antioch member once said to me. But they were a group each of whom had direct, unmediated experience of God, and that is a very powerful conviction indeed.

About three-quarters of an hour into the meeting there would be, though it was seldom called that, a period for intercession, that is, prayer for others' needs. Most Christian worship makes room for intercession, but the fellowship was distinguished by the number of people volunteering and the variety and specificity of their concerns. Wayward brethren were lifted up to the Lord. Illnesses of members and their relatives were reported, sometimes in great detail. Marital problems were mentioned (usually not in great detail). Material welfare, including the success of fishermen and loggers, was unabashedly assumed to be the Lord's business. Sometimes, although not often, a member would want to pray for political leaders. In all cases, the problem was something that was to be set before the Lord.

First, the concerns were aired and details, when appropriate, given. In effect, this ritual functioned as another announcement and sharing period, but women, who in general were outtalked two-to-one by the men, took a more prominent role. After everyone had a chance to raise his or her concern, there was prayer, opened by the worship leader. "OK, got all that?" he would say. "Now let's pray." The prayer floated from one person to another, with pauses long enough to make clear that one was finished and another could begin. It sounded like this:

> "Lord Jesus, we pray for those who have fallen away. Show us how to deal with them in love, Lord, but help us not to partake of their sin."
> "Yes, Lord," some added.

> "Lord, we remember those who are not with us tonight." Names were called out.

> "Lord, we ask you to watch over Bill and Ron out on the ocean tonight in their boat. Keep them safe, Lord Jesus. Let them prosper."

> "Oh Lord, we hold Rocky up to you. Heal his heart, Lord. Be with Linda and the children, Lord." There were many murmurs.

> "Lord, we hold Zeke and Wendy up to you. Let Zeke be strengthened, Lord, and not led astray. Be with Wendy, Lord, and fill her needs."
> "Oh, yes, Lord." "Thank you, Jesus."

"Lord, we pray for Steve Warner. We just ask you to meet him where he is and speak to him in a way he'll hear."

"Lord, we thank you that you're working in politics to redeem our sinful country. Lord, we just ask you to bear up those leaders who stand by you."

The "teaching" usually began soon after the period of intercession, about an hour into the meeting. Sometimes, though, there were other items in the proceedings: a baby dedication, the Baptist tradition's answer to infant baptism; a laying-on of hands to a member in particular need of prayer, featuring anointing with oil; a communion. These were special events, but they were celebrated in nascent style, the anointing with Wesson oil and the communion with jug rosé and matzos.

The major exception to nascent purity I was aware of at Antioch Fellowship meetings was that sometimes when the song leader was one of the fellowship's professional musicians, the praise-and-worship session would take on the aspect of a performance of original folk-gospel songs. Thus we heard, though no one could join in on, "I Like the Old-time Worship of the Lord," "No Man Comes To the Father But By Me," and "I'd Rather Have Jesus As My Savior Than Diamonds or Gold." These performances were musically outstanding, the songs were clever, and they were well received. But members still wanted to do their own singing, and the music was not often given over to the professionals.

The teaching was the high point of the meeting, something people eagerly awaited. When, however, it was done by Larry Redford, the acknowledged leader of the group, it was more a cognitive than an emotional high point. Redford was a former high-school teacher, and he often made wry reference to his addiction to an academic style. His talks were in form more like a Baptist adult Sunday-school lesson or a college lecture-discussion class than a sermon. Here is an example from late June.

Redford had not stood out during the worship, dressed as he was in a flannel shirt and work pants, but he had everyone's attention when he walked to the blackboard. He was older, at forty-four, than most of his fellowship regulars, but he was trim and athletic of build. On the blackboard, he copied a list from note cards in his hand:

> dentist
> garden
> change
> R 12:1–2
> L 8:1–21

"You're writing your shopping list, Larry," someone joked before he had finished. Someone else asked if he had written "chance." "No, that's *change*," he said, with strokes of chalk for emphasis. "There's nothing 'chance' about it." He spoke in a high-pitched voice, soft but penetrating. Many in the group sat poised with pens, note cards, and Bibles; some women stopped their needlework.

Larry began his talk by saying that he wanted to speak on a topic that had come up during the week when a "sister" complained to him of insufficient adventure in her life. He said that his topic would be personal change, and he asked everyone to turn to Romans 12:1–2. He read from his own Bible, the New American Standard version. There Paul says:

> I urge you, therefore, brethren, by the mercies of God, to present your bodies a living and holy sacrifice, acceptable to God, which is your spiritual service of worship. And do not be conformed to this world, but be transformed by the renewing of your mind, that you may prove what the will of God is, that which is good and acceptable and perfect.

Notice, Larry said, that in this passage Paul uses a passive construction in "be conformed" and "be transformed." (At this, several people underlined the words in their Bibles.) When we have problems with our teeth, Larry explained, we go to the dentist to have work done on us. We do not fix our own teeth, he said, but we . . . And here, Larry threw back his head and opened his mouth wide and pointed to his teeth. There were chuckles and murmurs of understanding from the group. That is the Lord's part, Larry said, to work on us.

He grinned and said that we need not worry that he would forget to remind us of "our part." That was his specialty, he knew. So he said that we should all turn to Luke 8, where Jesus tells the parable of the sower. He read through the passage and underlined its illustrations. Of the seed that lands on a rock and sprouts quickly only to die, he said, "You all know people who this has happened to. They seem to sprout up in the Lord but then they wither slowly, and pretty soon—poof!—it's all gone." (There were nods and murmurs of assent.) But Luke 8:8 shows that good soil works. It is marvelous how plants grow, Larry said. "You folks who garden know that." Getting into good soil is how we grow and change.

And how do we get into that good soil? he asked rhetorically. The answer was to be found back in Romans 12, where Paul says that we are to be "modeled" or "transformed" by our new *mind*, we are to worship God with heart, *mind*, and strength. At this someone volunteered that the same passage in the Jerusalem Bible has Paul saying, "Think of God's mercy, my brothers, and worship him, I beg you, in a way that is worthy of thinking beings, by offering your bodies as a holy sacrifice, truly pleasing to God." The reader stressed "thinking beings," and people again made notes in the margins of their Bibles. For the past ten years, Larry went on, the word has been, "Don't think; feeling is enough." But it is not enough to feel. We have to apply ourselves by getting our minds into God's word.

At this point a woman objected. "We're not spiritual junkies," she protested. Larry replied that he wanted to emphasize that the motivation for growth has to come from within. Then a man asked Larry for his interpretation of Luke 8:10, in which Jesus acknowledges that parables are such that some may see but not see, hear but not understand. Larry answered that parables are intended to stimulate those who truly want to understand God's message. But they also preserve our freedom. God did not want his incarnation to be so overwhelmingly material as to bypass the necessary redemption of the world.

A long discussion ensued, and eventually Larry tried to foreclose irresolution by assuming the role of theological expert. This is the old problem of the free will of man versus the sovereignty of God, he said. It's an age-old paradox that we just have to accept.

One of the young mothers made his point for him. She told a story (based on Matthew 14:28–33, I later found out) of a man who could walk on water as long as he kept his eye on Jesus. The minute he looked away, he began to sink. Holding her baby to her breast, she made this point with manifest conviction. "We just need to keep our eyes on Jesus," she said, her own eyes shining. Larry blushed and said he could not have put it better.

After an hour of teaching, Larry brought the meeting to an end. "Close your eyes and look up, or down, or wherever you think God is," he said. With his own eyes closed and head erect, he spoke a simple benediction.

Antioch Fellowship was a charismatic fellowship, but Larry Redford was not a "charismatic leader." As we shall see in chapter eleven, Redford offered no lip service to democracy in his organization. Yet each member was ideologically enfranchised to express his or her charismatic gift. Each was entitled to share a story, a prayer request, or a scripture passage, and Redford was bound to recognize their contributions. They accepted his leadership as legitimate and felt respect and gratitude toward him as a person. But they did not worship or adore him. This pattern, too, was more typical of 1970s charismatics than the notorious cases of Jim Jones and Reverend Moon.

In these meetings, members of Antioch Fellowship used the cultural resources of American Protestantism to make two kinds of statements. One statement was in the language of nascent religion, and it said that every aspect of life has religious significance. God speaks in mundane accents using blackboards, children's shoes, cooking oil, and dog-eared Bibles. God even makes jokes. No time, no place, no attitude, no person has a corner on religion. The religious life knows no bounds.

The other statement was in the language of evangelicalism. God cares about little things and wants us to pay attention to our loved ones. Men and women are different. Everyone—male and female, black and white, Jew and gentile—needs Jesus, not just the aid and friendship of Christians. Call on Jesus for help and you will see miracles in your life, including the built-in miracle of a spirit language. Use the Bible to hear God speak.

These two statements, and the languages in which they were spoken, were deeply intertwined at Antioch Fellowship in 1976, which consequently may be located in the lower right quadrant of our map (fig. 8). Yet liberalism can also speak in the nascent tongue, and the lower left quadrant of the map is not empty. *Sunday Morning*, by Michael Ducey,[5] focuses on the nascent state (he calls it "interaction ritual") in the theologically and politically liberal Church of the Three Crosses in Chicago in 1968–1970. Ducey found there the same prevalence of colloquial speech, quotidian dress, popular music, dispersed participation, and mixed use of space that I found at evangelical Antioch Fellowship in 1976. To put the matter in theoretical terms, religious form (nascent versus institutional) is analytically independent of theological content (evangelical versus liberal). Each conceptual dimension reflects underlying social dynamics proper to it. We will treat them in turn.

Nascent and Institutional Religion

Using the phenomenology of worship as a clue to an underlying social reality is one of the methods used by Francesco Alberoni, from whom I have borrowed the concept of "the nascent state." In religious life, Alberoni writes, we see a contrast between the "mystical, prophetic, enthusiastic, orgiastic" religious movement, "a community of believers who gather together, listen to the 'good news,' and are converted," as one state, and "the institutional, sacramental, and bureaucratic component," the "church, with its structure and congregations," as the other.[6] But the same contrast of two phases extends, according to Alberoni, to all of social life. In political life, there are periods of fervor, when new values and charismatic leaders emerge, which alternate with "periods in which organized life proceeds along the usual lines respecting bureaucratic rules or in the form of intrigue and patronage."

> And finally, in the lifetime of an individual there are also periods or moments in which experiences are of particularly vital intensity. These are times when fundamental decisions are made and the individual feels dominated by an interior necessity superior to his will—for example, upon falling in love or undergoing a conversion.[7]

Amorous rapture, political mobilization, and religious effervescence— these periods of vital intensity are alike instances of the nascent state.

Having been in love, having lived through the 1960s in Berkeley, and having witnessed Antioch Fellowship meetings, I know that Alberoni has put his finger on a fundamental feature of social life, the alternation between states of exhilaration and states of routine. Other students of comparative religion have pointed out the same basic principle. Victor Turner speaks of periods of "liminality," when the group becomes a relatively undifferentiated community of equal individuals, a "communitas," alternating with the "structured, differentiated, and often hierarchical system" we call society. Robert Ellwood contrasts "emergent" religion, experienced prototypically in the "cave," to "established" religion, which is enshrined in "the temple." Mary Douglas, taking her lead from Emile Durkheim, speaks of phases of "effervescence" and "ritualism." Max Weber wrote at length about "charisma" and its "routinization," and his lead was followed up in Ernst Troeltsch's analysis of "sect" and "church." Troeltsch's analysis, in turn, deeply influenced American church historians through its use by H. Richard Niebuhr, in his classic book, *The Social Sources of Denominationalism* (1929). I myself developed a parallel contrast between "monistic" and "dualistic" religion shortly after leaving Mendocino. Allowing for differences in emphasis, all of us were writing about the same thing[8] (see fig. 9).

Summarizing to this point, we have seen that there are two styles of religious expression, which styles, in turn, symbolically represent the two phases of religious social life, nascent and institutional. We have, then, a conceptual dimension along which we can place cultural expressions and social formations in American Protestantism. As such, our discussion so far has been primarily classificatory, but we will not leave it at that.

Alberoni's contribution is to show how the nascent and institutional states provide the keys to each other's dynamics. The nascent state is transitory; it "has a finite duration." But any given eruption of the nascent state—the intoxications of love, radical politics, and reli-

Author	Source (See References)	Conceptual Contrast	
Alberoni	1984	Institutional	Nascent
Caplow et al.	1983	Solemn	Holiness
Douglas	1969	Ritualism	Effervescence
Ducey	1977	Mass Ritual	Interaction Ritual
Ellwood	1979	Established	Emergent
		Temple	Cave
		Familiar	Excursus
Niebuhr	1929	Church	Sect
Schneider	1952	Body	Movement
Turner	1969	Differentiated	Liminal
		Structure	Communitas
Warner	1985	Dualistic	Monistic
Weber	1922	Routinization	Charisma

Figure 9   Conceptual Parallels to Alberoni's "Institutional" and "Nascent" States

gious conversion—is not simply doomed to a slow death. Rather, it may evolve into an institution. Indeed, Alberoni is interested in the nascent state precisely because the values at the core of every institution are the precipitate of an earlier nascent state. "The ideal, the vitality, the hope" of the nascent state are transmitted to institutions. Its "creative force remains imprisoned in the institution and nourishes it."[9] In the story to follow, we shall see how the vitality of Antioch Fellowship revitalized Mendocino Presbyterian Church.

Accordingly, we will treat Jesus' aphorism about new wine and old wineskins less as an oracle than as an enigma. It is a fact that many people in love wind up being married, revolutionaries become voters, and converts join established churches. When we probe into family rituals, political procedures, and religious symbols, we find that they are reifications of earlier nascent states. The congregational singing, pulpit Bibles, well-dressed laity, and clergy title of "minister" found in stodgy Protestant churches today are symbols of a time when popular participation and mass literacy were aspects of the new and radical idea of the priesthood of all believers. Many years from now, seating-in-the-round, guitars and tambourines, country gospel music, and group chanting may have become sacralized symbols dimly memorializing the religious revival of the last third of the twentieth century.

Interdependent as they are, the nascent and institutional states also repel one another. "The irruption of the nascent state into daily institutional life is a traumatic and incomprehensible phenomenon," writes

Alberoni. Those comfortable with the symbolic language of the institution are uneasy with the expressions of the nascent state, seeing them as impious, crude, vulgar, immature, erratic, and unreasonable. Whether we have in mind student rebellions in the 1960s, charismatic vocalizations in Protestant churches in the 1970s, or the disclosure of a serious extramarital affair in any decade, "the system's first reaction has always been to consider what was happening as something impossible and destined to expire quickly owing to its rashness."[10]

From the other side, those in the nascent state are convinced that they are bearers of self-evident truth. Old Testament prophets, Franciscan monks, Maoist cultural revolutionaries, SDS visionaries—"in every case, the 'infantile disorder' that characterizes the nascent state consists in taking seriously and literally the declared values that lie at the center of the institutions." What Dean Kelley identified as "strictness" as a property of strong religious groups—absolutism, intolerance, fanaticism—has its origin in the nascent state. As Alberoni says:

> Those who are in the nascent state discover precisely what institutions are in historical and sociological reality. This is the origin of the endless charges of hypocrisy that the movements have levied against institutions throughout the centuries. Taking the ideology word for word enables one to see that it is not being taken literally by others but has been diluted in a complex system of medium- and long-term means and ends in which the relationship between what is said to be wanted and what is really wanted is no longer apparent. Every institution is founded on a double truth, an ideological one and a factual one which are welded into a complex explanational system that legitimates its power and organization in terms of an ultimate end which is not after all very different from that experienced in the nascent state.[11]

Hence the movement sees the institution as blind to truth, hypocritical, and corrupt. Yet both movement and institution are dedicated, immediately or more remotely, to ideals that have their origin in some nascent state. As phases of social life both infused with values, movement and institution are equally "opposed to the universe of utilitarian relations."[12] This joint opposition is the heart of their symbiosis.

I have been speaking so far as if movements and institutions were endowed with personality, but such a mode of discourse is only a necessary convenience. "Falling in love" is an example of a nascent state between two human beings. A road-to-Damascus experience may involve only one earthly being, who makes sense of the experience using cultural resources. Movements in the nascent state, such as Antioch Fellowship in 1976 or the Free Speech Movement at Berkeley in 1964, are like scores of people falling in love at once and sharing the enormous power thereby created. Yet not everyone is equally in love. The Antioch Fellowship meeting described above was a collective attempt to symbolize the nascent state of the group and everyone present. Yet there was at least one acknowledged unbeliever regularly in their midst—the sociologist—and others had varying levels of commitment, as we shall see in chapter ten.

By 1976, the institution, the revitalized Presbyterian church portrayed on bicentennial Sunday, had begun to beckon many movement members into its midst. The new wine was pouring into the old wineskin. Yet even in 1976 new lovers of the Lord were still being converted in the movement, and its level of collective effervescence remained high. Without individuals in the nascent state, the movement could not exist; yet the very presence of the movement helped bring people into the nascent state. Though not a mystical entity, the movement was nonetheless an emergent social phenomenon the existence of which transcended any one of its members.

Nor is the nascent state unfathomable, as powerful and exhilarating as it may be. Just as we are beginning to learn some of the conditions under which people fall in love, so also Alberoni, Douglas, Ellwood, and Turner have looked into the roots of what they variously call the nascent state, effervescence, excursus religion, and liminality. Chapter six of this volume is one such explanatory inquiry. Movement leaders themselves are aware that the nascent state must be sustained by effort. The Antioch Fellowship elders tried to balance elements of structure and spontaneity by appointing a weekly worship leader and briefing him, if he was a neophyte, on the standard order. Sometimes the efforts at encouraging spontaneity failed because of too heavy or too light a guiding hand, and the meeting would be flat. Such manipulations are an aspect of institutionalization, but they cannot alone create either the nascent or the institutional state. Neither can be manufactured out of whole cloth.

The nascent state is no conceptual fiction. It was present in Antioch Fellowship in the early 1970s, and it exists today in countless prayer-and-study groups. It continues to threaten and refresh crusty old churches all over the country.

Theological Warfare: Evangelicals Versus Liberals

For the past quarter century, American Protestants wishing to break out of religious lethargy and to revitalize churches have taken up the symbols of either liberalism or evangelicalism. Enthusiastic, militant Protestantism in the 1960s spoke out for social justice, committing itself first of all to the civil-rights struggle and later to the antiwar movement. In the 1970s and 1980s, an equally militant evangelicalism crusaded for personal morality in the name of Jesus.

One of the leading figures of the 1960s was William Sloane Coffin, chaplain at Yale. His autobiography, *Once To Every Man*,[13] took its title from an abolitionist poem of James Russell Lowell, which had been made into a stirring hymn of liberal Protestantism. When I was a young Presbyterian in the 1950s, it was one of my favorites:

> Once to every man and nation
> Comes the moment to decide,
> In the strife of Truth with Falsehood,
> For the good or evil side
> Some great cause, God's new Messiah,
> Off'ring each the bloom or blight,
> And the choice goes by forever
> 'Twixt that darkness and that light.

It is the duty of individuals and collectivities to spurn comfort and stand up for the right. The Messiah appears, capitalized, not as a person but as a principle, identified with goodness, truth, and light. The hymn reflects the courageous spirit of liberal Protestantism at its best, and Coffin sang it at a draft-resisters' church service in Boston in October of 1967. The result of that event was his indictment on federal conspiracy charges.

I first grasped the sharpness of evangelicalism's ideological confrontation with liberalism when, on a tape recording from 1975, I heard the organist of Mendocino Presbyterian play the familiar music of that great hymn only to have the congregation begin singing some strange and different words. I looked them up in a hymnal:

> O the deep, deep, love of Jesus,
> Vast, unmeasured, boundless, free!
> Rolling as a mighty ocean
> In its fullness over me,
> Underneath me, all around me,
> Is the current of thy love
> Leading onward, leading homeward
> To my glorious rest above.

The author, one Samuel Trevor Francis (1834–1925), expressed sentiments more comfortable than Lowell's to Mendocino's 1970s evangelicals. Whereas Lowell wrote in the third person, Francis wrote in the first and second person singular. Where Lowell wrote of men confronted with stark moral choices, Francis's speaker swims in Jesus' love. Partisans of these two views set the poems *to the same music.* Such radically different contents within the same form epitomize the theological alternation within established institutions that has for decades been immanent in American Protestantism and that actually took place in Mendocino from the 1960s to the 1970s.

There are many terms used to describe the theological divide, and "liberal/evangelical" is only one of them (see fig. 10). Probably the most influential discussion is that of Martin Marty, in the chapter of his *Righteous Empire* entitled "The Two Party System." American Protestantism, says Marty, has been internally divided for a century.

> One party, which may be called "Private" Protestantism, seized that name "evangelical" which had characterized all Protestants early in the nineteenth century. It accented individual salvation out of the world, personal moral life congruent with the ideals of the saved, and fulfillment or its absence in the rewards or punishments in another world in a life to come. The second informal group, which can be called "Public" Protestantism, was public insofar as it was more exposed to the social order and the social destinies of men. Whereas the word "evangelical" somehow came to be a part of the description of the former group, the word "social" almost always worked its way into designations of the latter. They pursued a Social Christianity, the Social Gospel, Social Service, Social Realism, and the like."[14]

Contemporary evangelicals, including those at Antioch Fellowship, are less otherwordly than Marty's nineteenth-century partisans.[15] Moreover, Marty's very labels—"private" and "public"—misleadingly prejudge what is at issue in the literature, the extent to which the two ideologies promote collective life. We shall see that in the past fifteen years it is liberals who have become "privatized" in an organizational sense. For this reason, I will not use Marty's terminology in this book. Yet all observers agree with him that there is a clearly drawn, persistent division between the personalistic, pietistic, Biblically conservative party of the right and the societal, ethical, modernist party of the left.

Evangelicalism today is found in fellowships like Antioch in Mendocino, within institutionalized denominations such as the Southern Baptist Convention, and in the audience of the television evangelists. What these groups have in common is their stress on "confession of faith in Jesus Christ as personal savior." Such confession is what Antioch members' prayers, songs, and testimonies accomplish and what Larry Redford's teachings enjoin. The slogan, "Jesus Christ as personal savior," befuddles liberals and secularists, but its meaning can best be appreciated as a counter to the liberal interpretation of Christ as, in effect, a prophet, a teacher and example of righteous living.[16] For the

Author	Souce (see references)	Left	Right
Coleman	1972		
Hunter	1983	Liberal	Evangelical
Quebedeaux	1978		
Warner	1983		
Mouw	1976	Ecumenical	Evangelical
Hadden	1969	Liberal & Neoorthodox	Conservative & Fundamentalist
Cox	1966	Political	Metaphysical
Pratt	1972	Modernism	Pietism
Quinley	1974	Modernist	Traditionalist
Marty	1970	Public	Private
Hoge	1976	Protestantism	Protestantism

Figure 10   Designations of the Theological Divide

evangelical, humans are not self-sufficient beings who need only to be prodded to do their duty. They are fundamentally needful of external help, as Larry Redford's dentist analogy made vividly clear.

"Confession," in turn, means the public acknowledgment of such needfulness *using Jesus' name*. By contrast, "naming the name" is deemed counterproductive to the liberals' task of building a more just world.[17] Evangelical skid-row missions trumpet their religious message, but liberals' outreach programs are often carried out through interfaith ministries and secular agencies where mention of sectarian Christian auspices would be offensive at best. Presbyterians can combine organizational forces with Jews to combat racism, but only if they avoid divisive labels. Let the Jew remain a Jew, the Moslem a Moslem, and the Presbyterian a Presbyterian, the liberal argues, so that they can unite to win equal rights for all in voting, housing, medical care, and education. Evangelicals respond that they are uninterested in organizational labels although they are concerned about human welfare. Above all, they say that they are concerned about the spiritual welfare of individuals, and they insist that the Jew can become a Christian.

This contrast between liberal and evangelical produces a surprising conclusion. In terms developed by the social theorist Talcott Parsons,[18] liberals preach a "universalistic" ethic on the basis of "ascribed" identities. Evangelicals are "particularistic," caring primarily for the near and dear of like persuasion; yet they regard that persuasion as an "achieved," equal-opportunity status. For this reason,

Table 2   Evangelicals Are a Large Minority among Americans Today

	1976	1980	1984
Percent saying they . . .			
Have been "born again"[a]	34	38	40
Have attempted evangelism[b]	47	44	48
Interpret Bible literally[c]	38	39	37
Agree with all three (strong criterion for "evangelical")	18	19	22

[a]"Would you say that you have been born again or have had a born-again experience—that is, a turning point in your life when you committed yourself to Jesus Christ?"

[b]"Have you ever tried to encourage someone to believe in Jesus Christ or accept Him as his or her Savior?"

[c]"The Bible is the actual Word of God and is to be taken literally, word for word."

Source: "Religion in America, 50 Years: 1935–1985," *The Gallup Report*, no. 236 (May 1985), p. 38.

though the *client populations* of liberal benevolence are socially heterogeneous, to be found all over the world in every rank and station, the *constituent membership* of evangelical fellowships is more diverse than that of their liberal counterparts. From a relatively homogeneous base, liberals reach out to the world; evangelicals look after their own but are continually trying to enlarge the circle of their own. Evangelical religiosity is more likely to appeal to those whom the liberal wants to help.[19]

Depending on our definition of "evangelical," no fewer than one-sixth and as many as one-third of all adult Americans fall within that category. George Gallup, Jr., himself an evangelical, has been carefully monitoring the religious life of Americans since the 1970s. He has asked three questions of his respondents, corresponding to three criteria often taken to define "evangelicalism." (See table 2.) Over one-third of his samples in the past decade have claimed to be "born again." Nearly half (and considerably more than half among the Protestant subsample) have attempted evangelism. And three-eighths adhere to a literal understanding of the Bible. Between eighteen and twenty-two percent assented to *all three* of these questions and would therefore qualify as evangelicals under the most stringent of definitions.[20]

James Hunter used a different, no less strict definition (with a national sample drawn in 1978–1979) and arrived at the figure that 22.5 percent of adult Americans (thirty-five million persons in 1978) are evangelicals.[21] Clearly, evangelicalism is numerically important.

It is more difficult to estimate the number of those in the Protestant party of the left. Hunter simply defines "liberal" residually, as a Protestant who does not meet his strict criteria for "evangelical." This is not as questionable a procedure as it might seem, though it does inflate the number of liberals. As we shall see in chapter seven, one clue to the ascendancy of the theological right is that many within the churches who would like to oppose them do not know quite what they stand for and what to call themselves.

Probably the best data we have come from a series of studies conducted in the early 1960s by Rodney Stark and Charles Glock to ascertain the religious mood of Americans. One study assessed the degree of "orthodoxy" (that is, adherence to traditional, official doctrine) of 2500 church members in Northern California.[22] Stark and Glock found considerable doctrinal dissensus both within and among the historic Protestant denominations. We can turn some of their orthodoxy items upside down, as it were, to estimate the size of the constituency for a liberalism that would be more than a residuum of nonevangelicalism. (See table 3.)

Several things are apparent from these data. With the exception of the idea of original sin, Protestants disagree theologically more among themselves than they do as a group with Catholics. The Southern Baptists are easily the least liberal of the major Protestant bodies. The Congregationalists are most liberal, with the Presbyterians falling in between. Some elements of the liberal creed more readily receive assent than do others. Taking the first three items as indexes of a respondent's willingness to affirm belief only in this world (a pure humanism), very few church members can be found in this category. Even among the least orthodox group, the Congregationalists, most persons still adhered to the notion of the existence of a personal, supernatural realm. Yet the next three items (measuring what we can think of as acceptance within religious discourse of the world on its own terms) show substantial support, ranging from a quarter to two-thirds of members of Protestant churches and as many as one-fifth of Catholics. Finally, most Protestants (and Catholics, too) believe that altruism is necessary for salvation, and one-quarter extend this ethical requirement to race relations. There is a powerful current of ethical universalism among lay Christians.

Based on a sample of northern California in 1963, these figures suggest, though they do not prove, that the liberal party in Protestantism

Insert Table 3

Table 3   *The Liberal Constituency is Greater for Ethical than Theological Issues*

Percent of Church Members Responding with "Liberal" Answers to Questions:

	Southern Baptists	Presby-terians	Congre-gationalists	All Protestants	Roman Catholics	
Belief in God as "Higher Power," not Person	0	7	16	7	3	⎫
Jesus as Great, Extra-ordinary Man, not Divine	1	7	28	11	4	⎬ "Pure Humanism"
Probably or Definitely no Life After Death	0	7	21	9	5	⎭
Probably or Definitely no Second Coming	2	20	48	23	23	⎫
Probably or Definitely no Devil	1	48	78	43	14	⎬ "Worldly Optimism"
Reject Doctrine of Original Sin	55	68	94	65	19	⎭
Doing Good for Others Absolutely Necessary for Salvation	29	48	58	52	57	⎫ "Ethicalism"
Discrimination Against Other Races Would Definitely Prevent Salvation	16	22	27	25	24	⎭

Source: Stark and Glock (1968), pp. 28, 33, 34, 37, 40, 47, 53.

has its greatest support in the area not of doctrine but of an optimistic, socially responsible attitude. What holds the liberal constituency together, in other words, is less religion, narrowly conceived, than worldly morality. This is precisely what Jeffrey Hadden found in his study of clergy/laity relations later in the decade. Across denominations, members of the clergy professed very different theological ideas, but the younger clergy were more likely to be in ecumenical agreement, liberal both theologically and especially politically. In the 1960s, a pro-civil-rights consensus emerged among younger clergy across denominations and theological positions. On racial issues, many clergy could come together as a body.[23] Consequently, the core of contemporary liberalism is an attitude toward the world; of evangelicalism, doctrines about God.

The implication is that liberalism and evangelicalism should be able to coexist, because they do not directly contradict each other in the collective mind. They do coexist in left-wing evangelical fellowships (such as the Washington, D.C., *Sojourners* group), within large, heterogeneous denominations with room for all kinds of people, and among the sixteen percent of Stark's and Glock's Southern Baptists who think the fate of their souls depends on just treatment of members of other races, and among the forty percent of Congregationalists who still have no doubt that Jesus was the divine Son of God.[24] Both the evangelical party and the liberal party have substantial popular support among American Protestants.

Moreover, there is a self-conscious, academically creditable theological school, called Neoorthodoxy, which (one would think) might be in a position to bridge the gap between the two parties. Neoorthodoxy, articulated most influentially by Reinhold Niebuhr, affirmed both the historic faith of Christians in a sovereign God and the contemporary need of men to take the world seriously on its own terms. Niebuhr's thought greatly appealed to American intellectuals in the 1930s, and as a young Presbyterian in the 1950s I got in on the tail end of its intellectual reign. But Neoorthodoxy was deeply imbued with a tragic, European stance toward history and a realism about politics bordering on the cynical, and it never took root among the American laity.[25] Furthermore, many of its young clerical disciples were radicalized by the events of the 1960s and effectively cast their lot with the liberal party of optimistic social reform. Morally committed to the civil-rights movement, neoorthodox realists were stung by Martin Luther King's "Letter From Birmingham Jail," which condemned political ambivalence as deriving from "a strange, unBiblical distinction between body and soul, between the sacred and the secular."[26] In the

1960s, the nonevangelicals—from death-of-God theologians through old social gospel reformers to young scions of neo-orthodoxy—made common moral cause.

At the same time, however, evangelicalism was emerging from several decades of self-imposed exile to become less defensive and more assertive in American culture. As we saw in chapter one, the dominantly evangelical Southern Baptist Convention surpassed the United Methodist Church in 1966 to become the largest Protestant denomination in the United States. As individuals, evangelicals moved up the social ladder into the middle class. Their schools, such as Wheaton College and Fuller Theological Seminary, became increasingly respectable.[27] Notwithstanding deep differences over the nature of Biblical authority, the authenticity of contemporary pentecostal practices, and the urgency of social problems, theological conservatives from fundamentalists to neoevangelicals were united in suspicion of liberalism's apparently exclusive emphasis on worldly social action as a religious duty.

Thus, despite the sophistication of academic theology and the overlap in public support of both parties, the partisan polarization between liberalism and evangelicalism in the 1970s was as severe as it had ever been. One source of this polarization was that articulate spokesmen of extreme views, who themselves had only minority support on their side, were taken by the opposite side as representative. They could then be made scapegoats. Thus, in the 1960s, Harvey Cox spoke out for a secularized Christianity in *The Secular City*, popularizing ideas of the German martyr Dietrich Bonhoeffer, and became anathema among evangelicals:

> We do not speak to [our neighbor] of God by trying to make him religious but, on the contrary, by encouraging him to come fully of age, putting away childish things. . . . We speak of God to secular man by speaking about man. . . . God wants man to be interested not in Him but in his fellow man. . . . In Jesus of Nazareth, the religious quest is ended and man is freed to serve and love his neighbor.[28]

On the evangelical side, Harold Lindsell, theorist of Biblical infallibility, enraged moderate churchmen in the 1970s with his *Battle for the Bible*, a book-length manifesto for a purge of theological deviants from traditionally conservative denominations.[29] Lindsell sided with those who caused the ouster of most of the faculty of Concordia Seminary in St. Louis (Missouri Synod Lutheran), and he fueled the fires of the bitter conflict that rages today in the Southern Baptist Convention. Lindsell thus became the very incarnation of fundamentalist intolerance. In the 1980s, Jerry Falwell's "Moral Majority" has similarly served the American Civil Liberties Union as a dread symbol of a would-be right-wing theocracy.

Partisan polarization does not stem from a bimodal distribution of individual religious attitudes. It is a second- or third-order phenomenon in which highly committed spokesmen for extreme positions excoriate each other and thus provide symbolic targets of highly negative valence for the rank and file. Conservative polemicists are inclined to see liberals as apostate, promiscuous, and insidiously clever. Harold Lindsell called Paul Tillich, preeminent twentieth-century liberal theologian and professor for many years at Harvard, Chicago, and Union Theological Seminaries, a "neo-pagan," "whose personal life was a scandal" and whose theology was unChristian. The influence in the churches of men such as Cox and Tillich was likened by Lindsell to "treason," a "cancer," an "infection," and Union Theological Seminary was called "a poisoned well."[30]

Partisans of the left, for their part, returned the insults in tones of condescension and disgust. We have already read Harvey Cox's remark about "childish things" in reference to supernatural beliefs. Add to that intellectualist jibe the thinly veiled snobbery behind liberals' expressed disdain for the cultural tastes of television evangelists.[31]

Beyond snide dismissals, liberals bring out their most serious critical contention about evangelicalism: that its roots lie in a craven refusal to overcome narrow self-interest. Radicals of the left think their conservative opponents merely use religion to mask their class interests. Here, for example, are the words of John Fry, militant white Presbyterian minister and 1960s pastor of a Chicago ghetto church, excoriating conservatives in his denomination:

> I'll tell you about those conservative evangelicals. They are a small contingent of Presbyterians whose ability to shout very loud makes them appear to be an army. . . . We see all this fog besetting the church, hear all this sick populist noise, hear so many Jesus Christs it would seem we were in a Methodist revival, only to discover that the fog is not a general climatic condition, sent from On High, but is coming out of a tiny fog machine located in the church basement. [The conservative evangelicals] want to say that social action is all right *in its place*, but that the more directly mandated activities of preaching, teaching, and evangelism must always be considered the main business of the church. . . . You will not catch conservative evangelicals admitting that society shouldn't be changed however. All of which is so much sand in our eyes.[32]

Fry's statement is unusual in its bitter sarcasm but not in its deep-seated suspicion of evangelicals' motives.

We see that the two parties are polarized partly by their rhetoric. But they are also socially insulated from each other to a remarkable extent, so that a partisan of one side may know no one personally from the other. James Hunter shows that, taking the United States as a whole, evangelicals are disproportionately found among women, the elderly, those living in rural areas and the South, and those "in the lower echelons of educational achievement, income level, and occupational status."[33] Such findings (and Hunter here only confirmed long-standing beliefs about evangelicals' status) seem to make it easy to dismiss evangelicals as those living in the backwaters of society. Yet it is also true that evangelicals or, more broadly, *theological conservatives are the pillars of the local church.* Stark and Glock found, among their northern California church members, that the theologically orthodox were more likely to attend church, belong to church organizations, and contribute money than were the nonorthodox. Hunter's 1978 data revealed the same picture, with evangelicals being about twice as likely as liberals to do volunteer work (64% vs. 36%) and give more than five percent of their income (62% vs. 29%) to the church.[34]

Wade Clark Roof provided a careful explanation of the parochialism-conservatism complex in a study of North Carolina Episcopalians. Roof found that theological orthodoxy and church involvement went hand in hand, and that together they were both predicted by members' attitudinal orientation toward the local community. According to Roof, "the results are unambiguous."

> The active participants even in the mainline religious institutions are the orthodox believers, who increasingly as the nonorthodox stray away are left as the remnant of the faithful.[35]

Conservatives therefore make up in commitment whatever they lack in numbers, and the local church is their natural locus of activity.

And what of liberals? They tend to be located, an equally consistent set of findings has shown, disproportionately among clergy, particularly clergy employed in nonparish positions as denominational executives and seminary teachers. Hadden first documented this pattern using data from a number of mid-1960s surveys of American Protestants. He found an alarming gap between conservative laity and liberal clergy on attitudes toward the civil-rights movement. He found that clergy in what he called "structurally free" positions away from the constraints of the parish ministry were more likely to be involved in 1960s protest activities. He found that, among delegates to the (dominantly liberal) National Council of Churches Triennial Assembly of 1966, clergy were more likely than laity to be agnostic, less likely to be orthodox. A structural division within the church was the result.

> As has been demonstrated throughout this book, one of the major schisms . . . is between clergy and laity. . . . The depth of the schism is increasing [in 1969]. A significant proportion of young men who are choosing the ministry today are doing so out of a commitment to the solution of critical social problems in society. The seminaries reinforce and help internalize this commitment, because a large proportion of the seminary professors share this set of values and role expectations for the clergy. The same is true of many church administrators who seek to create structures in which the new breed can work.[36]

Later studies have replicated Hadden's general finding of a laity/ clergy division, whether on matters of theology, strictly speaking, or social attitudes. A national sample of 1,500 Presbyterians in 1973 revealed huge differences between clergy and laity on the issue of the authority of the Bible and the relative importance of the spiritual and material condition of humans.[37] A 1973 Indianapolis survey of 2,400 persons from seven mainline denominations (Episcopal, Lutheran, Methodist, Presbyterian, etc.) found a similar pattern of a liberal clergy taking cues from their denominational judicatories against a conservative laity oriented to a more dispersed social network.[38] A 1980 survey of Presbyterians' views of the Bible shows the same thing again (see table 4). *Protestant liberalism has its most secure niche away from the local church.* The theological divide has its most striking sociological expression in the gap between committed laypersons in local congregations, who tend to be theologically conservative, and clergy in seminaries and denominational administrations, who tend to be liberal.

Interactions and Ironies

Due to the social processes we have just explored—partisan polarization and movement dynamics—the potentially infinite variety within American Protestantism tends to reduce to the two-dimensional typology that we mapped in figure 8. On the basis of the preceding generalizations, we can now state some expectations, or hypotheses, about where we will expect to find representations of these types. (See fig. 11.)

The lower-right quadrant, "nascent evangelicalism," is the religiosity of Antioch Fellowship, as well as of the far-flung culture of the Catholic charismatic movement. In their study of churches in the

Table 4   Attitudes toward the Bible among Presbyterians Vary by Location Within the Church

	Percent giving evangelical, neoorthodox, or liberal response to questionnaire item on Biblical authority, by status within Presbyterian church			
	Evangelical[a]	Neoorthodox[b]	Liberal[c]	Preponderance of evangelicals over liberals
Members	37	45	16	21
Elders	44	46	10	34
Pastors	39	49	11	28
Clergy in non-parish ministries	24	51	23	1

a. Sum of those choosing
   (1) "The Bible, though written by individuals, has been so controlled by the Holy Spirit that it is without error in all that it teaches in matters of science and history as well as in matters of theology and ethics."
   (2) "The Bible, though written by individuals and reflecting their personalities, has been so controlled by the Holy Spirit that it is trustworthy in all it teaches in matters of theology and ethics, but not necessarily in matters of science and history."

b. Those choosing
"All of the Bible is both the inspired Word of God and at the same time a thoroughly human document."

c. Sum of those choosing
   (1) "Portions of the Bible, including some of its theological and ethical positions, may not be the inspired Word of God."
   (2) "The Bible is merely a record of the moral and religious experiences of Hebrews and Christians."

Source: "Presbyterian Panel Findings, The January, 1980, Questionnaire." United Presbyterian Church in the United States of America, Advisory Council on Discipleship and Worship. (Labels "evangelical," "neoorthodox," and "liberal" are my own. The study's authors use the terms "more" and "less" "authoritarian."—RSW)

Hartford, Connecticut, area, David Roozen and his colleagues call it the "evangelistic" orientation.[39] We should expect it to arise in times of social dislocation among those people who are most concerned about their relationships with their immediate loved ones, people who likely live in neighborhood enclaves, suburbs or small towns.

The lower-left quadrant, nascent liberalism, called the "activist" orientation by Roozen et al., is also a concomitant of rapid change, but

	Institutional *Liberalism*	*Institutional* *Evangelicalism*
INSTITUTIONAL	The "Civic" Orientation (e.g., Chicago First Methodist Church, 1982) (e.g., Mark Gallagher, pastor, Mendocino Presbyterian, 1967–1972)	The "Sanctuary" Orientation (e.g., Northtown Presbyterian Church, California, 1978) (e.g., Eric Underwood, pastor, Mendocino Presbyterian, 1973–1983)

(Religious Form)

	Nascent *Liberalism*	*Nascent* *Evangelicalism*
NASCENT	The "Activist" Orientation (e.g., The Church of the Three Crosses, Chicago, 1968–1970) (e.g., Peter Hsu, pastor, Mendocino Presbyterian, 1962–1966)	The "Evangelistic" Orientation (e.g., Antioch Fellowship, 1976) (e.g., Larry Redford, member, Mendocino Presbyterian, 1964–1978)

LIBERAL   (Ideological Content)   EVANGELICAL

Figure 11   Cultural Map: Varieties of Contemporary American Protestantism

we would expect to encounter it among well-educated people, particularly seminary students, and in college towns. Activist fellowships currently devote themselves to overcoming apartheid in South Africa, providing sanctuary for Central American refugees, and promoting the nuclear arms freeze. In the past, there were other, also liberal, issues.[40]

The upper-left quadrant, institutional liberalism, is called the "civic" orientation by Roozen et al. This orientation should characterize stable churches most under a cosmopolitan influence: downtown churches in major metropolitan areas, churches affiliated with denominational headquarters, university chapels. I have seen it in Chicago's First Methodist Church, in San Francisco's Grace Cathedral, and in Stanford University's Memorial Church.

Finally, institutional evangelicalism, the Roozen "sanctuary" orientation, should predominate in stable but relatively insular communities. Small-town, suburban, and metropolitan parish churches should disproportionately display this orientation.[41]

Testing these hypotheses must wait for another study, for this book is a close look at one church informed by the concepts developed in the present chapter. While the attributions are imperfect, we can nonetheless approximate the religious leanings of the four individuals most prominent in the story of Mendocino Presbyterian in the 1960s and 1970s using our four types.

Larry Redford was the prototypical nascent evangelical, the Bible his textbook, the Lord his constant companion. Peter Hsu, dynamic Chinese-American, was the nascent liberal, the activist. Though he was a life-long member of the Presbyterian Chuch, he was from the point of view of the Mendocino congregation an exotic and a radical, who insisted on breaking down the barriers that separated the church from the world. Mark Kimmerly was by theological conviction neoorthodox, but the polarized climate of the late 1960s pushed him to side with the party of his political conscience, the liberals. Yet he also worked hard to understand and enhance the traditions of his parish, including its pride in its architectural heritage and its role as the oldest institution in town. Kimmerly's was the institutional liberal, the civic orientation. Eric Underwood was the institutional evangelical, at least in comparison to Larry Redford. Like Redford, he preached from the Bible a message of salvation through Jesus. Unlike Redford, he was comfortable with the structures and traditions of the Presbyterian church, locally and nationally.

In the chapters to follow, we will learn much more about these men and their times than such a typology can convey, and we shall have occasion to qualify these attributions. Yet it should be clear that we need *at least* two dimensions of comparison if we are to understand the variety within contemporary American Protestantism. What is remarkable, in that light, is that so many observers of the religious scene, especially partisans to it, reduce these differences to a *single* dimension. Radical evangelicals tend to divide the ecclesiastical world into the camps of the living and the dead. The living churches are their own, spirit-filled and faithful to the Lord. The other churches have been killed by "churchianity," which may be translated as bureaucratic apostasy. Enthusiastic evangelicals do not easily recognize that theological conservatism is perfectly capable of desiccation. Nor do they acknowledge that activist fellowships can be full of life.

Activist liberals (and their academic sympathizers, as I argued in a 1979 article[42]) see a different single dimension of comparison among churches. There are those, they say, who "challenge" the natural human tendency toward complacency in the face of social injustice; these earn the liberals' respect. The others are those who merely supply spiritual "comfort" as an escape from the world; these are portrayed as fundamentally irrelevant and illegitimate for persons of good faith. Such perceptions ignore the radical (even if reactionary) aspirations of nascent evangelicals. They also disregard the smugness that ideologies of social justice invite among socially privileged liberals.

Such misperceptions may help account for the ironies in the story of Mendocino Presbyterian. Peter Hsu and Mark Kimmerly were inspired by the liberal ideal of opening the church to new constituents, perhaps not realizing that the new constituents would be happier with religious conservatism. Larry Redford brought an evangelical movement into the church, likely unaware that evangelicalism would strengthen the institution and sap his own resources. Eric Underwood preached a gospel of personal salvation, but his church bolstered the liberal struc-tures of the United Presbyterian Church through its financial success.

Religion is not only a personal commitment, or an I-Thou relation-ship. Nor is it defined solely by sophisticated theologies.[43] It is also, and for the purposes of this book, primarily, embodied in systems of mutual action (social organization) and shared meaning (culture). The societal and cultural levels are such that what individuals accomplish is often very far from what they intend. Peter Hsu, Mark Kimmerly, and Larry Redford contributed willy-nilly to the heterogeneity, vital-ity, strength, and theological conservatism of Mendocino Presbyte-rian Church, a combination that only Eric Underwood can be said to have wanted.

While these men were thus shaping the history of a church in Mendocino, I was a student, then a teacher, of sociological theory at the Berkeley campus of the University of California, then at Yale University. I had never carried out a major piece of empirical re-search on my own, and I did not consider myself a sociologist of religion. I had not read most of the research studies I have used to develop the generalizations presented in this chapter, but my igno-rance of religion was only partly attributable to the fact that many of them were not yet published in 1976. In fact, the two social worlds of the small-town church and the university social-science faculty could hardly have been further apart. The potent nexus of parochial-ism and evangelicalism was nearly invisible from our cosmopolitan and secular position at the opposite end of the culture. I lived in what studies of the academy have shown to be a consistently and overwhelmingly liberal subculture: young, high-achieving, social sci-entists in elite universities.[44]

As an American sociologist, I was part of the least religious stratum in the most religious modern society in the world. For us, religion was either a thing of the past or, in Chaplain Coffin, the politicized conscience of the liberal academy. Even sociologists of religion shared this perspective, treating liberal churchmen with respect and fellow-feeling but dismissing conservatives with contempt and incomprehension. It would have strained credulity to propose that a vibrant, popular evangelical movement would shortly make a serious bid for the soul of the nation.

3.

Sojourn in the Field

I think I can say . . . that I have been spared the chief ambiguity that afflicts intellectuals, and this is that civilized individuals hate and resent the civilization that makes their lives possible. What they love is an imaginary human situation invented by their own genius and which they believe is the only true and the only human reality. How odd! But the best-treated, most favored and intelligent part of any society is often the most ungrateful. Ingratitude, however, is its social function. Now there's an ambiguity for you!
—Saul Bellow, *Herzog*

On the Tuesday before Memorial Day, 1976, I moved into a lovely guest suite in a converted Victorian farmhouse two miles south of Mendocino. I had come, I said to all who asked, to study the Presbyterian Church and "the Christian community of Mendocino." I was prepared to live off my savings and stay until the end of the year, when I would begin a job that was waiting for me in Chicago. I was alone.

Preconceived Ideas

Mendocino was not wholly new to me. Once a year since 1970, during vacations from the job I had in Connecticut, I had come up to Mendocino to visit with my son and the new family of my former wife. Like most visitors, I had stopped to walk around the Presbyterian church grounds and admire the English gothic sanctuary with its white siding, shingled roof, and tall steeple. It looked like hundreds of others in the United States but for its extraordinarily good condition and the bronze plaque that proclaimed it to be a state historical monument, "congregation organized 1859, building dedicated 1868." But the church had begun to be more than an item of scenery in 1973 when I learned in a strange letter from my former wife, Jane, that she and her family, including my then eight-year-old son, Alan, had "come to Jesus" and joined the Presbyterian church. A New Haven friend deciphered Jane's letter to give me the alarming news that Alan was now living among charismatics. (Indeed, it turned out that he was one himself.)

During my next visits I was concerned to see whether this bizarre religious involvement would hamper Alan's education, but my worries were mollified by the fact that he continued to excel in school. Because I did not enjoy the witnessing that accompanied dinnertime discussions of religion at Jane's house, I did not ask many questions on my visits. Yet I wondered about a Presbyterian church where people could speak about "coming to Jesus."

My professional curiosity was piqued, and this project was begun in May 1975, when I heard a tape recording of Sunday worship in that church. The tape had come with a note from Jane responding to an anguished letter of mine. I had just been denied promotion at Yale University, where I had taught sociological theory for five years, and I was wallowing in self-doubt. But I rather resented receiving a tape-recorded sermon in response. More evangelism! I thought. So I let it sit a few weeks before finally deciding to listen to it on a day when I had nothing better to do. What I heard made me take notice.

The preacher, Eric Underwood, gave an excellent sermon, and he addressed himself, as Jane had promised, to people, like me, in distress. But long before the sermon commenced, I heard what sounded like an effervescent revival meeting. Hymns were sung with enthusiasm by a congregation full of young people. (Age shows in the singing voice as well as the skin and hair.) A period set aside for welcome and greeting of visitors, a deadly ritual in many churches, was a bedlam of happy voices. A ceremony of farewell to a longtime member leaving for another town featured familiar, affectionate references to events and persons in the church's history, which brought on more cheerful laughter.

The sermon I would be hearing, I thought, would not be a solo act, expressing only the preacher's beliefs. It would reflect on this congregation. So when the preacher spoke of Jesus as a living reality, as much alive today as two thousand years ago, and ended his sermon with what I only later learned to recognize as the equivalent of an altar call, I thought that this church was just begging to be studied. A Presbyterian church full of Jesus people, with a pastor who speaks to them! Eureka!

I thought I knew a bit about Presbyterians, having been one myself in the late 1950s. As a youth officer of my own congregation in Los Gatos, California, an officer of the youth Presbytery (regional) and youth Synod (interstate), and a delegate to the triennial youth National Assembly in Iowa in 1957, I had visited lots of churches, met many other young activists and would-be seminarians, and become close to several members of the clergy. What I thought we serious Presbyterians had in common was, first, an austere, existentialist faith in an unfathomable principle of transcendent justice, called God, and, second, a commitment to intellectual integrity in public affairs. I considered the ministry myself when I found that beat poetry like Allen Ginsberg's *Howl* excited discussion among the seminary students I knew.

I recognized even then that my motives were not entirely pure. I enjoyed the sound of my own voice reading scripture from the lectern, and I had a much more rewarding social life in the church than in the high school. But the pure religion I did embrace was cool and righteous. I loved to read aloud the first five verses of the Gospel According to John, hearing a Greek rationalism more than a Jewish mysticism in its logos. I was stirred by such hymns as "Once to Every Man and Nation" and "Our God Our Help In Ages Past."

To this day I remain grateful to the Presbyterian Church for providing a place for a teenage boy to exercise his mind and sense of moral seriousness without risking the ridicule he feared would have been the response of his schoolmates. But even then I was made nervous by any talk of "religious experience," and I was relieved that my local congregation celebrated communion only the required four times a year. At the national meetings of 1957, I shared a Grinnell College dorm room with seven other young Presbyterian boys, two of whom spoke of being "saved" and "knowing Jesus," to the embarrassment of the rest of us. We six were intent on getting the most out of our daily lectures on neoorthodox theology and staying comfortable in the muggy Iowa summer, and I recall that we attributed the Jesus talk to the origin of its speaker in exotic West Virginia. Back home in California, I knew no one who spoke that way among the youth leaders of the Presbyterian church, though we took ourselves and our religion very seriously.

Mendocino's Presbyterian church in 1975, though, seemed to be full of Jesus people, and their religion was a very experiential thing. To make matters even more interesting, I learned from Jane that her group of charismatics worshipped and spoke in tongues openly every Friday night in the church's meeting hall. How would my old-line Presbyterians feel about that? Wouldn't the pastor, who seemed to delight the Jesus people, be under great pressure from the old guard? Indeed, shortly before I moved to Mendocino, I read a newspaper story of a Presbyterian pastor in Virginia who had been sacked for condoning charismatic practices in his church. Wasn't that the more typically Presbyterian response to enthusiastic, experiential religion?

Taking such a response for granted, I thought of Mendocino Presbyterian as an ideal, delicate little laboratory where I could look firsthand at some social processes that had long interested me as a political sociologist. How can people with unusual ideas ("deviant cognitive structures") maintain them in the face of social pressure? What is the role of valued verbal symbols (God, peace, justice, democracy) in bringing about practical agreement? How is consensus forged out of ideological disagreement?[1] Following the social theorist Peter Berger, I expected to find elaborate mechanisms of ideological insulation that would allow the Jesus people and the old guard to coexist: pluralistic ignorance, social segmentation, coded language, euphemism. And I expected that underneath the surface of evangelical enthusiasm I would find, if I were to keep my ear to the ground, the resentment of an old guard who at worst would be scheming to get rid of the Jesus people and their pastor or, at least, would be devoutly awaiting the day that the born-again Christians might grow up.

I decided that an ethnographic study, and not a formal attitude-and-opinion questionnaire, would be required. I did not want to ask, "What do you think of people speaking in tongues in worship at your church?" if one of the factors in the apparent harmony of Mendocino Presbyterian were that large numbers of its members were unaware of such goings on. I would tread softly, question delicately, listen carefully, and read critically everything that I could get my hands on, always assuming that the presumed evangelical/conventional split would be at the base of all expressions of tension. Had there been a resignation from the session, the board of elders? Had there been a turnover of leadership in the choir? Was the nominating committee finding it hard to fill slots? Did the stewardship committee worry about people fulfilling their financial pledges? Aha! I thought. Here we see evidence of ideological discontent with the evangelical take-over. I did not recognize that those problems plague every church.

Despite my conviction that I was approaching a fragile and deviant organization, my expressions of interest in doing the study were warmly received by the pastor, Underwood, when I came up for a visit in August to meet him. My presence was also welcomed by Larry and Sue Redford, the leaders of the group of charismatics, during a subsequent visit on the New Year's holiday. They invited me to the regular Friday night meeting of their group, and I heard tongue-speaking for the first time early in January in the Presbyterian church social hall. During these two brief visits to Mendocino in 1975 and 1976, I met and was welcomed by other members of the Presbyterian church and the charismatic fellowship. I conducted some interviews, picked up a roster of church members, put my name on mailing lists, subscribed to the local newspapers, and arranged with Jeannie Baker, the person in charge of tape recording the church's Sunday services, to receive cassettes by mail until my planned arrival the next spring. I studied these materials and thereby knew a lot (and imagined more) about Mendocino Presbyterian by the time I moved in.

My other, very abbreviated, preparation was in the methodology of sociological field studies. I read some books, took a four-hour seminar at the American Sociological Association annual meetings, and discussed my project with several friends who had fieldwork experience. I am grateful for the advice I received, and I took much of it to heart.[2] Write down everything you see, hear, and do, including your own reactions to your experience (Rosalie Wax, John Lofland). Do not tell anyone, including a sociological confidante, what you have observed until you have written it down (Howard Becker). Leave wide margins in your written notes so that you can later add analytic codes (Lenore Weitzman). Be absolutely confidential; do not disclose to one member of the community what another has confided in you (Joyce Kozuch). Your own role is part of your research kit (Marcia Millman). Do not be afraid to probe, to nettle people in interviews; people like to expound on their ideas (Janet Lever). Beware of ideological accounts of personal change, especially from men; women are more prosaic (Bruce Hackett, Diane Rizzo). Don't go native; don't convert; remember that you have friends; call; come down for a visit (several Bay Area friends and my father, sister, and brother). Take a vacation midway during your fieldwork.

Getting Started

When I moved to Mendocino in May, I was therefore determined and ready, and I had the advantage of a point of entrée. (I was Alan's biological father.) I had an evidently genuine welcome from the church pastor and the charismatic fellowship leader, and I had a comfortable apartment with a view of the ocean framed by fields of scotch broom and wild roses. I unpacked the stereo equipment I'd had sent by UPS, picked up the key to my post-office box, and deposited my savings in the bank. It was an ideal setting, I thought, for a scholar who was writing a book. The trouble was that I did not yet have anything to write and was not sure of how to go about finding it.

For two days, I listened to more tape-recorded church services, read my accumulation of newspapers, and took notes at my desk, while my field research consisted of unconscionably long trips to the post office, the grocery store, the organic produce store, the fish market, and the bank. I knew I had to take advantage of opportunities as they arose, but the first two meetings I was able to attend—and on which I dutifully kept extensive notes—did little to assuage either my loneliness or my unsureness. One was a public meeting to discuss issues of town development, at which I heard spoken what I had already read in the newspaper, and the other was a woefully under-attended and unsuccessful Friday meeting of Antioch Fellowship, where I learned that most of the members had gone down to Sonoma County for a weekend Christian campout.

So the next day, Saturday, I put my tent and sleeping bag in the car and drove to Petaluma, where my fieldwork began in earnest at a huge charismatic rally. All of a sudden, I was immersed in a foreign culture, but I relished the feeling of being a real anthropologist at work. The field notes alone kept me busy for three days of writing back at my desk.

The 1976 "Festival of the Son" was held at a large KOA campground. Several thousand persons, mostly young adults and their hundreds of children, camped out for the weekend in orderly groups of families and fellowships like Antioch. They were there to hear "teachings" and performances of Christian folk-rock music, to discuss topics such as "the Christian attitude toward sexuality," and to meet with other groups of new evangelicals from all over northern California. It was the regional Jesus movement's annual answer to the rock festivals of only a half decade before, but it was anything but anarchic. Monitors, identified by armbands, were everywhere to direct traffic and care for minor first-aid problems. Everyone entering the grounds was handed a three-page leaflet with a list of rules (no dogs, no drugs, no alcohol, no open fires, wash dishes carefully). There were particularly explicit rules for the child-care service, and all children registered were to wear a gummed label badge. I was shocked shortly after I arrived to see my son walking around camp with the label affixed to his shirt, "_____ALAN_____ is His sheep."

In truth, the apparatus of authority was only lightly engaged, for the huge group behaved with remarkable docility and cheerfulness despite discomfort and inconvenience: windy cold in the mornings, burning sun in the afternoons, dust and chaff in the assembly grounds, and long lines in front of water faucets and chemical toilets.

A spirit of determined enthusiasm and willful cooperation suffused the weekend. One person, for example, volunteered that the lack of a drinking fountain (there was nary a one on the entire grounds) was a "blessing," especially for the women, because there were also few toilets.

Above all, I was struck by the evangelical language in regular official and unofficial use. "Hi, Steve. When did you get here?" "Just now." "Praise God!" Later, as I roamed around, I overheard this encounter:

> "This is Ron. He's a new Christian."
>
> "When were you saved, Ron?"
>
> "Just two weeks ago."
>
> "Praise God!"
>
> "I'm Jewish, and some people think that's a problem."
>
> "That's a double blessing!"
>
> "Hallelujah!"

By the end of my stay (I was exhausted after a day and a half), I had assembled the beginning of a lexicon of new evangelical jargon: "anointed," "the Body," "brother," "fellowshipping," "to minister," "saints," "sheep," "the walk" (meaning proper behavior). I had also learned that the question "are you a Christian?" did not mean "don't tell me you're not Jewish!" as it did around Yale. "Christian" was not an inherited, taken-for-granted, ascriptive status. It was a chosen, aggressively proclaimed, achieved one.

Never again in my months of fieldwork would I experience an event of such sustained, self-conscious ideological concentration, and never again would I feel so utterly foreign. Yet I had undergone a crash course in evangelical culture, had seen in the flesh some west coast and national Jesus movement leaders, and, I suspect, had demonstrated my seriousness to the people of Antioch Fellowship.

By the next weekend, I was able to take in the regular Friday night fellowship meeting without embarrassment, to spend much of Saturday at an Antioch work party, and to hobnob around town Sunday morning before church with Sol Bloom, one of the extroverts of the fellowship. I was cordial, helpful when I could be, and only mildly inquisitive, and my new friends struck me as very down-to-earth in contrast to the ideologues of the Festival of the Son. I could recognize "Praise God!" as the syntactic equivalent of "Far out!" and "Hallelujah!" as an alternative to the ritualized profanity of the early seventies.

In less than two weeks, I was established as a sociologist in Antioch Fellowship and the evangelical wing of Mendocino Presbyterian.

There was a reason for my easy entrée, and a corresponding pitfall. I was not only "Alan's father" and the sociologist doing what many took to be, I was surprised to learn, a master's thesis. I was also a potential convert, whose sympathetic mien and active involvement were taken as evidence that "the Lord has his hand on Steve." In truth, unlike the stock anthropologist among the aborigines, I knew there were no barriers of race, ethnicity, or language to my going native, and I had plenty of improbable models, new Jewish Christians among them, to show that there was only the verbal confession of faith separating "them" from me. I recognized that I would have to struggle to preserve my objectivity, not to get too close to these people who had welcomed me and helped my research get off to a good start. So, at the end of my second weekend, I made a written record of that very recognition and called a friend in Berkeley for a date the next week.

Self as Instrument

For the seven months before Christmas, I attended as many meetings and accepted as many invitations as, given my time and strength, I felt possible. There were the weekly meetings of Antioch Fellowship and the Sunday services at the church, including the periods of socializing that bracketed them. Later on, I became a regular at the Thursday evening prayer group at the pastor's house and the Wednesday evening choir practice at the church. I went to a couple of other prayer-and-study group meetings, spent another weekend at an evangelical campout, volunteered for more Saturday work parties, and took in every church social and picnic. Later on, as my social circle broadened, I was invited to meetings of the church's trustees and session and was several times a guest at the Rotary club. On first Mondays, I went to the public hearings of the Mendocino Historical Review Board. There were other public meetings, festivals, and parades; concerts, plays, lectures, and exhibits; and scenes in stores, bars, and dance halls—nearly all of which impinged on the church or the Antioch group and all of which I saw as part of my research.

I estimate that I have records of about four hundred hours of such identifiable events, and I learned at the outset that each hour of observation required a later hour of writing. My notes changed over time from a record of what the setting looked like and what was done and said, when I was new, to a record of who was there, who was not, and who said what, when I had learned more names. I found that, when I followed Wax's, Lofland's, and Becker's advice, my recall was extraordinary, and I could reconstruct a two-and-a-half-hour prayer meeting in great detail when I went straight home to my typewriter. So I usually got to bed hours after midnight.

I also discovered a complex cybernetic pattern in my observational work. Lonely for human company in my apartment, I could go to some more-or-less religious event, since the evangelicals were always ready to welcome me. Such social encounters, however, carried the risk of emotional dependency on those who were my subjects, with the ultimate peril of going native. But the obligation to record the encounter itself in written form both diminished the allure of accepting an invitation (one potentially pleasant hour of human company means one arduous hour of notetaking) and, when accomplished, helped objectify and thus distance me from the sentiments of affection and gratitude I was obliged to record. My notes thus became the surrogate for the friend or secular confessor I did not have living with me. More than the stereo, the phone, or my friends and family, my notes were my guarantor of sanity.

The type of research I was doing is called, somewhat inaccurately, participant observation. I did not disguise my role as a sociologist, and I did not undergo or feign conversion. But I otherwise tried to fit in unobtrusively and do what others were doing. That was not a problem when I was basically part of an audience, as in most Sunday worship and Monday public hearings, but it was more difficult when I went to prayer meetings or other highly participatory gatherings.

My rule was not to say anything I did not believe, and therefore I never offered a prayer. Since communion was always explicitly defined as a token of acceptance of Jesus's atonement for human sins, I never partook of it. However, I would not disdain to join hands in a circle of prayer, and I regularly shared some matter of personal concern in small prayer groups. I always sang the songs I knew or had come to learn, since I enjoy singing and sensed that unison singing represented, compared to spoken prayer, the lowest level of religious commitment. Indeed, by late August, when it had become clear to me that the director of the church's adult choir and a half dozen of her singers were known not to profess an evangelical commitment, I became a regular member of the choir.

My ambivalent participation—I was by no means the least active participant in Antioch's Friday meetings or the church's Sunday worship—misled some who were themselves marginal to the groups. Though I was introduced to the fellowship on a couple of occasions as a researcher ("This is Steve, from Yale, who is surveying us," Larry

Redford once said.), and although I routinely introduced myself to individuals as one engaged in a sociological study, worship services and prayer meetings were not regularly prefaced by the statement, "the bearded, graying fellow over there is a sociologist who is recording what is going on." Thus a few awkward moments, when a newcomer or irregular attender took me for a "brother," are recorded in my notes.

The notes themselves were less of a problem than one might suppose. At fellowship and worship sessions, many members took notes on the teachings, often in the form of marginal notations in their Bibles, and Sue Redford, a writer herself, took notes incessantly during every meeting. So I too wrote notes, on a pad propped on my Bible, taking a roster of attendees and shorthand memoranda on earlier prayers and testimonies during the teachings. Sometimes, I used other devices to take notes unobtrusively: in my tent during campouts, in the men's room during church socials, along the ocean headlands during extended shopping trips into town. Most often, though, I stored information in my head until I was home with the typewriter.

Observation was only the first aspect of my research. A second part of "field methods" is the gleaning of information directly from individuals, whether as casual informants or as formal interviewees. I recorded opinions and items of gossip from scores of conversations, and eventually I came to have friendly relations with more than a dozen informants. At first, my friends were firmly committed evangelical/charismatics, including Jane, my former wife, and Larry and Sue Redford. Over time my network broadened. Jane and her family, including Alan, left the area in July in a long-planned move. Meanwhile, my presence in Mendocino had become known and taken for granted. I got to know an artist, an architect, and the choir director, all deeply involved in one or another aspect of the church but not themselves evangelicals. I shared dinners with the county librarian and the Catholic priest, neither of whom was involved in the Presbyterian church but both of whom were knowledgeable about the community. Over time, I became especially close to the pastor himself, Eric Underwood, with whom I shared a frequent coffee break and an occasional beer.

Compared to the sixty persons I interviewed formally, the two dozen who were sometime informants were closer in age to me and more likely to be college educated. I flocked with those of like feather. But I also tended to hang out with women as much as with men, and that raises another aspect of my status in Mendocino. I was happy to be Alan's father, on an extended visit. I claimed to be a sociologist doing research. I acknowledged that I was seen as a potential convert. Soon, I also realized that I was taken as an eligible male.

When I first went to Mendocino, I was oblivious to something that almost everybody knows, that thirtyish single men are in short supply around churches. In fact, until two weeks prior to my departure from Yale for Mendocino, I had been planning to share that cozy apartment, although not the research itself, with a woman friend. That plan fell through, and I was therefore in the mood as well as the position to accept the many invitations I began to receive from people in and around the church. Since I am a decent cook and had a nice apartment, I was able to reciprocate. My social network, consisting of potential informants, expanded rapidly. Once I recognized the advantages of my eligibility, I determined to maintain it.

As any field researcher knows, personal relationships in the field are profoundly asymmetrical. I was in Mendocino to do research, to gather information, eventually to write a book. Most of those I came to know, to respect, even to love, were there to stay. That certainly does not mean that every encounter or every relationship was calculated. I was not so single minded. I gravitated toward those I found attractive, for one or another reason, and with whom I could be comfortable. Although many of the evangelicals radiated warmth and genuine concern, the nonevangelicals did not proselytize, witness, or adhere to a moral code I found astoundingly old-fashioned. I did not ask and tried not to cajole any new friend into violating his or her rules, and, in particular, I never pumped anyone for information of an officially confidential nature, for example, deliberations of the church's nominating committee. I shared my own talents and resources, so I made some dinners and offered rides to hitchhikers. I spoke freely about my past and future, professionally and personally. But I did not share the results of my research in Mendocino, above all the secrets and opinions people had confided in me.

One reason I so much enjoyed Eric Underwood's company was that he shared with me his infatuation with the rich lore of his congregation but he never, ever, asked my opinion of anything or pried for gossip about anyone. Early on, in fact, I was miffed when he seemed conspicuously uninterested in my report of what I took to be public knowledge about the Festival of the Son, which he had not attended. As a college professor, I was used to being listened to, but I learned my lesson on the spot and let Eric do the talking from then on. Larry Redford, by contrast, made me uncomfortable with an occasional request for advice. I shied away from those who were too curious about my findings.

The information, perspectives, and gossip that I learned through watching and listening helped me plan the formal interviews I conducted. At first, many of my interviews were little more than prerehearsed testimonies, nonetheless valuable, but owing little to my design. Other early interviews that I stumbled into proved to be strategic later. Thus on July 5 I was given a very full story by a member of the search committee that had brought Eric Underwood to the pulpit three years earlier, and, in August, I had a couple of hours with Underwood's predecessor, Mark Kimmerly, when he showed up in town for a nostalgic weekend. As my sense of the structure of the community grew, however, I began to target interviews to sample opinions I might otherwise be missing and to fill in pieces of the puzzle.

I usually went by appointment to the home or place of business of my interviewee, although some, for convenience, came to my place. I would usually have prepared a list of questions, jotted down for my reference. Since tape recorders make me nervous and I had no money in any event for transcriptions, I took written notes on a legal pad as the interview proceeded. The interviews usually took at least an hour and a half, and most lasted longer, some taking five or more hours over two days. As soon as possible, I would return to my desk to record a typewritten account, with as many direct quotations as I could remember or reconstruct. Sometimes, I interviewed two persons, a married couple, at one time. My interviews of Larry Redford, for example, were always done in the presence, usually with the collaboration, of his wife, Sue. (Those with Eric Underwood, by contrast, were always one-on-one.) Occasionally, some two-on-one sessions failed as interviews, when one spouse was clearly inhibited from expressing a view that the other could be expected to disparage. But often they were valuable, when each would jog the other's memory or one would contradict what the other expressed as a matter of fact, giving me insight into some matter of contention. Roger Ebert, the film critic, has this to say about his similar method.

> I don't use a tape recorder when I do interviews because it gets in the way: it inspires the subject to start dictating, and puts him on guard with every word. The notepad is much more confidential. When you think the subject is about to elaborate on an indiscretion, you keep writing, so that the silence hangs in the air and must be filled. During moments of revelations and confidences, you don't write at all. But you remember.[3]

Whether it was the notepad, the expression of sympathy and promise to listen and not leak, the wide circle of informants, or something else, I did hear many an indiscretion and many a revelation of disputes among Mendocinoites, all of which I kept to myself. I heard a lot of criticism of Larry Redford, a bit of Mark Kimmerly and his liberal predecessor Peter Hsu, but almost none of Eric Underwood, even from those who professed not to agree with him. My method of hanging around to hear expressions of discontent was working, and I had been right not to impose on my subjects my preconception of the structure of their dissensus. But I was right for the wrong reasons, for the axis of the dissensus was not between Underwood and the ideological heirs of Hsu and Kimmerly, but between Underwood and Redford. That was abundantly clear.

The pressure of keeping things to myself, the self-imposed lack of any fully symmetrical relationship, the sheer hard work of writing, and my bewilderment at not finding what I had expected all made an early fall vacation as necessary as my colleagues had advised. So I took off for three weeks in September. I had a thrilling High Sierra climbing trip, I picked the brains of two University of California friends who knew something about religion, and I relaxed in the homes of my brother, my sister, and my father. Above all, I spent a week going over my notes and began to sort out what I had found and to plan out the time I had left.

In front of me was evidence that the evangelical takeover was overwhelmingly popular and that the salient disputes were among the evangelicals, within the camp of the theological right, rather than between the right and a nonexistent left. Significantly, I read in my notes that people spoke of Underwood as a "healing presence." But what had he healed, and why, aside from the personal charm that had already begun to beguile me, was he so popular with every camp?

Shortly before leaving on my vacation, I went to a meeting of the session and was offered access to the church archives by the clerk of that body. Now I realized that I would have to take him up on his offer. I also knew that I would have to seek out those—some whose names I was to learn from the archives—who had ceased participating in the church. I had to dig deeper into the background of Antioch Fellowship. In short, I must become more the historian. I did not cease my watching and hobnobbing on my return to Mendocino in October, but I added many hours of work in the church office and sought out those who were strategic but less convenient interviewees.

The archives turned out to be a gold mine. Underwood gave me a file of old, carefully unfolded and flattened cereal boxes on the backs of which Dwight Perkins had been keeping Sunday worship attendance records since 1959. I copied the numbers, too faded for xeroxing, onto a huge matrix of fifty-two weeks by eighteen years. (Since then, I have added the figures through 1982.) Underwood also gave me the official report of the search committee that had called him and the resume he had provided them. From the church secretary I borrowed the annual reports for the past fifteen years. One of the veteran ladies of the choir lent me her copy of the 1959 centennial souvenir booklet. Larry and Sue Redford filled in my set of their fellowship's newsletters. Above all, the minutes of session, which I eventually read carefully for 1957 through 1982, were indispensable.

The minutes recorded the officers elected at the annual congregational meetings and their subsequent records of service; church members added to the rolls and whence they came; members deleted and deceased; dates of service of pastors; and a careful, literate, and discreet record of deliberations of the session itself. This being a Presbyterian church, the minutes were subjected to regular scrutiny by an official of the Presbytery, and they were kept in bound volumes of heavy bond paper, typewritten and increasingly detailed since 1960. Without my interviews and my own observation of a session meeting, I would have found it impossible to decipher many cryptic references. Nothing was sharply worded, all the hard edges of controversy having been sanded down by the clerks in the four weeks between meetings. But history was there to be read between the lines.

The Emerging Picture

Eventually, I had about nine hundred single-spaced pages of field notes, a file of four-by-six index cards with notes on five hundred individuals, tape recordings of a hundred worship services, a chronological precis of session minutes entered longhand on seventy-five legal-size sheets, file copies of attendance and budget records, and stacks of bulletins, newsletters, newspapers, and magazines—a mountain of data from Mendocino. I was bewildered by the gulf between its abundance and particularity and the relative elegance of the ideas of Marx, Weber, Parsons, and Shils, with which I had long worked. Even if I had not needed some years to become familiar with a new field, the sociology of religion, it would have taken a long time to wrest this material into shape. I told people in Mendocino not to hold their breath.

The first and most obvious step was to collate what I knew about all the individuals in and around the church and the fellowship. In effect, I needed retrospectively to conduct the sociological survey my methodological scruples had earlier forbade. All along in Mendocino I had kept an index file on all church members, fellowship regulars, and other members of the community. (There were many active participants in the life of the church who, for one reason or another, were not formal members.) Jane, my former wife, and Eric both gave me a great deal of information on the rough age, marital status, and occupation of individuals on the church roster, and another early informant, Ernie, the generous and outspoken man who installed phones, gave me the lowdown on family histories, who was sister to whom, who used to be married to whom. The session minutes told me when people had joined the church and where they had moved from. I got political party affiliation data from the county clerk's rosters in polling places on June 8, the day Jimmy Carter won the California Democratic primary. Some of my cards were to remain empty but for name, phone, and address. Most were filled in with bits of information, and many were packed. My assiduous but unsystematic methods did not reveal family income, an item of importance for many sociologists, but they did usually provide occupation and education data and, as important as income in the booming real-estate market of the mid-1970s, whether people owned their homes. By November, during dessert in Preston Hall at the close of an evening-long progressive dinner, I was able to win a personal information trivia quiz about individuals present from my store of knowledge. My file cards are on my desk for reference as I write.

A second step was to depict the evangelical culture I was immersed in. Here my earliest field notes were most valuable, those I took from the campouts, work parties, and meetings that I shared with the people of Antioch Fellowship in May and June. I got used too soon to their special language and their customs and ceased recording them in detail. But I did have the lexicon from the Festival of the Son, and I had recorded my astonishment at seeing fellowship members marking their Bibles with highlighter and ballpoint pens during Larry Redford's teaching.

Early on I had noticed that evangelical customs—carrying a Bible, having a "Jesus Loves You" bumper sticker, asking questions like "Do you know the Lord?"—served as markers of the community. Those of like mind were instantly recognizable from these signals, and that was welcome in an otherwise anonymous world. "Oh, yes! We love the Lord. Bless you." "Praise God." A sense of intimacy in new social contacts was thereby provided.

As a partially acculturated member of the community, after a few months I came to use the evangelicals' recognition of like-mindedness as my own index of respondents' evangelical identity. Having decided against an attitude survey, I did not have systematic data on my subjects' conversion history, Biblical literalism, or willingness to prose-lytize, the standard opinion-poll items used to identify evangelicals. I also discovered that no one other than the Underwoods and the

Redfords even used the designation "evangelical." ("Born again," "loves the Lord," "spirit filled," "Jesus freak," or just plain "Christian" were the labels used.) So I used the evangelicals' own criteria of involvement in evangelical culture—regular attendance at prayer meetings; habitual carrying of a Bible; recent baptism by water immersion (unorthodox among Presbyterians); and, especially, the use of evangelical language—to supplement self-description as my operational definition of "evangelical."

The rapidity with which I became accustomed to the evangelicals' idiom (though I did not use it in my own speech without oral quotation marks) was itself significant. It was a clue to the permeability of the culture itself, a validation of many new evangelicals' reports of the alacrity of their conversions, and, despite my preconceptions, evidence of the continuity between the culture of the evangelicals and the surrounding secular society. I discovered how it was that one who had only recently converted could become an "elder" within a year or two. I learned that the dramatic event of conversion, in which one agrees to take on the identity of one who loves the Lord, is not the end but a midpoint in the process of evangelical socialization, a turning point around which the neophyte often cannot see what lies ahead. So my careful and therapeutic notes on my own state of mind—my dreams, musings, and afterthoughts—were a source of data on the anxieties felt by the convert.

It is easy to grasp the idea of studying persons, known by their names and faces, and cultures, marked by their strange customs. It is more difficult to perceive social structure, which is the sociologist's special interest.[4] A legal entity, such as the California corporation called "Mendocino Presbyterian Church," or indeed the licensed marriage of Larry and Sue Redford, is only a small part of the corresponding social institution, often merely a piece of clothing rather than even a skeleton. We must also not regard as definitive what the participants in an institution or movement claim it to be. How misleading it can be to take at full face value the notions that a church is "an open caring community," a marriage is a "life partnership," or a university is a "temple of learning." Most often, these idealizations are half-truths.

Sociologists therefore amass information from which they hope to extract a sense of the social structure. Much of the information may prove to be dross, however. For example, we shall see that it matters for the evolution of Antioch Fellowship whether its members are single males or married couples, but it took close reading between the lines of several years' worth of highly rhetorical newsletters and close rereading of interview notes to see the one pattern fade into the other. We shall see also that a church organized as a set of age- and sex-specific activity clubs is very different from a church made up of heterogeneous prayer groups, but the hundreds of pages of session minutes have almost nothing to say directly about the corresponding shift within Mendocino Presbyterian between 1960 and 1975. That discovery came first of all from looking at formally posed photographs of church groups in the centennial booklet of 1959 through the eyes of a participant of the mid-1970s.

One of the first things I began to do with my data after I left Mendocino was to organize systematic chronologies and surveys. For example, I mapped Dwight Perkins's cereal-box attendance records onto a continuous sheet sixteen feet long, and the fall and rise of activity in the church since 1960 became graphically apparent. A running roster of members of session, elected annually for staggered three-year terms, with occasional resignations, took days of close scrutiny of annual reports and session minutes to assemble, but since then it has provided at a glance the particular makeup of the church's ruling body for every month over twenty years. A four-foot-long piece of butcher paper, divided into columns, was a matrix upon which I entered dated events in the intersection of the fellowship and the church from 1969 to 1978. An informal survey of ages of church members done by the pastor-search committee of 1972 served as a base of comparison to the survey I constructed for 1976 out of my own knowledge. Comparing these two surveys showed that the church had proportionately more young adults in 1976 than four years earlier, which in turn made it likely that the upbringing of children would become a higher priority.

Though my own eyes and my informants told me much, the patterns that emerged from these time-series data were striking and sometimes surprising. For example, the differing appeals of Peter Hsu and Mark Kimmerly, both political liberals, were first made clear by a statistical comparison of the church backgrounds of the members who joined during their ministries. And the funneling of Antioch members into the church was more vivid in statistical retrospect than at the fellowship and church meetings.

Accurate, detailed, sensitive description of individual, cultural, and organizational patterns is most of what we mean by sociological analysis. Most "why?" questions can be usefully reformulated as "how?" questions, as trial lawyers know. Thus I tried to understand how some hippies had become fundamentalists, how some successful exurban dropouts had joined a charismatic fellowship, and how a struggling, politically involved church had become a prosperous evangelical church. Trace the process, and you answer the question.

It was an inchoate conviction of the importance of processual knowledge that dictated the chronological outline of the heart of this book, chapters four through twelve. Rather than provide a snapshot portrait of the church and the fellowship at one point in time, 1976, which turned out to be a time of rapid change, I decided to show how the two organizations had evolved together. Yet there were difficulties with the historical approach.

The ideological loading of "history" and "the past" in Mendocino was the biggest problem. Like many charming rural communities in the 1970s, Mendocino had attracted artists and cosmopolitans who were fascinated by its quaintness. They wanted to know the stories of the century-old houses they had bought and begun to restore. Who built it? When? For whom? Who inherited it? A Mendocino Historical Research Association was founded, and there was already a Mendocino County Historical Society. Both published journals and monographs, and I was a subscriber. For the "historically" minded, however, history seemed to end around 1915, by which time most of the interesting houses, storefronts, and churches had been built. Struggles over historical authenticity—reflections of underlying disputes over development—were rife at the monthly Historical Review Board hearings. Newcomers' nostalgia for turn-of-the-century buggies and lumber schooners clashed with natives' recollections of Depression-era movies and Model As. When I expressed interest in "history," I was regularly referred to a couple of nonagenarians who had been too feeble to get around and see what was happening during the two decades of interest to me.

The past was even more salient for many of the new evangelicals, who defined themselves as being saved from a former life of sin. Converts often exaggerate the depravity of their past, because such exaggeration helps justify the often considerable sacrifices of old ideas, old associations, and old pleasures that the new life of sanctification requires. In fact, some Mendocino converts seemed to compete for the inverse honor of having led the most dissolute pre-Christian life. So I knew that I had to treat accounts of the past with a certain skepticism.

Despite the salience of the past, recollections were often partial, conflicting, and downright inaccurate. Events remembered as significant would be only vaguely placed in time ("a year or two ago"). The wrong names would be attached to an important event. Having myself been locked into academic schedules and saved annual engagement calendars for twenty years, I can date events in my own life with great precision. That was not so for many people in Mendocino.

To establish chronological and thereby causally significant sequences, I took the church's archives as fundamental. They were a skeleton on which to hang the rich but often fuzzy accounts given me by informants and interviewees. I knew from the minutes just when Larry Redford served on session and just when Eric Underwood was voted in as new pastor. But I also had to make adjustments to that framework and inferences on it. Once I had to take a clerk's reference to "last Sunday" in the minutes to mean the Sunday after the meeting being recorded but before the clerk's actual transcription of the minutes, because other evidence, including Dwight Perkins's records, suggested that construction. Session minutes, attendance records, and informants' stories complemented each other's incomplete perspectives to provide an estimate of the impact of a sexual scandal on the congregation in 1965.

The resulting history is biased toward processes that I can document through archives, informants' diaries and letters, triangulated recollections and, given the eventual length of my involvement in the research, my own longitudinal observations. Some of the more dramatic stories I was told do not receive much play. I did not find out, for example, whether Ben Moss, whom I knew on and off from 1975 to 1982 as a self-styled fanatic Jew for Jesus, was indeed the world's greatest sinner prior to his conversion in 1973. And I cannot say a great deal about the militant postconversion organization of a hippie commune in 1973. But I can recount with confidence the commitment trajectories of Burt Rogers (chapter five), Pat Wakefield (chapter five), Dan Whitman (chapter twelve), and Bruce Douglas (chapter twelve), and I have carefully reconstructed the social processes of the entry of Mendocino Presbyterian into the world of postwar public life (chapter four) and its subsequent turn to the theological right (chapters seven and nine), of the wholesale conversion of a hippie commune (chapter six), and of the rise and fall within the church of a radical charismatic movement (chapters five, ten, and eleven).

I did not simply discard misinformation and tendentious accounts. In the beginning, of course, I did not have the wherewithal to distinguish truth from falsity. Moreover, testimonies, whether slanted or not, were part of the culture I was coming to know. Later, I found that several half-truths were sufficiently widespread for me to wonder why. Church veterans misattributed public issues stemming from Peter Hsu's ministry to that of his successor, Mark Kimmerly. Some did the reverse. Many church members and other Mendocinoites thought of Antioch Fellowship in 1976 as a commune of underemployed hippie Christians, which it had long ceased to be. Many knew that Antioch had expelled a woman member in the recent past, but few knew who she was or when it had happened. I took these patterns of misinformation as strategic for the analysis of strains in the community. They were the mechanisms of stress maintenance Peter Berger would have told me to look for, but they were in the wrong place. By the time I came to write the book, the tensions they were reflecting had long been resolved.

Exit

People praised God at Thanksgiving that the rain had finally come to break a record drought. Thirsty wells were refilled, and sprouting grasses began to poke through chaff and fallen leaves. Days were short, and families turned inward to the hearthside warmth of the holidays. But I felt chilled and was depressed by the slow disappearance of the sun. November is my cruelest month, and I picked up a cold that I couldn't shake.

My person and welcome were wearing out. For six months, I had worked harder than ever before. I was lonesome, knowing that I was only a sojourner and avoiding the social pairing that well-meaning hostesses tried to impose. I still went to Friday fellowship meetings, but I had successfully resisted conversion. Though my evangelical friends still prayed over me, they seemed to have given up hope on me. There was still much I did not know, persons I had not spoken with, scenes I had not scouted, and records I had not perused. But I was tired.

Late one night in November, I was enjoying a rare moment of relaxation, just listening to the foghorns, when I heard a trucker on the highway downshift to take the curve into Little River Bridge, and the sound in my imagination took me to an unremarkable motel somewhere in Nebraska, on the way to Chicago. There I felt peace.

What a vision! I was ready to leave.

There was a great deal I did know, and I had discovered two ingredients in the success of Mendocino Presbyterian. For some, the young evangelical veterans of the counterculture, the Christian life was an exciting challenge. They were living, as they had in now legendary moments in the sixties, in the nascent state, on the edge of existence. They were not all perfected in their walk with the Lord. They were not all prosperous. But the Lord's presence was all about them, and everywhere there was His will to be done.

For others, the evangelical turn of the church was nearly the opposite, a period of relief from overwrought times. These churchpeople were comforted to know that God was still in His place after all the turmoil. The accents of the language they used with him might have changed from ah-men to ay-men, but he was still there to bless and keep. His house was sturdy.

Before I could work these ideas of the challenging and comforting faces of 1970s evangelicalism into the generalizations presented in the previous chapter, I had a good deal more work to do. There had to be more sifting and sorting, guided by the questions and advice of my sociological colleagues and my repertoire of social theory. I had to read up on the sociology of religion, now that my original idea of studying ideological dissensus in the abstract had washed out. I needed to survey the ideological range of contemporary mainline Protestantism by visiting as many churches as I could. I would also need to return to Mendocino to conduct more research (and would find that I was not the only person privy to knowledge of conflict in the church). But on my next research trip to Mendocino I would be no longer an ambivalent participant, always present while emotionally aloof, but a researcher meeting by appointment with interviewees and spending office hours with the archives, leaving other hours for a private life.

The response as I prepared to leave Mendocino gave me the key to the coexistence of the two types of evangelicals, the challengers and the comforted, the nascent and the institutional, under the regime of Eric Underwood. "How can you leave?" everyone asked, as if to commiserate. Never mind that I was leaving six months of unemployment for a good job. Never mind that a Chicago friend had found me a spacious, affordable apartment in the midst of one of Chicago's trendy lakefront neighborhoods. "It's too bad you have to go."

Eric had deliberately set me up for this chorus with two of his trivia questions at the progressive dinner dessert. By tablehopping and hobnobbing you were supposed to match each of thirty gossip items to one of the hundred persons present. One item was "lived in Chicago for thirty years and never wants to go back." Another was "will begin teaching in Chicago in January." How like Eric to combine puckish humor with an astute estimate of Mendocinoites' self-image! To be sure, there were those, including Eric himself, who had enjoyed having me around. There were also those who knew and dreaded the midwest and its winters. There were no doubt still more who found life in any big city distasteful. But for nearly all of them, Mendocino itself was the ideal place to live, and fully four-fifths of the persons at that dinner had come there to stay within the past twenty years. Three weeks earlier, I had been one of only two native Californians at an election-night TV party of two dozen Mendocino County Democratic Party activists. In August, I had sat in on a small meeting of no-growth conspirators who discussed such measures as letting air out of tourists' tires and spreading rumors of Legionnaire's Disease at the Mendocino Hotel. Suggestions from friends in Aspen, Colorado, and Marboro, Vermont, informed their discussion. These defenders of small-town life called themselves "progressives."

Eric's social-engineering exercises had a goal, to promote integration in his diverse, cosmopolitan congregation. But they also had a factual premise: that what the people of Mendocino shared was a determination, often a costly one, to make this place their home. They were small-town people by choice, elective parochials.

I pondered these things as I drove eastward along Interstate 80. Mixed with the sense of loss of my Mendocino friends was my relief at getting away and my anticipation of a new life in Chicago. I arrived on Christmas Eve, the day of Mayor Daley's funeral, and picked up the keys to my apartment, where I showered and changed for a holiday dinner. When I showed up at my friends' place, they were glad to see me safely arrived. And I was glad to see them, the sort of group I had naturally found congenial until a few months before. Four sociologists and an editor. Two employees of Northwestern University, one each of Yale and Illinois, and one of *Playboy*. Three Jews and two Protestants. Nobody religious.

"Tell us about Mendocino," they all said.

4.

Reorientation: Mendocino Presbyterian, 1959–1970

Yet it is only too evident that the religiousness of America today is very often a religiousness without religion, a religiousness with almost any kind of content or none, a way of sociability or "belonging" rather than a way of reorienting life to God.
—Will Herberg, *Protestant-Catholic-Jew*

Churches prospered in the proreligious atmosphere of the 1950s, and Mendocino was no exception. In Mendocino, the fifties saw a finally successful climb out of the Depression of the 1930s for both the town and the church. Mendocino's population—so far as we can tell from the records—reached by 1960 the numbers it had registered between 1900 and 1910 (before the post–World War I slump), and the Presbyterian Church in 1957 registered 160 members, topping its previous peak membership of 126 in 1913–1914.*

Any small-town church is affected by the local and national economy. Mendocino's earlier peak coincided with the closing of the lumber mill, and its varying fortunes up through the 1950s were still closely tied to the prosperity of the timberlands and mill towns nearby. Economic opportunity and geographic potential do not spell automatic social success, however, and particular, local factors shaped the experience of Mendocino Presbyterian in the fifties. This church, for example, might have gone the way of other small, old churches on the north coast, its properties sold or its buildings demolished by fires or highway projects. The Presbyterian Board of National Missions, which subsidized the church budget for nearly thirty years, might have felt the

*For a discussion of Presbyterian Church "membership" criteria, see chapter 8 below.

burden unjustifiable. The town physician, a leading citizen, might not have decided to lend his active support to the church. The area's Presbyterian seminary might not have provided the series of student ministers who found the church's tiny salary offering ($480 in 1931, $2400 in 1953) acceptable. Fewer able and dedicated and more inept and disreputable men might have served as regular pastors. A whole series of personal and organizational decisions in fact helped Mendocino Presbyterian realize its potential.

The Congregation in the 1950s

After an unsuccessful pastorate ended in 1952, Frederick Althorpe, who had pastored the church in its grimmest days of the 1930s, early in his career, returned to Mendocino Presbyterian at the age of sixty to take up a final challenge. A man of commanding physique, Althorpe had been a sailor in his youth, and his sermons were salted with stories of the sea. In his maturity, he had become an expert counselor and a capable churchman. Mendocinoites were thrilled to have him return.

Here are the highlights of the church's life in the fifties. Reverend Althorpe was installed as pastor in 1952, and more than fifty people joined the church in the next two years, many of them being restored to the rolls after long periods of inactivity. In 1954, Dr. Preston, beloved town physician, died, bequeathing to the Presbyterian Church a block of real estate, the sale of which was to finance a new social and educational hall adjacent to the church. Additional funds were raised from church members and townspeople, a loan was made from the Presbytery, and the new building—containing classrooms, offices, a kitchen, and a large assembly hall—was dedicated in 1957 as Preston Hall. Preston Hall having opened, Reverend Althorpe retired at the age of sixty-five to a home in Little River, and he was honored by the congregation as lifetime Pastor Emeritus. (In the years to come, he would be called on repeatedly to serve as interim pastor.) Althorpe's successor, Ward Higginson, served from 1958 until 1962, and it thus fell to him to preside over the church's centennial celebration in 1959, which was an occasion for understandable self-congratulation and a twenty-five-page souvenir history (on which I have drawn). A congregation of 114 people turned out on Sunday, November 8, for the centennial worship service. It was, except for Easter Sundays, the largest turnout of Higginson's four-year pastorate. Nineteen-sixty was the first year of full self-support for the church since 1931; no longer was Mendocino Presbyterian on the denominational dole.

Thus, as it entered its second century as a congregation, Mendocino Presbyterian was in healthy condition. Though its membership was down to 152 after the peak of 160 two years earlier, the loss was more nominal than real, since a pruning of fifteen inactive members in 1958 betrayed a previous slackness in membership standards. Average Sunday attendance was approximately fifty percent of the membership, a respectable, if not outstanding, figure. Average giving was sufficient to support a budget of over $11,000 in 1960, and to put the church on a self-supporting financial basis.

The physical properties of the church symbolized its well-being. The sanctuary, built in 1868, was the grandest building in town, indeed, the grandest building on a fifteen-mile stretch of coastline. Its ninety-foot steeple was a local landmark. The manse, built in 1909 during another period of prosperity, was a spacious though drafty house with an enviable living-room view. The new social and educational building, Preston Hall, was a modern, much-needed facility, which enhanced the impression of prosperity on the church grounds without detracting from the stately glory of the old sanctuary.

The internal life of the congregation was busy and convivial. The congregation, as was typical of Protestant churches of the fifties, was organized into a system of social clubs. First was the women's association, then (and still) the oldest social club in the church. Officially the "United Presbyterian Women's Association" and known informally as the "Ladies' Aid," it had regular meetings, provided hostesses for church functions, and conducted an annual fund-raising bazaar. More recently constituted were a couples' club and a youth club, called, according to 1950s Presbyterian practice, the "Mariners Club" and the "Westminster Fellowship." The choirs—adult and youth both—were also organized as clubs with designated officers, and each group had about twenty members. A men's club was organized in 1959, and in that same year a Brownie troop was sponsored by the church.

These groups were religiously sanctioned social circles. They met for social events, to sing, to raise funds for the church, and to enjoy fellowship. There is no indication in the records I have seen or from my interviews that they were of a religiously devotional nature, and given what we know about the churches of the 1950s, that would not be expected. For example, the Mariners' gift to the church for 1960, it is reported unabashedly in the session minutes, was a set of ashtrays for Preston Hall. One Mariners couple told me that they sometimes met off the church grounds so that they could enjoy beer and pretzels with their meetings, since alcoholic beverages in Preston Hall were prohibited by the trustees on their reading of Dr. Preston's will. One hears little about prayer in the records.

The church was, therefore, aside from its weekly worship service and Sunday school classes, a collection of age- and sex-based associations. The church's formal annual report included the clubs' separate financial reports, and the Mariners, the choir, the women's club and the men's club all had delegates to the annual committees to nominate new trustees and elders and to the pastor-seeking committee that replaced Althorpe with Higginson. Higginson had a reputation of being "good with youth," and, despite his own middle age, was reportedly a devoted fan of the high-school football team. No one I spoke with in Mendocino could recall much about his preaching, but he was remembered for his regular visits to the homes of his parishioners. One informant called him "the village parson." Wholesome and appropriate socializing seems to have been the accepted function of the church in those years. Higginson may have wanted more distinctively religious activity, since it is recorded that he proposed to the session in 1961 that an altar call be used to bring the service to a close. But that idea was scotched by the elders, and there is little evidence that more "religion" was desired by any significant element of the membership.

Veterans of those years remember religion as one of the ways in which people expressed their social identity. The Portuguese predominated in the Volunteer Fire Department and worshipped in the Catholic mission church. The Finns ran the Masonic Lodge and the school board, and some of them joined the old New England families in the Presbyterian church. To say that one was a Presbyterian in 1959 was to say more about one's ethnic ancestry and social life than about one's beliefs.

Advent of the Sixties

In this way Mendocino Presbyterian coasted into the sixties on the religious momentum of the fifties. But the sixties were to be different. To begin with, Mendocino's economy changed fundamentally. For a century, Mendocino had been dependent on primary production. Lumber, fishing, stock-raising, and agriculture had been the economic mainstays through boom and bust. But starting at the end of the fifties, growing through the sixties, and accelerating in the seventies, Mendocino became a tourist mecca. In 1947, the architectural quaintness of the village and its church had been discovered by Hollywood, when the motion picture *Johnny Belinda* was filmed there on location. (A $2000 rental fee to the Presbyterian Church was a windfall that kept the church afloat in some lean years.) In 1954, the town was again used as a movie set for *East of Eden*. *The Russians Are*

Coming, the Russians Are Coming, Summer of '42, and *Racing With the Moon* brought more Hollywood money to Mendocino over the next decades and made its citizens aware of its value as a living museum. By 1975, Mendocino had been legally declared a historic district in order to protect its architectural values.

Bohemian artists (dubbed "beatniks" by San Francisco columnist Herb Caen in 1958) discovered the weathered charms of Mendocino and its depressed land values at about the time that their North Beach habitat became uncomfortably publicized and prohibitively expensive. Gregory Mazzocco, a San Francisco painter, established the Mendocino Art Center in 1959, bringing with him what townspeople nervously called a "new element" of artists and cultural radicals. The demographic change in the early 1960s was sweeping: highly cosmopolitan newcomers moved in, but local youth in pursuit of careers found it necessary to move out. The immediate vicinity offered scant opportunities for a young adult to make a start in life. The jobs in retail stores, building trades, school teaching and government service were mostly taken. Later in the sixties, large numbers of other young adults—hippies—began to arrive from the cities, but it was not until the tourist boom of the 1970s and the later boom in marijuana cultivation that the economy of Mendocino would attract the economically ambitious. In sum, the 1960s saw a massive replacement of the younger native population by exurbanites. In turn, the new people were less conventional in their cultural values than those they supplanted.

A long view on church records of the 1960s—more geographic transfers, fewer baptisms—betrays this demographic shift. But the church felt its impact more immediately and dramatically. Two young religious radicals arrived in Mendocino, bringing their versions of the nascent state to the Presbyterian church. The first was Peter Hsu, a Chinese-American from San Francisco, who became pastor in 1962. The second, whose story we will take up in chapter five, was Larry Redford, a schoolteacher from Los Angeles. Both were visionaries, the one of the religious left, the other of the right. Between them, they shook the church to its theological foundations.

The pastor-seeking committee that brought Peter Hsu to Mendocino Presbyterian was undramatically constituted. A congregational meeting in May of 1962, after Reverend Higginson had resigned, saw about sixty people (forty percent of the church membership) elect six of their number to call a new pastor. There were four women and two men on the search committee; all were faithful members of the church, and there was a range of opinion from conservative to liberal among them. By the time I came to Mendocino to study the church, most of these people had died, but from one member still living, from other veterans of the time, and from the official records, this story was pieced together.

The committee was presented with five resumes of candidates in the geographical area and in the salary range the church could offer (about $4800). According to my informant, the only one who remotely fit the criteria was Peter Hsu. He was young (thirty-four), well-educated, and highly recommended, and he seemed far and away the best man for the job. But he was Chinese! Reverend Althorpe, acting as interim pastor, assured the committee that their judgment was sound. In fact, Althorpe had been disappointed with the lackluster pastorate of Higginson and welcomed Hsu's infusion of young ideas. So the committee invited Hsu to deliver a trial sermon in Fort Bragg. They found him to be everything he'd been said to be, and more. He was energetic, quick-minded, and even handsome. He had to be their man. They set a date (July 1, 1962) for the "candidating sermon" in Mendocino, and worked to persuade their fellow church members. One woman on the committee called all the members of the Ladies' Aid to convince them that such an appointment would be in keeping with the Presbyterian Church's long-standing mission to Chinese-Americans in northern California. Other members of the committee were given roles to play in the congregational meeting that would follow Hsu's sermon.

Two weeks in advance, the candidating sermon was announced, and one hundred twenty people, a large turnout for that time, attended the service to hear Hsu preach about the church as a corporate body. Those who were members stayed for the congregational meeting while Althorpe ushered the candidate outside to pass the time. Hsu was won over by the older man's wry remark, "You know, the last time we had a Chinaman in this town, we ran him out." But inside, things went according to plan. The chairman of the search committee, a highway patrolman, read Hsu's resume. By arrangement, there was a motion to approve the call, and someone else moved that there be a standing vote. As my informant told me, "I was in the back of the church, and when the vote came, everyone stood up. They didn't have the guts not to. We did our work, and we delivered the congregation to Peter Hsu. No sour grapes were allowed." It may be related that in his more than four years of pastoring this church of 150 members, Hsu saw Sunday morning attendance top one hundred on only nine occasions, four of them Easter Sundays, when Protestant churches traditionally bulge with once-a-year churchgoers. By the end of his term at Mendocino, average Sunday attendance was hovering below forty percent of the membership. The many reasons for this relative disaffection, as well as the achievements of Hsu's pastorate, will be elaborated in a moment. But that July Sunday in 1962 was not forgotten. When asked to explain their reasons for disaffiliation from the church, the wife of one previously active couple said, "Perhaps it was the way he [Hsu] was voted in."

Liberalism Nascent

Peter Hsu thus became the first nonwhite pastor of a white Presbyterian Church in California. He came to Mendocino with a personal mission to bring what he called progressive religion from a ghetto church to a majority church. His model was the Presbyterian church in San Francisco's Chinatown, in which he had been spiritually raised. "In this church," Hsu wrote years later, "life and liturgy blended together. Daily events took meaning from the profound truths demonstrated at the Lord's Table. Life was seen as holy, love was expressed through fellowship, and mission was accepted as the natural outcome of having worshiped together."[1] Hsu did not encounter Christianity as an obligatory, taken-for-granted extension of life at home, but as a whole round of life within a community. In his very person, Hsu brought youth, race, and nascent religion to Mendocino in the early sixties.

Peter Hsu was an educator, a scholar and writer, and he emphasized the teaching part of his role above the pastoral, administrative, or priestly functions. He began the practice of opening the monthly meetings of the church's board of elders (or "session") with a half-hour study of a specially chosen Bible passage. (The session spent much of 1963 studying the social theory in Paul's letter to the Colossians.) Hsu raised the consciousness of church members in his sermons, and he was an active participant in the denomination's system of hierarchical judicatories (the Presbytery and the Synod). He also served a term on the county grand jury.

Hsu's pastorate had two overall thrusts. One was to streamline the church's internal organization, a program of rationalization. The other was to open the church to the wider community, both local and cosmopolitan, a program of ecumenism. He presided over a restructuring of the session set in motion by Althorpe, and he established a new body, the deacons. Before Hsu's time, the business side of the church's affairs had been the responsibility of the five-member board of trustees, and the spiritual side was supervised by the seven-member session. In 1963, the two bodies were merged into a twelve-member board, four members being designated as trustees, legally responsible for the properties and financial affairs of the church but no longer holding themselves aloof from religious concerns. The deacons, with five (after 1970, nine) members, were an elected body specially designated to be visitors to the sick and lonely. This was by tradition a major aspect of the pastor's role, but Hsu did not believe in "stroking" members with regular visits. He saw pastoral care as the responsibility of the whole congregation, not only of the minister. He led the first class of deacons through Dietrich Bonhoeffer's *Life Together*, the foremost theological statement of the ideal of church life he had experienced in Chinatown.

Hsu despised "fluff" in the church, and he watched the age and sex-based activity groups, one by one, die off (with the exception of the venerable Ladies' Aid). From time to time during the sixties the church even lacked a choir. (A drop-in program for town youth, quite different from the clubby Westminster Fellowship, flourished under Hsu's guidance for a while in the mid-1960s, until the church member who was its particular inspiration moved away.) One other group within the church, "Albion Chapel," six miles away, clung stubbornly to life. A small group of older residents whose own church had been demolished by the state highway department in the 1940s, Albion Chapel came under the care of the denomination in the 1950s and was merged with Mendocino Presbyterian in 1958. Throughout the 1960s, this group's fading life is chronicled in the church's records, until the early 1970s, when their building—a run-down old house—was taken over by young evangelicals.

The rationalized church structure was not all Hsu's doing, but it did serve his educational agenda. Moreover, he was both credited and blamed for its effects, and resentment against his relative neglect of traditional pastoral care seems to have been widespread. Speaking of the establishment of the deacons, one disaffected person said, "They decided that there were too many other things for the minister to do. Before, the ministers had always done it, but Peter never called on anybody."

By all accounts, the most damaging event during Hsu's pastorate was a scandalous affair within the congregation. It was none of his doing, but his response was widely criticized. Even twenty years after the fact, it would be tactless to identify the principals, and it will suffice to mention the parameters of the case. There was a romantic triangle, with a homosexual side, involving a married couple long active in the church and a newcomer. The family was wrecked, one parent was left with the children, and many members of the church were outraged at the behavior of the newcomer, who was accused of "corrupting one of our own." The scandal was, said one informant, "an almighty upheaval from top to bottom." "Everyone was appalled," said another. "It was one hell of a mess," said Hsu.

In the face of calls for action from excommunication to lynching, Hsu insisted that the church must have room for sinners. He became privy to intimate details of the case (which he told me he would not divulge to his own wife, let alone to a sociologist) that convinced him that the sin was not one-sided. Some session members supported him, but others sympathized with the cries for vengeance. The October 1965 meeting of the session was virtually given over to discussion of the issue. Romans 12, with its reminder that vengeance is God's prerogative, was Hsu's Bible reading for the month. Several session members called for punitive action, and they were quelled, though not calmed. Finally, a motion was passed "that we do not condone" the activities of the alleged culprit "that have led to difficulties over the past few months." The compromise motion added a note of forgiveness and an offer of continued Christian fellowship for the outsider, who, however, felt unwelcome and soon left the congregation.

The wounds of this affair were deep. Many people felt that the actions taken against the "outsider" were insufficiently severe, and many also thought that Peter Hsu did too little for the now-separated former mates and their children. Hsu, in turn, felt that the scapegoating of the outsider reflected the narrowness of Mendocinoans' attitudes. For the last year of his pastorate, in the wake of the scandal, Hsu's regular Sunday congregation was a knot of about sixty members, and 1966's Easter service saw a turnout for that usually jam-packed service of only 128, a record low. Hsu felt grateful to those who stood by him and the church in the crisis, and he realized that they were not identical with those who backed him on social justice. In later years, as a seminary professor, he warned his students, "You can do your politics if you're a good pastor."

One longtime member who counted herself a friend of Hsu's told me that he was not in fact a good pastor but that he had a real gift as an educator. His achievement at Mendocino Presbyterian was to make the congregation as a body aware of its inherent membership in a larger world. Hsu knew that he was helping write social history, and it was he, several informants said, who brought the church "into the twentieth century."

Soon after his arrival in Mendocino, Hsu saw a need to open Preston Hall to the community. The argument hinged in part on the fact that townspeople had given donations for the building under the impression that it would be used for "social and educational purposes," primarily for the church but also for worthy groups. Newspaper reports of the fund-raising campaign had been studiously ambiguous about Preston Hall's sacred/secular status. For example, a reporter saw the building as "a focal point for Christian fellowship in the community of Mendocino and the immediate coastal area." One speaker at the building's dedication was reported to have lauded Dr. Preston's "Christian purpose [of] increasing the educational and fellowship opportunities of the church for the community." But in 1958, shortly after the building opened, the trustees authorized its use for social, cultural, and educational activities sponsored by church members only, and in the ensuing years its use was denied to such groups as the 4-H and the public school teachers' association on the grounds that the requests did not come from members. But in February of 1963, a half year after Hsu's arrival, the session passed a new policy. "Recognizing its responsibility to the community," the church made its building available to "community organizations" "to promote programs of civil betterment and awareness." This opportunity was immediately seized by groups and individuals in the town, and the disposition of Preston Hall became a political sore point and the single most time-consuming issue for the church session in the next decade. But higher church officials approved of the new policy, and the Mendocino session soon received an official letter of commendation from the Presbytery.

Hsu's overture to newcomers was another ecumenical effort. A jazz buff and something of a bohemian in personal style, Hsu reached out to the burgeoning artist's colony. One of his new friends was a noted left-wing artist, known among her detractors in town as a communist, whose paintings of children, doves, and flowers were popular among pacifists in the early 1960s. She lived across the street from the church, and, though she came to worship only once, she immortalized the Sunday School children (including the Hsu children) in her canvases. Other artists, some of whose lifestyles were disliked by conservative townspeople, were welcomed by Hsu, both as church members and as decorators of Preston Hall. In a town not previously known for its cosmopolitanism, Hsu could point with pride to the church's role in the integration of the new bohemians to the life of the community. "Beatnik," he reported in his annual summary for 1964, had become a term more of humor than of scorn in Mendocino.

At least of equal significance for Peter Hsu were his initiatives to bring state, national, and international social issues before his parishioners. "Basically, our church exists for mission," he said in his year-end report for 1963: "Our church must move ahead." A year later he urged, "We must continue to stand for justice and equality and human values." He frequently brought social action messages from Presbyterian judicatories to the attention of the congregation.

In 1963, the big issues were at the state level: the Rumford Fair Housing Law, in which Hsu had a deep-seated personal and ethical interest; and the death penalty. In 1964 and 1965, attention turned to the American South, and a Presbyterian civil-rights curriculum was the study material for several months of session meetings in 1964. In March of 1965, use of Preston Hall was granted for an arts fair benefit to help rebuild black Mississippi churches that had been destroyed by segregationist arson. (Frederick Althorpe was cochair of this event.) In 1966, Hsu brought to the session a draft of a revised United Presbyterian confession, featuring new language concerning social justice. Near the end of his pastorate, he began to speak out against the war in Vietnam.

The Gathering Storm

Hsu's activities caused discomfort for some and brought inspiration to others. A few members resigned. Others came to worship less often and gave less generously. Four longtime members, whose participation in the life of the church began to fall off under Hsu and who were finally suspended from membership during the 1970s, spoke to me of the church's politics as a reason for their disaffection. Still others, grumbling perhaps about Hsu's partiality to "beatniks" and "the town Red," stood by the church nonetheless. One outspoken person, a faithful, conservative member of the church, became active as a layperson in the affairs of the denomination in order to keep tabs on the "wild things" it kept cooking up in politics. Then there were those—about thirty people—who joined the church during Hsu's years, at least some of them attracted by his policies.

It could not have been easy to be a young pastor in the 1960s preaching social justice to a conservative congregation. So we have been told by sociologists of religion. Fewer have pointed out that it also must have been difficult to have been a parishioner in disagreement with one's pastor when he claimed to be speaking with biblical and theological sanction. Just as the liberals of the 1980s fear that those in the middle of the road are being intimidated into acquiescence by the "Moral Majority's" invocation of God, so also moderates in the 1960s must have been cowed by articulate, zealous, liberal preachers like Peter Hsu. He succeeded in securing formal approval of his first annual pastoral report, but the tone of the session's action was querulous. "All were in accord on the point that 'the church is a servant to the community.' " When Hsu asked his elders in March of 1965 for permission to take an emergency leave to lend a hand in the civil-rights struggle in Alabama, the response was cool. The session agreed, however, to grant the permission "if the Holy Spirit calls him." Hsu's purpose was to get his session to declare itself concretely for civil rights, and he won.

When he spoke out on the war in Vietnam, he was "called on the carpet" by the elders, as one informant put it. One session meeting early in 1966 had this outcome:

> After a lengthy discussion, it was decided by common consent that the church should be concerned with social issues such as the war in Vietnam and that Reverend Hsu should prepare a sermon soon attempting to show how a Christian can show his concern about current moral problems and how a church and its members can do their parts in fulfilling Jesus' commandment "to make peace." It was hoped that the sermon would point out that the church does not align itself with any particular group on social issues.

After the sermon was preached, the session again went on record as approving its content.

Though he was under suspicion, Hsu did not slacken his activities. He took the prophet Amos as his model, and he was inclined to see in his own unpopularity an index of the effectiveness of his prophetic witness. There was a blitheness in him that gave him a remarkable ability to concentrate on essentials and disregard sidetracks. One informant said that Hsu was "puzzled" by lack of support for his initiatives, and the record shows that he made a yearly complaint about poor attendance. But he was no fool. He simply would not heed such a reproach as this one, voiced to me ten years later by a member of his board of deacons:

> I believe the church should not get involved in politics; the sermon should speak from the Bible and show how we ought to deal with our everyday lives. I don't see why religion should change.

The evidence shows that sentiments such as this, voiced or tacit, articulate or bewildered, were widespread in the church, without being predominant.

Conflict was muted, but not absent. It took subtle forms, as Jeffrey Hadden found to be true of Protestant churches across the land in the 1960s:

> For example, a minister who has become involved in some form of protest may suddenly find himself subjected to criticism for neglecting his visitation duties or absenteeism from the ladies' missionary society. In one sense, these criticisms may be legitimate, for the more he becomes involved in activity outside the church, the less time he has for

local parish duties. But in another sense, the criticisms are a covert way of handling dissatisfaction with his involvement in social action.[2]

Studies done of Presbyterians elsewhere in the country a few years later show on the basis of carefully analyzed quantitative data that church members who favor pastoral care and Biblical teaching over liberal social action as the preferred agenda for their churches do so out of genuine theological rather than hidden political convictions.[3] So we should not dismiss Hsu's opponents simply as political conservatives annoyed with liberal social action. Yet whatever the alternative agenda to Hsu's might have been does not appear in the contemporary or retrospective accounts. Some people were clearly unhappy, and, as Hadden was finding at about the same time, there was disquiet in the church.

Controversy engulfed not Hsu but his successor. During Hsu's ministry, church membership grew slowly, as did the budget, on a per-capita basis. But average attendance dwindled steadily, and Hsu and his elders did little pruning of the rolls. The 150-plus membership rolls of Mendocino Presbyterian were seriously inflated when Hsu left in October 1966. The church body was slack.

Four years after accepting the call from the Mendocino church, Hsu received an offer from Presbyterian headquarters in Philadelphia to take a staff position in the Board of Christian Education. The salary was double that of his present job, but the job itself, full-time in his specialty, was the primary attraction. Four years earlier, immediately after accepting Mendocino's call, he had received a similar offer, which he was obliged to decline because of his commitment to Mendocino. After four years as a pastor (the average term for the many pastors Mendocino Presbyterian had had), and receiving the blessing of his mentor, Althorpe, Hsu felt free to leave. At a meeting of the Presbytery, he sounded out Mark Kimmerly, a fellow alumnus of San Francisco Theological Seminary, about the upcoming Mendocino vacancy. In Mendocino, he advised the elders to seek out another young minister as his replacement, but he made no particular case for Kimmerly.

Hsu's charm and talents won him many friends even among those who did not agree with him, and today even his erstwhile opponents express pride in his subsequent career as a writer, teacher, and church executive. Some now acknowledge that he was right and they were wrong about the action taken in the scandal of 1965. Hsu left behind few personal enemies and several partisans of his community-oriented brand of Christianity. He did not leave behind a united congregation.

Evidence of disunity surfaced at the congregational meeting held

after worship on November 13, 1966, to elect a pastor-search committee. The members were presented by the elders with a balanced slate
of nominees, five names for a committee intended to number seven,
two additional people to be nominated from the floor. But five people
were nominated from the floor, including an outspoken conservative
who is remembered by contemporaries as a "retired career army sergeant with a temper to match."

Unique in the twenty-year period I have scrutinized, the ensuing
election was a contested one, with ten nominees for seven places. The
vote was by written ballot. The result was a relative victory for the
friends of Hsu. The sergeant was not elected, and of the other contes-
tants, newcomers were elected over old-timers. Reactionaries defaulted by staying away, and the new committee was unlikely to seek
a successor who would turn his back on the direction Hsu had set for
the church.

While the pastor-seeking committee began its work, the congregation turned once again to pastor emeritus Althorpe to provide interim
leadership. He took on the task at $400 per month under a job descrip-
tion carefully qualified to protect his health (he was seventy-four), but
he did more than was required for less than was offered. He led a
committee to write the job description for a new pastor. He presided
over busy and contentious session meetings in which the new year's
budget was planned. Because 1966/1967 was a season of drought, the
church had to buy water from a neighbor. When finances got tight,
Althorpe suggested reducing his pay to $300 per month. After the
new pastor had been chosen, a grateful congregation thanked Althorpe again for "leadership, inspiration, and his work in uniting the
fellowship."

The pastor-seeking committee presented its candidate to the congregation eight weeks after its own election. He was the man Hsu
himself had sought out to take the job, Mark Kimmerly, and eighty-
eight people came that Sunday morning to hear his candidating sermon. In response to hard feelings about the calling of Peter Hsu,
someone moved that the vote on the motion to call Kimmerly be by
written ballot. The call was approved (there is no record of the tally,
though Kimmerly remembers hearing that there might have been a
dissenting vote), and Kimmerly became the new pastor at the beginning of February 1967.

Mark Kimmerly was thirty-four and was completing work for a
master's degree in Christian Social Ethics at the seminary. He had
earlier pastored a church in Plantation, a San Joaquin Valley farming
town beset with class and racial conflicts, and he had returned to
seminary to refresh theological convictions that had been put to the

test by a contentious congregation. He and his wife, Carol, came to Mendocino, despite the low salary offered, thinking that such a small town would be a good place to begin raising the family they had theretofore postponed.

Longtime members recall Kimmerly as less zealous than Hsu had been, and, while appropriately blue-eyed and ruddy-faced, Kimmerly was introspective where Hsu had been outgoing. His intellectual model was the chastened, realistic Neoorthodoxy of Reinhold Niebuhr rather than the heroic martyrdom of Dietrich Bonhoeffer, Hsu's ideal. Kimmerly was characterologically sensitive to diversity in his congregations, and he quickly learned the makeup of his new constituency: the old-time townspeople, the now-established bohemian artists, the conservative and liberal church pillars, and the flowering counterculture. His initiatives in the congregation were more likely to be consensus-building mechanisms than call-to-action sermons. He proposed opinion-sharing congregational meetings, goal-clarification session meetings, and weekly feedback hours after the sermon. He was more inclined to notify the congregation of divisive political initiatives sent down from denominational hierarchs than to urge action on them. Relative to his predecessor, he seemed to care more about this particular congregation, this community and these people, than about general social issues. Above all, he put the congregation to work on its physical properties, a project calculated to unite them.

Not only had Peter and Emma Hsu paid little heed to personal criticism; they had also put up with the disrepair of the once-stately manse. But the Kimmerlys arrived in February, and Carol Kimmerly would not tolerate it. It seldom freezes during the north-coast winter, but there are five or six months of steady, damp cold that can put a chill deep into the bones. So the drafts had to be stopped up and the heater replaced. The glint of the sun off Mendocino Bay was glorious when the sun could be seen, but the more frequent sieges of fog cast a gloomy pall. So the walls had to be painted and papered in new, bright colors. Bob Gamble, church trustee and chair of the pastor-search committee, virtually moved into the manse for a month to supervise the work that would make it worthy of the new pastor and his wife.

In his first week on the job, while strolling around the grounds, Kimmerly was asked by a tourist, "Is this building still in use?" One year short of its centenary, the sanctuary showed its age. Over the years, the building had deteriorated, and its architectural integrity had been compromised by tiny classrooms being parcelled out of its south end. The matter of the building centennial was discussed at Kimmerly's first session meeting in 1967, and later that year the congregation approved an ambitious building improvement plan, involving structural restoration, painting, carpeting, and stained-glass windows. The necessary loans were guaranteed by the Synod, and the restorations were completed in 1968 and 1969, leaving a large deficit. Within the next two years, a series of bequests and memorial contributions discharged it. Among veterans of the congregation, Kimmerly is most fondly remembered as one with a gift for rebuilding.

Neoorthodoxy is more assured in its rejection of liberal self-deception and conservative nostalgia than it is in its own worldly credo. So Kimmerly came to Mendocino not, as did Peter Hsu, with an agenda, but with generalized sympathies for the left in the movements of the 1960s and a particular scorn for those who opposed them in the name of propriety. When an issue presented itself, Kimmerly would take the stance he felt was just. He thus earned among church conservatives the reputation of being partial to dissidents, but at the same time his skepticism did not truly inspire those on whose side he stood. He stood for social justice, for peace, and for openness to the youth of the sixties, but he was less a leader of these causes than a would-be conciliator between their advocates and opponents. That role was little appreciated, and much of the time Kimmerly seemed discouraged. Yet he ultimately left the church in a strong position that was seized upon by his successor.

It took no clergyman to mobilize movements for political and cultural change in Mendocino in the second half of the 1960s. Though a small town, Mendocino was only hours away from San Francisco, the west-coast capital of radical politics and cultural experimentation, and Mendocino's reputation as a haven first for bohemians and then for hippies had spread along the coast. The church had been swept up in the tide through Peter Hsu's ideas and his new constituents. But it was through Preston Hall that the church was most irretrievably enmeshed in the cultural currents of the sixties.

Through Hsu's initiative, Preston Hall had become a center of community activity. It also became a chronic bone of contention in the session. In the words of one veteran church officer, "Preston Hall has been a beast," "a thorn in our sides," "a cross for the church to bear." Under Peter Hsu, as we have seen, the church officers decided to make the hall available to the community at large, under monitoring by the trustees. This policy pleased not only liberals in the Presbyterian hierarchy and in the community but also those Mendocinoans of various political affiliations who had been led to believe by the building's fund-raising campaign in the 1950s that the facility would not be monopolized by the church. Once the new policy of openness was established in 1963, it developed its own momentum. Precedents were set, and constituencies of users developed. After a few years, moreover, it became clear that the hall was a source of revenue for the church. The church incurred costs by opening the building for nonchurch concerts and meetings, and "donations" were expected for such use. But the church incurred costs simply by maintaining the building at all, and by 1971 the trustees found that the church budget had become dependent upon Preston Hall revenue. Some of the hall's uses had raised hackles, and church officers frequently found themselves explaining and amending Preston Hall policy. (Today, after thirty years, the only rule that has been consistently in force is the prohibition of the use of alcoholic beverages.)

The first skirmishes over Preston Hall were episodes in the cultural conflict of the 1960s. It was loud noise and rock dancing that most upset those who complained about the use of the hall in 1965 and 1967. Session committees were set up to clarify policy, and compromise solutions were tried: placing curtains on the windows, limiting the power of amplifiers, allowing bands to rehearse but not to perform, and locking the doors on rehearsals lest they become performances. Feelings ran high over "wiggly dancing" and "Beatle-y music," and one vocal complainer was the retired sergeant mentioned earlier, who lived across the street from Preston Hall.

Six months after Kimmerly came, the session hit the ceiling when the chairman of the trustees granted use of the hall for a dance to benefit a counterculture school in the nearby town of Caspar. By formal vote, the elders rescinded the action of the trustees and took to themselves the prerogative of deciding who might use the hall and for what purposes. For the next three years, every request to use the hall had to be approved by the entire session, and approval was by no means automatic. Preston Hall began to consume the lion's share of the time of their monthly meetings.

Having acted in haste against the trustees, the session had to be ready to respond to important requests quickly, and a bylaw amendment was passed later that year allowing special meetings of the session to be called on fewer than five days' notice, with two-thirds of its twelve members being a quorum. The result of these procedural changes, in which Mark Kimmerly was not particularly implicated, was to hold him as well as other church officers on a very short leash. The leash was soon used, and the issue was a demonstration sponsored by the Southern Christian Leadership Conference soon after the assassination of Martin Luther King, Jr.

Throughout 1967 and 1968, the congregation had become increasingly polarized. One active member, the wife of the retired sergeant and herself the former church treasurer, complained of publicity for a peace rally that appeared in the church bulletin. Another conservative resigned his post on the session in the spring of 1968, giving no formal statement but leaving no doubt that the liberal inclinations of the pastor and the denomination were too much for him and his wife. In this atmosphere, it may have been naive for Mark Kimmerly to grant, as he did, permission to use Preston Hall on an upcoming July 4 weekend for a "Poor People's Campaign Benefit." Folksinger Malvina Reynolds had been invited, and some townspeople thought her a communist. (Reynolds denied the allegation in a letter to the local paper.) A study group within the church had requested the use of Preston Hall for the benefit, and Kimmerly gave permission. He had articulated his reasons in his master's thesis. "The Christian faith," he wrote, "cannot be locked safely in a narrow box, painted red, and used solely for extinguishing the fires of hell."[4]

When the word got out about Kimmerly's action, there was an outcry from conservatives in the congregation and on the session, and a special meeting of the session was called on four days' notice. Opinions were strong and divided. The retired sergeant called Kimmerly a communist. Kimmerly bristled and responded that he was an officer in the naval reserve. A less extreme conservative could not understand why Kimmerly had taken an action that obviously violated the procedural guidelines set down the previous year. Others agreed with the pastor that the planned event was not political in a partisan sense. But one of his staunch allies had recently moved away and left the session, and the pastor was backed into a corner.

A motion was made to rescind Kimmerly's action, and, on a secret ballot, the vote was four in favor, three opposed, and one abstaining. (Three resignations—two because the individuals left town, one for political reasons—had reduced the session temporarily to nine members, and one was absent.) There being no majority, it was decided to reconsider, and, when the vote was taken again, it was a four-four tie. As moderator, or chairman of the meeting, the pastor cast the tiebreaking vote against the motion, thus affirming his original action. Before the meeting adjourned, a committee consisting of the pastor, the sergeant, and Larry Redford, the evangelical school teacher, was appointed to write a letter to the church membership and to the local papers explaining that the use of Preston Hall for the Fourth of July rally did not constitute an endorsement by the church of the SCLC.

The rally delighted town liberals, who got "good vibes" from Malvina Reynolds. But reactionaries were outraged, and one person painted a hammer and sickle on the garden gate of the "town red" artist. The congregation was divided. At the next regular meeting of the session, three days after the Poor People's Benefit, a motion was passed requiring written application for future use of Preston Hall and designating one member of the session to receive the applications and maintain the calendar for the Hall "with the cooperation" of the Pastor.

Two months later, an elaborate new policy for the Hall was passed by the session. Recognizing the precedents established for the previous five years, the new policy made the hall available for community nonprofit organizations and activities. It reaffirmed the compromise that "public dancing" would not be allowed. (In practice, this seemed directed more at "social dancing" and "rock dancing" than at "folk dancing.") It left standing the traditional prohibition against alcoholic beverages. It formalized the role of keeper of the church calendar. (These policies stayed in effect until the fall of 1971, when, having tired of the trivia of running the calendar and having seen political passions cool, the session again delegated responsibility for the hall to a committee.)

The new 1968 policy added a guarded provision, which illuminates the touchiness of the compromise:

> Permission [to use the Hall] will not be granted to groups who represent a political or social position likely to cause separation within the church family. However, under certain circumstances involving our Christian position, the session may grant permission for use of the hall if both sides of a volatile issue are fairly presented. Or, at the discretion of the session, a poll of the membership may be taken in the form of a hearing to present and clarify the issues involved.

In fact, these elaborate procedural devices went unused for ten years until they were invoked against a church committee's application to show a right-to-life movie in Preston Hall. Instead, the most intransigent of the conservatives withdrew, including our sergeant, who resigned from the session that fall. Social action items coming from the denomination were reported directly to the congregation in newsletters and at worship services by an active but conservative participant in the Presbytery. Kimmerly did gain on session one valuable new ally, an artist who was active in the peace movement, when the year's four resigned slots were filled. But Kimmerly could no longer offend the prickly sensibilities of the elders by opening Preston Hall to controversial causes. Moreover, he had never wanted to be a crusader. He wanted to be a healer. He was sensitive to pressure from the right, and he recognized from his prior pastoral experience that good churchmanship was to be found on both conservative ar. `b-eral sides of a dispute. However, when basic values—including his political convictions—were invoked, he would stand up for his beliefs and not be intimidated.

By 1970, Hsu's and Kimmerly's openness to new elements in the community began to pay off in the increased participation of artists in the life of the church. Shortly after coming to Mendocino, Kimmerly had hosted a meeting of the Presbytery and had asked Arturo de Grazia, a potter prominent in the local art world, to put on a "happening" for the visiting dignitaries. De Grazia's efforts—a light show and pottery-making exhibition—were well received by the outsiders. The art colony became more accepted in the community, and two people on the session, a decorator and a musician, were specially mandated to develop arts-in-worship programs. For the next two years, "experimental worship" programs were held on a monthly basis, employing the talents of musicians, poets, painters, sculptors, and photographers, whether or not they were members of the church. One event had de Grazia reading from the Beatitudes, a marijuana leaf marking the place in his Bible, while his wife sang verses from Simon and Garfunkel's "Sounds of Silence," their young child in a sling over her shoulder. Such activities were part of the attraction of the church for avant garde newcomers to the community.

De Grazia and his wife would eventually join the church (in 1974) along with dozens of other veterans of the counterculture, making it a very different Presbyterian church in the 1970s than it had been in the fifties and the sixties. But de Grazia and the others were not drawn in directly by Kimmerly's ecumenism but by a radically unintended effect of it. It was not Hsu's and Kimmerly's liberal Christianity that ultimately attracted the counterculture. Instead, it was the nascent evangelicalism of another newcomer to Mendocino, Larry Redford, which had that effect.

5.

From Mission to Parachurch: Antioch Fellowship, 1969–1973

For charisma is by nature not a continuous institution, but in its pure type the very opposite. In
order to live up to their mission the master as well
as his disciples and immediate following must be
free of the ordinary worldly attachments and duties of occupational and family life. Those who
have a share in charisma must inevitably turn
away from the world.
—Max Weber, *Economy and Society*

Mark Kimmerly's proudest achievement in "stewardship"
and social engineering was the cooperative effort to rehabilitate the
church properties in observation of the building centennial. He intended and planned this outcome. But his greater impact on the
church came through his outreach to a community beyond the ken of
the church family. For this man of Neoorthodox theology and liberal
social conscience was a prime mover in the establishment of a theologically conservative, even fundamentalist, enclave in his own congregation, an enclave that began, in his mind, as a mission to the counterculture. This chapter tells the story of that enclave, later known as
Antioch Fellowship.

Mission to the Counterculture

The social fault lines dividing Mendocino in the late sixties
were unlike those Kimmerly had known in his previous pastorate in

Plantation, as well as unlike those he had read about in preparing his master's thesis. The divisions were not of race and social class; Mendocino was not like Little Rock, Gastonia, or Detroit.[1] At issue in Mendocino was culture or "lifestyle," and the parties were the straight and the hip. Mendocino was a haven for flower children and a way station to Canada for war resisters. Some young immigrants went "back to the land," pitching tents or building unconventional shelters on out-of-the-way plots of forest land. Transients camped on the beach just below the town and cooked and kept warm by driftwood fires. Townspeople vented spleen at "vagabonds" and "undesirables," random rifle shots broke the stillness of the forest, and more than one handmade house was destroyed by a fire of mysterious origin. Nasty letters appeared in the paper.

> Can't Mendocino be cleansed of its growth of "noxious weeds"? This wouldn't be holding progress back. It would be preserving the fine old North Coast traditions that built Mendocino and kept it going through thick and thin. Wake up, Mendocino. Keep the CRUD off your doorstep.

Kimmerly was appalled at such sentiments, though he himself first viewed the sexual freedom of the newcomers with distaste. He was saddened by some hippies' neglect of their own children. But his home—the manse, next door to the church, right above the beach, and just off the main road into town—was an obvious spot for refugees from the draft or from San Francisco's increasingly violent drug scene to seek solace and shelter. Some wanted to talk. Some even came to church. But few found whatever they were looking for. As the most prominent, most stable institution in town, the church ought to be doing something for these people, thought Kimmerly. But what?

The answer came from a strange quarter. Larry Redford was a thirty-seven-year-old science and physical education teacher at Mendocino High School and an outspoken evangelical. In the new year of 1969, he was just coming off a three-year term on the church session. Redford felt frustration both in his service to the church and in his job at the high school. The session he served on, he later told me with disgust, would rather discuss where flags should be placed in the church than ask how church members' faith could be deepened. At school, neither the hippie kids nor he had much interest in what they were supposed to be learning.

Kimmerly knew that Redford's concerns for spiritual nurture were far from his own concerns for social reconciliation. But he knew of Redford's restlessness, and he also knew that Redford owned and lived on a twenty-acre ranch five miles east of town, an underutilized parcel of sheep pasture, pear orchard, and redwood grove set on a ridge, with a small but well-built house and a few outbuildings. When Redford unloaded his woes to Kimmerly over a family dinner one night that winter, Kimmerly's answer was a startling but practical suggestion: "Why don't you open your ranch to the hippies?"

It was, in fact, an opportunity that the Redfords had been waiting for, not so much to run a mission or a hostelry, but to spend all of their time in what they called "Christian adventure." They were spirit-filled Christians, but for most of their four years in Mendocino they had found that mention of Jesus as a living person or the Bible as a textbook for living invited ridicule, especially in the church. They were starved for spiritual companionship and eager to see the heartache and confusion of Mendocino's transients answered by Christian commitment. Kimmerly's suggestion fell on responsive ears.

Evangelicals in the Nascent State

Larry Redford had been raised in a nominally Presbyterian family in Los Angeles, but he became a born-again Southern Baptist while serving in the air force in Texas in 1954. After marrying a girl he'd met in church and completing college at Baylor, he began training, three years after his conversion, at the new, independent evangelical school in Pasadena, Fuller Theological Seminary. He was not sure he wanted to become a minister, for he was suspicious of institutions and lacked self-confidence, but he wanted to learn more about the faith he had chosen to embrace. He went to school only part-time, while he worked to support himself and his wife and child, but his devotion to his work and his studies—what he called devotion to the Lord—was a strain on his marriage. He was devastated when his wife left him for another man, and he dropped out of Fuller and took a job servicing vending machines to try to get her back. When that did not work, he returned to the seminary and finished in 1963. Soon after, he got a California teaching credential at Valley State.

Once burned, Redford gave more thought to a second marriage. He met Sue, than a twenty-year-old nursing student, during his two-year hiatus from Fuller, through an evangelical group called "The Navigators." The two were mutually attracted but cautious, since divorce is regarded with disapproval by Southern Baptists. Sue's own parents had been divorced, which she says gave her compassion for Larry's plight as well as determination about her own marital future. When their mutual interest became obvious, they decided to spend a month without seeing each other, in prayer and Bible study, to seek confirmation of their inclinations. Only when they had found confirmation did they proceed, quite deliberately, to fall in love. I can only imagine what went on in Larry's and Sue's minds as they searched the scriptures that month. Knowing them both, I have no doubt that they did as they say. For our story, what matters is that "bringing it to the Lord," with Bible and prayer, was part of the Redfords' marriage contract.

When Larry got his job at Mendocino High School in 1964, he and Sue joined the Presbyterian church. Such new blood was welcomed, and they were both appointed to the church's membership committee. But they met no young couples who shared their intense evangelical commitment. A year after joining the church, Larry was elected an elder, and over the next three years he was a faithful participant in the monthly meetings of session. But he disapproved of the way the pastor, Peter Hsu, used the Bible to make points for his social ideals. He found Mark Kimmerly more to his liking, but Kimmerly did not preach the evangelical message of personal salvation through Christ that Larry was committed to.

When Kimmerly broached the idea of opening the Redford ranch to hippies, Ted Brown, pastor of the Mendocino (Southern) Baptist Church and more connected to the evangelical network than were the Presbyterians, suggested that the Redfords look into "Sonlight," a street ministry in San Francisco, part of the new Jesus movement that was channeling youthful antinomianism in theologically conservative directions. So Larry and Sue went to San Francisco. As cultural conservatives, they were put off by the bizarre decor and dress at Sonlight, but they met people who shared their faith and its vocabulary. They saw Sonlight as a rescue mission that could identify those converts who wanted deeper spiritual training and send them up to Mendocino.

Meanwhile, Mark Kimmerly followed up on his opportunity. Having received a favorable reply from Larry, Mark set out to mobilize what support he could in his congregation. Many of his old-timers looked with scorn on the hippies, and he knew that a pastor had to prepare his ground well when entering controversial territory. He planned a series of sermons on the theme of brotherhood, beginning with the least objectionable platitudes but moving toward a declaration of the congregation's obligation to young people with unconventional lifestyles. On Easter of 1969, he concluded his sermon with the suggestion that the church sponsor a hostel for young people who were seriously trying to escape the drugs, prostitution, and violence of San Francisco's Haight-Ashbury scene. He anticipated some angry phone calls, but to his relief, everyone approved. One even said, "That's the first time I've been proud to be a Presbyterian."

Kimmerly invited Redford, at this time a "past active elder," to present the youth hostel idea to the session. Sentiments of support were mixed with delicately phrased suspicions and level-headed business questions. How would it be paid for? What about legal liability? Would Redford be open-minded about people's beliefs? Should we inflict these hippies on Sue? Do we need to bring yet more hippies to Mendocino? Redford responded with a formal prospectus, which he brought to the next session meeting. He stated his intention to comply with county building and health standards. He asked Ted Brown and Mark Kimmerly to sign on as codirectors. He assured the church membership that the hostel was "not going to be a hippie commune" but rather "an attempt to help young people to find themselves in life, and to put Jesus Christ at the core of the life they discover." He called it "Antioch Ranch."

After a long discussion, the session agreed to "give approval and encouragement" to the program and to publicize it to the church members, but not to provide any direct funding. The Baptist church— which was too tiny even to provide its own pastor with a salary— would have nothing official to do with the Ranch. Nonetheless, the lukewarm endorsement of the session and good offices of the Presbyterian and Baptist ministers were vital. Despite the later misconceptions of some of its members, the Presbyterian church did not establish the Ranch, as Larry and Sue stressed to me. On the other hand, without the church's umbrella, "Larry wouldn't have lasted the night," as an unsympathetic elder told me. Antioch Ranch opened in June 1969.

With the endorsement of the session, Mark Kimmerly arranged small grants from two other California Presbyterian churches. Redford secured two food scholarships worth a total of $500 from the evangelism committee of the Presbyterian Church's regional governing body, the Synod. Most important, the Mendocino session approved in October a procedure to channel individual and corporate contributions for Antioch Ranch through the church. As the church's trustees saw it, this procedure would allow the church to keep tabs on where the money was going, while allowing contributors to the Ranch to claim a tax deduction.[2] In the next seven years, nearly thirty thousand dollars was so channeled to Antioch Ranch and its projects.

Such financial support, however, was not forthcoming overnight. Antioch Ranch was what is known among evangelicals as a "faith ministry," a bit of jargon meaning that its financial support was irregular and insecure. The first year, Larry Redford continued to work for his salary as a teacher, but his desire was to give up public-school teaching altogether. Labor-intensive ventures, donations in kind, surplus foods, odd jobs for cash, the farm land itself, and frugality kept the ranch together.

Sonlight sent up five new converts, all young men, and they spent the summer tearing down an old house that had been donated by a sympathetic local realtor in exchange for the demolition work. With the still serviceable redwood lumber, the crew built the frame and roof of a mess hall before the winter rains. Sue did the cooking for her enlarged family, now numbering a dozen, and Larry led Bible-study classes three days a week. At first, the Ranch was intended to house a core group of four to six young men, who would stay for several months and divide their time between physical, outdoor work and religious instruction and devotions.

Transients were expected and were welcomed when they arrived, but they were not actively sought out. Plenty of transients—staying for as short a period as a day or as long as several weeks—did come to the Ranch, and by the end of the first year provision had to be made for women as well. The women were enlisted to help Sue with the cooking, washing, mending, and cleaning and, in Larry's words, "other aspects of the general work God expects of women." In December, the Redfords sent out an "Antioch Ranch Newsletter," which at first was simply an elaborate version of their family's regular Christmas letter to friends but became a somewhat irregular bimonthly publication in the next two years. When spring came, Larry decided to take an unpaid leave of absence from his job to devote his full attention to the Ranch.

Sociologists who have written on "commitment" have pointed out that a commitment is not simply an inner determination or a promise to oneself.[3] It can be a deliberately arranged social trap, where other parties (spouse, children, in-laws, employers, creditors, the community) are witnesses to and guarantors of a bargain. The bargain is that one gets something one wants in return for the risk of loss of face if one backs out. The greater the risk, the greater the commitment. People can gain social credit by piling on more obligations, since others perceive the awful costs they would pay if they were to renege. In this sense, the Redfords were increasingly committed to running their lives as a religious enterprise. They had let a great many people in on that bargain: the church, the evangelical network, their guests, and their children. When, at the end of Larry's one-year leave of absence from his teaching job, he had to decide whether to return to teaching or to resign his tenure, the commitment was deepened. His father offered the family $1000 to add a much-needed bedroom to the main house if Larry would return to his teaching job, and Larry saw that temptation as his signal to resign. "Satan attacks with his doubts, but we are getting to know his voice," he wrote in his May 1971 newsletter. (Did he see his father as Satan? No. But he saw the voice of Satan in his own inclination to accept his father's offer.) "That clinched it," he told me in 1976. He resigned his job and with it the financial security enjoyed by middle-class Americans. In effect, he and Sue had become Antioch Ranch.

Antioch Ranch as a Patriarchal Household

Antioch Ranch evolved into a "Christian growth center" in its first two years. Never a "rescue mission" (that job was left to others) or even exclusively a haven for refugees from the "counterculture," it was a relatively secluded, partially self-sufficient, highly intentional extended family whose members were related by affinity rather than by blood. It provided temporary shelter to scores of transients in the expectation (or faith) that its own needs would be met in similarly unstructured ways. Here is how it worked.[4]

1. Material needs were met by cash income, gifts in kind, and the work of Ranch members. Gifts in cash came from the two California Presbyterian churches (joined by a third in 1970), from the Synod, and from a few individuals. In the first few years, income of this sort never amounted to more than $3000 per year. More significant was the cash income earned by ranch projects and through the labor of Ranch members. Young men and women from the Ranch found occasional employment as caretakers and cleaners in the area, and, beginning in May of 1971, the Ranch contracted to supply janitorial services to the Presbyterian church. Larry Redford himself made jewelry from abalone shells. Seaweed pickles were made and sold to health-food stores and restaurants. Hogs were raised, mostly for ranch consumption, but some pork was sold. A Christian bookstore brought in a few dollars as well as spreading the gospel. Ranch men raised chickens, rabbits, goats, pigs, and a few cattle, tended the pear and apple trees, and began a truck garden. The women cooked, cleaned, and sewed in, as Larry had it, the manner sanctioned in Proverbs 31. (The good wife "rises while it is yet night and provides food for her household and tasks for her maidens.")

Gifts in kind included used clothes, furniture, electrical appliances, and farm equipment. Someone gave baby chickens; another gave fruit trees. Valuable services were provided without charge by local and visiting well-wishers: upholstering, butchering, haircuts, dental work, and optometry. With so many gifts in kind, the Ranch family—fourteen full time residents and over 700 visitors—was able to survive in 1971 on a bit less than $9000 in cash income.

2. Leadership was effectively in the hands of Larry Redford, but he and his household agonized long hours over the basis of authority. Nominally, the Ranch was entrusted to Brown (the Baptist pastor), Kimmerly, and Redford. But Mendocino Baptist Church had frequent changes of pastor, and by the end of 1971 not only Ted Brown but also his successor, both of whom gave help to the Ranch, had left the area. Kimmerly occasionally attended the weekly open potluck dinners of the Ranch fellowship, where neighbors and friends were welcome, but he could not provide day-to-day guidance for the intense activity of the Ranch. Moreover, his wife, Carol, was a feminist and could not abide the Redfords' sex-role ideology. So Mark Kimmerly was a visitor to, not a member of, the Ranch household. He could see that Redford was putting a distinctive stamp on the ministry, but he also had confidence that it was not becoming a "cult."

Larry Redford clearly had the last word, by virtue of his ownership of the property, his gender, his age (forty in 1971), and, after 1970, his full-time commitment to the Ranch, and he liked things to go the way he believed the Lord wanted them to go. Yet he was not a man of overweening self-confidence, and he was uncomfortable with the responsibility his position entailed. He did not claim a special God-given aptitude for leadership. He would rather persuade than command, and he would seek to bring others to his way of thinking by persistent coaxing.

Redford's desire to share responsibility began to be answered during the third summer at the Ranch when a longtime evangelical couple was added to the Ranch family. They were David and Jeannie Baker. David Baker was a state park ranger recently transferred to Mendocino who had helped Redford bring the Ranch prospectus to the Presbyterian Synod. Baker had since joined the Presbyterian Church and been elected an elder-trustee, acting as a liaison between Antioch Ranch and the session. The Bakers were the first couple of roughly equal age and status with whom the Redfords could share their idea of Christian fellowship since their move to Mendocino. As this relationship developed and the Bakers wanted to settle permanently in the area, Redford sought out the owner of a seven-acre parcel of land adjoining the Ranch, and the Bakers were able to purchase the land at a very modest price on a no-interest loan, in which transaction they saw the hand of the Lord. Despite his wife's trepidations, David became a lieutenant of Larry's, and the Bakers' land was informally brought under the Ranch's management. With the Bakers on the scene, the Redfords were able to take a two-week vacation in the summer of 1971.

3. Discipline—what sociologists call "social control" and new evangelicals call "the walk"—was both a precondition for and a goal of Antioch Ranch. From the outset, the leaders and sponsors of the Ranch wanted it understood that "no drugs or sexual irresponsibility [i.e., nonmarital sex] will be tolerated." Single men and women were put up in different "dormitories" (one being nothing more than an old house trailer), and the turnover in their numbers made difficult any collusion among them against the official norms of chastity and abstinence. Daily devotional meetings, meals in common, and group chores not only absorbed what might have been idle hours but also served as occasions of surveillance and indoctrination. The Redfords felt particularly fortunate, "blessed," when they recognized the applicability to their enterprise of Paul's injunction, "If any one will not work, let him not eat" (II Thess. 3:10, RSV).

Proscriptions and restraints loom large in the rhetoric of some evangelicals, and it is tempting to attribute this emphasis to their peculiar psychological makeup. In fact, evangelicals are divided among themselves, and many are personally ambivalent, about the emphasis that should be placed on external behavior.[5] At least one goal of Antioch Ranch at its inception was to reach out to those of unconventional behavior and lifestyle, and the Ranch thus shared the commitment of many evangelical missions not to exclude those with long hair, shabby clothes, or uneducated speech. If a godly walk required conventional styles, presumably that would follow the Christian nurture one received through the mission. Not only did simple human generosity and patience demand such a policy, but so also did the evangelicals' doctrine of salvation, which was an important part of their appeal to the counterculture.

The common coin of evangelicals is their insistence that salvation is available to all persons through confession of faith in Jesus Christ. One does not earn salvation, one accepts it. Salvation is not based on worldly attainments or sins; it transcends these. This message has always appealed to those who scorn the standards of the institutional world, and "faith, not works" became a byword of the posthippie Jesus movement.

Given the theological goals, the social constituency, and the practical requirements of the fellowship, it is understandable that a doctrine of "discernment" arose in order to handle the problem of social control. Particularly during the summers, when large numbers of youthful transients (up to 100 per month) dropped in for short visits, Larry and Sue felt exploited by those who flouted the Ranch's strict but plain behavioral code and shirked their share of the chores. During the third year, they paid increasing attention to screening out "problem people" and arrived at some sociological rules of thumb. Young, newly converted, married couples were not encouraged to become residents of the Ranch, and neither were teenagers. "Emotionally disturbed" persons were referred to other ministries. Sobriety, tractability, and helpfulness were looked for in potential young adult recruits. "We are increasingly careful who we choose, feeling much like Jesus must have felt as he chose His 12 disciples," wrote Larry in a newsletter. "He prayed all night before making any decisions."

4. "To aid in the nurture of Christian young people" had been the first objective for the Ranch specified in the prospectus approved by the Presbyterian session, and nurture continued to be its mission for Larry Redford, though some of its supporters might have been surprised to know what nurture came to mean. It did not primarily mean providing a refuge of love and concern for seekers or providing a home community for those who were practicing some form of Christian service in the wider world. It meant above all the inculcation and practice of the conviction that the Bible and prayer have answers to all questions about conduct: interpersonal, especially man-woman, relationships; raising children; commercial dealings; citizens' obligations; health; and priorities among everyday chores. Christian nurture, as it came to be at the Ranch, was nothing less than the total sanctification of everyday life.

Accordingly, the teaching program of the Ranch was all-absorbing. Bible-study classes were held three mornings a week, and separate men's and women's Bible classes, to which neighbors as well as residents were welcomed, took place on Wednesday nights. One weekend night would be given over to a neighborhood potluck dinner leading up to a teaching, sometimes by Larry Redford and sometimes, via cassette tape, by a prominent evangelical leader, especially Bob Mumford, of Christian Growth Ministries in Fort Lauderdale, Florida. The fellowship met on Monday nights as a corporate body to thrash out the week's problems. On Sundays, Ranch members were expected to attend a local church. Individuals were urged to use their little spare time in Bible study and prayer.

"Bible study" was highly concentrated. During the whole third year of the Ranch's existence, the topic was the single, quite brief, letter of Paul to the Colossians. Faithful students of "Larry's Bible study" would pay at least as much attention to each verse of a Pauline epistle as would a doctoral candidate to a stanza of Shakespeare, and their Bibles had a lived-in look: dog-eared, underlined, and cross-indexed. People of the Ranch were admonished to take Paul's teaching to heart in an utterly prosaic manner.

> Therefore consider the members of your earthly body as dead to immorality, impurity, passion, evil desire, and greed, which amounts to idolatry. For it is on account of these things that the wrath of God will come, and in them you also once walked, when you were living in them. But now you also, put them all aside: anger, wrath, malice, slander and abusive speech from your mouth. Do not lie to one another, since you laid aside the old self with its evil practices. . . . And whatever you do in word or deed, do all in the name of the Lord Jesus, giving thanks through Him to God the Father (Col. 3:5–10, 17; NASV).

Traditional religious rituals also took place at Antioch. From the beginning, adult baptism by immersion was practiced, Redford being of the historic Baptist persuasion that baptism is a sign of the individual's freely chosen acceptance of the gift of salvation rather than an ordinance to be administered to infants by an institutional church. A baptism was an occasion for celebration by the fellowship, and the group would drive down to the coast and perform the rite, even in the chill of winter, in the tidal estuary known as the Big River, within sight of the Presbyterian church. Weddings were celebrated on the Ranch, with some legally authorized minister performing the ceremony and large numbers of friends and relatives of the couple in attendance. It began to appear to Larry that performing the marriage ceremony might become a proper function of his leadership of the Ranch.

Two Patterns of Recruitment

By the fall of 1971 the Ranch had taken shape as an extended household with haphazard financing, paternal authority, pervasive social control, and intense ideology. What Antioch Ranch meant to its clients can be illustrated through the stories of two of its early recruits, Burt Rogers and Dianne Hunter.

Burt Rogers was twenty years old when he came to Antioch Ranch, a half year after it opened. He had dropped out of school at sixteen to escape an unhappy home and spent three years as a vagabond and marijuana pusher. He was a shrewd dealer and made a go of it, but he never felt love for his hippie clients. More than a year before coming to Antioch, he determined that the drug scene was not for him, and he had landed a straight job. But his life still lacked meaning. At a street ministry in San Francisco and then at Antioch Ranch, however,

Burt discovered human relationships that seemed to be based on freely offered love, love even for a sour kid like him, and he cast his lot with these ministries.

At Antioch Burt was baptized, and he became a steady hand on the Ranch. His conversion to Larry Redford's brand of Christianity was gradual. On one occasion he felt obliged to reciprocate Larry's care for him by informing on another Ranch member, who was still surreptitiously using drugs and was then asked to leave the Ranch. Burt credits Larry with being his "father in the Lord," and his familial obligation was such that he was willing to inform on a peer.

During his first year at Antioch, Burt made weekend trips to San Francisco to see Lucille, whom he had met through the street ministry. Lucille, a couple of years older than Burt, was the daughter of a Baptist minister and an undergraduate at San Francisco State. Though she was no hippie, she sensed she had disappointed her father because of her half-hearted involvement with her college studies and her more absorbing involvement with men.

After one particularly painful episode, Lucille recalls she got down on her knees and asked God to reveal His presence to her. She intended to stop breathing but, she recalls, "the Lord just breathed for me." Thus was she born again. What had been only a nominal Baptist identity became an experienced reality. Having asked God to take charge of her life, she felt even less inclined toward college (seeing spiritual shallowness and darkness in San Francisco State's political activism) and more inclined toward a traditional female role. She felt her Lord say, "You'll never know me until you are married," and she felt the need of a Christian man to be her husband. Though Burt was a high-school dropout and a former dope dealer, he was that Christian man, and he courted her tenaciously during her last year at State.

When Lucille finished college, Burt, with the Redfords' permission, asked her to move to the Ranch. One month after, the Rogerses became the first couple to be married on the Ranch. Then, I was told, the fireworks began. Burt wanted to assert himself as head of his new household, but that need ran afoul of Lucille's now independent membership in the fellowship and the single-head patriarchal authority system of the Ranch. Larry owned the property and the pickup truck, and cash income earned off the Ranch—Burt had some gardening jobs in town—was, in effect, subject to substantial tax (through methods that kept changing until Larry hit on the concept of the tithe). The resulting negotiations, Redford always having the last word, were bruising on Burt's ego, and the Rogerses left the Ranch after a few months, to work out the terms of their relationship on their own.

Burt Rogers represents an early success of the Antioch mission.

Never a derelict, he was an unhappy, cynical young man who found direction for his life through the fellowship. He has since become a doting father of two and has been reconciled with his siblings and divorced parents, who have found his home a welcoming place to visit. He and Lucille were solid members of the fellowship in 1976. The lesson for the fellowship was that Burt's sort of person can be opened up but that such "baby Christians" do grow up and want to be independent. How the Redfords were to combine this lesson with their longing for a stable Christian community was a problem to be solved.

Without knowing it, Dianne Hunter, who lived across the road from the ranch, began to point the way. A smart and popular girl in high school, Dianne had turned on to drugs and dropped out of her studies at the University of California's Davis campus during the height of California's summer of love (1967). In Davis's drug subculture she met Steve Hunter, a young radio disk jockey and guitar player who was also a college dropout. Both Dianne and Steve had trust funds, giving them the freedom to live anywhere, and hearing of Mendocino as an artists' colony, they came up for a visit and bought a thirty-three-acre parcel of forested land a few hundred yards from the Redfords' property.

For their first year, just as Antioch Ranch was starting up, Dianne and Steve lived in a tent as they built a redwood cabin. Do-it-yourself building was the basis for a purely secular acquaintanceship between Steve Hunter and Larry Redford, but Dianne found the Redfords much too square for her taste. She was absorbed in her new rustic world, pregnant, dabbling in meditation and witchcraft, frequently bored, and still doing dope. Her curiosity was piqued, though, when younger, hipper people from the Ranch began to drop by, speaking of Jesus as someone you could have as a friend and bubbling over with cries of "Praise the Lord!" One day she went over to the Redfords' intending to ask how one can actually communicate with God, and as she walked into the house, she saw on Sue's kitchen table a book with the title, *Prayer: Conversing with God*. She decided that a supernatural force was trying to reach her.

Dianne dates her salvation from that point (August 1970), but there ensued a year of what she remembers as terrible trials. At first she did not think that behavioral changes were required by her new faith ("There was no walk then," she said), but she did begin serious Bible readings on her own. Then she began to listen to evangelical teachings on tape, one of which brought her a message about the ways of Satan. Dianne began to see that "Satan had been ripping me off. I saw *why* I should be reading the Bible, *why* I should be getting into fellowship with other Christians, *why* I should be stopping dope." Antioch Ranch, with no overt rule-bound barriers, evidently open to people of hip backgrounds, was a fellowship she could take.

Conversations with other Antiochers and taped teachings began to burden her with the fact that Steve had not converted. He found the enthusiasm of the young converts at the Ranch obnoxious and their religiosity fit for simpletons. He was more interested in learning from hip neighbors about righteous, back-on-the-land styles of life, and he spent a lot of time with his electric guitar. He was determined to ride out Dianne's Jesus phase, as he had her infatuation with Transcendental Meditation. Dianne took to heart a Bible passage she'd been given: "In the same way, you wives, be submissive to your own husbands, so that even if any of them are disobedient to the word, they may be won without a word by the behavior of their wives, as they observe your chaste and respectful behavior"(I Pet. 3:1–2, NASV). With that advice on her mind, but feeling very distant from Steve, Dianne took a week-long visit to her mother in the summer of 1971.

It was a time of great activity at the Ranch. Larry had decided to quit his teaching job; the Bakers had moved into a trailer on their newly purchased property; the ranch's second wedding had taken place; and an intense, impressive young saint named Terry had joined the work crew and become the Presbyterian church custodian. Terry was also a guitar player and he knew that Steve Hunter was willing to share music, if not religion, with Antioch people. One night during Dianne's absence, Terry and Steve were jamming, and Steve asked, without arguing, how Terry could believe what he professed. Terry set forth a simple gospel, centering on sin and forgiveness. Very late into the discussion and into the night, Steve asked Terry to lead him in prayer, and he was saved. "I was overtaken. A tide like in the Bay of Fundy came over me. I felt warmth and peace." When Dianne returned three days later, early in the morning, she awoke Steve to hear, "Guess what? I've accepted Jesus Christ as my Lord and Savior." She felt that she had obeyed the Lord, and He had kept His promises.

Steve Hunter's conversion was celebrated at the Ranch. Everyone was relieved to see Dianne's burden lifted. Moreover, the Hunters soon became a model for recruitment to the fellowship. Young couples, most with small children, who were recent migrants to the country began coming to Jesus and the Antioch fellowship, the wife first, then the husband. Instead of a ministry to urban singles, the Ranch turned into a neighborhood fellowship of poor but financially independent young Christian families. As Larry Redford put it when Steve Hunter converted, "We have a very strong enclave for Christ in our geographical area."

Converting the Neighborhood

In 1971–1972, mass conversions swept through Mendocino's counterculture, and we will look at that process more closely in the next chapter. For Larry and Sue Redford, the revival meant that a spiritual wind was moving in their direction. Just as they were finding that they could not deal effectively with the problems of emotionally disturbed or utterly unconventional individuals, so Jesus movement communes were reaching out precisely to social outcasts. The experience of 1972 for the Redfords was that, though they offered hospitality to seekers and sojourners, they preferred a more stable, more settled clientele.

Antioch Ranch did not overnight cease its outreach and mission functions. In 1972, 500 people stayed at the Ranch for overnight visits or longer. In October alone, the Ranch made room for an additional eleven persons who were invited to stay indefinitely; thus its population almost doubled overnight. But the Redfords' emphasis was on other couples on the Comptche road, the five-mile-long, half-mile-wide ridge between Big River and Little River, where "mellowed out" exurbanites were expanding their handmade houses and dooryard gardens and searching for spiritual forms in tune with their newly primitive mode of existence. Alongside the oriental philosophies and disciplines that many had brought out of the counterculture—TM, Yoga, the *Upanishads*, the *I Ching*—now, in the midst of a charged atmosphere of revival, Christianity presented itself as a live option. In May 1972 Larry noted with excitement, "There are literally hundreds of sparkling, growing, enthusiastic brothers and sisters in Christ in this area." The Ranch took its part in this small-scale cultural revolution, and it then adapted itself to the vastly improved local conditions.

At that time the Ranch was holding weekly, sex-segregated Bible-study classes, led by Sue and Larry. Women and men from the neighborhood responded to their own curiosity and to the invitations of friends, and they came, in small numbers, to these meetings. Anne de Grazia's rabbit-raising ventures gave her contact with Audrey Greene and Jeannie Baker, who were Antioch members, and one day she decided to accompany them to the Wednesday Bible study. She saw there a vibrant religious presence that she had never before seen in a church. Within weeks she and Arturo both felt the Holy Spirit enter their lives. They, in turn, piqued the curiosity of their neighbors and friends, the Wakefields. The two couples first began to read the Upanishads and the Gospel of John as an exercise in comparative religion, and then the Wakefields began to attend the Wednesday Bible studies at Antioch.

Jeffrey Wakefield was adding a room to his house and, anticipating a rainy California winter, he asked his friends to come over one Saturday to help raise the roof. "I asked a lot of friends," he later said, "and only the Christians came. There were about eight of them, and some I hardly knew." Larry Redford and Steve Hunter were among them. One night in October at the women's group, Sue Redford recounted a vision, a prophecy, that she'd had. With great warmth and graceful gestures, she told the group that she had seen a flower, a petunia, closed and in darkness, and then opened into a brilliant light. Pat Wakefield said nothing, but her heart leapt. "Petunia" had been her mother's pet name for her when she was a child, but no one in this group knew that. She felt like saying something but didn't want to make a fool of herself and so kept silent. But later, Sue gave another word from the Lord: "Be not afraid, be not ashamed." Presently, when the group was in prayer, Pat felt the Holy Spirit come into her. "Suddenly Jesus was as real as the other people in the room. I saw through new eyes." Still saying nothing to Sue or the other women, she went home and announced to her husband, "I've been born again." A few weeks later, at a prayer meeting, Jeffrey answered a call to conversion and accepted the Lord. Both soon began to spend all their spare moments with the fellowship. Within a year, they joined the Presbyterian church.

The Greenes, the de Grazias, the Wakefields, and others—so many local people came into fellowship! Here is what Larry wrote in his October newsletter: "It is exciting to watch the love of God and His gospel spread like leaven in this area. People are being drawn out of darkness in such a strong mystical manner that before one realizes it, there are whole new crops of baby Christians running around. It is like one of our hens suddenly walking out of some secret place with an unexpected brood of young chicks. Only she knew what was going on until it was time for the world to know."

To Larry Redford, the mass conversions were exciting and mystical. To their unbelieving neighbors, they were startling and irrational. Antioch fellowship rejoiced in the harvest of souls. Stubborn rationalists mourned (that is not too strong a word) the loss of kindred spirits. And just as Larry saw people being drawn out of darkness, his opposite numbers saw an insidious obscurantism settle in among the brave homesteaders of the Comptche Road. But the process of conversion was neither magical nor sinister. It was a process of cultural diffusion propelled by personal, emotionally significant ties between specific individuals, and it would be, in principle, quite possible to map out the elaborate person-to-person networks through which the gospel was spread in Mendocino in those months.[6] The effect of personal networks is great if it operates within marriages, as it did during Mendocino's conversion, many women bringing their husbands into the fold within a span of a week to a year. (This pattern was recognized among fellowship leaders, and Larry Redford once told me that "women are usually ahead of the men since they have more time to think about it.")

Converts have a way of exaggerating the changes their lives have undergone, and sociologists of religion have learned to be skeptical of stories (I heard quite a few) of great sinners becoming humble saints, the more so when those stories come from the erstwhile sinner himself. I have not emphasized such stories here, and I have sought (not always successfully) some independent confirmation of life histories. Nonetheless, some converts did suddenly abandon rather dissolute habits, as did Dianne and Steve Hunter. Some consolidated and strengthened through their conversion a preexisting resolve to change: Burt Rogers comes to mind. Others, such as Lucille Rogers, met their social destiny, confirming a deep-seated religious propensity. For still others, the change was more radical culturally than behaviorally, and Antioch was beginning to gather in newly minted saints who were putting behind them not so much the sins of misbehavior as the sin of unbelief. The Wakefields and the de Grazias all experienced conversions the most striking features of which, so their friends thought, were the sheer amount of time they began devoting to evangelical activities and the prominence of the name of the Lord in their speech.

Sol Bloom presents an extreme but not unique instance. Sol, whom we met in chapter two, is a Jew who was converted toward the end of the mass conversion in 1973, and he was, by the time of my fieldwork in 1975–1977, one of the most engaging, witty, and enthusiastic new Christians in Mendocino. Born in the mid 1930s in New York City, Sol had a thoroughly Jewish secular upbringing through public schools in the Bronx to a teaching credential earned at Columbia University Teachers College. Sol met Jane Christopher, a Berkeley graduate (and nominal Protestant) through the civil-rights movement of the early 1960s, and she became his wife. Through the late sixties and early seventies, Sol and Jane made their way through California's hip underground, he having a succession of teaching jobs in alternative schools and she caring for their growing family. They gravitated toward the neoprimitive scene of Mendocino County and came to live on the Comptche Road in 1973.

Jane's friends introduced her to Antioch, and she converted. But Sol had a difficult time accepting her new faith, and when he was in a religious mood, he preferred the original Jewish scriptures to the New Testament stories that Jane began talking about. But Sol wanted more than anything else to keep his wife, and after six months he relented and simply said, "Jesus, if you're real, come into my heart." At the moment of that invocation, he told me, nothing happened. But about ten days later, while he was driving into town, it dawned on him that he had been "born again," and from then on he spoke about his Lord at every opportunity. On his first trip to visit his parents in New York, two years after his conversion, he amazed his mother by asking Jesus to repair her kitchen stove, and he distressed an old Jewish friend from the east one Friday during my stay in Mendocino by bringing her along to an Antioch Fellowship meeting. As a "fulfilled Jew," Sol had undergone a radical change in identity, which was most evident simply in his speech.

Some new Christians seek out God; others insist they are sought out by Him. But for everyone, the moment of conversion is a deliberate act, when God is invited into one's life.[7] When this decision is made in the company of a community of professing evangelicals, it is likely to be a highly consequential decision, with results that the convert does not foresee and frequently would, in prospect, scorn. The convert does not know what he or she is getting into.

One consequence of conversion is the adoption of the language of the evangelical community. This is not typically as radical a change as it was for Sol Bloom, but it is significant. Turo de Grazia designed a new logo for his pottery, a descending dove, to represent the Holy Spirit. Other Antioch members gave business enterprises unmistakably religious names like "Hallelujah Redwood Products," or more ambiguous ones like "The Fisherman Restaurant" and "Christian Brothers Painting Company." For many converts, the adoption of an evangelical vocabulary meant that "witnessing," often so vexing to nonevangelicals, was a constant feature of speech. "Witnessing" is the willingness to speak about one's religious faith, simply owning up to the facts of one's life, according to many evangelicals. It is not proselytizing in itself. Nonetheless, "We're doing the Lord's work"; "We just held it up to the Lord"; "Before I came to Jesus"; "We've really been blessed"; and "Praise God"—these locutions are obtrusive to the irreligious or to the conventionally religious. The result for many converts was that sooner or later most of their friends were also evangelicals, whether by conversion or selective elimination.

Behavioral codes demanded changes, too. Converts learned to shun the kinds of temptations that had in the past been associated with guilt and despair. For this reason, many gave up alcoholic beverages, since they invite intoxication. The mind-altering quality of marijuana was cited as a reason to give it up, but it was also shunned as a symbol of secular protest. Some new Antioch affiliates gave up rock music, political involvement, organic cooking, and long hair as symbols of excessive devotion to or rebellion against the standards of the secular world. Some rules were simply seen as dictated by God: no swearing, no lying, no stealing, no adultery (or, more generally, no sex outside of marriage, probably the strongest new Christian taboo). It even turned out that some practices of little salience, such as reading the astrology column or dressing up the kids for Halloween, were regarded in the fellowship as dangerous flirtations with the works of Satan; they also were to be given up. The new "don'ts" are not the same for all persons or for all fellowships. But there are always new proscriptions, and they are often surprising to those who come to be bound by them.

There were new prescriptions as well at Antioch. Honesty and charity were extolled, particularly toward friends, neighbors, and relatives. Simplicity, not the time-consuming primitivism of the counterculture, was enjoined for clothing, cooking, and housing. Economic self-reliance, trusting in individual hard work and the Lord rather than in an organizational career or the state, was idealized. These standards and others like them were impressed willy-nilly on the new convert, sometimes by explicit precept and sometimes by concrete example, but always by increment.

Above all, the new Christian was advised, and was very frequently already motivated, to pay closer attention to his or her family. Grown men, such as Burt Rogers and Larry Redford, felt impelled to repair strained relations with parents. Women were told to submit to their husbands, whether or not the husband "knows the Lord," and experiences like Dianne Hunter's were held up as inspiring examples. Men were told to respect their wives, especially to be faithful to them sexually. Children were told to honor their parents, and more than one child of the counterculture had to learn to address his parents as "Mom" and "Dad" instead of by their first names. Parents were told that they should "dare to discipline" their children for misbehavior. In general, when a family issue came up in prayer meetings or counseling sessions, the advice received was to turn in traditional directions: to men, give up alcohol and other women; to women, give up independent ambition; to children, give up material demands and criticism of parents; to all, give up pride and symbols of vanity. A few months after his conversion, Jeffrey Wakefield wrote in a letter to his parents, "Our Christian fellowship here is a great help. We are trying to serve God and our neighbors, [and] it helps us get on better with each other and the children." In another letter, he said of his son, "We're getting Paul to clean up his mess and he cooperates."

When Dianne Hunter or Jane Bloom or Pat Wakefield met the Lord, it was a deliberate and far-reaching decision. But they did not know in advance where, how far, and by what route its consequences would reach. Even their spiritual elders, the Redfords, could not know where in particular they would attempt to lead their flock, for their ministry itself was changing in constitution precisely with the influx of these new, older, educated couples. Always self-conscious and reflective, always trusting in the Lord, Larry gave voice to a sense of this development in successive Antioch Ranch news sheets.

June 1972: The Bible Study was working through the post-exilic, old testament books Ezra and Nehemiah, finding valuable principles. "The undergirding principle of the whole thing is that in 500 B.C. the job was done on something *apart* from themselves, a physical building, while today the job is to be done *on* ourselves. We are the workers, and we are the construction project, for we are the temple of God."

September 1972: "Some things we are beginning to understand, some things are still vague. This we do know, God is up to something, shifting gears with us in some way and we need to be sensitive."

October 1972: An upbeat report speaks of the "Comptche Road Bible Belt." "We are beginning to experience 'koinonia!' " [a biblical Greek term meaning deep sharing].

December 1972: "The other evening we were asked once again by a young man, 'What is the purpose of Antioch Ranch?' As usual we ended up taking half an hour to say what we probably should be able to focus into a single sentence. Looking back I realize once again that the concept of *nurture* covers a great deal of what we're here for. As individuals we are pressing on in the Spirit's help to become more like the Lord Jesus in our character, and exercise the gifts He has entrusted to us. As a fellowship we seek maturity in our unity, koinonia, our love for each other and others. At the heart of our fellowship we see forming a core of 12–14 resident (to the area) brothers and sisters. We are beginning to spend more time together. . . . We feel we are on the crest of a wave."

February 1973: A year-end informal accounting of visitors and expenses is given, and Eric Underwood's appointment at Mendocino Presbyterian Church is announced. "At this time there are over 30 adults who regularly look toward this ministry as more or less their source of fellowship and edification. At the heart of the work we now have 6 couples who meet weekly along Acts 2:42 guidelines to set the pace for the larger ministry. There is a sense in which this is a neighborhood ministry as most of the folks live on our road or close by. . . . We have longed for this for a long time."

It was thrilling for the Ranch fellowship to ponder the laconic record in Acts 2:42 of the activities of the infant church after the first Pentecost. ("And they devoted themselves to the apostles' teaching and fellowship, to the breaking of bread and the prayers"—RSV.) This simple account inspired the day-to-day doings of fellowship families, and each of these Biblical rubrics took on enormous symbolic weight as enthusiastic evangelicals, led by Larry Redford, wrung homely implications from them. "Fellowship" meant everything from Christian encounter groups to financial contributions. "Breaking bread" meant not only communion but an elaborate, enthusiastic weekly prayer-and-song worship meeting. The more than nineteen hundred years since the first Pentecost seemed to vanish as the fellowship fleshed out this spare Biblical model.

Fellowship of Independent Households

From an outsider's secular viewpoint, the Acts 2:42 model was far from Mark Kimmerly's rescue mission concept. No longer an extended household, no longer a ranch, Antioch was becoming a fellowship, or "parachurch." By 1973, Antioch was a religious federation of independent evangelical households, with increasing spiritual self-sufficiency and decreasing economic self-sufficiency, relative to its predecessor Ranch.

1. The Ranch concept required a supply of labor for home industries, particularly the abalone-shell jewelry. Jewelry-making was a skill of Larry's, and it was one that took some time to impart to Ranch residents, just as Larry was increasingly occupied with teaching and personal counseling. Meanwhile, the newer recruits to the fellowship were families resident only "to the area," not to the Ranch, and they had their own needs to meet and their own occupations.

Antioch continued (through 1976) to receive support from churches outside Mendocino, and gifts in kind continued to help maintain the Redford household. But a new concept of material support began to emerge in 1972–1973, the tithe from Antioch members themselves. Those members who wanted income-tax records could send their checks through the Presbyterian church conduit. Others used a number-ten can, marked "tithes," placed on the book table at fellowship meetings. By 1975, the Redfords were on a "salary" of $750 per month from the fellowship. Slowly, Antioch became a ministry in which Larry and Sue Redford's spiritual expertise and full-time commitment were traded for contributions from their own clients, who had their own sources of income in the secular economy. Larry called it "material koinonia."

2. Correspondingly, the leadership structure of the fellowship was broadened and decentralized. There are many indications from my informants and from Antioch newsletters that Larry Redford had perennially longed for "shared responsibility" in his ministry, but a stable system of plural eldership waited upon the incorporation of independent households into the fellowship. The first was that of David Baker, who owned the seven acres adjoining the Redfords' land on the west and worked full-time as a park ranger. David was part of the older Ranch extended household and in 1971 was appointed an "elder" by Larry. In 1972–1973, Larry appointed three new elders, all relatively "new in the Lord." Monty Greene was an expert woodworker with an independent income who had converted in the late summer of 1971, a few months after his wife, Audrey. The Greenes were about thirty, college educated, and they had two preschool children.

Turo de Grazia is the potter we met in chapter four. Along with his wife Anne, he had come to the Lord in the summer of 1972. After raising Turo's children by a previous marriage, the de Grazias—he in his middle forties, she in her late twenties—had just begun to raise a family of their own and had two infant daughters.

Steve Hunter had been saved in June of 1971. He was twenty-four, and the Hunters, too, had two infant children, both boys. As their inheritances were exhausted, Steve began to develop a cabinetry and woodworking business, Hallelujah Redwood Products.

With Larry Redford, forty-one that winter, and David Baker, thirty-two, these were the new "shepherds," elders, or presbyters (in New Testament Greek terms) of the Antioch Ranch fellowship. Larry was acknowledged as first among equals, but he had the shared responsibility he had desired. His shepherds had in common that they owned property, were husbands and fathers, and lived near, but not on, Antioch Ranch.

By abandoning the patriarchal extended model and turning Antioch into a presbyterian federation, Redford answered some of the problems he and Pat had encountered. "Sharing responsibility" with others allowed Larry to concentrate on the teaching and counseling that he felt to be his true vocation. Granting others rights of authority mobilized their participation. Recognizing worldly maturity, particularly that of Turo de Grazia and Monty Greene, helped solve the question of "discernment" that had bedeviled the Ranch during its first three years.

Yet the federation model brought in a new problem. From the point of view of the radical, New Testament ministry Antioch was aspiring to become, the secular standards that led Larry to designate some men as elders—education, property ownership, superior craftsmanship, age, and gender—were a centrifugal force, potentially tending away from a pure scriptural ideal. In theological terms, the new presbyterian organization gave too much recognition to "works" in the appointment of "babes in the Lord" to leadership. We shall see some of the consequences in chapter ten.

For the two years of five-man rule, the system worked well. The elders met regularly and lengthily to consider personal, spiritual, and organizational issues. The key concern was always to ascertain God's will, whether a couple should be encouraged in their courtship, whom to send to the Presbyterian Church as custodian, how to conduct the weekly worship meetings, and (as we shall see in chapter six) whether to become part of a larger paradenominational ministry. All five were men of intelligence, learning, and evangelical enthusiasm, and Larry Redford and David Baker particularly were accustomed to spending long hours in discernment of God's will. These must have been at once exhausting and exhilarating sessions.

As the "shared responsibility" pattern developed, Larry asked the elder couples to "shepherd" their own "koin" groups, and so Monty and Audrey Greene led a group consisting, among others, of Burt and Lucille Rogers. Still later, the Rogerses took a hand at leading a group in their neighborhood. The Hunters were able to accommodate houseguests for long periods in their household, called "Still Waters." Other couples organized neighborhood potlucks and led Bible-study meetings. Not all of these ventures were successful, since not all the leaders had the experience of the Redfords or the sheer time and energy that they could devote to the effort. But the decentralized, hierarchical model came more and more to be an accepted ideal.

In November 1973, Larry and Sue initiated personal contacts with leaders of the fast-growing number of charismatic fellowships in America. Supported by special contributions of Antioch sympathizers, they attended a conference for over a thousand charismatic leaders, held in Miami, Florida, the Christian Growth Ministries Conference. For three years at occasional Antioch meetings they had been using the tape-recorded teachings of Bob Mumford, one of the Florida conference convenors. During their week-long stay at the conference, they not only met Mumford and his colleagues Derek Prince, Don

Basham, David Edwards, and Ern Baxter, but they also talked with other leaders of local fellowships who had experiences similar to their own. Sue Redford recalled that this conference helped allay the "paranoid feeling" that she and Larry were "oddballs." In fact, many groups—under some influence from Mumford and the others, it is true, but also as a response to similar changing conditions—were developing similar notions of community and authority.

3. As the fellowship matured, Larry Redford was able to devote more of his effort to his teaching role. Less the paterfamilias, less the harried employer of a transient collection of ranch hands, he was now the minister of a relatively settled congregation. As minister, he provided ideological resources for social control, and the concept of a division of labor received his attention. Paul's famous metaphor of the church as a body with distinct organs contributing to the well-being of the whole was expounded by Larry and others as a legitimation of diversity, including inequality, within the fellowship. "Now there are varieties of gifts, but the same spirit; and there are varieties of service, but the same Lord; and there are varieties of working, but it is the same God who inspires them all in every one" (I Cor. 12:4–6, RSV).

The principle of a division of social labor is familiar to sociologists from the writings of Karl Marx and Emile Durkheim,[8] and its articulation in a religious organization might be unremarkable but for its obvious ideological function in the case of spirit-filled Christians. When each person is directly, intimately in touch with the Almighty through the Holy Spirit, each can justify idiosyncrasies as God-given, including uncooperative or disorderly leanings. The doctrine of specific, spiritually equal but practically distinct gifts is a clear counter to centrifugal tendencies. One person has a gift of teaching, another a gift of healing, another a gift of praise in music, another a gift of humble service. In this way were the various contributions of individual fellowship members given spiritual value and social stability.

A clear implication of the division of labor is that there is no place for an isolate. All Christians are members of "the body" and "being in fellowship" was advanced as the sine qua non of the Christian life. The notion that one could have a relationship solely to God was scorned as a "Lone Ranger Christian" fantasy, and that epithet was applied to the growing number of "hippie Christians," revival converts who persisted in old lifestyles of dope smoking and nonmarital cohabitation. The ideal of Christian fellowship was symbolized in the figure of the cross, a vertical aspect (God to person) and a horizontal one (person to person). Sole concentration on either aspect (antinomian spiritualism in the first case, social gospel in the second) was regarded as deviant.

This differentiated, stratified social group extended in principle around the world, but one's greatest worldly obligation was to pay attention to the needs of immediate kin and neighbors, above all one's spouse and children. "Love everybody" was scorned as an escape from mundane duties owed to particular others, and the Christian unity that Paul commended in his letters to first-century churches was said to begin at home, with the family. "If our families' lives are not in Divine order, warm and loving, then our broader fellowship, yes, the church, will be weak and unable to grow into maturity," said Larry in his newsletter. Families that had begun with casual liaisons or unplanned pregnancies took on the highest level of moral significance and traditional legitimation.

4. The greater maturity and more varied resources internal to the fellowship intensified the religious activity of the group. With less attention needed to guarantee sheer survival and discipline, there was more place for nurture and celebration. Antioch body meetings, as I called them in chapter two, were the central, anticipated, weekly event. Held in Redford's living room, they consisted partly of Larry's teaching on some scriptural passages, with application to the lives of fellowship members. There was time for "sharing," in which implications of Larry's teaching and other Biblical citations were given by individuals speaking of personal events of the week. Those in physical or psychic distress were encouraged by laying on of hands and prayer. For the first time, music and singing became central to the worship experience. Guitar players, pianists, and fine singers abounded in the maturing fellowship. Meanwhile, Larry Redford, very much unlike his wife, was indifferent to music, and it was not an activity that he could control, even unknowingly and subtly. Music became one of the means for the practical decentralization of fellowship authority.

The most striking aspect of worship at Antioch Fellowship was the practice of the gifts of the spirit, or the charismata. It was in 1972–1973 that the body meetings became more charismatic in the manner described in chapter two. The Redfords had long been charismatics, since their southern California days of the early sixties, but they did not hurry to introduce their newfound Christian friends in Mendocino to spirit baptism. They sensed as much prejudice against pentecostalism as they did against fundamentalism, and they were not anxious to be martyrs to divisive slogans. Some members of the fellowship had negative preconceptions of pentecostalism prior to their own spirit baptism, and even after it many continued to disdain the emotionalism of classical lower-class pentecostalism. Indeed, the term "charismatic" was preferred to "pentecostal" for its less negative connotations.

One after another, however, Antioch members were introduced to "the baptism," sometimes as an intensification of the conversion experience, as it was for Pat Wakefield, sometimes as a "second baptism," months or years after the decision to accept Jesus. David and Jeannie Baker both received the baptism in a small fellowship session at the Ranch when hands were laid upon them, but the gift of tongues came later—weeks later for Jeannie and a year and a half later for David. Lucille Rogers asked about spirit baptism at Sue Redford's women's group, and she received the baptism and the gift of tongues together when hands were laid on her during a revival meeting in Caspar. Burt Rogers distrusted "pentecostal theatrics" and resented social pressure. So he had the experience when he was out hunting, alone.

Speaking in tongues is a dramatic manifestation of charisma, and David Baker recalls the inner doubts he had in the many months that intervened between Jeannie's reception of the gift and his. But the gift of tongues does not exhaust or define spirit baptism. Theorists and participants in the movement agree on this, insisting that tongue-speaking is only one manifestation of a much broader experience, which is at the heart of the New Testament message. They cite the story at the beginning of Acts in which Jesus, after he had risen from the dead but before he was taken up into heaven, promised his disciples that they would be "baptized with the Holy Spirit." He said, "You shall receive power when the Holy Spirit has come upon you" (Acts 1:5 and 1:8), and the early church saw the events of the first Pentecost as the fulfillment of this promise. Paul's teaching that puts tongues in the context of other spiritual gifts (I Cor. 12–14) was cited in meetings and to those who inquired. Accounts of the charismatic movement agree that tongues, prophecy, interpretation, and healing are widely recognized and widely practiced identifiable gifts.[9] Spirit baptism is a feeling of serenity for some and an audible wind for others, but for all it is a remarkably invigorating experience. Charismatics have a sense of increased "power," they say, but I find "vitality" or "intensity" to be a better way of putting it.

Lucille Rogers recounted that her spirit baptism in 1972 helped heal her marriage. "I learned to be submissive to Burt, but he learned to treat me with respect and to give me space. We also learned to deal with our kids and to be reconciled with our families." Evidently, spirit baptism had this effect through an intensification of the Rogerses involvement in religious life. Lucille said that she and Burt made new friendships through the charismatic community. They spent more time studying tape-recorded teachings of charismatic teachers. They listened solely to gospel music. "We felt to be more a part of a family. . . . We experienced the Holy Spirit as a teacher and comforter."

The Holy Spirit infuses the life of the charismatic, but the experience is not Dionysian for middle-class converts. Charismatics seem to have no difficulty articulating their experience. Here, for example, is an excerpt from one of my conversations with David Baker.

RSW: How do you use it [your gift of tongues]?

DB: Jeannie uses hers mostly in personal prayer. I use mine daily to build up my relationship with the Lord. I speak in tongues on my way to work. But I sometimes also feel the gift during meetings of the body. There is a difference between these two uses. One is more of a praise thing; the other is a prophecy.

RSW: Would a linguist be able to hear the difference?

DB: I think so. At Antioch, it's the Lord speaking through me. The other times it's me addressing the Lord.

When David used his prophetic gift, he would expect an English interpretation to be forthcoming from one with that gift, according to Paul's teaching (I. Cor. 14:13). On the one occasion in 1976 when I heard clearly audible prophetic tongue speech at Antioch, it was David Baker; his prophecy was immediately interpreted by Steve Hunter. The overwhelming preponderance of tongue-speech in contemporary neopentecostal groups is of David's first sort: individual praise, which does not require interpretation.[10]

Antioch became a charismatic fellowship. But that does not mean that worship was ecstatic, in the ordinary sense of that word. Worship was emotionally stirring indeed, but it was restrained and quite under rational control. It also does not mean that speaking in tongues was a qualification for membership. Individuals who had not experienced it might feel like second-class citizens, but they were by no means excluded. Finally, "charismatic" applies to the social integration and doctrine, not to the authority structure, of the fellowship. Insofar as *each member* of the fellowship was endowed with charismata, Larry's authority, and the authority of the leader of any similar fellowship, was continually vulnerable to principled challenge. The "body," more than the "head," was charismatic.

The Fellowship and the Church

Intended by Mark Kimmerly as an instrument of the church's concern, Antioch Ranch became for its participants an end in itself: Antioch Fellowship. Whether or not they were aware of this evolution (Mark Kimmerly says he was), the leaders within the Presbyterian church did not oppose it. David Baker began a three-year term on session in 1971, and he presented regular reports on the activities and population of the Antioch group. He did not stress its neopentecostal theology, but his own manifest humility and decency reassured skeptics among the elders. Conservatives could support the Ranch as a way station for the rehabilitation of derelicts. Liberals liked the social concern that the Ranch symbolized. Though one elder grumbled that the Ranch was simply a way for Larry Redford to dip into church funds and others wondered about baptisms and weddings happening on the Ranch, the enterprise continued to be regarded by most, when they thought about it at all, as a "mission to the counterculture," thus a salve to the conscience, or a "hippie ranch," thus a minor cultural nuisance.

These misconceptions were fed by Antioch's own limited interaction with the church. The Redfords and the Bakers were members of the church, and they and few others attended Sunday services, sitting always on the east side of the sanctuary and smelling of wood smoke from their stoves and heaters. Larry preached the sermon on some Sundays when Mark Kimmerly was away, and other Ranch members now and then gave "testimonies" of leaving the drug scene for the Christian life. The young man from the Ranch currently acting as church custodian would become known as a symbol of the church's interaction with the Ranch. Even the Ranch's own formal posture in its infrequent publicity brochures did little to portray to the average Mendocino Presbyterian the religiously radical nature of the enterprise the Redfords were engaged in. "A community for Christian fellowship and growth," as a 1971 leaflet portrayed the Ranch, was an acceptable rubric for it, but a phrase far too vague to delineate much of anything. By the summer of 1972, moreover, Mark Kimmerly was out of the picture, and Larry Redford was soon busy trying to turn the church itself in his spiritual direction.

With the coming of Eric Underwood, a fellow alumnus of Fuller Seminary, to the pastorate, the Presbyterian church seemed to become an institution worthy of Antioch's leavening influence. For the next several years (1973–1977), Antioch played the part of an *ecclesiola in ecclesia*, never wholly removed from, never merely part of, the Presbyterian church.

6.

A Hippie Commune Comes to Jesus: The Holy Land, 1969–1974

It was the best of times, it was the worst of times, it was the age of wisdom, it was the age of foolishness, it was the epoch of belief, it was the epoch of incredulity, it was the season of Darkness, it was the spring of hope, it was the winter of despair, we had everything before us, we had nothing before us, we were all going direct to Heaven, we were all going direct the other way
— Charles Dickens, *A Tale of Two Cities*

Three ridges to the south, five miles by air but forty minutes by car, a radically different counterculture outpost was in its heyday during the first year of Antioch Ranch. "Therese's Land," or simply "the Land," it was called, and it was known on the north coast and to hip collegians in Berkeley as the "Queen of the Communes." During the turbulent year of 1969–1970, which came to a shattering close with the invasion of Cambodia, the shootings at Kent State and Jackson State, and the de facto closing of scores of universities, the Land was a pastoral mecca for those in search of freedom, peace, and authenticity.

Therese's Land straddles Navarro Ridge three miles inland from the ocean cliffs. The south slope drops through brush and vines to the Navarro River, whose tidal estuary is a natural channel for cooling ocean fogs. The north slope is steep, well-watered, and heavily forested, draining into a small creek. The ridge top itself is broad and rolling, like Iowa farmland, but only a quarter mile wide. Unlike the other ridges of Mendocino, it was mostly open pasture, with a few second-growth redwood groves, stock fences, barns, and farm houses dividing up the fields. On Therese's property the nineteenth-century loggers had left huge, blackened redwood stumps, ten feet in diameter and twenty feet tall, some of them hollow, some covered with vines, which became the eerily beautiful trademark of the Land.

Two Communards and Their Patroness

There came to the Land that winter two visitors who were to play opposing parts in its history. Laurie was a senior at the University of California, and she divided her time that year between an urban commune in Berkeley and the Land in Mendocino. A talented semiprofessional musician originally from New York, she decided to give up urban life and move permanently to the Land in the summer of 1970 to escape the turmoil at Berkeley. She had already written in the spring of 1970 a brief sociology term paper describing the setup of the commune. Six years later, she was embarrassed by its naivete, but she lent it to me for my research.

The other visitor was Judy, a slender, blonde high-school girl from Santa Barbara. Judy's parents had enrolled her in a "free school" to conquer her boredom with studies, but she found its lack of discipline an opportunity to do even less work than she had at public school. In January 1970 the free-school group came to the Land for a one-month field trip, and Judy fell in love with Pete Mateo, the Land's most free-living, high-spirited, energetic, and persuasive hippie. She was fifteen; he was nearly thirty. Judy returned to the Land as soon as school ended that spring and spent the summer with Pete in northern California and Oregon. A brush with the police and a visit from her older sister convinced her to return to Santa Barbara for the new school year in the fall. But she left again to rejoin Pete on her sixteenth birthday in October, having asked a girlfriend to tell her parents, at home with a birthday party, that she would not be returning. From then on, her main home has been the Land, and it was there, on New Year's Day, 1976, that we sat in the field outside her cabin in bright winter sunlight as she told me her story.

Laurie and Judy are only two of the dozen or so persons I queried about their experiences with the Land. Among my other informants were members of a University of California research team who had come to the Land to study hippie childraising.[1] But the points of agreement between Laurie's and Judy's accounts, despite their radically opposed evaluations—Laurie as diehard pagan, Judy as an early convert—make their intersecting experiences a point of entry to the story of the upheaval that shook the Land, and much of Mendocino, in 1971 and 1972.

The land of the Land was owned by Therese, a German-American woman who had invested the proceeds of a divorce settlement first in a house in Santa Barbara and then in this 160-acre parcel on Navarro Ridge in Mendocino County. Therese was a short, somewhat plump, woman of forty-five (in 1970), who is libeled by such a spare description. The beauty she had been in her youth had not left her in middle age. Her figure was womanly. Her skin was tan, with fine lines of age. Her hair was thick and blonde, with threads of silver. Her eyes were clear blue, with a slight squint. Her smile was radiant, and her feet were always bare. As the owner of the Land, and a person of privileged European upbringing and more recent married wealth, she carried herself with natural authority. As a woman, and the mother of two young teenage sons, she was an image of idealized motherhood. To the vagabond young, she was the hippie queen of Mendocino. To the local straights, including the new evangelicals at Antioch, she was a witch.

After a divorce in 1962, Therese kept what she thought of as an intellectual salon in the growing retirement and college town of Santa Barbara, and she was influenced by her avant-garde friends to investigate the movements for new freedom then springing up at Esalen, in Big Sur, and Haight-Ashbury in San Francisco. Esalen charmed her. She met Fritz Perls, worked on hangups in gestalt therapy and joined the nude bathing in the famous hot springs. She also met Pete Mateo there. "Everyone loved him," she later told me. "He was constantly stoned and utterly irresponsible." She did not have to tell me that he was dark and very handsome.

The scene in San Francisco challenged her. The hippies wanted peace, freedom, love, and unity, she thought, but they were unhappy in the city. Country living might bring them their desire. They'd be able to grow their own food, tend animals, play their music, and be open and trust one another. And so she bought land in the country for thirty thousand dollars and opened it up to her young friends and their friends and their acquaintances, to anyone.

The Commune, 1970

When she was first shown the property by a Mendocino realtor, it had many buildable and tillable acres, plenty of water, and the shell of a large barn. She invited people to join her under the condition that they help her build a house and contribute to the mortgage and commissary. The work was enjoyable and the money contribution was small (about $20 per month). By the time of Judy's and Laurie's visits of 1970, the Land presented itself to them as a happy and successful family of two dozen persons.

1. Material support. The most obvious symbol of the family's success was its buildings. The barn had been refurbished as a community center. Therese's house was underway, one of the great stumps had been made into an enclosed shower and another into a tree house, a giant tipi and a wood-frame geodesic dome had been built, and various members of the family had begun to build their separate cabins. Therese bought some new materials for her house, but other materials, including the stone for her fireplace, were gathered from the countryside. Still other things—sound old wood, bricks, and machine parts—were salvaged from Mendocino area buildings on the same arrangement that Antioch Ranch had used: we'll tear the building down, haul the refuse away and leave you a building site if we get to keep the salvage.

Some family members had become renowned in the area for their skills—Jerry the stonemason, Nick the plumber, Al the carpenter—and they were lovingly crafting a righteous house for Therese. "The Big House," they called it. Its post-and-beam construction was solid and true, and its finished surfaces were of redwood, a soft but durable and beautiful wood. A stone and used-brick fireplace stood at the center of the house and brought the kitchen and living room together. Large single-pane windows looked out across the canyon of the Navarro to the south. Unlike other buildings on the Land, it had indoor plumbing and electricity. More—stained-glass windows, heavy, hand-carved redwood doors, a glorious varnished redwood floor—was to come.

The other major community project was the barn. "The progress of the barn is everyone's concern," wrote Laurie in her term paper. The first floor held a kitchen, a family room, and a workshop. Even in an unfinished state the kitchen was the center of community life: the assigned day's cooks (men and women both) prepared vegetarian stews there, the family gathered on benches at a long plank table for their meals, and a message board above the table announced things of concern. The family room had a fire pit and space for sleeping mats. The workshop held a sturdy table and a wealth of old and new tools. On the second story, up a ladder, was a library and sitting room, where the family kept its collection of old college texts and books on organic gardening, do-it-yourself building, practical botany, art, religion, and fiction, and its musical instruments and art supplies. "The barn has a unifying effect on the people of the Land," wrote Laurie.

Life in the country at the end of the 1960s could be easy for young people willing to accept primitive conditions. Therese provided the all-important space. The family members provided labor. The Land itself provided water. Standing, dead trees for wood were easy to come by on nearby lumber-company properties. Much of the needed food, especially vegetables and herbs, was grown in an organic garden, and the staple of the diet, brown rice, was bought in wholesale lots. Chickens and goats provided some eggs and milk. The small monetary contribution expected of everyone was garnered by some through welfare and disability payments, but others could use their skills on the external market: musicians did occasional gigs; weavers, woodworkers, painters, and leatherworkers sold their wares; gardeners, typists, housecleaners, and babysitters sold their services. Beyond the obligatory $20, pocket money was needed for "zu-zus," but it wasn't hard to come by. Only Therese had utility bills and taxes (as well as the mortgage) to pay, and those small amounts were well within her means, especially with the young people's contributions.

2. Governance was minimal. Major decisions concerning the community were made at "family meetings," described by the dewy-eyed Laurie as "a close equivalent to the town meeting of colonial America." In this setting, the family would commit itself to major collective undertakings, such as the rehabilitation of the barn. For short-term and crisis questions, there evolved a "family council," consisting of Therese, Pete, Nick, Jerry, Al, and a handful of others. Other chores, notably cooking and dishwashing, were distributed according to an agreed formula: two cooks per day, with a repeat stint every two weeks. In the crises that changed life at the Land in the next two years, this rudimentary governance system could not overcome the great personal influence of the patroness, Therese, and her hero, Pete.

3. Social control. The reputation of the Land spread far in the counterculture, and many transients visited. Like all "open" communes, the Land, itself living off the society, was vulnerable to exploitation by others. One young mother, for instance, was known for leaving the care of her children up to the most compassionate of the communards. But the population of the Land stayed relatively stable at about twenty-five plus a handful of children. There were recognized duties of membership in the family and a stable core of insiders who had many subtle ways to "vibe off" the unwelcome. Moreover, the reputation of the Land included the notion that it was a place for the "hippie elite." Steve and Dianne Hunter, in their preconversion hip enclave on the Comptche Road, thought that the Land had a "code of proper hipness." "It seemed," Dianne said, "that you had to be outstanding as a hip person, really beautiful hip,

to make it there." Steve said that he had been afraid to venture to the Land.

This hippie elite enjoyed the salient freedoms of the era on the Land. In warm weather, nudity was the standard of dress, and Pete was said to have gone naked all one winter for the sheer experience of it. Sexual freedom was another norm, and Therese makes a point of saying that her older son was "sleeping around" at the age of fourteen with the full consent of his mother and the other adults. Psychedelic drugs—LSD, mescaline, psilocybin, marijuana, hashish—were joyously indulged in, and peyote was the focus of a virtual cult.

The accounts I have heard differ on the scandalousness of these practices. Therese and others who converted now emphasize the dissolute mores of the pagan Land, seemingly delighting in a latter-day horror for the sins of the past: promiscuity, drug abuse, and welfare chiseling. Others, including Laurie, acknowledge that their behavior was "weird" from the point of view of those who had been brought up to feel guilt about sex, but insist that the Landers were "just a bunch of young people who were finding out what was going on." Laurie says that the sexual norm was a pattern of one partner at a time, new partners usually being met off the Land. (In anthropological jargon, this would be "exogamous serial monogamy.") Mark Kimmerly, a less closely involved observer, saw it differently. He was not bothered by the nudity, but he was repulsed by the "sharing of each others' wives," suggesting a pattern of symmetrical polygamy. Whatever the practices, it seems to be agreed that the Land at its height in 1970 was a cooperative, peaceful commune. An elder of the Presbyterian church, who knew Therese through her real-estate dealings, brought a distinguished visitor to the Land during the summer of 1970 (the visitor was a Presbyterian minister from Northern Ireland on a pulpit exchange with Mark Kimmerly), and, at Therese's request, the communards put on their clothes for the occasion.

4. Religious expression. The group activities at the land wore a religious halo. Unlike so-called "intentional communities" (such as Oneida and New Harmony in the past, the Bruderhof and Twin Oaks today) the Land family was not united by an articulated ideology prior to their move to the country.[2] Most, however, found one or another level of meaning in an eclectic mix of religious notions, from the legendary Native American peyote cult through Tibetan Buddhism to Vedic Hinduism. By 1971, some were even experimenting with Christianity. The tipi became a site for those who did the peyote ritual, the library was the site for study and quiet contemplation, but above all mealtime in the barn was the place for communal ritual. This is how Laurie described it:

When dinner is ready a large bell is rung. The food is set out with dishes, buffet style, on the central serving table. [Then] Everybody joins hands around the fire and says a silent grace. Children, babies, visitors, everybody is included. [Later] around the fire is the place where the day's adventures and stories get told. . . . Sometimes the fire is surrounded with people playing drums and flutes. The atmosphere around the fire reminds me of a peaceful American Indian tribe.

No one was more central to this impression than Pete: half-Mexican, clown, storyteller, leader in matters hedonic and spiritual, and—with his dark hair, shining brown eyes, wide smile, and muscular build—gift to women. His special contribution to the Land was less his skill as a builder than his sheer vitality and his manifest conviction that this was the life to live. He was permanently in the nascent state.

Mass Conversion, 1971–1972

On Halloween night, 1970, or rather at three in the morning of All Saints Day, the big barn burned down. "God erased it," said Therese later. "The fire wiped us out," said Laurie later.

The barn went up fast. A peacock in the coop shrieked. A stained-glass window on the second story flared and then burst out. The heat was intense and the colors glorious. Everyone stayed up all night, and the sunrise seemed to be some sort of omen. "The sunrise was spectacular," said Laurie. "The sky was outrageous, an expanse of orange and red. I'd never seen anything like it." Therese, equally impressed, remembers different details: "The sky was one half black and the other half blue. Such a sign!"

Now a major structural fire in the coastal mountains of California is not like a fire in the cities of the urban northeast. Buildings are not very tall, the ground is unpaved, and few persons stand a chance of being hurt. But buildings are wooden and dry, fire crews are volunteer, trucks are slow and distances long. The chances are that if the fire is not extinguished immediately, the building will be totally consumed, not just gutted. In the cities, fires bring fear of death, grateful stories of escape and rescue, and dirty salvage work. On the Land, however, there was alarm, excitement, spectacle, and a total, purging loss of the community's physical center.

After the fire Therese's Big House was needed for the family, and she, her sons having left to live with their father, moved down to a tent on the Navarro. Laurie, two other Landers, and three other friends went to Baja California for a month. Meanwhile, Pete had already been away for a month, having met the runaway Judy in San

Francisco on her birthday and gone with her to Hawaii, where they lived on the Big Island that fall on a diet of fruit and nuts. Therese returned from the river and Laurie from Mexico by Christmas, but Therese—still on a spiritual search and still valuing her privacy—went again next spring on a pilgrimage to India and Nepal, leaving a request that the family build her another handhewn house to compensate for the Big House. In the aftermath of the fire, leadership on the Land had defaulted.

Soon, too, the paradoxes of the Land's freedoms were made clear. Pete and Judy contracted hepatitis in Hawaii and returned to the Land to be taken care of by the family. Laurie's lover was sent to prison far to the south in Lompoc on an LSD conviction. Laurie's friend Linda found that she was pregnant after the trip to Mexico. As Pete recovered, he began an affair with another woman on the Land, and sixteen-year-old Judy found that she, too, having abandoned her family, was pregnant.

While Therese was in Katmandu learning meditation, a newcomer to the Land set about providing a new religious focus. Marge Schulenberg was a forceful Texan with a fundamentalist background. She had left Mendocino by the time I came to do my work there, but I heard many stories about her, one being that she succeeded in converting her outlaw husband, Bart, within one week of issuing an ultimatum. The Schulenbergs were there when the barn burned down, and they led some of the family in hymns around the ashes. Therese says that Marge found a cross and a Bible in the rubble, and Laurie recalls, with some distaste, that Bart read from the Bible and "spoke to God" that morning. Dianne Hunter remembers hearing a cassette tape on "the reality of Satan" played by Marge one night soon after the fire, and Sue Redford recalls her coming to Antioch meetings while Bart waited outside in the car. The record shows that Marge joined the Presbyterian church in January 1971 to become the first hippie Christian on its rolls, and Mark Kimmerly says that it was she who introduced him to the Land two months after the fire. Most important, however, it was Marge who converted Judy, and Pete followed.

In midwinter, 1971, just over a year after her first starry-eyed visit to the Land, Judy was lonely and frightened: she was pregnant and estranged from her own family, and her lover was seeing another woman. In her recuperation from hepatitis, she had stopped smoking marijuana, and she now felt alienated from the drugs-sex-and-nudity customs of the Land. In her loneliness, she accepted the Schulenbergs' offer of friendship, and one night she found herself being proselytized in their cabin. She remembers resisting their Jesus talk and wanting to leave their company, and she took what she thought might be the easy way out, agreeing to utter the stereotyped formula of a confession of faith. It might have been this one:

> Lord Jesus, I need you. I open the door of my life and receive You as my Savior and Lord. Thank You for forgiving my sins. Take control of the throne of my life. Make me the kind of person you want me to be.[3]

With that, she left Marge and Bart to go home.

On the dark footpath back to the tipi that was her home, she suddenly felt Jesus with her. "Did you really rise from the dead?" she asked. "Are you really there?" Then, as she put it in testimonies as well as to me, she received "new eyes," a sort of new perspective on the world, and she knew that Jesus *was* with her. Within the week Pete, a lapsed Catholic who had no use for the church but plenty of religious sensibilities and a conscience pricked by Judy's plight, also "found Christ" (as Judy, with naive disregard for theological niceties, put it).

Judy's conversion seemed to take hold immediately, Pete's only later. Judy's career as a hippie came to an end after only one eventful year. The southern-accented evangelicalism she received from Marge Schulenberg was unfamiliar to a formerly sheltered daughter of a well-to-do Presbyterian family, but the message of Jesus' eternal devotion and God's merciful forgiveness was far less alien to her than her desperate circumstances, alone in a tipi on a remote ridge top in the country. Surrendering her will to Jesus must have released an enormous rush of energy. In the years to follow, she would have many crosses to bear: Pete would wander again, the child she was carrying would die of a congenital heart defect four months after birth, her next pregnancy would bring twins, she would have to care for her growing family in cramped, dark, primitive quarters. But six years later, during the year that I spent among her Christian friends, Judy—pregnant again on her twenty-second birthday—was a leader in song and a valued member of the fellowship.

For Judy, the Christian life meant, among other things, a regularized home life with Pete, but there were other new converts whose lifestyle was not so suddenly changed. Among them were Linda and Peggy, single women who "still had men and stuff," as Judy put it, and Pete himself, whose involvement with his other woman came to an end only after a bitter three-way confrontation in which Judy asserted her rights. Judy's life did not attain the wholeness she longed for until the next summer, in August, when she, now six months pregnant, and Pete were legally, religiously married with Therese and her parents in attendance. She treasures the photographs of her wedding. Looking back, she says that she and Pete would never have stayed together but for the Lord. She alluded to continuing ups and downs in her marriage, "but we have a solid rock on which our marriage rests, the Lord." Such has been Judy's salvation.

The conversion of the community was less poignant but more ironic, less sudden but more dramatic. The presence on the Land of a few professed Christians—the Schulenbergs, Linda and Peggy, then Judy and a handful of others—was at first merely an aspect of the Land's religious eclecticism, creating more concrete religious opportunities for the spiritually inclined. Months after Judy's radical and Pete's nominal conversions that winter, Therese returned from her visit to India and introduced the practice of early-morning Buddhist meditation for those who were interested.

Christian missionaries of various sorts, though, were active among the Landers. Eleanor Kearney, a well-educated, trained Bible teacher, offered a Bible-study class at Albion Chapel, five miles up the road. "I had thought that just little old ladies would come," she told me. "But instead the hippies and heavy Jesus freaks came." Some of them frightened her, and she wondered if there was too much similarity between "the drug thing" and "the Jesus thing." But she persisted for over six months.

Later on that year, Mark Kimmerly himself was invited by Marge Schulenberg to lead a Bible-study group at the Land on the book of John. For about four months, the group met once a week. One of the regulars was Turo de Grazia. The choice of John's gospel, said Kimmerly, was the Landers', and it was appropriate, since John is at once the most comprehensive and most mystical of the Gospels. It was Kimmerly's intention to promote humane values at the Land, but most of those who were members later became converts to a fundamentalism far more doctrinally conservative than his own intellectualized faith.

Indeed, one of them guffawed when telling me about the group five years later when I said that it seemed that Kimmerly had been at the time one of the few Christians in the group:

> Ha! Kimmerly a Christian! No! We were studying the Book of John, really going over it line by line. It was boring. We were all dead, including Kimmerly. Once Bart Schulenberg came to one of our meetings filled with the spirit, and we were blown out. We didn't want any more fanatics to show up. We wanted to make sense of the Bible intellectually.

This man himself, a Jew who called himself Carlos, converted within a year and became a notorious zealot.

As Christianity became a legitimate religious alternative, some people from the Land began to attend churches in the area, including the Presbyterian church. Some, less interested in leavening the institutional church, went to Antioch Fellowship meetings. One of the Land's well-regarded couples were married by Kimmerly on the Land: the bride, a beautiful and talented painter, was the daughter of one of the left-wing artists who had joined the Presbyterian church in the days of Peter Hsu; the groom, raised in a fundamentalist family, was Al, the Land's most skilled carpenter. So far, however, Christianity was still only one religious option among many: Presbyterian minister Kimmerly could perform a marriage ceremony on the "pagan" Land with a quasi-Buddhist Therese as a legal witness.

Christianity became more than an option (or less, if you prefer) through the mobilization of Pete's profession of faith. During the spring, the invocation by others of his commitment had turned Pete away from another woman and had served to calm him down when he was in a fight with another man, an event observed with astonishment by Laurie. But for Pete that spring, Christianity was mostly a new religious idiom. He did not yet have the "new eyes" that Judy had. Judy and Pete planned to spend a summer month at the Marin county Renaissance Pleasure Faire, where Pete hoped to make some money and have fun, but at the last moment he heeded a plea from one of the Christian missionaries on the Land that he, who had presumably given his life to the Lord, ought to go to Eureka's "Beacon House" to learn about the Lord. According to Dianne Hunter, it became the norm that year "to go up to Beacon House when you got saved." Pete may have felt that his life was out of order. Therese had returned from another trip abroad and was manifestly disappointed that Pete and Al had not, as they had promised, finished her new house.

At Eureka, Pete and Judy found an intensely organized religious community. No drugs or alcohol were tolerated. No one received government welfare. Single men and women lived in separate dormitories, as, despite her obvious pregnancy, did Judy and Pete. The day began before sunrise and was filled with programmed work, worship, and religious instruction. It was at Beacon House that Judy and Pete decided to get married and to invite Judy's parents and Therese to the wedding. Therese says that she was appalled by the fanaticism of the organization. Having herself been a member of the Hitler youth in Germany in the 1930s, she saw a frightening replay in Beacon House. "If this is what heaven is like, then I don't want it," she thought.[4]

When Pete and Judy returned from Eureka, he was on fire with the Lord, and she was shortly to give birth to their daughter. His friends found the change in Pete unnerving. One—who later converted—

thought he'd had "too much acid." Therese wondered, when she first saw him after his Eureka sojourn, "Why doesn't he stop smiling?" Laurie, who did not convert, said she was "really sad" that he became a Christian. But Pete's magnetism and his influence had not waned. As a neighbor across the road remembered, "the Land exploded through the force of his personality." One after another, members of the family converted, and Judy remembers the exciting news of miracles daily sweeping the commune. "Paul has accepted the Lord!" "Praise God!" "Jerry has been saved!" "Hallelujah!"

Pete invited other lambs and missionaries down from Eureka, and soon activities organized in the name of the Lord began to be part of many Landers' lives. Visitors from Eureka stayed on the Land and elsewhere (including the homes of Antioch members like the Hunters). The Eureka people virtually took over a small Four Square Gospel church in Caspar, and for two weeks straight a revival meeting was held there in which many of the area's young persons were baptized in water and the spirit. The chief of the Eureka organization, Jack Boyle, came to Mendocino to add his weight to the revival. He made a formal request of the Presbyterian session to use the nearly abandoned Albion Chapel as a youth hostel. (The request was rejected under the influence of Mark Kimmerly, who was suspicious of Boyle's methods and, like Therese, caught the scent of Hitlerism in his organization. But evangelical Landers nonetheless used the Albion house over much of the next year for worship and potluck meetings.) It was Boyle's intention to make the Land a satellite community of his organization, and for that he needed more than bodies. It was necessary to convert the Land as a collectivity and as a locale. He even hoped to get legal title to the land itself.

Therese vividly recalls the battle to convert her. She returned from a trip to Europe in the spring of 1972 to find the Land teeming with baby Christians. They spoke about little besides the Lord. She closed her ears. Pete told her, "You lost, Therese. I won. I've been saved. I've been born again." She thought he was on another trip. He said that he'd prayed over the new house, and now it was finished. Christian madness or not, she moved in to her new quarters.

But then a special missionary came down from Eureka with instructions to convert Therese and reorganize the Land. His name was Jimmy Young. "I was suspicious of his motives. They just wanted me to sign over the commune to them, I thought." Jimmy and Therese argued fiercely. She was turned off, she said, to Beacon House Christianity. It was for weak people. The Bible was too narrow to be followed literally.

The encounter went on for seven days. Therese began to be impressed by Jimmy's idealistic, selfless, total dedication. "I love conviction" is one of her mottoes, and she loved his. Jimmy made her feel ashamed of her pride—"you're a good woman but you pile glory on your shoulders"—and guilty for misleading her young charges with spurious religious whims. She began to feel the struggle inside: "My heart knew Jimmy was right, but my mind said 'no.' " A voice within her said, "You're either for him or against him."

"So after seven days, I just accepted." Therese made her confession of faith, and a few days later, her conversion took hold when she had to confront some hostile curiosity seekers who barged onto the Land. "God help me," Therese thought. And she turned away the trespassers' hostility with a strange love that just poured out from her. "I was so amazed. I didn't like those people. It wasn't me. That's when I realized Jesus is living inside of me. Jesus took me over. He broke me totally." From this point on, Therese submitted herself to the new Christian leaders. "I had nothing more to say on the Land." But she did not sign over the property to Beacon House; on this, she took Kimmerly's advice.

Not everyone on the Land had converted or would convert. But by the spring of 1972, there was a substantial majority of new, fundamentalist converts, some old family members, some newcomers from Eureka. The converts began to demand behavioral changes from the holdouts. Smoking in the dining hall and public nudity were now deviant. Laurie tells this story: "I kept doing the old things. Like one day I was in the garden working. I was naked, and there were some Beacon people around. Pete told me that I should get dressed. I asked him why, and he said something about stumbling. I was still idealistic, and I didn't like what I heard." A meeting was called to discuss the issue, and Al's bride, a rather moderate new Christian, suggested a compromise such that she and Laurie and other idealists could wear light, filmy dresses. But that idea was rejected as being even more provocative to the new Christian sensibilities than nudity. Laurie's answer was to withdraw from collective activity.

Collective activity, especially meetings of the family council, became unpleasant for the minority of nonconverts. After returning from Eureka, Pete resumed his participation on the family council and swayed many to his side. After her conversion in April, Therese simply flowed with the fundamentalist tide. Several family members left the Land; others stopped coming to council meetings. Mark Kimmerly, who wanted to provide "a counterbalance to the judgmental, hateful style" of the Beacon House organization, was invited by Al, the last holdout on the family council, to intercede. But Kimmerly infuriated the new majority by likening their style to that of the Nazis, and his standing welcome on the Land was withdrawn. Soon, Kimmerly accepted another call and resigned his position at the Presbyterian church, and another barrier to Beacon House control fell. Al was outgunned, overwhelmed. He extracted a promise from Therese for the title to the plot of land he'd been living on (which was fulfilled in 1975), talked it over with his bride, and gave up. He left the Land.

The revolution was not bloody, but it was radical. Both its victors and its victims agree on that. In a legal deposition, written to defend a tax exemption for the Land ministry, Therese said flatly, "the Land became a Christian commune under the supervision of Beacon House, and godly laws were established in it," but this verbal formula glossed over a momentous change. A week after her conversion, Therese "went all the way" and burned all the non-Christian books in the new library in the big house. (She made no secret of her plan before the fact or the deed after, and Laurie was able to rescue a few books, including the *I Ching*, from the threatened bonfire.) "Godly laws"—my very mention of the expression in the interview with Laurie made her choke with frustration—meant no drugs, no nudity, no sex outside of marriage, no music other than gospel music, no dancing, and corporal punishment for children's misbehavior.

Recalcitrants were "booted off" (as Mark Kimmerly put it). "We kicked them off," said Therese. Hoping to gain my sympathy, it seemed to me, Judy acknowledged that some of the non-Christians were loving persons; they had taken care of her and Pete when they had had hepatitis a year before. But they were also selfish, she said, unwilling to give up any of their personal rights. Some stubbornly flaunted their nakedness and were therefore hard to be around. "They were, you know, the sort who never *would* change." So they were asked to leave.

It is clear to me now that Judy had Laurie in mind, though I did not know at the the time and heard Laurie's side of the story only after another year had passed. The beginning of the mass conversion had taken Laurie by surprise, since she was spending a lot of time away visiting her imprisoned lover, but she took notice when Pete began speaking about the Bible and she was alarmed when, much later, Therese announced to her during a family meeting, "You know this is a Christian commune now." Laurie resisted. She stopped going to family dinners and cooked for the few remaining non-Christians in her own house. "I saw it that this was my home, and people from outside were coming in and telling me how to work and live and wrecking the place." After the political confrontation over nudity, "I became the 'evil woman,' though I didn't see it that way. It was a shock to be living in the place with that going on." Laurie sought out

Mark Kimmerly's aid ("I thought Mark was O.K. In fact, he got kicked off because he was thought to be too liberal."), and her doing so increased the resentment against her. But Kimmerly's efforts to moderate the extreme fundamentalists had already failed, and he was leaving Mendocino.

Laurie did not give up easily. One by one her friends converted or left. "It was real uncomfortable. I was the only woman among the nonconverts. Linda and Peggy had converted. I wanted to show that the Beacon House was on a power trip, not a love trip. It was my home, and these guys were impostors. This went on for six months. There were all sorts of attempts to convert me. All manner of tactics were used. I was pressured into going to one of their religious meetings, and I went to see what they did. There, in a room full of forty people, Jack Boyle tried to convert me. They were very expectant that something was going to happen. I was fighting for survival."

Finally, as we have already heard from Judy, they realized Laurie wouldn't convert. Jerry, one of the family members who did convert and, as a male, one of the leaders, offered Laurie $110 for her house. "Then they said they'd give me wood to build a new house if I left. So eventually they gave me a pile of wood. Nick [the plumber, the next-to-last diehard] helped me move the wood. I left." It was September 1972, the pagans were gone, and the Land became "The Holy Land."

Spiritual Bootcamp, 1972–1974

Life on the Holy Land was a far cry from what it had been in the old days. For two years after Therese's conversion, until the Eureka organization decided that the Land had no more place in its mission, it was a "beehive," a "madhouse" of new Christian activity. It was a highly structured yet imperfectly organized youth camp, some of whose members were converts from hippie days. "It was the largest way I've ever seen the Lord move," said one. In the following ways their lives had changed.

1. The work life of the group ceased to be a by-product of an ideological, aesthetic, and personal quest for meaning and became more a means to a vastly expanded need for material provision. No longer two dozen but upwards of a hundred persons were now to be accommodated on the Land. Accounts differ, but the population increased by a factor of at least three, perhaps four. Many of the new members were not talented craftspersons, and some were recent refugees from social and economic dereliction. Work was no longer expressive but instrumental, and members were no longer encouraged to

"do their own thing" but to contribute much more purposively to the food supply, building program, and cash income of the group. They established a pottery factory and a tree-planting service, and some members worked in regular, forty-hour-a-week jobs on the outside, being expected to turn their wages over to the group. One veteran of those days told me he didn't mind the small ($10 per week) allowance that was returned to him because, with his full time job and off hours fully taken up with praising the Lord, there was little use for spending money. Money, food, and shelter were scarce, and the new organization at first did not have the wherewithal to care for its exploding population. Times were hard, and the Land called out to sister Christian communities, including Antioch Ranch, for aid.

Jobs on the outside were taken without an attempt to change the terms offered, with two qualifications. First, the employer might be asked to accept the dictates of "the Lord's will" as a reason for a day's absence. Second, women were not allowed to take jobs that the fundamentalist sex-role concept found inappropriate. One would-be employer in the community was furious to find that the services of one new woman convert, an expert welder, could no longer be hired.

2. Decision-making was reserved for male "elders." Family meetings were now held for religious but not political purposes, and the council was reformed to exclude women and to concentrate authority in the hands of those with more substantial "Christian" credentials. The counterculture rejection of formalization did not disappear overnight, however, and one could progress from lamb to elder in less than a year. Still, the concept of an office (of elder) was reintroduced into legitimate discourse. Moreover, the entire commune on the Holy Land was supervised by or "submitted to" an external authority, the Eureka ministry. Such submission was more than theoretical, and Therese, along with several other converts, was ordered near the end of 1973 to leave the Land, first to go to Eureka for training and then to New York City for an eighteen-month tour of street evangelism. A formal, many-layered hierarchy, which some would liken to an army, others to an ancient episcopate, was instituted, with Jack Boyle at its head.

Boyle tried, in effect, to bring all the new Christians of Mendocino, including Antioch Fellowship, under his authority. Boyle and the Redfords had first come into contact through Marge Schulenberg and the Caspar revivals, and when Larry was preaching against "Lone Ranger Christians," he could not lightly dismiss Boyle's vision of a higher level of Christian unity in Mendocino. Boyle came armed with effective Biblical ammunition, Paul's very teaching on the diversity of gifts. "Now you are the body of Christ, and individually members of

it. And God has appointed in the church first apostles, second prophets, third teachers, then workers of miracles, then healers, helpers,
administrators, speakers in various kinds of tongues. Are all apostles?
Are all prophets? Are all teachers? Do all work miracles?" (I Cor.
12:27–29, RSV)

Boyle presented himself as an apostle, Redford claimed to be no
more than a teacher, and throughout the summer of 1973 Boyle and
his lieutenants harangued Larry and Sue and the Antioch elders with
the demand that they "submit" to his apostolic authority. After long,
prayerful deliberations, the elders rejected Boyle's bid in a "Dear
Brother Jack" letter. "We rejoice to see the good fruit with which your
work has been blessed," they wrote. "You come to us inspired with a
vision, but we too have been given sight and are bound to follow as
the Word is revealed. . . . Jack, we regret the pressure we have felt
from you because we believe that an apostle does not demand submission but receives it through his service. . . . We love and embrace you
in Christ." Boyle's ambitions came up against the inherently centrifugal force of scriptural authority in a literate population.

3. Rules of behavior were, as Laurie's experience has already
shown, radically changed. Drugs, drinking, smoking, nudity, "forni-
cation"—many old freedoms, some that had been precious—were no
longer tolerated. Enforcement of these rules for children was through
spanking, for adults through overwhelming social pressure on the
converted and witnessing to the unconverted. One couple from Berkeley came to see their old friend Bobby, a new convert on the Holy
Land, but he was away at work. The Christian communards learned
that the visitors were—who would conceal such a thing among California hippies in 1973?—living together without benefit of marriage.
Before Bobby got home, his friends, disgusted at being called fornica-
tors, had left.

The new regime was given credit by many—friend and foe alike—
for changing lives that had been dominated by drugs, corrupted by
promiscuity, and ruined by aimlessness. But the vigorous reassertion
of traditional gender-role expectations led to polarized evaluations.
Women were to avoid being provocative; not only nudity but bare
legs were proscribed. Men were supposed to have short hair. Sleeping accommodations were segregated: there were "sisters' houses"
and "brothers' houses." Women and men were to follow appropriate
occupations: housework and horticulture were female; building and
forestry were male. The sexism of the new converts was without
doubt the most contentious matter I encountered in my interviews
and conversations in Mendocino.

4. The most obvious change at the Land was the supplanting of a

diffuse spiritualism and religious eclecticism by a specific and exclusive commitment to a radically conservative variety of Christianity. Religion was no longer pluralistic and merely facilitated, it was unitary and prescribed. Religious observance—Bible study, worship, grace before meals—was incumbent on all who chose to stay, but religious observance (the "outrageous praise of the Lord") was no burden for most but rather the most joyous part of the new life.

The new, mobilized Christian life was not for everyone. Judy and Pete found themselves hemmed in by their own success as evangelists. Judy found the expectation of daylong involvement in the community to be a distraction from the family she wished to build, and Pete was temperamentally disinclined for the day-to-day discipline of the Christian commune. He wanted to combine his new religion with his individualism. (In 1976, his cabin was festooned with a wholly idiosyncratic collection of slogans: "Honk if you love Jesus," "Sierra Club, Kiss My Axe," "Stop the Whale Killers," "Support the Right to Bear Arms.") So Judy and Pete moved off the Land to a trailer in the woods, moving back only when the Eureka organization pulled out in 1974 and left the Land in the charge of Larry Redford.

In fact, the conversion cannot be understood without seeing the spiritual continuity that bridged the abyss between the old and the new Land. Before and after the conversion, the communards devalued the institutions of the wider society and rejected what they saw as the superficial, routine lives it offered. The standards of the Land—old and new—were spiritual. Honor in the established world of education, business, and the professions was scorned in favor of honor as (at first) an authentic, whole, or (later) a spirit-filled, saved person. Before and after, one was a "freak," then for peyote, now for Jesus. The rejection of the merely routine, rationalized, standardized ways of the world in favor of the excitement of the extraordinary, the miraculous, and the meaningful was the link of nascent sensibility between the old Land and the new. When that sensibility later saw manifestations of the spirit in the old institutions of the society, including the Presbyterian church, a pathway of reintegration for the aging counterculture and revitalization for the crusty establishment could be cleared.

The Land and the Evangelical Community

The legacy of the Holy Land to the developing evangelical community of Mendocino was twofold. First, the Land was an agency of resocialization, a place where new ideals and new commitments were thoroughly inculcated. It was a center of indoctrination, aptly called a bootcamp for the convert. Not all who went through that experience have stayed within the evangelical fold, but the wonder is that so many have, particularly such influential persons as Therese. Many of the moderate evangelicals I spoke with credit the steadfast-ness of their faith to some vigorous and thorough, even rigid, early training: the parental home, a collegiate Christian house, or a camp like the Holy Land. After departure, the proselyte has a "solid founda-tion" that will permit free involvement in pluralistic society without loss of basic evangelical identity.

Second, the Holy Land was only one wing, albeit an extreme and unbalanced one, of an evangelical movement that spread through Mendocino in the early 1970s. It incarnated some inherent aspects of a rich orthodox Christian tradition: total commitment, divine presence, redemption from sin, Biblical authority. Just as, for many Americans of broadly leftist political sympathies, the Communist Party makes the Americans for Democratic Action look good, so for latent evangeli-cals the Holy Land made Antioch Ranch (and later the Presbyterian church) look good. Just as bitter conflicts among organizations on the political left (think of the Stalinists and the Trotskyists) do not pre-clude individual mobility between those organizations, so a convert to Antioch's style of evangelicalism could appreciate the Land's mission. Antioch and the Land (as later Antioch and the Presbyterian Church) played a symbiotic soft-sell–hard-sell game.

Here is the story of Bobby, raised a Southern Baptist but in 1972 a free-living, likeable, thirty-five-year-old hippie. He lived on Woody's Land, another hippie commune, but used to visit Therese's Land, in its pagan days, to meditate with Therese and Carlos. "When they went Christian all of a sudden, I still had a lot of love for Therese, and Carlos and Pete, and I'd go there and talk. [But] I didn't like their idea that Jesus is *the* way; I couldn't take that. I had a really bad argument with Carlos." Bobby then got introduced to Antioch Ranch by "a real pretty woman" who lived on the Holy Land and with whom he fre-quently shared a ride from work. "Then she moved to Antioch Ranch and there I met Christians I could talk to. The Land was too heavy, and I couldn't see much love there. Therese was mostly OK, but with the others it seemed to me to be an ego trip. But I saw love at Antioch Ranch. They listened. So I started hanging out at Antioch. At Anti-och, there were Turo and Anne and Jeffrey and Pat, and I thought, 'These are respectable, serious, reliable people, not blown-out hip-pies.' After the teaching at Antioch one night, Turo and two other guys and I prayed for me, that I would accept the Lord. Suddenly I wanted to have what they had. I wanted to have again what I had as a kid. I prayed, and I cried. It was like when I was eleven. I felt like a light bulb. I sure got zapped by the Holy Spirit." Two months after his conversion, Bobby moved to the Holy Land for the training he thought he needed. "The best and the hardest times in my walk with the Lord were there."

The Land gave Antioch a spiritual boost, a cadre of zealous evangelists, and a bootcamp for recruits. Antioch gave the Land a favorable public image as part of the Christian ministry to the counterculture. One and a half years after her conversion, Therese, former hippie queen, preached the Sunday sermon at the Presbyterian church. But by then, not only had the Land gone through its radical change, but the evangelical revolution had come to the Presbyterian church itself. Antioch Fellowship—strengthened through its symbiosis with the Holy Land—was the agent of that revolution.

7.

Evangelical Victory in the Church

When a handful of wholly committed human beings give themselves fully to a great cause or faith,
they are virtually irresistible. They cut through the
partial and fleeting commitments of the rest of society like a buzz saw through peanut brittle.
—Dean Kelley,
Why Conservative Churches Are Growing

Just as Mark Kimmerly unwittingly gave a boost to fundamentalism in his early sponsorship of Antioch Fellowship, so Larry Redford, leader of the charismatic fellowship, advanced the fortunes of the
institutional church when it fell to him to play a leading role in it. For it
was Larry Redford, more than any other person in Mendocino, who
was responsible for bringing Eric Underwood—evangelical preacher,
astute administrator, affable neighbor—to the pastorate at Mendocino
Presbyterian Church. This chapter tells the story of how Redford and
his allies had their way.

Liberal Exhaustion, Institutional Persistence

The last few months of Mark Kimmerly's ministry brought
discouragement. The Christian message he had tried to bring to the
counterculture backfired when the hippies at the Land went far beyond the mystical message of the Johannine Gospel to the radical
fundamentalism of the Jesus movement. Larry Redford was going his
own way with Antioch Ranch, a direction that Kimmerly did not
oppose but could not embrace. His own deep-seated personal opposition to American involvement in Vietnam gained him as many ene-

mies as allies. His last even mildly political official act at Mendocino Presbyterian was to cast a tiebreaking vote in the session to permit the local chapter of the War Resisters' League to hold a meeting in Preston Hall, and he knew his position would be resented by conservatives. This worried him, for his experience and his studies told him that conservatives are often more faithful to the organized church than liberals. He feared he could not long do without the former but could not count on the latter.[1] His discouragement showed in his preaching. One of his officers said that she came to dread the scoldings she could expect to get in Mark's sermons.

Above all, he told me four years later, living in the manse had become unbearable. He was the only full-time clergyman in Mendocino and effectively chaplain for a community of a thousand. He and his family had little privacy, and his wife was increasingly disinclined to bear the burdens of incessant phone calls and knocks on the door. He took it personally when the building restoration fund collection box located in the historic sanctuary was plundered twice in early 1972, feeling both anger and responsibility.

The Kimmerlys were in the process of searching for another home in Mendocino in order to leave the manse when he was contacted by the Presbyterian Church in Arena, California, a politically liberal and socially diverse congregation in a growing university community. He accepted the position there and announced his resignation to the Mendocino elders in June.

He preached his last sermon on June 25 to 149 worshippers, the second-largest congregation (not counting Easter services) he had addressed in Mendocino. The church voted a motion of appreciation to him and his wife, and many came to a reception to wish him well. He was remembered with respect four years later as a builder, an intellectual, and a person of courage and conscience, but he was perceived as personally standoffish. Political conservatives felt that he was friendly to the left, and theological conservatives questioned his spiritual leanings. A close friend of his remarked that Kimmerly took personally his failure to lead the church toward a liberal consensus; he was "crucified," said this friend.

He was, of course, very much alive as he went to take on his new pastorate, but he was also more successful in Mendocino than he or his opponents realized. The church had turned a corner toward new vitality. The physical properties of the church were in much better condition when he left than when he had come, and the church was organizationally stronger as well. Kimmerly had led campaigns to prune inactive members from church rolls, twenty being suspended in 1967 and twenty-seven in 1970, and the result was that membership was down by a nominal ten percent but the ratio of attendance to membership was up by more than thirty percent. This leaner, more active membership had volunteered the funds and the labor for the centennial building campaign, and overall per-capita dollar giving had increased by nearly sixty percent (from $60 to $95 per member) in the five years of Kimmerly's ministry.[2]

The physical upgrading of the church and the social diversity that Kimmerly encouraged meanwhile began to draw in some of the new faces that were made available by Mendocino's demographic changes. Average attendance was increased by the frequent but irregular visits to Mendocino Presbyterian of busloads of Jesus people from the Land and the surrounding woods. And just as deadwood was being pruned, new arrivals to the community, most of them retired or semiretired from careers pursued elsewhere, began joining the church. Over thirty people joined the church in the last year and a half of Kimmerly's ministry, and a third of them took very active roles in the growth of the church through the early 1970s.

The healthy state of the congregation was thus due in part to demographic changes beyond the minister's control, but the church was able to capitalize on those changes through its outreach to more liberal, more recent residents of the community. Yet the "creative worship" that Kimmerly and his artistic friends sponsored did not itself appeal to the alienated youth who were its intended audience. In the view of one of the artists who participated in it, the attempt to reach out to the counterculture through contemporary poetry, painting, and music was "a very bourgeois thing." It was Larry Redford and, even more, Jack Boyle who, with an evangelical message and paternal guidance, were successful in that outreach.

When Kimmerly left, the elders set in motion the procedure to choose a regular successor, and they asked the eighty-year-old Frederick Althorpe to become interim pastor once again on a part-time basis. Through the summer, Althorpe led Sunday worship and meetings of the elders and gave the congregation a welcome sense of continuity. In the fall, however, he found the demands of the position too taxing, and an advanced student from the San Francisco Theological Seminary, Craig Everett, was hired as a part-time interim pastor. From November into January, Everett preached at Sunday services and attended, but did not preside over, meetings of the session.

Few persons remembered much about Everett in 1976, but one event was spontaneously cited by several persons as a symbol of "the times" the church had had to go through. Christmas Eve of 1972 happened to fall on a Sunday, and although Christmas does not traditionally draw Protestants to church the way Easter does, an evening musicale brought over one hundred persons to the sanctuary. Christmas Eve, 1972, also happened to be the day chosen by President Nixon to bomb North Vietnam into aquiescence. Everett, I was told, was so outraged by the bombing that he interrupted the musicale to deliver a scathing attack on American foreign policy. Some people walked out, and Everett was subsequently disparaged as "Prophet Craig." Everett evidently helped some members put Kimmerly's more reserved political stance into perspective, but he also added to the antipathy felt toward the Presbyterian seminary on the part of two powerful lay members of the congregation. In effect, he made both his predecessor and his eventual successor look attractive.

In fact, the congregation was held together by its laypersons in the nine months between Kimmerly's departure and Underwood's arrival. The artists' contingent continued creative worship. A newcomer couple, both early retirees, began a fund drive to buy a new organ. An evangelical woman led a Bible-study course. The newsletter was written, printed, and distributed. Sanctuary doors were opened for worship and locked after. The offering was counted and banked. A trustee was ready to preach a "canned" sermon if the interim pastor, who had a long distance to travel, should be late for worship. After-worship refreshments were served. The bills were paid. The myriad little ways in which a social organization enlists the variously motivated efforts of ordinary persons endured. The pillars of the church stood straight.

The regular cycling of formal lay leadership also continued. At the end of 1972, the terms of four elders (one-third of the session) expired, and one other elder resigned after two years of her three-year term. The congregation's nominating committee, chosen each year at the January annual meeting, enlisted five persons (who could expect to be elected by acclamation) to fill the positions on session. The political balance of the board remained fairly even between Democrats and Republicans, but the new board, the one Underwood would chair, had on it two fresh articulate conservatives who were to play important roles in the years ahead.

The officer-nominating committee operated entirely independently of the pastor-search committee, and the deliberations of the latter, which I shall soon recount, were kept "top secret," as several outsiders told me. But one of the eventual trustee nominees, Ed Kearney, was married to a member of the pastor-search committee, and he did know who the new pastor was to be prior to his own election. Thus one of the conservative newcomers to the session, who led the effort to keep the church free of political involvement in the ensuing years, knew before agreeing to serve that the new pastor would be an evangelical. We shall return to this matter in chapter twelve.

Evangelical Mobilization

While the organization was thus working away, continuing to occupy a routine place in the lives of most, absorbing most of the free time of others, its surface appearance was becoming more evangelical and less conventional. Larry Redford and one of the elders at the Holy Land encouraged their charges to act as leaven in the "straight" churches of the area, and, although the Caspar church particularly catered to their style of worship, a recycled hippie bus painted with Jesus slogans would disgorge a dozen enthusiastic new Christians into Mendocino Presbyterian Church about every three weeks. Reaction was mixed. One townswoman notorious for her vitriolic temper was said to have demanded her husband cease singing in the church choir, so as not to lend approbation to a church that would countenance bare feet and the smell of wood smoke among its communicants. A conservative grande dame, a pillar of the church, opined that she did not like the newcomers but she was glad they were in church. A more revealing—albeit stereotyped—response came from a young liberal who was irritated by the new evangelicals' obtrusive vocalizing: "I thought, 'wouldn't they be happier in a Southern Baptist Church?' or actually I thought, 'wouldn't I be happier if they were in a Southern Baptist Church?' "

But even as the new evangelical troops were praising God in strange tongues, some of their leaders were engaged in a sophisticated effort at social change. A congregational meeting to elect a pastor-seeking committee was called by the session for the earliest possible date after the pulpit was declared vacant—the first Sunday in August—and announcement of the meeting was given for several weeks in advance at Sunday services. On August 6, 1972, eighty-four persons attended morning worship, and, after the few who were not members of the church had left, Reverend Althorpe called the special congregational meeting to order. He suggested that a small and odd number of persons "representative of the whole congregation" be elected to the committee. When seven persons had been named and had accepted nomination, motions were made and carried to close nominations and to elect the seven by unanimous ballot. The meeting—including opening and closing prayers—was over in less than half an hour, and, without the contentiousness that had characterized the last such congregational meeting in 1966, Mendocino Presbyterian had chosen a representative group, indeed, but one with an evangelical bloc.

The seven members, in the order their nominations were entered into the record, were:

Katherine Lamphear, a young single woman, who was an artist and student and the daughter of a respected elder of the church. She had been active in Mark Kimmerly's "creative worship" program and had joined the church in December 1970.

Grace Silva, the recently retired Mendocino grammar-school principal, a pillar of the church and the community, and by far the most senior person on the new committee. Though a native to the area and a member by birth and by marriage of two of its prominent families, she was a political liberal and was proud of her rapport with the young. She had served the church in many capacities and had been a member since 1925.

David Baker, thirty-two, the park ranger introduced in chapter five. At the time of the pastor search, he was serving on the session of Mendocino Presbyterian and as an elder of Antioch Ranch Fellowship. He had joined the church in December 1969.

George Helms, a recently retired civil servant, new to Mendocino but long active in the wider organization of the Presbyterian church. A man of establishment sympathies and civic spirit, he, along with his wife, had joined the church in 1972.

Dorothy Lendler, public-school librarian, who had moved with her husband and child to Mendocino to escape the climate of Los Angeles a few years earlier. She was of politically and cultural liberal inclinations and had recently been elected to the church session, on which she was serving as "clerk" (or recording secretary). She and her husband had joined the church in January 1971.

Eleanor Kearney, about forty-five, a housewife and mother of five, who had moved with her wealthy lawyer husband to Mendocino about two years before. She was an enthusiastic evangelical Christian, having had a conversion experience in 1967. She had not served the church as an officer, but she had been leading Bible-study classes, including one that attracted people from the Land prior to the mass conversion there. Eleanor and Edward Kearney had joined the church in December 1970.

Larry Redford, forty, beginning his fourth year as leader of Antioch Ranch. A political and theological conservative and full-time worker for Christ, he had been a member of the church since 1964.

Redford and Baker had agreed beforehand to be ready to nominate each other, but neither was able to recall to me whether they had in fact done so. Along with Kearney, they constituted a strong bloc of three on the committee. Redford became the leader and guiding spirit. But in another respect, Kearney was the pivotal member. She was in the middle of the age range and, although a newcomer to Mendocino, of unassailable social respectability. Yet she was also, like the missionaries to the counterculture, a born-again evangelical Christian, which was a religious inclination heretofore not associated with respectability at Mendocino Presbyterian.

Given the election procedure, it was a balanced committee and reasonably representative of the congregation. There were four women and three men. The age range was late 20s to late 60s with the median (early 40s) being somewhat younger than the congregation's. There were three registered Republicans, three Democrats, and one nonvoter. All had some college education, and several had postgraduate training. All were property owners, and all were ascriptively Protestant. The most significant statistical imbalance was that most were newcomers to the church, and only Mrs. Silva and Redford had been members for longer than the duration of Mark Kimmerly's pastorate. This imbalance, in turn, allowed the evangelical plurality on the committee—Redford, Baker, and Kearney—to determine its direction, in the absence of any competing bloc of experience and determination.

During my sojourn in Mendocino, I came to know all of these persons, and I interviewed most of them formally. Their recollections, combined with the terse official records of the church, have allowed me to piece together the story of their work despite the policy of secrecy that the committee observed during the search period itself.

Immediately after their election, the committee members were convened to establish their organization. Redford was elected chairman, and the group set up a schedule of weekly meetings into the fall. Redford, who began to devote great chunks of time to the task, made himself familiar with the most recent United Presbyterian Church pastor-search procedures. The committee followed them closely, and their progress was monitored by Althorpe, who chaired the meetings of the ruling elders when they met with the committee, and by Willard Pratt, pastor of the nearby Presbyterian church in Fort Bragg, who was their official liaison person to the denomination.

The first formal step was for the committee to complete a "church information form," which served both as a kind of internal stock-taking for the church and as a job description for potential candidates. The committee pooled their knowledge to compile a survey of the composition of the congregation (age, sex, race, occupation, and education of members), the physical properties of the church, and existing programs and church groups.

More consequential were the policy decisions that the official form called for, from the simple question of what salary could be offered to a new pastor through less tangible questions about the "mission goals" of the congregation and the kinds of abilities that would be looked for in a new pastor.

Larry Redford knew what he wanted: a "Christ-centered" pastor, whose teaching would be "biblically based" and who would make it his mission to shape Mendocino Presbyterian as a "new testament church." The fragmented majority of the committee, having no consensus among them on Christian humanism, political liberalism, or even antifundamentalism, had no such clear agenda, and they contented themselves, for the most part, with assuring that proper procedures were followed.

Redford led the committee to seek the endorsement of the session for the direction he wished the committee to take. Regarding the tangible aspects of the job opening, the committee sought to increase the salary offering by ten percent and to sweeten the position by establishing a budget line for a quarter-time office secretary. Primarily, however, Redford so shaped the substance of the job description that "biblically based teaching" assumed primacy as the criterion for selection. The church information form prepared by the committee was a thoroughly evangelical document, and it was approved by a specially called meeting of the session, after long discussion with the pastor-seeking committee in attendance, five weeks after the committee's election.

The job description left little room for any nonevangelical agenda. The officers of the church agreed that they would consider candidates of either sex and any race, but, having already had a Chinese-American pastor, expressed no interest in special affirmative-action procedures. Experience of candidates in particular kinds of ministries—inner city, urban, rural parish; large or small congregations, staff or pastoral responsibilities—was declared unimportant. No special competences were expected of applicants in psychological counseling, community organizing, or ecclesiastical politicking. Instead, the committee spent its time determining its answers to the information form's questions regarding the candidate's "preaching ability" and "other capabilities." Regarding preaching, the committee stated three criteria: "1. Biblically based teaching" (which was decisive for the evangelicals and could not easily be countered by the others); "2. Relevant to personal growth and social needs" (which was not one criterion but two usually opposed ones, and hence lost significance as a factor); and "3. Readily understood by varied age groups" (a criterion that all members could readily agree on, but with significantly different models in mind).

Regarding "other capabilities," the denomination's information form offered seven areas and invited the local committee to specify three. The seven possibilities were (a) administration; (b) Christian education; (c) community involvement; (d) evangelism/recruitment; (e) parish program development; (f) pastoral care; and (g) steward- ship. The committee passed over items that sounded too worldly or too controversial and chose (d), (e), and (f). Here the nonevangelicals on the committee took a stand, backed up by the majority of the elders, to state that the three additional criteria were listed in no particular order of priority. Redford acceded. The resulting job de- scription, however, was one that a parochially inclined evangelical clergyman could find distinctly suitable. Thus "above average capabili- ties" were stated as desirable in three areas, "not listed in order of priority," but nonetheless listed in this order:

Evangelism/Recruitment: Spiritual enrichment and outreach, contacting visitors and gathering new members.

Parish Program Development: Working with youth, families and small groups, reconciling and establishing an empathy between the conserva- tive and contemporary elements.

Pastoral Care: Personal contact, counseling, visiting in homes, and hos- pital calls.

The most remarkable and most radically evangelical aspect of the completed information form was its articulation of the "goals and objectives" of the congregation. Presbyterian procedure required the committee to "identify and describe the mission goals established by the session," and Redford's answer was diametrically opposed to the equally radical goals articulated by Peter Hsu ten years earlier. It was the concept (which Redford had already begun to articulate at Anti- och Ranch) that "the mission of the church is the church." He wrote a statement of the "goals and objectives" of the church, which, sound- ing harmlessly utopian in its religious language and ecumenical in its concrete language, won the assent of the committee and the session. But Redford meant every word of it.

Overall Goal of the Church

Our goal is to become a local New Testament Church, a fellowship of those who are true followers of Jesus Christ. Our purpose is to *become* individually mature Christians and corporately unified in our commit- ment to Christ and to one another. It is to be an organism that is continually building itself up in love through the grace and knowledge of its leader, Jesus Christ.

Objectives for Reaching that Goal

1. Teaching: We need to be under solid, consistent teaching from God's word in an atmosphere where there can be discussion, questioning, and a hammering out of practical application.

2. Koinonia (deep fellowship—oneness): Our members need to be deeply involved with one another in our joys, trials, and everyday concerns. There needs to be a real sharing with one another of the life we have in Jesus Christ.

3. Lay Leadership: Our men and women need to be trained how to minister to one another in spiritual and material ways so as to allow a pastor the time and energy to fill his unique ministry in the local body.

Outflow from the Goal—Result

We believe that the more we become a mature people in Christ the more we will be "a light on a hill" as Jesus described. That is, we will serve as a very real force for good and love in our community, which has a unique challenge. We must relate to (in no particular order):

1. Long-time established families.
2. Large numbers from the "hip culture" as permanent members of the community and with undetermined goals.
3. Migrating numbers traveling the favored route between the San Francisco Bay area and the Pacific Northwest.
4. Unreached young families living in the area.
5. Recently retired new arrivals of all ages.

We feel that lay leadership, with various skills and potential, is available within this congregation. Our need at this point in our church life is for an energetic pastor-teacher to train, motivate, and guide us.

In the terms introduced in chapter two, what Redford had received endorsement for was a manifesto to turn a *social institution* into a *social movement.* An institution is a consensually recognized, relatively stable set of social roles and norms that takes its place among other institutions in the society and harnesses the commitment of participants even as it tends to last longer than the involvement of any one of them.

A *social movement,* by contrast, is much more dependent on the intense commitment of its individual constituents, and it tends to absorb all their energies, as was true of Antioch Ranch for the Redfords and others in the nascent state. A movement does not usually have a recognized, legitimate place in the society, and its social function is to produce change, sometimes radical change, rather than to reproduce the status quo.

In theological terms, it was Redford's goal that the actual, "visible church" of Mendocino, populated with hereditary Presbyterians, socially concerned artists, and Sunday Christians, as well as religious virtuosos, should become in fact the "invisible church," embracing only those who have experienced God's gift of salvation. The idea was to turn a compromised human institution into a "fellowship of true followers," a radical aspiration indeed.

Institutions generally are vulnerable to the ideological appeals of movements, which usually claim to be acting in the spirit of the values to which the target institution gives only lip service, such as peace, justice, reason, love, or God's glory.[3] The session of Mendocino Presbyterian had no reason at hand not to endorse the insurgents' motives.

The information form being approved, it was forwarded to the denomination's central bureau for clergy seeking new calls, the Department of Ministerial Relations, in Ohio. In turn, there were sent to the pastor-seeking committee more than 200 resumes of candidates meeting the broad requirements of the committee (primarily geographical proximity). A copy of the form, minus a few confidential items like maximum salary, was sent to candidates who expressed interest in the newly announced job opening. Responsibility for perusal of the resumes was divided among the committee members, and some of them also received telephone calls putting in a good word for various hopefuls. In the buyer's market for clergymen, there were many attractive candidates, and Lamphear was particularly interested in one who had a strong background in counseling psychology.

One candidate, however, caught the eyes of Redford, Baker, and Kearney, and when they decided that Eric Underwood was the man for the job nothing could stand in their way. Underwood was an associate pastor of a large church in the city of Salinas, about 250 miles away, and he had listed his name a year earlier as one generally, but not urgently, interested in a new call. From Redford's point of view he stood out first of all as a fellow graduate of Fuller Theological Seminary, having overlapped there with Redford from 1961 to 1963 (though the two were not acquainted). More to the point were the manifestly evangelical terms Underwood used to describe himself, this in a denomination where theological liberalism was the predominant accepted idiom.

Thus, in outlining the responsibilities of his current position, Underwood mentioned at the head of the list his role in fostering the "Biblical literacy" of his adult membership, through eight-week classes for prospective members and an extensive adult Sunday-school program. Stating his viewpoints, Underwood said that the role of the pastor is to be the "spiritual coach" of the church, and the mission of the church is "to make disciples of Christ by preaching and teaching the gospel." He listed his "major capabilities" (choosing from the same set as had the Pastor-seeking Committee) as "evangelism/recruitment," "christian education," "administration," and "pastoral care," manifesting a close affinity with the committee's evangelical bloc and satisfying two of the officially stated three criteria. The liberals on the committee could see that Underwood felt that church members should be "catalysts in society," and they noted that he had been serving for five years as chairman of the Hospital Chaplains' Board of Monterey County. But there was nothing in his resume to suggest that he would lead the church as a collectivity in social or political action.

Beyond his ideology, Underwood had other attributes that appealed to the committee. His undergraduate degree (from UCLA) was in business administration. He had done postgraduate work in clinical psychology. He declared himself open regarding salary and the type of community he wished to live in. He had seven years' experience since ordination and was young (thirty-four) with a wife and two children. Though the committee knew that it was unfair to seek a "two-for-the-price-of-one" deal by requiring the pastor's wife to be Pastor's Wife, they noted with approval that Mrs. Underwood was a graduate of a Presbyterian College, a member of her husband's church, and, without apology, a housewife by occupation.

So the committee agreed with Redford to take a close look at Underwood. The next step was for the committee, acting discreetly, to hear a sermon preached by the candidate, and Underwood was invited to the church in Fort Bragg one Sunday for that purpose. He passed that test with flying colors, though he implied a more politically liberal stance (quoting with approval some words of Martin Luther King, Jr., in his sermon) than had been apparent from the self-description on his resume. (The resume did not include information that, unlike Kearney, Redford, and Helms, he was a registered Democrat.) The committee decided that he was their man, the evangelicals with enthusiasm for a like-minded Christian. Among the nonevangelicals some felt that Underwood would unify the church (having the experiences of Craig Everett and Mark Kimmerly in the background), while others were stymied by their sheer inability to suggest a convincing alternative.

Underwood himself was persuaded. He met Mark Kimmerly for

lunch one day near Santa Cruz to discuss Mendocino, and he learned that the church was on the verge of new growth. He negotiated more secretarial help with the committee and signaled to them his intention of phasing out the dying Albion ministry (which Kimmerly had advised). But he was unable to win a housing allowance in lieu of the existing manse, and he therefore paid a large capital-gains tax when he could not plow back the proceeds from the sale of his Salinas house into one in Mendocino. (Two years later, the congregation would make it possible for him to buy his own house.).

Before the committee could bring their candidate to the congregation, they had to seek the approval of the responsible agencies of the denomination. For that approval, in turn, they were required to comply with affirmative-action procedures, described by one committee member as "farcical." So four of them agreed to conduct what was reportedly to all parties a pro-forma interview of a nonwhite clergyman who, though his name appeared on the job-seekers' list, had expressed no interest in the Mendocino opening. That exercise concluded, the committee went to the Presbytery with their choice, and they received approval.

These procedures took much longer than any other pastor search in recent memory, and it was not until January that Underwood could be invited to deliver his candidating sermon before the congregation. For over four months, with first Althorpe and then Everett acting as interim pastor, the committee had been at work, and the congregation had been told nothing of their deliberations. Only on the first Sunday of the new year did the fifty-odd persons attending hear that a candidate for pastor was to preach two weeks hence. That announcement and a notice in the church newsletter brought out over a hundred persons, about two-thirds of the number of church members, to hear Underwood's sermon. At the end of the worship service, Underwood was conducted outside by Althorpe while a congregational meeting heard Redford deliver the report of the pastor-seeking Committee. Without the machinations that the 1962 committee felt necessary or the contentious atmosphere that greeted Mark Kimmerly in 1967, the vote was unanimous and enthusiastic. Underwood received the call.

A few days later, Redford exulted over the victory in his Antioch newsletter:

> The situation at the Presbyterian Church is at an exciting point. Our candidate, Eric Underwood, from Salinas, was approved by the church and hopefully will begin his ministry here in early March. We feel he is uniquely fitted to lead this church into greater maturity during these days of renewed life here on the Mendocino Coast. Mendocino needs a

light set on a hill winsomely and faithfully glorifying the Lord Jesus, and we sense we are on the brink of a new era.

Three years later, when I first met him, Redford still spoke as the triumphant leader of a benign conspiracy. Referring to himself, Baker, and Kearney, he said, "We three had a bond and knew what we wanted. We knew that the way we went, the committee would go. We picked Eric." This account was corroborated to me from the other side of the committee as well.

With the help of Antioch crew, the new pastor moved into the freshly scrubbed manse, and he took up his duties on March 12, 1973. Having the memory of the inexperienced student pastor, Craig Everett, freshly in mind, the congregation expected a lot of Eric Underwood, and the evidence is that he did not disappoint them. Whereas attendance had been hovering around seventy, it immediately jumped to well over 100 and grew. For years, only a fraction (one-half to two-thirds) of the church's membership had attended worship on a given Sunday, but under Underwood's leadership the number of Sunday worshipers frequently exceeded the number of members. Many of them came from Antioch Fellowship. To put it another way, the Sunday attendance surpassed 100 only a dozen times in the preceding three years but fell below 100 only six times in the next three years.

Evangelicalism in the Institutional State

The new pastor had described himself well in his resume. He was a loyal alumnus of Fuller Seminary who regarded the Bible as the final arbiter in matters of Christian faith. He had learned his lessons in homiletics well, and he was an engaging, at times dramatic, preacher. He was old enough to be experienced and stable but young enough to be flexible. His wife, of Lebanese ancestry and also an evangelical, was an unearned bonus for the church, a musically talented, energetic extrovert, who seemed to relish her role as pastor's wife.

Underwood had other qualities that did not appear on official paper, as his new congregation soon learned. He was a convivial and popular person who had been president of his college fraternity and a glee club singer. He knew how to delegate responsibility. He was skilled in business administration, not so much on the accounting side as on the marketing side, and it soon became apparent that he was more inclined to balance the books by increasing income than by holding down expenses. He was a practical evangelical who attributed his fiscal liberalism to his faith that God would stimulate the flock's generosity. He was a Presbyterian by convenience, who spent only an obligatory year at a Presbyterian seminary in Texas, after his three years at Fuller, in order to be ordained. However, to Larry Redford's ultimate chagrin, he was an institutional clergyman, a person who had deliberately and successfully pursued a worldly career conformable to his evangelical belief. He was no antinomian, and he more than once confessed that his own strongest temptation was to forget God and to live as a "good, Godless man." Only his conscience and his theology told him of the impossibility of that worldly dream.

Above all, Underwood was a self-conscious, sophisticated evangelical, neither, he would state when asked, a charismatic nor a fundamentalist. To the uninformed unbeliever, there may appear to be no significant difference between evangelicals (those who believe in the resurrection, miracles, conversion, and the Bible as the final arbiter for Christian faith) and fundamentalists (who add a belief in the literal truth of everything in the Bible, including its creation stories and its dominant patriarchalism), and charismatics (who believe in the contemporary relevance of the Pentecost gifts). The Redfords were all three; Underwood was only an evangelical.

Underwood's conversion had occurred when he was twenty, and he went from being an unchurched ladies' man to a chastened, more serious college student who moved in with a fundamentalist living group. Since then his Christian experience had been in the supportive atmosphere of evangelical institutions in southern California, Texas, and Salinas. He was not a radical who had done battle against a perceivedly hostile environment, as was Larry Redford. Underwood was more inclined to accept the world, to see, with Martin Luther, all callings as religiously significant or, as several of his congregants told me, to "meet people where they are."

He had begun to do that already in his dealings with the pastor-search committee. On the occasion of his trial sermon in Fort Bragg, he had stayed with the Kearneys, the wealthiest family in his congregation-to-be, in their luxurious home perched on the very edge of the ocean headlands. Two months later, when he returned to preach his candidating sermon, he was a guest of the Redfords, sleeping in a borrowed camper truck amongst rustic cabins, pear trees, children, dogs, and goats. He thus gained a vivid picture of the range of evangelical life styles in Mendocino.

Underwood's prosaic, parochial evangelicalism was most pointedly revealed to me one night in 1976 during a prayer-group meeting in his home. Ordinarily, participation was elicited from every person in attendance, often simply by their being asked "How goes it with you?" the end and climax of the meeting being a long, round-robin intercessory prayer in which these personal concerns were put before God.

On the evening in question, at the suggestion of Underwood's wife, Vonnie, we played a variation of the usual theme, a meditation exercise she had learned at a recent prayer workshop. Bobby, a veteran of the Land and one of the regulars in the group, offered to lead the exercise, and Vonnie offered (ever the helpmate) to shield us and her husband against interference from the phone or doorbell for the hour it would take. Bobby was greatly skilled in meditation techniques, and had been tutored not only under evangelical auspices but also through the Esalen-based human-potential movement. His leadership of this exercise was effective, and the meditation was a moving experience, especially for the usually rather impatient Underwood.

Bobby began gently by asking each of us to find a position in which we'd be comfortable for a long time without moving. Then he asked us to close our eyes and sit up straight so that all our vertebrae were stacked on top of each other. After a pause, he said, "imagine you have a searchlight going through you and mending all your sore spots." He added more soothing words. Imagine then, he said, that you're in a special place in which you feel at home, and he allowed time for images of that place to enter our minds. Now, he said, you have a guest. . . . You entertain your guest. . . . Your guest gives you a gift. . . . Your guest leaves. . . . All of these suggestions were to be imagined and enjoyed by us, and Bobby allowed us to mull them over thoroughly, each to his or her own thoughts. Finally, easily, Bobby said that we could "come back." We did so, but none more slowly than Eric Underwood.

The exercise was only half over, for now, Bobby said, we were to share our imagery. Many persons had Jesus, or one of the persons of the Trinity, as a visitor, and their comfortable places—from a hippie Christian's thatched hut through an arthritic woman's warm, small house to my own imaginary Chicago Gold Coast apartment—reflected their needs and desires. Eric Underwood, who uncharacteristically took his sharing turn first on this night, exposed his own worldly evangelicalism.

As he imagined his ideal place, he said, he kept wondering, "How much is this place per month?" It was a small house with a wide deck, built up on pilings from the shore of Mendocino Bay. It was accessible only by ladder, and it had everything he'd need: a study with all his books, a bathroom, a couch with two chairs, and a bathroom. (Living with a wife and two daughters, he *meant* to say "bathroom" twice.) He had several visitors, one of whom was "the Lord," and another was an old pal from seminary. For entertainment, he'd had a drink with the Lord. And he got two gifts. From his seminary friend he got a "perfect Bible translation, so that I wouldn't have to keep seventeen translations on hand." And from the Lord, he received a blank book, which is "your life and yours to fill in."

As I came to know Underwood, I saw how well this symbolic portrait suited him, and it is a tribute to Bobby's skill that Eric, affable and frank but seldom emotionally open in the way that Larry Redford was, revealed so much of himself and his practical theology at one moment. "The Lord" was part of his vision and part of his life, but not all of his life. His professional work, his need for privacy, his localism and his voluntarism were all given expression.

These characteristics suited him well for the task of bringing harmony and vitality to the congregation, and it was his good fortune to arrive in Mendocino just as a truce had been declared in Vietnam and the enmities of the war years began to recede.

8.

Church Growth and Decline in Context

Only real people can do things. "Structures" are a
way of talking about the patterns of what they do
in groups. . . . Any causal explanation must ultimately come down to the actions of real individuals.

—Randall Collins, *Conflict Sociology*

The response to the new pastor was immediate and lasting.
One hundred and twenty-two persons came to hear Underwood's
inaugural sermon on March 18, 1973, and by the end of the year
average Sunday attendance, which had hovered just under eighty
during Mark Kimmerly's last year, was 120. In 1974, it was 160, in
1975, 172; then, during my period of field research in 1976, it was 186.
Church membership grew from 138 when Underwood arrived to 154
at the end of the year, and 181, 186, to 223 at the end of 1976. Total
spending grew from the $17,000 range during Kimmerly's pastorate
to $40,000 in 1976, in real dollars adjusted for inflation, while spend-
ing per capita jumped from about $120 under Kimmerly to $180 under
Underwood, again in real-dollar terms.

Within those first three years the properties of the church were
enhanced with a new Allen organ, a new roof for the sanctuary, a set
of chimes, and a set of several hundred new hymnals. The Preston
Hall mortgage was burned. Traditional activities—choir, Sunday
school, summer camps, scout troops, progressive dinners—were re-
invigorated. And distinctively evangelical activities—a telephone
prayer chain, a men's breakfast group, Bible-study groups, and especially Christian "Koinonia" groups—blossomed. In the face of the
nationwide decline of Presbyterian churches, the church in Mendocino all of a sudden started enjoying the good fortune of the Assem-

blies of God. (See fig. 12.) What might have been merely Larry Redford's leadership coup, calling a pastor to his own liking, became a revolution in the institution.

Those in Redford's fellowship said that the Presbyterian church had become far more magnetic under the leadership of Underwood than it had been before. The officers of the church were also elated, in their established way. In November of Underwood's first year, the session's worship committee went on record with the opinion that "the increased attendance showed that the congregation as well as the session was very pleased with the way worship services were being presented and especially the sermons." Two years later, the session approved a gift of $3000 "in gratitude for the progress of our church under Eric Underwood" to be allocated to worldwide Christian work. Then, in 1978, a grateful congregation surprised Underwood with a $5000 gift for a summer trip to Scotland, one of the historic founts of Presbyterianism. During my months of field research, formally and informally asking questions, eavesdropping on gossip, attending meetings and reading whatever I could get my hands on, I found that this attribution of the evident success of the church to Underwood's leadership was widely shared.

Sociologists are professionally inclined to doubt stories of heroes. It is our business to be skeptical, and it is not our business to praise men, famous or otherwise. I have already shown in chapters four through seven how the way was paved for Underwood's evangelical regime by the Mendocino revival of 1971–1972 and by the exhaustion of political activism. Underwood came at the right time. It might be further supposed that 1973, in growing rural California, was simply a good time for churches and churchly people and that there is nothing extraordinary about the turnaround at Mendocino and the role of Underwood in it. This chapter examines such a supposition, a "null hypothesis," in light of the professional literature on church growth and decline. We shall see that the trajectory of Mendocino Presbyterian does stand out as remarkable, and Underwood's role was essential.

Membership in Presbyterian Churches

What is true for many social facts is true for church membership: the single best predictor of this year's statistics is last year's. As social institutions, churches are organizationally conservative, and we should not expect to observe much year-to-year change, other things being equal. For churches, that stability is due to their members' commitments taking on the force of habit, regularly setting aside Sun-

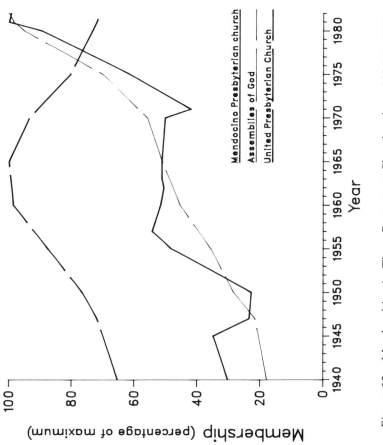

Figure 12 Memberships in Three Protestant Churches from 1939 to 1982 Measured in Percentage of Maximum Membership

day morning for services and a pledge for the offering plate. Yet no church can afford to take members' commitments for granted.

Members are mortal, and American churches have disproportionately aged populations. Gallup reports that forty-eight percent of all American Presbyterians are over fifty years of age,[1] and the Mendocino congregation was even older. It comes as no surprise that Mendocino Presbyterian lost seventy-two members to death in the quarter century 1959–1983, about three per year. Replacement is not automatic, moreover, even if other, younger members produce children. Although Presbyterians practice infant baptism, no one is entered on the church rolls as a member until he or she professes faith in Christ and agrees to unite with the church, a step that usually occurs in adolescence or young adulthood.

In contemporary America, church members are liable to be geographically mobile, and that is especially true in California. When people leave the community, sooner or later they will be lost to the congregation. When there are many newcomers, as there began to be in Mendocino late in the 1960s, the church has an opportunity to recruit new members. But the newcomers may not be of a churchly bent, and those who are so have the freedom, in our pluralistic society, to shop around before settling on any particular congregation. One aspect of the American pattern of denominationalism discussed briefly in chapter one is that transfer of membership for the geographically mobile is effectively automatic among the mainline churches. In such a way have the churches adjusted to the facts of mass mobility. At the same time, however, mobile Presbyterians are thereby offered greater choice in their communities of destination. The Methodist or Episcopal church might suit them as well. Net in-migration to a community is no more than an opportunity for recruitment.[2]

Change of heart is a third cause of membership loss and gain. People get fired up, and they get tired. They may find the new minister exciting or insufferable. A change in personal circumstances— marriage, parenthood, divorce, widowhood—may make participation in the life of the church more or less rewarding, more or less convenient. Some people, as we saw in chapter five, experience a radical conversion that compels them to organized religious activity.

Membership turnover is thus a fact of Protestant church life, and it was particularly prominent in Mendocino in the late sixties and seventies, with about one fifth of the membership being added to or subtracted from the church rolls *each year*. What is remarkable given our personal freedom in America is that churches, which are entirely voluntary associations, persist at all. Yet no fewer than two-thirds of all adult Americans regularly claim to be church members.[3] At

Mendocino Presbyterian since 1970, members lost to death, migration, and disaffection have been more than balanced by new recruits.

Presbyterian practice recognizes several categories of membership gain and loss corresponding to the foregoing account, and each constituent congregation keeps a yearly record accordingly. These categories have changed from time to time during the twentieth century, but in Mendocino for our quarter century the practice has been consistent. First, there are gains and losses by "certificate," or letter of transfer from or to another church. The net of such transfers in Mendocino was negative from 1957 through 1966, a rough index of the negative impact of migration on the church in those years. It was strongly positive from 1967 through the end of the 1970s. Second are losses by death. Mendocino Presbyterian was hit particularly hard by deaths in 1959, 1961 and 1962, 1969 and 1970, and 1980, but the numbers are too small for analysis. Third are gains by "profession, reaffirmation and restoration," a category of the newly churched. Profession of faith is to make the formal vows of faith in Christ and of affiliation with this church for, as it were, the first time. Reaffirmation of faith is the return of one whose membership in some church had long lapsed. Restoration is the return of a lapsed member of this particular congregation. Finally, there are losses by suspension due to the action of the local session. This may occur at the request of the disaffected member, but more commonly it takes the initiative of the pastor and the elders to prune from the rolls those who have ceased participation.

Inactive members are costly, for the congregation's annual dues to the judicatories of the denomination are based on its nominal membership. The requirements of membership are diffuse and undemanding—a single communion or a few dollars in the offering plate every other year will usually suffice—yet the willingness of the church's officers to enforce them is wildly variable. In Mendocino, pastors Higginson, Kimmerly, and Underwood evidently worked to keep their rolls free of deadwood. Althorpe and Hsu did not. The significant drops in membership in 1947, 1958 through 1960, 1967, and 1970 were primarily due to the removal of members who had been inactive for some time. The rate of suspension, therefore, is ambiguous as between an indicator of members' disaffection (with a lag of several years) and congregational strictness.

Each congregation reports annually to the General Assembly, the governing body of the denomination, and the statistics are published yearly.[4] The effect of aggregating statistics on nearly nine thousand congregations is to smooth out the idiosyncratic swings of the local congregation into the pattern characteristic of the denomination as a whole. In figure 12, two of the curves are smooth ones, aggregates of whole denominations. One is the bumpy record of Mendocino Presbyterian. It is clear nonetheless that the Mendocino church curve after 1970 is unlike that of its parent denomination. What can we learn about these curves from the literature?

Explaining Church Growth and Decline

In an influential collection of research reports, *Understanding Church Growth and Decline, 1950–1978*, sociologists Jackson Carroll, Dean Hoge, and David Roozen suggested that

> a useful framework for organizing and interpreting the wide variety of factors that contribute to church growth or decline can be developed by crosscutting two distinctions. The first distinction is between contextual factors and institutional factors. Contextual factors are external to the church. . . . Institutional factors are internal to the church and are aspects of its life and functioning over which it has some control. The second distinction is between national and local factors.[5]

I will adopt their terminology, assuming it is clear to the reader that they use "institutional" very broadly to include the activities of what we have been calling both institutions and movements. One might as well speak of "endemic" or "indigenous" factors.

Four types of factors result. *National contextual* factors include "the broad sociostructural, economic, political, and value commitment changes that have occurred in the United States over the past quarter century." *National institutional* factors include "the activities of the national denominational and interdenominational bureaucracies." For the purposes of this book the policies and actions of the United Presbyterian Church in the United States of America (UPCUSA) and its judicatories are national institutional factors. *Local contextual* factors are characteristics of the local secular community over which the congregation has little or no control. "These may include population shifts, neighborhood changes, local economic trends, and so on." *Local institutional* factors include "the quality and scope of program and leadership" internal to the congregation. These are the factors— style of worship, preparation and delivery of sermon, quality of music, building design and maintenance—that most immediately attract or repel newcomers to the church.

All four types of factors play a role in our story. The civil-rights movement of the early 1960s and the antiwar protests of the late sixties and early seventies were national contextual factors whose influence was felt in Mendocino. California voters, for example, were offered a chance in 1964 to approve an initiative constitutional amendment to nullify a statewide fair-housing law passed by the legislature in 1962. Peter Hsu and a local realtor friend went on the road up and down the coast to debate the amendment—con and pro—thus helping activate the issue on the local scene. (The amendment passed by a two-to-one margin but was later declared unconstitutional.) Later on, Mendocino's population was swelled by young men trying to stay on the move to escape an unpopular war. Developments in the economy—the energy crisis, inflation, and the real-estate boom of the 1970s—were other national contextual factors that impinged on Mendocino.

The estimate of religion in popular opinion is another factor that undoubtedly affects the church. We have seen that the 1950s were a period of indiscriminate proreligiousness in the United States. To some extent, church participation in those days was a matter of conforming to the expectations of the wider culture. One was "supposed to" go to church in the fifties, but that is certainly no longer true as a rule today. One question asked repeatedly by the Gallup poll for the past three decades gives us an index of the climate of religious opinion. "At the present time," the interviewer asks, "do you think religion as a whole is increasing its influence on American life or losing its influence?" Although the precise meaning of one's answer to that question is ambiguous between neutral perception and wishful thinking, subtracting those who think religion is losing influence from those who see it increasing gives a simple index of popular opinion on the centrality of religion.[6] (See fig. 13.) By this measure, pastors Althorpe and Higginson enjoyed a proreligious climate in 1957–1962, but public opinion began to turn against religion during the time of Peter Hsu. Mark Kimmerly, if we assume Mendocino reflected American trends in 1967–1972, had an uphill battle to wage to have the church taken seriously, whereas Eric Underwood faced a much less hostile climate of opinion.

National institutional factors probably mattered more in the 1960s than in the 1970s in Mendocino. The eight to nine thousand local congregations of the Presbyterian church have a fair degree of autonomy (less than most Baptist congregations but more than Roman Catholic parishes), and the Mendocino church in its evangelical heyday of the 1970s paid little attention to its parent denomination. For example, Mendocino adopted in 1974 a nondenominational but distinctly evangelical hymnal rather than one of the hymnals published by the denomination.[7] Another instance was the lack of regard shown to the annual UPCUSA General Assembly by the Mendocino congregation during my period of fieldwork in 1976. As an unusually

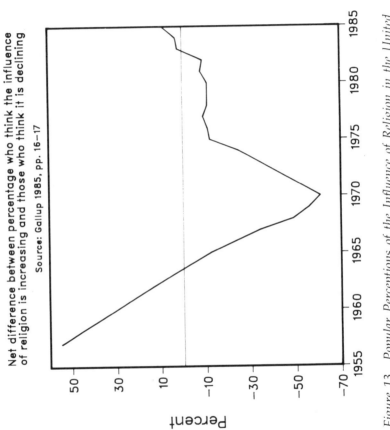

Figure 13 Popular Perceptions of the Influence of Religion in the United States from 1957 to 1985

attentive visitor to the Mendocino church's meetings and a reader of its bulletins, I learned only that a report from the General Assembly would be presented in the nearby Fort Bragg Presbyterian Church one night in July. Deciding that my research interests required me to go, I found I was one of only two Mendocinoans in attendance, the other being George Helms, introduced in chapter seven, whose pattern of activity in denominational affairs had been set long before coming to Mendocino. I heard nothing about the General Assembly in Mendocino from him or anyone else.

Yet some Presbyterian rulings and policies were felt in Mendocino. Elaborate search procedures for new pastors are mandatory under Presbyterian law, and these procedures were instrumental in bringing men of social conscience to Mendocino's pulpit in the 1960s. In 1972, however, these same procedures were skillfully used by Larry Redford to bring about a conservative revolution.

Another denominational policy had ironic results in Mendocino. In 1971, the UPCUSA Council on Church and Race granted $10,000 to the Angela Davis Marin County (California) Defense Fund. It was a gesture of solidarity with an outspoken critic of injustice in America, who was accused of conspiracy in abetting jailbreak and murder, and who, the Council felt certain, would not receive a fair trial unless many outsiders came to her aid. There was, understandably enough, a great outcry from attentive conservatives in the Presbyterian church. In the recollection of John Fry, introduced in chapter two, the outcry was an unholy melange of "disgust, rage, hatred, vengeance, ignorance, bigotry, [and] lying," tinged with guilty lust for a "sensationally good-looking woman, thoughbeit Communist, black, and a professor." Conservative local churches vowed to punish the UPCUSA agencies by redirecting contributions.[8] Not much was heard one way or another in Mendocino about the Angela Davis grant, but Larry Redford's struggling evangelical mission was the recipient of some other congregations' pledges thus diverted from the denomination.

We have seen that other Presbyterian policies—one favoring secular community access to church meeting halls, the other approving income transfers to Antioch Ranch—were taken note of by the Mendocino elders. Yet the most powerful way that the denomination can affect the congregation—its control over education of clergy—was effectively nullified by Larry Redford's 1972 pastor-search committee.

Local contextual factors are of obvious importance. In the 1970s, Mendocino was bustling with tourists and new residents, attracted by its small-town charm but cosmopolitan culture. Indeed, Mendocino and Mendocino County typified a national phenomenon of the 1970s: the relative repopulation of rural America. Throughout the first two centuries of United States history, Americans steadily became proportionately more urban and less rural. (This does not necessarily mean that rural America actually lost population, only that it did not keep up with the mushrooming of the cities and suburbs.) But sometime between the 1960 and 1980 censuses, this flow reversed itself for the first time, and Mendocino was only one of thousands of rural settlements far beyond the metropolitan areas that grew rapidly in the 1970s.[9]

Mendocino's economy, too, changed in the third quarter of the twentieth century. Tourism and highly specialized retail shopping meant an expansion of low-paying service-sector jobs and risky opportunities for the self-employed. In-migration meant construction jobs. Oscillating interest rates translated into instability in the lumber industry, historically the dominant source of jobs in the region. Rising taxes, land values, and processing costs made agriculture less feasible. An expanding counterculture market, an understaffed county sheriff's department, and the development of sinsemilla cultivation in the mid-1970s brought a boom in commercial marijuana cultivation in Mendocino and neighboring Humboldt County.[10] In a moment, we shall return to a more detailed discussion of local contextual factors.

Most of this book concerns what Carroll, Hoge, and Roozen call local institutional factors. But such a focus does not mean that local leaders always have things their way. We will see that one result of Hsu's and Kimmerly's activism was a lean church, a church that was able to respond rapidly to the new evangelical leadership of the 1970s. We have witnessed another irony in Kimmerly's sponsoring of a mission to the hippies that became the springboard for the successful effort to turn the church's pulpit from liberal to evangelical. In my detailed recounting of this story, with its colorful setting, human protagonists and powerful ironies, I risk obscuring the wider context in which it took place and which in part accounts for it. This discussion of contextual and national factors is intended to compensate for any such impression.

The Carroll-Hoge-Roozen framework is not perfect. For one thing, they use "institutional" more broadly than we have elsewhere in this book, to refer to those factors that are potentially under the control of religious leaders. The activities of both Mark Kimmerly and Larry Redford are "institutional," in their sense. Another problem is the effective arbitrariness of the framework's distinction between those matters out of church leaders' hands and those within. Thus the authors treat the antireligious climate of the 1960s as a national contextual factor that affected all churches. Dean Kelley, who wants to preach to the churches, responds:

The cultural climate may indeed be a dominating causal factor in the growth or decline of mainline churches, which are apparently very susceptible to transient shifts in public opinion about what's "in" and what's "out" this decade, year, or month. But other churches are not as clearly affected by the cultural climate. Not knowing perhaps or more likely not caring what that climate is supposed to be, they go on attracting and retaining members, even young adults, in spite of the supposedly adverse cultural climate.[11]

Peter Hsu was one of the young men who went against the complacency of the 1950s and who made the sixties what they were. Larry Redford swam against the liberal tide a decade later and thus contributed to its ebb. Technically, then, cultural climate should be seen as a contextual factor that *interacts* with institutional factors.[12]

Similarly, when we find, as we have in chapter five, that the evangelical tide in Mendocino engulfed young adult couples, do we then treat the coming of a younger generation, their own children, as a contextual or as an institutional factor?[13] On the one hand, whether young adults will desire children: whether, having given birth to them, they will seek to pass on their own beliefs to them; whether their churches will succeed in acting on these needs—these can be interpreted as institutional factors, factors, that is to say, over which local religious leaders can have considerable influence. Care for the younger generation's upbringing will be part of our story in chapters 10 and 12. On the other hand, reproductive biology is not under the direct control of the local church. Thus I have used the Carroll-Hoge-Roozen framework not as a set of pigeonholes but rather as a checklist of reminders that developments outside the Mendocino church may play an unsuspected role.

Population Change as a Local Contextual Factor

Let us, then, look immediately at community population growth and decline as a local contextual factor in the Mendocino church's growth and decline. Is the latter a function of the former? Just that question was put to me by sociological colleagues who commented on this research, and so I set out with an assistant to answer it.[14]

We immediately ran up against the problem that Mendocino is unincorporated and unrecognized by the U.S. Census as a unit of enumeration. Thus we do not know exactly what its population is now or was in the past. The best approximation we could find was the "Mendocino-

Table 5   Census Population of Mendocino Area and Membership of
Mendocino Presbyterian Church from 1900 to 1980

	Census Population	Church Membership[a]
Year		
1900	4,516	68
1910	5,559	91
1920	5,126	70
1930	3,383	60
1940	3,355	87
1950	4,766	72
1960	5,947	146
1970	5,623	136
1980	8,997	284

Source: UPCUSA (PCUSA) Annual Statistical Reports
[a]Mean of end-of-year membership for the three years surrounding each decennial census.

Anderson Census County Division," a region of western Mendocino County about forty miles long and twenty wide, far larger than the community Mendocino Presbyterian serves, yet the smallest enumeration unit available. To add to our woes, the Mendocino-Anderson division has been the unit of enumeration only since 1960. In 1950 and earlier censuses, "townships" (now a nearly obsolete designation in California) were enumerated, *approximately* three of which (Anderson, Big River, and Cuffey's Cove) are geographically equivalent to the post-1960 county division. With these qualifications, we arrived at census population totals since 1900 for Mendocino and its hinterland, including the settlements of Caspar, Little River, and Albion on the coast and Comptche, Philo, and Boonville in the interior. These statistics—along with contemporaneous membership totals for Mendocino Presbyterian church—are given in table 5 and figure 14. Clearly, there is a correlation between population and church membership. Obviously, the church had a rapidly increasing population base to grow on in the 1970s. Moreover, a population decline in the 1960s, whether in Mendocino or the surrounding countryside, probably reflects at least a weakness in the economy that affected the local church. Population and church growth are paralleled in the 1950s, and decline in both set in after the lumber boom caused by the rebuilding of San Francisco after 1906. Even so, membership and population change were inversely correlated in the 1930s and 1940s, which informants told me was the result of a particularly strong pastorate (that of young Frederick Althorpe) followed by a series of weak ones.

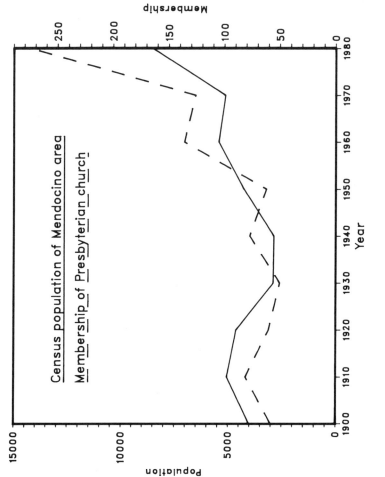

Figure 14   Census Population of Mendocino Area and Membership of Mendo-cino Presbyterian Church from 1900 to 1980

There also seems to be a long-term trend for Mendocino Presbyterian to enroll a larger proportion of its area population over time. We may speculate that the improvement of local transportation—the building of roads and bridges—made it feasible for more coastal area citizens to attend Mendocino Presbyterian. Moreover, with the shift in the local economy toward tourism in the 1960s, Mendocino became the mecca, more central to the region than it had been in the more decentralized era of lumber, fishing, and stock-breeding.

It is clear that this local church was affected by population shifts. The question is: "How much?" Do newcomers to the community automatically sign up with the Presbyterian church? Are those who leave drawn proportionately from its rolls? Is there a constant population/membership translation factor? Any local church leader in a growing community might pray that there were such a factor; in a declining community, that there were not. Our task was to discover one if it existed.

Accordingly, we looked into membership change and population change for sixty-odd rural and small-town northern California Presbyterian churches for the two decades 1960–1970 and 1970–1980. We confined our attention to other country (i.e., nonmetropolitan) churches for two reasons. One was the pragmatic one of avoiding arbitrary divisions of the population of cities with more than one Presbyterian church. The second was in response to earlier findings that town and country Presbyterian churches behave differently from those in cities and suburbs.[15]

We found membership totals for each church for 1960, 1970, and 1980 from the UPCUSA General Assembly Annual Statistical Reports. We then found the U.S. Census population for the smallest geographical unit including the given church, usually incorporated municipalities, Census Civil Divisions, or Census Designated Places, from the three censuses. We calculated the percentage change in membership and in population for each church and community for 1960–1970 and 1970–1980 and plotted the results (see figs. 15 and 16).[16]

The figures show that in both decades the majority of the communities grew (more dots are to the right of the vertical axis) and the majority of the churches declined (more dots are below the horizontal axis). But community growth was more prevalent in the 1970s than it had been in the 1960s, which our previous discussion of the recent repopulation of rural America would lead us to expect. In fact, only three communities are shown as declining in population during the 1970s, and these only slightly. Nonetheless, relatively few (less than one third) of the churches in growing communities are shown as growing in the 1970s.

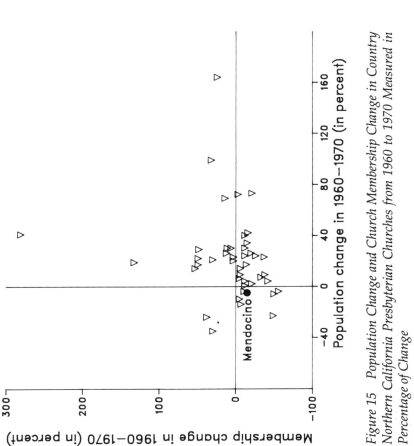

Figure 15 Population Change and Church Membership Change in Country Northern California Presbyterian Churches from 1960 to 1970 Measured in Percentage of Change

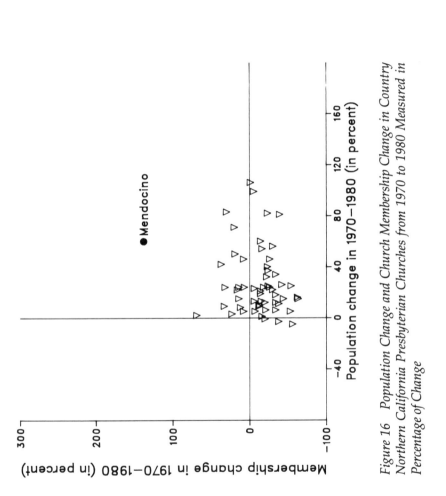

Figure 16 Population Change and Church Membership Change in Country Northern California Presbyterian Churches from 1970 to 1980 Measured in Percentage of Change

One of them, which is Mendocino, stands out far above the others in membership growth, even though its community growth, while rapid at sixty percent, is below that of six other towns. Churches in four of these six towns in fact declined in membership.

Figures 15 and 16 are called, appropriately enough, "scattergrams." The two variables—population change on the horizontal axis, membership change on the vertical axis—seem largely uncorrelated with each other. Indeed, for each dataset, statistical tests disclose that only two percent of membership change is explained by population change.[17] Mendocino Presbyterian church, which moves from being one of the points in the lower left quadrant in the earlier figure to being the extreme outlier in the upper right quadrant in the later figure, is unusual in its fit with population change. (If population change did account for membership change, we would expect most observations to be clustered about a line moving from lower left to upper right.)

Clearly, population change alone does not explain church growth and decline. We have seen that Kimmerly's rigorous roll pruning in the late sixties led the way for Underwood's capitalization on population influx in the 1970s to produce Mendocino's dramatic jump from lower left to upper right in the diagrams. Roll pruning and evangelism, though, are local institutional factors, not contextual ones. Most northern California Presbyterian churches, in other words, failed to capitalize on the opportunities offered by population growth in their communities. It is likely, on the basis of this statistical examination, that Mendocino church had something special to offer to the influx of newcomers to its community that the general run of Presbyterian churches did not.[18] So it is to the internal life of this church that we must turn for an explanation of its trajectory. Particular events and persons in Mendocino brought about the general sequence that was characteristic of American Protestantism as a whole.

The picture of the local institutional trajectory of Mendocino Presbyterian that emerges from the statistics conforms to impressions I received from informants and from narratives in the session minutes. The 1960s were a time of out-migration from Mendocino and the church was relatively weak. But Peter Hsu's courageous public witness did attract a few new members. At the same time, however, his regime alienated members, as is most clear from attendance records. Meanwhile, he did not employ the sanction of suspension either to cajole recalcitrants back into church or to formalize their nonparticipation. The church thereby, despite the presence of newly enthused members, grew slack in the mid-1960s.

Kimmerly's regime was one of holding ground with respect to

active members. He seems to have attracted into the fold mostly those who were moving into the community, and they began to amount to significant numbers in the early 1970s. At the same time, he led efforts to prune Hsu's "deadwood" from the church rolls, and thereby fostered a leaner church, composed of members with a higher average commitment.

Underwood continued the pattern of relative strictness in the use of suspensions. (He, in fact, instituted a yearly roll-cleaning operation.) At the same time, he capitalized, as Kimmerly had begun to do, on the net immigration into Mendocino by attracting scores of new members, many of whom were, as they had been in Hsu's day, newly churched. But unlike Hsu's, his regime elicited a far higher average rate of financial commitment and Sunday attendance.[19] He attracted many and alienated few. In the 1970s, Mendocino Presbyterian grew quantitatively, qualitatively, and rapidly. What was Underwood doing? Especially, what was he doing from the very outset?

9.

Beachhead for Christ: Mendocino Presbyterian, 1973–1976

Let every one of us stay each in his own parish, where he will discover more useful work than in all the making of pilgrimages, even if they were all combined into one. Here, at home, you will find baptism, sacrament, preaching, and your neighbor; these are more important to you than all the saints in heaven.
—Martin Luther, *Appeal to the Ruling Class*

On a winter Saturday night in 1973, Larry Redford enthused about Eric Underwood to his Antioch Ranch flock. "We've got this new preacher coming, and he's really neat," he said in his best upbeat gym-teacher style. Larry and Sue began to encourage their people to check out the new pastor as soon as he arrived. So it was a crew of mostly Antioch men who responded to the call to help move the Underwood household into the manse on the first Monday of March. When Underwood began preaching, two weeks later, one hundred twenty-two persons, including many from the Ranch, came to hear him. By the end of the year, attendance was never again to drop below one hundred at Mendocino Sunday services. Within a year, average attendance doubled; within six years, the membership doubled. When I came to Mendocino three years later, you could still feel the excitement in the congregation.

Figure 17 indicates graphically the nascent state of Mendocino Presbyterian in 1973–1976. Easter-size crowds showed up every Sunday, and soon the membership rolls swelled as well. We have seen in chapter eight that we must look inside the congregation, particularly

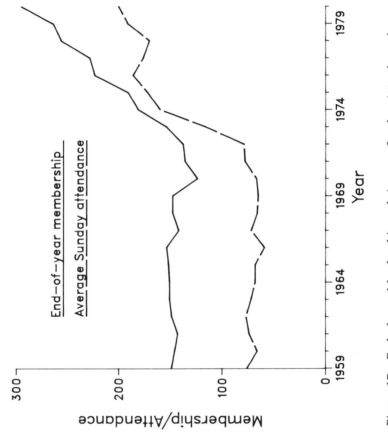

Figure 17 End-of-year Membership and Average Sunday Attendance from 1959 to 1980 (Easter Attendance and Periods between Pastorates Omitted)

at the new pastor, to understand what was happening. We find that he preached an evangelical message which immediately attracted new Christians from Antioch Ranch, longtime evangelicals among new immigrants to the community, and other church-inclined immigrants, while at the same time holding on to the church's veterans. Over the years his message was heard and heeded by lapsed churchgoers of all sorts, who began to join his church in large numbers. And over time, his message, his leadership style, and the new talents that his regime attracted combined to create a magnetic ecclesiastical presence in Mendocino. But the message itself came first. What was it?

To answer that question, I have used interviews from 1975 through 1982 and the written record of the period 1973–1976, but I have used most of all my own eyes and ears as a vistor to Mendocino worship services, participant in a prayer group run by Underwood and his wife, and as Boswell to Underwood's Johnson, recording his conversations with me and many others. I have drawn especially on tape recordings of the worship services he conducted, a rich, verbatim record.[1]

Underwood's teaching—in his sermons, prayers, choice of hymns, pastoral counseling, and administrative leadership—had two consistent intertwined themes: an evangelical Christian theology and a particularistic social ethic. In both respects, the message he brought to Mendocino differed from that of his predecessors of the 1960s. In place of a demythologized theology, Underwood asserted an orthodox Christian doctrine. In place of an emphasis on cosmopolitan concerns of international peace and domestic civil rights, he urged his parishioners' attention to the needs of those very close by, especially their spouses and children. I shall call these two aspects of his teaching the "evangelical" and the "parochial" appeals.

Worldly Evangelicalism

The evangelical appeal challenged those who, in the interest of ecumenical cooperation and in the light of liberal education, had learned to play down exclusivist Christian doctrine, above all the doctrine that the historic Jesus is not merely a great man, prophet, or representative of godliness but God himself incarnate. In a series of sermons on the gospel account of John, Underwood emphasized the claims to divinity Jesus is reported to have made. Discussing the story of the washing of the disciples' feet (John 13:1–17), Underwood said that in this discourse Jesus revealed his nature to the twelve.

Here Jesus bares his nature for them. All through the public ministry there was great restraint in telling them who he was. Here he says, "You're right. I am Master and Lord." *Didaskulas* and *Kyrios.* Master and Lord. He seldom asserted himself in this way but at this particular point he wanted them not to mistake who he was at all. All the way through the gospel of Mark, every time he does a healing what he says to the person who wants to give gratitude to him is this: "Give glory to God the father." But here he asserts his lordship and his leadership. When Jesus affirms their assessment of him as Lord and Master, he is making a statement that is entirely in line with the great declarations we have read all the way through John's gospel, those great "I am's." "I am the bread of life. I am the good shepherd. I am the door. I am the way, the truth, and the life. I am the vine and you are the branches. I and the Father are one." Those who claim that Jesus never represented himself as a rightful object of worship are clearly wrong. They've not read the gospel accounts.

Time and again, in this fashion, Underwood declared his departure from the modern Presbyterian tendency to soft-pedal these historically particularistic orthodox claims. To the new evangelicals, hereditary Presbyterians, and social gospel Protestants in his congregation, he reiterated the evangelical polemicist's favorite dilemma: either Jesus of Nazareth was the Son of God or he was a crazy man.

Jesus is not only God, he is a living person, the evangelical appeal maintained. Personalistic, sentimental hymns like "What a Friend We Have in Jesus" and "O the Deep Deep Love of Jesus" began to be featured in Sunday worship. Folk gospel musicians from Antioch Ranch and the Land were welcomed by Underwood to bring their message of intimate life with Jesus to the Presbyterian church. Underwood minced no words in his sermons:

> Jesus Christ, I believe, is just as much alive today as he was when he walked upon the earth approximately two thousand years ago. It is he who saves men. It is he who gives life. Not any teaching about him, not some institution that serves him, nor his followers—it is he alone, the living Christ who is with us this morning who gives life.

Bringing his flock into a relationship with this Christ was the manifest goal of Underwood's evangelism. He had, he said often, no interest in making new Presbyterians or Protestants, and his orientation toward the Presbyterian church as a denomination was more of convenience than ultimate commitment. The living god transcended worldly organizations.

As Underwood preached the doctrine of a sovereign and living

God, so he also led his congregation in prayer to this God. A long and stately but intimate and extemporaneous pastoral prayer was a regular feature of Underwood's Sunday worship. Confession, thanksgiving, petition, and intercession were offered in these prayers on behalf of the congregation. Sufficient time was allowed at the beginning for silence to settle on the congregation and thoughts to concentrate for the worshipper. Here, word for word, is a pastoral prayer from April 1975, with pauses indicated by ellipses and paragraphs. (A representative from the Gideons, a Bible-distribution society, had spoken briefly earlier in the service.).

> Now let us join our hearts together in a time of quiet prayer as we bring before God those things that are of importance to us, as we take a time of confession, laying our lives before the living Lord. Let us pray.
> [Full minute pause.]
> O God our Father, we thank you that you have put into our hearts the desire to pray.
> We thank you that you have made us such that in a time of trouble we instinctively turn to you.
> We thank you that you have given us the gift of prayer, that your ear is ever listening to catch our every word . . . and to hear even the heart's unspoken cry for help.
> We thank you that the door to your presence is never shut . . . to him who enters and seeks you.
> We thank you that you have given us the confidence to pray.
> We thank you that you have told us that you are our father . . . and that your name is love . . . and that you love each one of us . . . as if there was only one of us to love . . . and that no child of yours can be lost in the crowd.
> We thank you that you have given us unanswerable proof of your love . . . by sending your son Jesus Christ to live and to suffer and to die for us.
> You have heard our prayers this morning, Father. Give us now an answer to our prayers.
> We do not ask that we should be protected from all pain and sorrow, from all danger and distress. We ask for humility to accept whatever comes to us. We ask for courage and fortitude and endurance to come safely through it, to come out on the other side finer in character and nearer to you.
> We do not ask that you should answer our prayers as we in our ignorance would wish, but as you in your love and your mercy know best. Into your hands we commend our spirits, because we know that you are love to care, that you are mercy to bless, and that you are power to save.
> Father, we present to you this morning those in our number who are

ill and set aside. We pray for Margaret Lamphear, for Elmer Holden, for Agatha Johnson, for many among our number who for one reason or another are separated from us.

We pray for the work of your kingdom, and especially this morning for the work of the Gideons as they pass the word of God from place to place, to students and servicemen, into the motels and hotels of the major cities. We thank you for that work of planting the word of God. We pray that you would bless it and multiply their efforts.

We pray for the leaders of our nation this day in the very difficult decisions which they must administer and decide. We pray for President Ford, for the Congress, for the Courts, for all those in places that we have placed them there to govern over us. Give them wisdom. Guide them. Teach them. Make them humble before you.

In Jesus' name we pray. Amen.

The sheer length of this prayer—it lasted over five minutes including its pauses—is an index of the attention the congregation was asked to pay to prayer. For the sake of comparison, note that the Lord's Prayer takes about thirty seconds to recite, the Nicene Creed used in Catholic churches about eighty seconds, and the average choral anthem two and a half minutes. Next to the sermon, the pastoral prayer was typically the longest continuous element of the Sunday service.

The image of an authoritative, benevolent, and accessible God was thus reinforced week after week by Underwood in Mendocino. The new evangelicals loved it, and it was familiar to the old-timers whose religious sensibilities were formed prior to the intellectual reign of Niebuhr, Tillich, and Bonhoeffer. In other ways too, Underwood's gospel was just what Larry Redford and his Antioch flock hoped would be preached in the Presbyterian church. Rather than yoke his conservative theology to a staid liturgy, Underwood made it his practice to vary the elements and order of worship week to week, variations sometimes written into the printed order of worship, sometimes announced from the pulpit. A *Gloria Patri* might be sung, with or without the doxology. An invocation might lead into the Lord's Prayer. Or it might not. Underwood would ask for "ladies only" on one verse of a hymn, alternating with men on the next. The offering might be after or before the sermon (but usually before). Whoever read the scripture lessons would use his or her own Bible translation, those from the Land preferring the King James version, Antiochers using the Jerusalem Bible or the New American Standard version, the church's own lectern Bible being the Revised Standard Version. The musical literacy of the congregation allowed for frequent introduction of unfamiliar but thematically appropriate hymns. In this way, Underwood catered to the new Christians' antiliturgical ideology and their skepticism of desiccated Churchianity.

From the new Christians' point of view, it was Underwood's message of salvation by faith that was most thrilling. Here was an evidently successful man, speaking from the pulpit of the venerable Presbyterian church, who did not assume that those within his hearing were the comfortable who needed only to be brought to a sense of their moral obligations. Here was a man who seemed to know that everyone, regardless of outward appearances, was vulnerable to circumstantial disaster and inner turmoil and that all humans, straight and hip, were therefore reduced to common dependence on a saving providence. He thus justified the decisions they had made, both as former counterculturalists and as newborn saints, to reject the standards of the world.

In his first years at Mendocino, Underwood concluded each of his sermons with an evangelistic pitch that, in its rhetorical structure and personal manner, was as close to a Baptist altar call as one could find in a Presbyterian church. Here is an example:

> You know, I think of it every Sunday morning, but I wonder if there's someone here in the sanctuary this morning who is caught up in the midst of some sort of personal earthquake. Their life has been shattered. Everything seems to be crumbling. I think that person needs to hear loud and clear that God is able to save you in the midst of that disaster, that no one is beyond his help, that no one has a problem that he cannot handle, that he cannot correct, that he cannot make new. Perhaps there is someone who is full of fear, burdened with guilt, whether it be real or imagined. You may have come to the end of your rope, your own personal resources. If so I give you now that divine and ancient formula that has helped so many of us, "believe on the Lord Jesus Christ and you shall be made whole, be given life, you shall be saved." There is no one here this morning beyond the love of God, beyond his healing bond. Our savior is in the business of giving life. He alone can help us put together the pieces of a broken life. In the midst of this fellowship, it can happen to you. . . . Let us pray.

> Father, many of us can say by way of testimony that except by your grace we would not be here today. You have shown yourself to be a life-giving savior. We thank you, we praise you for your gracious help in all that we attempt. We pray for the one here this morning that is in need of your help. Lift them up. Heal them. Deliver them. Make them whole. Meet them in their hour of need. For Christ's sake and for their salvation. Amen.

This emotive appeal was thematically continuous with the sermon it concluded. The topic concerned the agony of failure, as represented by the story of Paul and Silas' Philippian jailer (Acts 16:16–40). But the hortatory tone and the personal form of address stand in contrast to the expository mode of the sermon itself. Underwood astutely mixes first, second, and third persons, singular and plural, to speak directly to whomever in the congregation, regardless of sex, is receptive to the appeal, but meanwhile to reaffirm the profound confession of faith of the indefinitely bounded body of believers. Week after week the message was thus conveyed that "we" are the mercifully saved *and* that the benign work of salvation is not yet done. The valuable gift of salvation could be shared, and no one was better prepared to share it than the babes in the Lord. "So the last will be first, and the first last" (Matthew 20:16).

Underwood's evangelical appeal did not, meanwhile, exclude the settled and successful. We shall see later that he affirmed the quotidian world out of the theological conviction that God's creation was good. His social ethic was optimistic and practical. But his hermeneutic method itself was compatible with the standards of his educated and worldly parishioners.

To begin with, his sermons were worthwhile educationally. He had learned in seminary to discipline his topical concerns and to focus his pedagogical efforts by teaching a series of sermons straight through a whole book of the Bible. First was the epistle of James. Then came a year and a half devoted to the gospel of Luke and its sequel, the Acts of the Apostles. These were followed by Paul's letter to the Philippians and the gospel of John, which series he completed during my period of field research, then to launch on the most ambitious series of all, on Genesis. Of course, there were occasional visiting preachers and Underwood would step out of sequence for some events (as he did on Bicentennial Sunday). But he generally adhered to a plan that, as he said, prevented him from abusing the pulpit to indulge a momentary enthusiasm while at the same time protecting him from being at sea over a limitless choice of topic.

Underwood used modern Bible scholarship while avoiding the contentiousness surrounding the "higher criticism" of the sources. So his explications usually spent less time on the identity of the author of the text than on what the text must have meant to its contemporaneous readers. He did not bother with the issue whether "John" wrote the gospel attributed to him, but he did devote himself to the message that the author had for his audience.

For the congregation, this had the advantage of making Underwood's sermons into something of an academic course, by no means inferior educational material on the Mendocino coast. The number of serious Bible-carrying believers outside the Antioch contingent was only a large minority of the congregation, but for the others—both the liberals and those for whom theology was of low salience—Underwood's method provided a readily comprehensible and cumulatively valuable education into one of the foundations of western culture. For the evangelical bloc, it was a challenging invitation to further Bible study, which was one of the chief goals of Underwood's ministry. So the "Biblically-based teaching" that Larry Redford wanted in Mendocino proved, in Underwood's hands, to be a unifying factor in the congregation.

In his preaching, Underwood took more notice of secular learning than did the more radical Redford. As an institutional clergyman, Underwood was more accustomed to the company of educated worldly persons than was Redford, and his own choice of informal associates leaned heavily in the direction of younger, college-educated persons like himself, whether or not evangelical. He found their mix of secular and religious culture more appealing than Redford's more austere, though no less intellectual, evangelicalism. So Underwood's sermons were sprinkled with quotations from great books and popular wisdom lessons culled from seminary courses, inservice training, and pastors' study guides. His learning, it might go without saying, was spotty, but he had no difficulty holding his own as a leader among his reference group.

Above all, unlike Redford, Underwood had chosen to coexist with, rather than to deny, the secular world. For him, secular learning was valid but insufficient. Unlike the theological modernist who takes the axioms of liberal learning as premises of his own religious doctrine, Underwood was also unlike the fundamentalist who rejects liberal learning whole and part as irremediably tainted. His stance toward the world of secular learning was one neither of capitulation nor of rejection but of parallelism. His theology was a doctrine, as we put it at the end of chapter seven, of worldly evangelicalism.[2] Preaching to a cosmopolitan congregation with, if anything, a relatively liberal tradition, he blurred the hard edges of orthodox evangelicalism.

In common with the historic Arminian response to Calvinist predestination, Underwood was a voluntarist who taught that God, while sovereign, expected humans to do all in their power. He always counseled his parishioners to seek professional help in the case of serious medical or emotional problems, and more than once I heard him reinterpret other evangelicals' accounts of prophecies and demons as being more plausibly matters of schizophrenia and indigestion. "Bringing it before the Lord" in prayer was to be done in addition to seeking the professional help available in the secular world.

Underwood expressed his secular-sacred coexistence doctrine in a sermon on intercessory prayer during his series on John. The text was John 4:43–54, in which Jesus heals at long distance the son of a colonial official who had sought him out in the Galilean town of Cana. Interpreting this passage for his congregation, Underwood said that prayer for the welfare of another is not an attempt to persuade a reluctant God to intervene. It is an attempt to cooperate with God on a spiritual level, using the medium of telepathy, just as doctors and nurses cooperate with God on a physical level. He added a caution:

> Not that prayer and telepathy are one and the same thing. I'm not saying that, for that would take God out of the picture entirely. But just as our study of evolution helps us to understand the machinery which God used in creating the world, so our study of telepathy—the influence of mind upon mind—helps us to understand more fully the machinery which God uses in answering our prayers for other people.

In this way did Underwood assist the ambivalent members of his heterogeneous congregation to adhere simultaneously to their religious and secular belief systems. The evangelical appeal did not exclude worldly commitments; it rather put them into a context of subordination to a higher, less tangible but no less demanding reality.

Underwood's evangelical doctrine embraced secular common sense and spiritual submission. Explicating the meaning of the concept to "believe in Jesus Christ," Underwood retold what he said was an old story. A man strings a rope across the lip of Niagara Falls and proceeds to ride a bicycle, on the rope, to the other side and back. You are among a crowd who gather to cheer him on. "And then he leans down and says to you personally, 'Do you believe I can do it?' And you say, 'Yes.' He says, 'Climb on the handlebars.' " "Believing in" Jesus Christ is thus not the same as "believing in" Abraham Lincoln, in the sense of assenting to the proposition that Lincoln lived and was President. The latter is merely an intellectual attitude. The former is an attitude of faith, trust, and personal commitment. In this sermon Underwood emphasized that the *faith* kind of "belief" was of a *higher* order than the intellectual kind, but a secularized member of his congregation could easily hear that it was a *different* order of attitude.[3] Again, the evangelical could coexist with the secular.

Elective Parochialism

Underwood's message had another aspect, a social ethic, which I call his parochial appeal. By "parochial" I mean to designate an orientation to things local, to be contrasted—as it is in sociologists' parlance—to "cosmopolitan."[4] Though "parochial" carries a negative connotation in the minds of many, the term is used here in a value-neutral sense. Indeed, it is my hope that the conventionally negative valance of parochialism might be reassessed by readers of this book. For parochialism was not the result of mere ignorance or prejudice on Underwood's part. Like the parochialism of Martin Luther, it was an emphatic choice.

Underwood expressed one theological cornerstone of his parochial philosophy during the sermon on intercessory prayer I quoted from a moment ago. Expounding on the work of healing Jesus is reported to have accomplished at Cana, Underwood extracted a lesson for intercessory prayers in public worship and in prayer circles.

> Our prayers arise from our intimate loving relationships. We don't pray for the sick of the world. We pray for those that we are in relationship to and that we are concerned about. Our prayers are not impersonal. . . . We pray specifically and name those who are in need of God's hand. We have only one reason to suppose that God will answer our prayers for those whom we love . . . Jesus answers prayer when it arises from a total relationship of loving concern on our behalf.

There can be no mistaking the normative as well as descriptive intent of this passage. We not only *do* pray particularistically; we *ought* to do so.

Well before I heard these principles enunciated in a tape-recorded sermon, I saw them put into practice over my several months of participation in LIFT (for "life in fellowship together"), the weekly prayer group Underwood and his wife conducted (the same group that is mentioned in chapter seven). Though this group was open to visitors (including me) and lacked the explicit contractual basis of encounter groups, it did have a regular format. When all had taken seats in a circle in his living room, Underwood (or in his absence his wife), would begin the meeting by asking the person to his side to let the group know of his or her concerns of the week. (Sometimes he more formally asked for "prayer requests.") This sharing, sometimes disparaged within the group as "show and tell" when the concerns seemed too impersonal, would continue for over an hour in order around the dozen or so persons present, each person contributing at least a few words and some launching into veritable recitations. At the end of the sharing, Underwood would call for a time of prayer, usually by asking one of the younger men to lead off. The prayer would move from person to person, in no particular order, for fifteen or twenty minutes, until a long pause signaled exhaustion. Then Underwood prompted "and all the people said . . ." for the group's unison "Amen!"

At my first several LIFT meetings I was astonished by the recall displayed by those offering prayers about the concerns that had been expressed during the sharing. It seemed that no one had to (indeed, no one was supposed to have to) pray for himself or herself. It occurred to me that members of the group were more or less openly competing with one another in their demonstrated capacity to recall others' concerns in prayer, and this interpretation was confirmed one night during my third month of attendance when Vonnie Underwood opened the prayer time by saying, "let's see how many of you can remember what were people's concerns." Once, when a LIFT regular who was known for his spaciness complained that the list of concerns was very long, implying that each person might pray for his or her own concern, Underwood spelled out the implicit contract of the group. The sharing and prayer, he said, were intended to stimulate solicitude about each other's welfare during the week between meetings.

I was also impressed with the humility and earthiness of the prayer requests. Frank prayed that Nancy, missing one night because of a week-long house-sitting job, "may be strengthened, Lord. We ask that you just be there for her." Martha prayed for her employers and surrogate family, who were known as nonevangelicals, "that you may show yourself to them, Lord." Buddy prayed for the family he had been living with, who were shortly to leave Mendocino, "that the melancholy of this time of moving may not dampen their looking forward to their new life." Underwood prayed for "those in this little congregation who need jobs and direction" and mentioned by name several younger couples. Over the months, particular persons' jobs, health, travels, and affairs of the heart were more or less concretely the topics of prayer in the group. Under the implicit assumption that extrapersonal affect and concern are limited quantities, it was the practice of Underwood's LIFT to concentrate them on those who were known and loved.

I learned that orientation to the local here-and-now was part of the Underwoods' personal way of life. One night when it was my turn to share I complained about my marginality to the Mendocino community, having important friends, family, and memories in such places as Berkeley, San Diego, Chicago, and New Haven. Underwood, who had lived as an adult in Los Angeles, Oakland, Pasadena, Salinas, and Mendocino, California, and Austin, Dallas, and Denton, Texas, responded to me that he and Vonnie had long decided that their home would have to be "in the present" and their "significant others" this "crazy group" here. I saw his point. The pressures on a pastor are overwhelming, as Mark Kimmerly also made clear to me, and they had abated only slightly after the Underwoods left the manse and moved into their own home in Mendocino (July 1975). The pastor's home is a crisis center and halfway house. The phone rings frequently, and there was almost always a young person of dubious social adjustment staying "temporarily" in the Underwood household. Eric and Vonnie Underwood had decided that the wiser course was to embrace this chaos. What I learned of them subsequently only confirmed this self-description of their choice.

The virtues that Underwood preached were those of interpersonal harmony: gentleness, humility, meekness, sweet reasonableness, fidelity, forgiveness, and concrete love. He frequently admonished his congregation, in prayers as well as sermons, to beware the capacity of words to hurt. He suggested, in the same ways, that apologies might be in order for harm one had committed. At the same time, he preached the importance of receptiveness, the readiness to receive an apology, a gift or other offering, and he made known his own delight at receiving his congregation's gifts and prayers. He indulged in conventional interpersonal rituals of conviviality and had no patience for those who felt themselves above a simple "how are you?" In Underwood's social teaching, there was nothing on earth more real than the other persons we encounter and no obligations more salient than those to one's family.

Interpreting the personal ministry of Jesus, he reiterated the orthodox theme of God's grace—His unearned mercy—as represented in Jesus' love and sacrifice for all humans, but he emphasized the particularistic element in Jesus' choice of the twelve disciples (he chose *these* twelve, not others). Underwood's intent was not to narrow the scope of God's concern but to highlight the particular love Jesus has for the listener. He recommended that attitude to his congregation: "If you hear nothing else this morning, then hear this. Take this home with you. We are missing the point of Christ's love in our lives if it does not duplicate itself in the lives of others."

He wished his congregation to bear in mind not "others" in general, not "the poor," the "despised," or the "underprivileged," but the particular other persons that they had recently wronged or disappointed. For Underwood parochialism was, ironically, a general philosophy: pay attention to the here and now. He called it "working with the given."

The outstanding exception to Underwood's parochialism that I was aware of during 1976 itself proved the rule. In August, he arranged a weekend visit to Mendocino by Benjamin and Carol Weir, longtime Presbyterian "fraternal workers" in Lebanon, who were temporarily in Berkeley for a well-earned leave. They spoke at a Saturday potluck dinner and presented the sermon the next morning. They gave the congregation a first-hand, informative account of issues and factions in Lebanon's ongoing civil war. They tried to make clear to the new Christians of Mendocino that "Christian" and "Moslem" in Beirut were ascriptive, hereditary identities, not achieved, born-again ones. They urged the congregation to continue its support of UPCUSA missions and suggested that, as citizens, Mendocinoans might reconsider their government's policy of massive military support of Israel. Most people I spoke with in the congregation, especially Underwood himself, were impressed with the intelligence and courage of the Weirs, and I shared their impression.

Underwood's mother-in-law, a member of the congregation, was herself Lebanese, and she brought Lebanese dishes to the potluck. Lebanon figured prominently in Underwood's intercessory prayers, and in the months after the visit of the Weirs a poster featuring their pictures and reminding people to pray for them and their work was displayed in the church narthex. "We pray for those that we are in relationship to and that we are concerned about. Our prayers are not impersonal." In 1984, when Ben Weir was kidnapped in Beirut, the Mendocino telephone prayer chain was mobilized.

For Underwood to enact the philosophy of parochialism required him to learn the particular cultures of Mendocino. His socialization to Mendocino began in his dealings with the pastor-seeking committee. When he came to give his candidating sermon, he brought with him his clerical robe. Having spent the night at Antioch Ranch, he decided to lay it aside Sunday morning in favor of a sport coat and tie. Later that evening, after he had been elected as new pastor, he attended the coincidentally scheduled annual congregational meeting dressed in jeans and a flannel shirt. In the ensuing months, he continued to experiment with modes of dress, and he felt free to grow the moustache he had been discouraged from trying before. He kept his clerical robe on hand for the priestly functions of baptism, weddings, and funerals, but he chose a conventional suit or sport coat, with shirt and tie or turtleneck, for most worship services. He never wore a clerical collar.

His relatively informal liturgy was also the product of evolution in a local niche. Like Peter Hsu and Mark Kimmerly before him, he invited Mendocino's artists to contribute to the church's worship, especially musicians. When the choir did an especially thrilling job on an anthem, Underwood invited the congregation to express its appreciation with applause. He himself, moved by his own message, would sometimes conclude a sermon singing a stanza of a familiar hymn— "Rock of Ages" or "What a Friend We Have in Jesus"—and the congregation would join him a capella.

Not all of these experiments were well received. Frederick Althorpe, still Mendocino's elder statesman, advised Underwood that the dancing that had been part of his installation service was perhaps a bit avant garde for the Mendocino congregation. An influential trustee protested every time Underwood allowed an otherwise beautiful service to be spoiled with the maudlin accents of folk gospel music. Several skittish older church members let it be known that they did not appreciate sharing with hippies a loaf of bread and goblet of wine for communion in place of the more traditional Presbyterian individual servings of bread and juice. Whenever added attractions in the service extended the worship hour much beyond noon, Underwood knew that he could expect a scolding from another veteran, who did not want to be late for her lunch table at the Sea Gull Inn. Most, however, enjoyed the experiments, and the relatively informal service that was their result by 1976 was hugely popular with the growing congregation.

Through the elders and other persons in the congregation who reached out to him, Underwood began to learn about and to experience firsthand Mendocino's heterogeneous culture. He visited the homes of the wealthy and walked down a steep, muddy, quarter-mile path to the tiny, hidden cabin of the Wakefields. He met the local characters and learned the new local typology: logger, fisherman, artist, Rotarian, tourist, doper, Jesus freak. He heard of anxieties over the housing code, coastal access, taxes, the price of gasoline, the commerical cultivation of marijuana, and the threats of clear-cut logging and offshore oil drilling. He found that many persons would wish to tell him as much about their past lives as their present circumstances: previous marriages or relationships, long hair, academic and other careers, worldly success foregone, bad habits and addictions overcome.

Above all he learned how special a place Mendocino was to its residents, particularly the newer ones. For them Mendocino was a utopia. There were contradictory notions about the nature of its uniqueness, some finding charm in its windswept quaintness, others in its disheveled funkiness. Some thought hippies desecrated it; others that they adorned it. And there were systematic, down-the-line disagreements on how to maintain its character, whether through orderly planning or a total ban on improvements. But bohemian and petit bourgeois, preservationist and developer alike knew that they had found the town of their dreams. I call those with this ideology "elective parochials," to emphasize the deliberateness of the migration and the heterogeneity of their backgrounds. Underwood called them, in a spiritual language, "saints," or the set-apart. In a corny secular idiom, he frequently called them "folk."

The new Christians and the newly arrived churchgoers in Mendocino had in common, therefore, not only their Lord but their propensity to speak ideologically about their geographical circumstances. It was in his half-conscious adaptation of that ideology that Underwood struck the most responsive chord in Mendocino. It was a case of what Max Weber called an "elective affinity" that Underwood's philosophic parochialism matched the elective parochialism of his new parish.[5]

Underwood best combined his own theologically informed philosophy with the particular culture of the Mendocino congregation in a series of sermons he gave on Paul's letter to the Philippians in the summer and fall of 1975.

His method in these sermons was by then familiar to the congregation. They could look forward to a slow march through each chapter and verse of the book, though Underwood promised them at the outset that the series would not be as long as had been that on Acts. (He told them to expect two and a half months, but it took him nearly four. The Epistle to the Philippians, by the way, occupies four pages in my Bible!) With each passage, Underwood would explicate matters that a first-century reader, especially the original recipients of the letter, would have understood by way of background knowledge. Where was Philippi? What relationship did this church have to Paul? What were "bishops?" What was Paul's "imprisonment?" Who was Epaphroditus? Who was Caesar? From each passage, Underwood would extract some principle or lesson for Christian life, and he spent a whole sermon on the next-to-last verse, in which Paul sends the greetings of the Christians "of Caesar's household." (Underwood's point was that one can be a Christian anywhere, even under adverse circumstances.) In time-tested homiletic fashion, he usually divided each lesson into three parts. In his comment on Phil 1:7–8, for example, Underwood said that Paul loved the Philippians for three reasons: (1) They were generous to him; (2) They were steadfast Christians in a pagan neighborhood; (3) They set an outstanding example of stewardship. Finally, he concluded each sermon with an evangelistic pitch. "How is it with you, my friend, today?" he asked. Or "how are you praying to Christ to change you today?"

From midsummer to advent this one brief book was Underwood's text, and he took every opportunity to draw parallels between his own congregation in 1975 and the one Paul had established at Philippi—his first on the European mainland—in AD 50. In the first of the fifteen sermons, Underwood said that the church at Philippi was "a bit of a model of our own congregation." Like the first-century model, it set an example of faithfulness and stewardship in unfriendly terrain. "I am confident," Underwood said, "that a major beachhead for Jesus Christ has been established along this coast."

Like the congregation at Philippi, that at Mendocino was internally heterogeneous. The first three converts at Philippi were a rich businesswoman, a clairvoyant slave girl, and the jailer, a civil servant: one Greek, one Asian, one Roman; one wealthy, one poor, one middle class; two women and one man. So too in Mendocino, said Underwood. People come from all backgrounds, a few from wealth, a few more from poverty, most from the middle; some with culture, others with little schooling. Women played a prominent role in keeping the faith here too, he stressed. All need the grace of Jesus Christ, and so all are brothers and sisters in one family.

Both congregations were filled with new Christians, some of whom were "fulfilled Jews," like the apostle himself, whom the new Roman Christians such as the jailer must have thought of as "that crazy Jew, Paul, filled with the love of the living Lord." (Underwood's congregation chuckled at this, thinking, I'm sure, of Sol Bloom.) Like Paul and his converts, many in Mendocino had "a past to live down," those "prodigal years of our past" that some recent converts in Mendocino took a bit too much pleasure in renouncing during Antioch Fellowship testimonies. The new Christians in Mendocino and Philippi were alike in a position to offer a behavioral witness for goodness in the midst of a pagan culture, but both had to beware the temptation of sinking back into lasciviousness. "Apart from transformed lives, the Gospel has no effective witness in the world," Underwood warned his congregation. The man on the street is a pragmatist who isn't impressed by the exhortations of Jesus freaks and wants only to share his community with "good neighbors." "Only let your manner of life be worthy of the gospel of Christ" (Phil. 1:27).

Both churches suffered bouts of internal dissension. Paul admonished two women to settle their differences, and Underwood used this precedent to counsel reconciliation. Some teachers in Paul's day insisted that circumcision was still a requirement for men of the faith, and Underwood used Paul's scornful reply (Phil 3:2–11) to puncture claims for the unique importance of a particular mode of baptism, particular spiritual gifts, an apocalyptic second coming, and renunciation of worldly goods and connubial sex, thus distinguishing his own preaching from that of charismatics and monastics. For the new Christians of the first and twentieth centuries, a spiritual libertinism or antinomianism, by which the convert declares the sufficiency of grace and the irrelevance of law, was an inherent temptation. Yet the old, the straight, the square proscriptions of immoderate indulgence and irresponsible sex were incumbent on babes in the Lord, and no one should live in such a way as to challenge others to confront their flagrant sin. Above all, both churches needed to take to heart Paul's plea that selfishness be put aside in favor of humility. The desire to implement some ideal or principle shades off into the desire to dominate others in its name, with the result that the church has an excess of would-be leaders and too few followers. None can compare to Jesus, at the name of whom "every knee should bow . . . and every tongue confess" that he alone is Lord (Phil. 2:10–11).

Week after week, the Mendocino congregation was thus cajoled, chided, admonished, educated, and greatly flattered by Underwood's likening them to Paul's favorite. "I can only echo Paul's thanks to you, the Mendocinoites, who have followed in the pattern of the Philippians." Unlike Peter Hsu, who regularly suggested that the church he pastored was too narrow as a community and who urged a more cosmopolitan awareness; unlike Mark Kimmerly, whose personal discouragement toward the end of his term was reflected in "scoldings"; unlike these, Underwood adroitly suggested that his congregation was precisely the place where the living God was doing his work. The institutional structures of the church were transfigured in spirit.

The message that Underwood brought to Mendocino exalted the church by affirming both the sovereignty of the God in whose name it was founded and the religious significance of the community that provided its present incumbents. Underwood's teaching was evangelical and parochial, but it was not ignorantly so. The evangelicalism was sophisticated and the parochialism was by choice. The distinctive ideological color of Mendocino Presbyterian church after March 1973 was that of worldly evangelicalism and elective parochialism. The evangelical appeal bestowed transcendent and catholic significance on the quotidian lives of the Mendocinoites while the parochial appeal fostered a concentration of energy on the home front. It was a potent mix.

Harvest of Souls

New and longtime evangelicals flocked to Underwood's church, about seventy-five joining in the first three years. Some of them had resided in Mendocino for years without becoming involved in a church. Others were new in town. They came from many parts of California and the United States and represented a cross-section of occupations. Within Underwood's first three years there came an evangelical dentist, a veterinarian, a computer troubleshooter, a retired minister, a couple of underemployed teachers, two real-estate brokers, a restaurateur, an air-traffic controller on extended leave, several nurses, a sculptor and a woodworker, a medical technician, a telephone operator, several clerks and handymen, a half dozen housewives, and five high-school boys—all evangelicals. There was one bloc of ten new evangelical members, kin to a deeply committed and wealthy evangelical architect, who joined the church within Underwood's first two years and became a corps of enthusiastic supporters.

First of all, though, there came many new evangelicals from Antioch Fellowship, about thirty joining the Presbyterian church by the spring of 1976. The Antioch contingent were themselves a mixed bunch. Fully a quarter of them were teachers either in the public schools or in the shoestring counterculture schools scattered through the hills. Several were artists, some of the "would-be" variety but some whose works provided a fully self-supporting income. Some were housewives and handymen whose livelihood was earned primarily in their own cabins and yards, supplemented by waitressing and odd jobs in town. Most had experienced periods of economic marginality, where the source of this month's income was neither secure nor the basis of a career identity. At least one was, even subsequent to his membership in the Presbyterian church, by reputation a marijuana dealer. A few others lived off trust funds.

With the increased and increasingly legitimate participation of evangelicals came an evangelical coloration to the worship and activities of the church, and not only in Underwood's sermons. Underwood welcomed the contributions of evangelical artists. A born-again sculptor fashioned a rugged driftwood cross for the chancel. A born-again seamstress crafted a banner incorporating the historic symbols—celtic cross, chi-rho, orb and ark—of the Presbyterian church. A born-again veteran of Therese's Land designed a new logo for the newsletter, a transparent descending dove superimposed on a line drawing of the church's famous steeple. Born-again guitar players added their talents to Sunday services.

After a lull coinciding with the long interregnum of 1972–1973, the church school was reactivated with an overwhelmingly evangelical staff (ten of twelve), half of whom were young adults affiliated with Antioch Fellowship. Membership classes were conducted every three or four months, and prospective members of all categories, including those transferring, were expected to attend and to hear Underwood's appeal for Christ and his church. The adult choir, which had been an on-again, off-again proposition since the scandal that had rocked the church under Peter Hsu in 1965, was solidly reestablished first under a born-again volunteer director and then, when she moved away, under an unpaid professional conductor who, though not an evangelical, was glad to have a choir during her several-year sojourn in Mendocino. The choir, the local talent for which was largely the result of the evangelical revival in Mendocino, and the new organ, the fruit of a fund-raising effort begun by liberal laywomen under Kimmerly's regime, were the star attractions of an increasingly appreciated music program. Meanwhile, Underwood influenced another lay committee's choice of the independent evangelical hymnal, *Hymns for the Living Church*, to replace the tattered denominational hymnals that had been in use for years.

Evangelical preachers visited, evangelical movies were shown, parishioners were invited to spend a week at evangelical summer camps, and, in 1975, over one hundred fifty persons attended a "fulfilled seder," a Christian-Jewish Passover dinner hosted by Benjamin Moss, a Jew for Jesus who lived on Therese's Holy Land. The church property in Albion, which both Mark Kimmerly and Larry Redford had described as an albatross, was itself made into an evangelical outpost in the summer of 1974, when Underwood asked Jeffrey and Pat Wakefield if they would live in it as caretakers and missionaries in exchange for free rent.

For the deepening of evangelical commitment, there was still Antioch Fellowship, which was more active than ever. For those who wished, however, to share faith and doubts with others in a more egalitarian context, Underwood began fostering fellowship groups, one of which was the LIFT group I frequented in 1976. The first such group, in 1973–1974, was deeply influential on its participants. For about a year, a handful of married couples, including the Underwoods, met one evening a week, rotating from one house (or cabin) to another, for discussion and prayer. Some chapters from an inspirational but nuts-and-bolts book would be discussed extensively. Personal implications of the book's message, including negative connotations and doctrinal disagreements, would be brought up. Then there would be a period of personal sharing, including prayer requests. The evening would be ended with the sort of extended round-robin intercessory prayer I have described earlier. "I suppose it's something like an encounter group," said one participant in a letter, "except having Jesus Christ as a basis makes it more meaningful."

In the years following there were more such groups. There was a men's prayer breakfast every Tuesday at a local restaurant. There was an adult group focused on childrearing. There was a group of hippie-Christian artists who met for devotions and to discuss innovations for the Sunday worship hour. There was a group organized around the study of the works of Francis Schaeffer, an influential Swiss-American evangelical intellectual. Another young couples' group got underway during my period of field research. Later there was a group discussing the evangelical Christian response to world hunger, using the writings of Ron Sider.[6] In a host of ways, Mendocino Presbyterian became an evangelical church.

The evangelicals felt a spiritual kinship with Underwood. "Eric is a fine pastor interested in preaching the Living Christ," wrote one Antioch member in a letter to her family a few months after joining the church. Others called him "Christ-centered" and "spirit-filled" and said that he fostered a "commitment to Christ." Another person, a longtime church member who said her religious identity had been confused by Peter Hsu and Mark Kimmerly, was delighted to have what she called a "fundamentalist" in the pulpit, as contrasted to a politicized preacher "with his head in the clouds." To other evangelicals, Underwood had a "gift for teaching" and imparted "spiritual food."

Though the evangelicals I interviewed were overwhelming in their approval of Underwood's ministry, they differed among themselves, corresponding to their varied backgrounds, on the rigorousness of his moral teaching. One man whose testimony to me revealed a checkered past of preconversion womanizing said that Underwood's church's pews "can get pretty hot sometimes. Eric can be very specific." But another, who had experienced the fundamentalism of the Holy Land, happily found Underwood to be "not in bondage to the law." An older woman who harbored bitter memories of her pentecostal upbringing recalls having first thought of Underwood's preaching, "Oh! oh! we're going to have altar calls." But she soon found that Underwood "made Christianity a joyful thing for me." I had the impression that most of my evangelical informants would have agreed with the young woman who admired his way of saying pointed things from the pulpit always with a smile. In sum, the evangelicals perceived that Underwood was one of them and that he had a way of meeting the varied intellectual and moral needs of their number.

No one disliked Underwood. One of his strong supporters and admirers—by no means an evangelical himself—claimed that Underwood was the person that everyone wanted to be his best friend. But those whose attitude toward Underwood's orthodox Christian message was ambivalent had other reasons to approve of his leadership.

A retired engineer praised Underwood for "superb analyses" in his sermons. Underwood doesn't take the easy way out but rather explains things about the Bible, this man said. But meanwhile, he doesn't give "a lot of hellfire and brimstone." A young woman said she found Underwood's sermons intellectually stimulating; she felt that she had learned something about early church history. A newly retired resident, recently widowed, quite avidly followed Underwood's series on Genesis, even though her own religious belief was in the Unitarian-Universalist tradition, far removed from Underwood's evangelicalism. Two other nonevangelical women were attracted to the "dynamism" or "looseness" of Underwood's worship services; they liked the way he shook things up from week to week.

There was no doctrinal consensus among the nonevangelicals. Neither Peter Hsu nor Mark Kimmerly had left a corps of politically liberal or theologically neoorthodox laypersons in the church. The lack of such a corps extended to the lack of a self-designation: no label suggested itself to those who could not embrace evangelicalism. When I asked one young woman to describe her religious orientation—it having become clear in the interview that she didn't share Underwood's—she first said "liberal" but immediately qualified that remark by saying "that's not the best word; maybe 'humanistic' comes closest." Her father's family had been evangelicals and she disdained evangelicalism in others, including Underwood, whom she otherwise liked. As the interview proceeded, it became clear that she had many labels—"rigid," "fundamentalist," "heavy," "emotional"— for those on the other side but none for herself. And she felt herself to be in a minority. A retired civil servant answered the same question in a similar context by saying that he was an "intellectualized" or "philosophical" Christian, "certainly not a fundamentalist." But he too supported Underwood's church. The evangelicals had preempted "Christian" as their own self-designation, just as, according to Martin Marty, they had successfully appropriated "evangelical" a century ago.

The consensus among these vaguely defined nonevangelicals was that Underwood appealed to the evangelicals *and for that reason also to them.* "People flock to him," said one. "He has a following," said another. "He's a magnet." Yet another person, an active member of the church for over forty years, under ten pastorates, was quite pointed in her comment. Underwood, she said, is an excellent speaker who directs his remarks to the "lost souls" in the congregation, and that is the reason that she could "only accept about forty percent" of what he had to say. But she was devoted to the church, proud of its diversity, and thrilled by the large number of male voices in the choir. (Meanwhile, five of the seven regular men in the choir at that time were evangelicals, five had joined the church under Underwood, and the talented director was, although neither an evangelical nor a member of the church, one of many newcomers attracted by the social mix of the congregation.) The retired civil servant, a man of considerable sophistication, admired in others the literalistic Christianity he rejected for himself. The fundamentalists, he called them, "may be naive intellectually, but they do live a Christian life." The resulting mix of young and old made Mendocino Presbyterian a "live church," he said.

In sum: Underwood drew in many evangelicals. Their numbers, their youth, their diversity, their energies, and their vitality created a nascent state that drew and kept others. In the meantime, the weariness and divisiveness that had been the domestic fruit of Vietnam had passed. Evangelicals were at the center of this process, and their man, Eric Underwood, was its agent. "He's a uniting force," said one of his supporters. He had "a healing presence," said a veteran of the Hsu and Kimmerly years.

10.

Movement and Institution

The ideals of prophets and saints can take root only when they are attenuated, moderated and compromised with other contradictory ideals and with the demands of the situation and the needs of 'the old Adam.' . . . That is why the ideologist, be he prophet or revolutionary, is affronted by the ordinary man's attachment to his mates, to his pub, to his family, to his petty vanities, to his job, to his vulgar gratifications, to his concern for the improvement of his conditions of life.
—Edward Shils, *Center and Periphery*

We have seen that Antioch fellowship was the decisive catalyst in the explosive growth of Mendocino Presbyterian in the mid-1970s. Its leader, Larry Redford, had maneuvered the church into calling an evangelical pastor. Its members were the clientele who began flocking to hear Eric Underwood's preaching, who offered their energies to the Sunday School, and who began to swell the church's rolls. Its spirit of youthful religious enthusiasm—its nascent state—added to the new magnetism of the old institution that captivated others in the community.

For four years, from March of 1973 until May of 1977, the fellowship constituted an *ecclesiola in ecclesia,* a little church within a church, always distinct from yet never fully independent of the Presbyterian connection. Underneath the surface, seismic tensions strained the bonds between the two organizations. Yet there were also significant areas of cooperation and, more tangibly, human bridges between them. Many of the individuals involved in both groups were only dimly or sporadically aware of these tensions, and the yoke between the fellowship and the church lasted a full nine years, spanning the ministries of Mark Kimmerly and Eric Underwood.

In this chapter and the next, we will explore the strains between the fellowship and the church. The present chapter focuses on the fellowship as a movement and the church as an institution, both dedicated to evangelical ideology. We will see that the fellowship and the church collaborated on the establishment of a Christian elementary school, in direct competition with the public school. Then, however, we will see how the movement's radical approach collided with the institution's moderate approach to the issue of deviation from the old-fashioned moral code that both espoused. Finally we will see that the relatively worldly institution attracted people who had come to evangelicalism through the more intense movement. As a result, substantial numbers of persons began to choose the church over the fellowship, thus exacerbating the tension between them.

The chapter to follow will explore the response of Larry Redford and his remaining followers to the threat of competition from Eric Underwood and his church.

Ecclesiola in Ecclesia

Antioch Fellowship was always intimately linked with Mendocino Presbyterian, and the link was obvious. As we have seen, about thirty of the new church members in 1973–1976 came to the church by way of Antioch Fellowship. A few church members became regulars at the weekly Fellowship meetings. During the period of my on-site observation in 1976, nearly half of those I took to be fellowship regulars were also church members.

During Sunday services the Antioch contingent—church members and regular visitors—were usually to be seen in their favored pews right beneath the pulpit. One Antioch couple, the Bakers, took charge of the weekly tape recording of the church services, for the particular benefit of shut-ins (and later, incidentally, of the sociologist). During the after-worship coffee hour, Larry and Sue Redford presided over the Antioch book table in the fellowship hall.

Members of the Fellowship being younger, on the average, than other church people and more likely to have young children, they were disproportionately involved in Sunday School and worship-hour child care. Half of the church-school teachers during Eric Underwood's first year were active Antioch members, and over the next few years they continued to staff such key church-school positions as teacher for Junior High and Senior High and Superintendent even as other evangelicals new to the church began to predominate among the teachers. Through 1975, Sunday baby sitters were more likely than not to be Antioch members.

The church and the fellowship were linked by leadership and finances, too. Larry Redford and David Baker had served on session prior to Underwood's pastorate, but Underwood began the practice of tapping a fellowship veteran for session at every yearly opportunity: Chris Fisher, a public school teacher, in 1974; Jeffrey Wakefield in 1975, Arturo de Grazia in 1976. (Were it not for these Antioch elders, Underwood might have been the youngest person on his session.) Thus the majority of Larry Redford's group of "elders" in 1972–1975 also became elders of the church.

We have seen in chapter five that the church lent itself to the financial needs of the Redfords and their fellowship. The fellowship had a $100-per-month contract to provide janitorial services to the church from 1971 to 1974. Later on, yearly gifts totaling $3000 came from other northern California Presbyterian churches, and members' and well-wishers' tithes and offerings totaling many more thousands of dollars came to the fellowship by way of the church. The giver would make out a check to the church; canceled, it could be used to document a tax deduction. The church treasurer would deposit that check and write another to the fellowship. This procedure, flatly called "laundering money" by one participant, went on for five years. The sums were small, but they were a large proportion of the fellowship's (and the Redfords') budget. The fellowship was in this way dependent on the good offices of the church.

The church and the fellowship were intimately linked in other ways. The fellowship newsletter was typed and mimeographed in the church office, so it had a look similar to that of the bulletin handed out at Sunday services. Musicians from the fellowship frequently performed for Sunday worship. For one year, at the time I was present in Mendocino, the fellowship had the rent-free use of Preston Hall for its "body meetings" every Friday night.

The church's outpost at Albion became a "youth ministry" under the "joint authority" of the church and the fellowship when Jeffrey and Pat Wakefield moved there in 1974 to be resident caretakers and missionaries. This same couple were later financially sponsored by both the fellowship and the church for Jeffrey's studies for the ministry.

The most ambitious joint venture of the fellowship and members of the church was the establishment of a "Christian" elementary school in 1975. The idea came up in the fellowship. Larry Redford had frequently complained about the "garbage" his kids picked up in the public schools, and one of the many teachers involved in the fellowship suggested that it might not be too difficult to set up a private school. Indeed, the Wakefields had themselves run a licensed counter-culture school prior to their conversions. Early in 1975, the formal legal work was done, space was rented from the small Mendocino Baptist church, a board was constituted, a sliding tuition scale was established, and teachers were hired. The "Good Shepherd School" opened in September with two teachers, an aide, a volunteer, thirty-two students (K–6), and a budget of $15,000, much to be met on "faith."

It was a remarkable undertaking. The principal and upper-grade teacher, Ben Moss (who also served on the board), was a former New York City public-school teacher who had quit that system in the wake of the 1968 teachers' strike. The primary-grade teacher, Pat Wake-field, had run the academically oriented "Headlands School" from 1971 to 1974. Her husband served on the board. The two teachers were members both of Antioch Fellowship and of the Presbyterian Church, as was Larry Redford, who also served on the board. Of the remaining board members, one was a school volunteer who later became a paid teacher (she and her husband were active in, but not members of, the Presbyterian Church), and the other was the South-ern Baptist pastor. Four of the board members were parents of chil-dren in the school; the principal's daughter was as yet too young.

Principles of evangelical justice governed the administration of the school. The (male) principal's salary was $600 per month, while that of his (female) primary grade teacher was $300. This disparity re-flected not only their differing responsibilities and credentials, but also the fact, as she put it, that "he supports a family." (Her husband was the main breadwinner in her household). For pupils, tuition was $35 per month for the first child from a family, $25 for the second, $15 for a third, $5 for a fourth. (Two families sent three children to the school and eight sent two in 1976.)

The curriculum was conservative Christian. The day began with prayer, "real prayer, not just token," in the words of a school bro-chure. Curricular materials were from a Florida evangelical publisher called "Beka Books." In the opinion of the primary teacher, they rightly emphasized the "godly virtues" of kindness, honesty, and courage, in contrast to the public-school materials (published by such companies as Ginn, Harcourt, and SRA), which, she thought, pan-dered to a presumed hip, jaded, and cynical attitude among school-children. "It's too bad," she added wistfully, "that Beka Books are so patriotic."

With a student/teacher ratio of about 15:1, quiet and disciplined classrooms, a dedicated staff, and determined parents, students got plenty of individual attention, and their test scores compared favorably with those of kids in the public school. The Good Shepherd School was, in other words, attractive on other than strictly doctrinal grounds, and some parents enrolled their children for the academic and behavioral values it adhered to. One mother was relieved to get her son out of the public school because he had been subject to teasing there. Another mother, a newcomer to Mendocino, enrolled her six-year-old daughter in the Good Shepherd School as soon as the child returned from her first and only day at the public school to ask, "Mommy, what's a motherfucker?" Another mother rejoiced, "My kids are learning to read!" Although I did not study the school as such, my impression is that it was as much or more its social values—obedience to authority, trust among peers, respect for cultural tradition—as its narrowly "Christian" rubric that was the key to its relative success.

Support for the school was not, therefore, solely a matter of showing proper evangelical colors. Not all Antioch families agreed about the utter "darkness" of the public school. Sue Redford, who still had one daughter there, and Jeannie Baker, whose son liked Mendocino sports, still held out hope for the public schools. But all Antioch parents of elementary-school-age children did send them to the Good Shepherd School by its second year of operation. (The last public school holdouts, the Bakers, decided at the last moment to enroll their two children in Good Shepherd in 1976. Their daughter missed her friends and wanted to be with them again.) But several families unafilliated with the fellowship or who were former members also opted for the Christian school. In all, about half the Good Shepherd School constituency overlapped with the church. The blue-and-white school sweatshirts were a familiar sight in Sunday School and at church picnics.

The school was not uncontroversial. Grace Silva, doyenne of the church session and retired public school principal, opposed it. The current public-school principal complained that his budget was losing about $50,000 in state per-capita aid for the kids who went to Good Shepherd. Most notably, Eric Underwood let everyone know that his girls, third grader and kindergartener in 1976, would stay in the public schools. He took the traditional American Presbyterian view that Christians should be leaven in the public schools, and he tried (unsuccessfully) to organize a P.T.A. in the public school. Board members of the Christian school, by contrast, took "a very separatist line," as one put it. "To have strong Christians, you need a Christian education." Larry Redford was disappointed in Eric Underwood's decision, but the church as a whole gave much more support than opposition to the school.

The link between the church and the fellowship was most clearly marked by the weekly meetings held by Antioch in Preston Hall in 1975–1976. Every Friday evening, for over two hours, the church's social and cultural hall was the site of charismatic worship, evangelical testimony, participatory prayer, and Larry Redford's Bible teaching. The room was well lighted and the curtains were left open to reveal the scene to passersby on Main Street even at the height of the tourist season. The Presbyterian church thereby entertained in its midst a combination charismatic prayer meeting and Southern Baptist adult Sunday School class.[1]

To gain both legitimacy and funds, the fellowship was dependent on the church. In turn, the church relied on the fellowship as a source of enthusiastic volunteers. There was a symbiotic relationship between the two organizations.

Among the many differences between the fellowship and the church, what stand out are their orientations to the surrounding society. Larry Redford alternately wanted to convert the community and to withdraw from it. He was uncomfortable with his undeniable dependence on "the world" and preferred to live on faith rather than by contract. His fellowship disdained to be merely an arm of this or that worldly institution. It was, ideally, a part of the true church universal, the ecclesia, the called out, set-apart, spotless Bride of Christ.

The Presbyterian church, by contrast, was the oldest institution, occupying one of the oldest buildings, in town. Its current pastor, like his predecessors, played by the implicit rules of pluralistic society, leaving taxes to Caesar, legal regulation to attorneys, and most education to the county school system, while maintaining a special interest in the promulgation of Christian doctrine. A pastor might do a better or worse job of educating his congregants and might wish to raise their consciousness in one or another direction. But he would expect to be accountable to his denomination and to his successor as well as to his flock. His church was inevitably in the world.

This is not to deny that there were other differences between the fellowship and the church, between Redford and Underwood. There were, and we have spoken about many. The fellowship was a hybrid product of the counterculture and served a younger clientele than did the church. The fellowship was openly charismatic; the church was not. Yet not all these differences were apparent to all participants in the organization, and some of them were in fact exaggerated to give a meaningful face to the deep-seated structural difference between

them. The most common perception of the fellowship-church relationship among Mendocinoites was that the former was the countercul-
tural complement to the straightness of the latter. The ex-hippies live
at Antioch and the blue-haired ladies go to church, the stereotype
went. Having lunch one weekday at the Sea Gull with Ernie, the
church's long-suffering volunteer gardener, I heard the town gas-
station owner—himself a church member—ask Ernie in a piqued
tone, "Why don't some of those folks up at the ranch come down to
help you?" This was in 1976, many years after Antioch Ranch had
ceased being a Christian work hostel and become a parachurch whose
members had their own families, jobs, and businesses.

The Redfords and the Underwoods implicitly conspired in the promulgation of this stereotype. Redford described Antioch Ranch as "an
interdenominational temporary country-farm home for young adults
seeking spiritual answers and new beginnings" on the church information form he annotated for Underwood in December 1972, just
when that description was becoming seriously misleading, and Sue
Redford continued in conversations to speak of the Ranch as a place
where people could "work out their problems with drugs" long after
her home had become a meeting ground for settled neighborhood
charismatics. On the other side, Underwood's capsule history of the
church and the community, which he gave to those attending his new
members' class in 1976, spoke of the Ranch as a place where Haight
people could go to get off drugs.

In fact, the "counterculture versus straight" rubric served both
Underwood's and Redford's interests. It allowed Underwood to put
some distance between himself and the more radical fundamentalists
and charismatics in the evangelical camp, who were threatening to
some church members. He could thus appear more moderate to those
on his theological left without invoking theological issues (such as his
skepticism of "the second coming") that would divide him from his
right. At the same time, it gave Redford the legitimacy of ministering
to a distinctive clientele and allayed suspicion of what was, in fact, his
competing organization.

Wayward Sheep

The basic movement-versus-institution difference between
the fellowship and the church is best seen by looking at their contrasting treatment of those who deviated from their shared moral code, in
particular, their code of sexual conduct. Shortly before my fieldwork
began, an event occurred which both expressed and shaped the na-

ture of Redford's fellowship and Underwood's church. Peggy, a veteran of Therese's Land and an early new Christian convert, was formally disfellowshipped by Redford and his elders for persisting in what they saw as a sinful relationship; Underwood, in response, invited her to his church. During 1976 and 1977, Redford's action was cited by several persons as a reason for disaffection from the fellowship. Others defended the action.

(Several informants having volunteered opinions about the event—without, however, mentioning Peggy's name—I set out late in 1976 and on my return in 1977 to query those involved about their actions and, having finally learned Peggy's name, interviewed her too, in August of 1977. The accounts agree as to the facts but differ drastically in evaluation.)

Peggy, a shy and soft-spoken member of Montgomery Greene's "Koinonia group," met Carl, a rock musician, at a bar early in 1975, and he soon moved in with her and her son. She had been, she told me, lonely and unfulfilled, and all the acceptable—i.e., "Christian"—men she knew were married or too absorbed with religion to be interested in relating to her. Carl used drugs, drank excessively, and brought in little money, and she knew the relationship was "not right." But she loved him and continued to do so until, much later, she grew tired of his drinking and failure to offer her security. As her involvement with Carl intensified, that with the fellowship weakened, though she had been an ardent worshipper at the Redfords'.

During her period of cohabitation she did sometimes show up at Greene's small group meeting, and her backsliding was an issue he tried to confront. "She knew what she was doing," he recalled. "She knew she'd be hurt." But he was unsuccessful in dissuading her from a course he felt wrong, so he asked Redford to step in, bringing Peggy's case up before the group of elders, then consisting of himself, Redford, David Baker, and Steve Hunter. The elders' discussions were long and prayerful, and guidance was sought from scriptures. But Redford's judgment was harsh. Peggy, he said, was "a sexually horny woman . . . living in blatant, obvious sin" with "a really raunchy guy." As we have seen, Redford's religious convictions held "sexual immorality" to be intrinsically sinful, but he also worried about the demonstration effect that Peggy's deviance could have on other "sisters" who were similarly tempted to stray. "It's hard for single women," said Sue Redford. "They want male companionship." The problem, everybody agreed, was in Peggy's heart.

The fellowship elders thought the meaning of scripture was clear. Did not Paul say (I Cor. 5:2) that those who indulge in sexual immorality should be expelled from the community? Did he not admonish believers not to cause a brother to stumble (Rom. 14:13)? Other scriptural advice—not to overlook one's own sins in judgment of another's and not to apply public sanctions before confronting the deviant privately (Matt. 7:3–5 and 18:15–17)—was considered by the elders, and no one who knew Larry Redford in Mendocino ever accused him of acting in haste. Nonetheless, Peggy was not aware at the time of these arduous deliberations and two years later could only vaguely recall a visit from Steve Hunter, intended as a serious personal word of admonition (Matt. 18:15), during the period when Carl and her conscience were keeping her away from the fellowship.

But then, early one evening in June, while she was making dinner for company, there was a knock at her door, and Larry Redford and Steve Hunter were there to hand her a letter of "disfellowship." She was overwhelmed with hurt and shame. When I spoke with her two years later, the wounds still had not healed, and I spent much of the next week regretting that I had opened them again. It did not seem to help when I assured her that her name was seldom mentioned in connection with the disfellowshipping. She spoke with bitterness, bewilderment, and fresh pain of the "martyrdom" she had experienced at the hands of those who had once extended to her the hand of love. Always professing to be a Christian, never denying the Lord, she said, "even in a bar," she had not returned to the fellowship or to the Presbyterian church.

Redford announced the disfellowshipping to the body at their next meeting ("everyone knew anyway"), and some members let their disapproval be known. Two young men sided with Peggy and soon left the fellowship. (They soon became regulars at Underwood's Thursday LIFT meeting.) Monty Greene felt remorse and shortly after resigned his position as elder, soon dropping out entirely. (He later apologized personally to Peggy.) The news made the rounds of the Presbyterian church, and I heard offhand allusions to the event (though not to Peggy's name) and to Redford's "dictatorial rule" during the next year. Most important for Peggy, though, was that "Eric told me right away that I would be welcome in the Presbyterian church."

Redford clung to the view that Peggy's cohabitation with Carl was "a very flagrant issue" (he said to me in 1982), and though his harshness was tempered by Sue's expressed solicitude for Peggy's spiritual and social well-being, he continued to defend his action in expelling her. At my first Antioch meeting in January 1976, I heard him relate a message from a book on pastoral care written by, he said, a man who had been an actual shepherd. Though I did not at the time fully understand the import of what he said, I wrote in my notes that the shepherd warned that deviation can be dangerous among sheep. "In fact it may be necessary for the shepherd to cut off the congenitally restless roamer from the flock so as to protect others." So I summarized Redford's lesson that night, and it seemed to me then an ominous warning not to stray, with the grave premise that Redford the shepherd was responsible for the rectitude of the flock.

As minister of the church, Underwood reacted differently. His message, as we have seen, was profamily, and he was as firm a believer as Redford in the sanctity of marriage. He did not approve of sex outside of marriage, and he preached traditional sexual morality. Yet his church was set in a community where old moral standards had been challenged and new ones—particularly a norm of serial but exclusive nonmarital relationships—had popular support. More than once, he found himself officiating in a wedding in which the couple's own children participated as flower bearers, and during the third year of his pastorate a socially prominent cohabiting couple lent their trained voices to the adult choir. Short of removing the church from society, he could not purify the sexual morals of his congregation.

So he made a point of letting Peggy know, as soon as he heard of Redford's action, that she was welcome in his church. "Eric still holds out his hand to me," she said in 1977. Though she did not take up the offer, the gesture was appreciated. "Now I know who my real friends are," she said. Had she taken up Underwood's offer, she might have heard him preach on the sins of the flesh (and Underwood did not approve of her relationship with Carl), yet she also might have found vindication in a sermon Underwood preached on the woman caught in adultery, when his series on the Gospel of John got to that point (John 7:53–8:11) in March of 1976.

Jesus asks those who would condemn the adulteress whether they were without sin themselves. No one volunteers, and Jesus is left alone to forgive the woman and tell her to sin no more. Underwood drew three lessons for his congregation from this story. First, he said, Jesus reaffirms traditional teaching on the sanctity of marriage. Second, Jesus taught that the sins of disposition are as grievous as those of the flesh. Third, we are encouraged by God's forgiveness and forgetting of our sin and by hope of renewal. Regarding the second of these lessons, the two kinds of sin, Underwood alluded to Redford's action against Peggy:

> These two kinds of sinners are always with us. They sit side by side in this congregation. And sometimes they're housed in the same per-

son. . . . [Our Lord] seems to have hated and feared most the sins of disposition . . . Jesus had more hope for this person than he did for her decent and respectable tormentors. How often the church has stood with the scribes and the pharisees and pointed the bony finger of the scripture at some poor soul that's gotten mixed up in the sins of the flesh! In being so zealous to pin them with the scripture, they have done a surgery that was successful but lost the person in the process. How often we have performed radical surgery and cut out the malignancy only to have the patient die!

Peggy had not died, but she was indeed lost to the Christian community in Mendocino.

The Peggy affair was only the most dramatic example of the difference between the fellowship and the church. When Buddy, a born-again gay Christian trying to go straight, was spotted one Saturday night at Toad Hall, the counterculture saloon, he was sought out the next day by two elder brothers of the fellowship. Buddy wanted to celebrate his victory over temptation, since he'd refused a toke from someone's joint and declined an offer to stay the night with some gay friends. But Sol and Tim, acting on the Matthew 18 principles they'd learned from Larry Redford, admonished him to stay away from places of temptation. Buddy was furious and let me know how much he preferred the supportive atmosphere of Eric and Vonnie Underwood's LIFT to the judgmentalism he felt from Antioch people.

Nancy, who also frequented LIFT, was a new convert trying at twenty-four to put a series of unhappy relationships behind her. The Redfords thought she ought to join the single sisters' ministry Therese had established at the Land after Beacon House moved out. About a half dozen women, mostly in their twenties, lived dormitory-style in the Big House and held daily devotionals led by Ben Moss. Nancy did agree to share her horticultural expertise with the sisters, but she refused Therese's overtures to become a resident (and member of the flock). Redford, however, still insisted that she ask his and Sue's permission before accepting a "date with a man." She felt fewer attached strings in her involvement with the church and the Underwoods. Whenever she was absent from LIFT, Vonnie Underwood, her "prayer partner," expressed concern for her, but Eric and Vonnie did not seek her out to pass judgment.

The fellowship's and the church's (and Redford's and Underwood's) contrasting modes of social control, different responses to backsliding, were only personal experiences to Buddy and Nancy, whom I had come to know well. But other cases, those of Peggy and Elise, became issues between the two organizations. Elise, a very pretty girl of sixteen who lived at the Land and was a volunteer at the

Good Shepherd School and a regular at Antioch Meetings, was in love with Matt, a high-school boy whose parents were new members to the church. Her parents, in particular her mother Sandra's new husband, Curt, disapproved of the affair; Matt's parents accepted it. In the face of Curt's demand that Elise stop seeing Matt, the kids "eloped," declaring themselves to be married. The two sets of parents were at loggerheads—his providing a cabin for the new couple, hers refusing consent for the marriage of an underage woman. The fellowship and the church were drawn into the conflict.

Ben Moss, Good Shepherd School principal and Antioch elder-in-charge at the Land—thus twice Elise's "shepherd"—and longtime acquaintance of both sets of parents, felt "a leading" to intervene. He used his influence to dissuade Sandra from giving permission for Elise to marry. He felt that the situation needed "the surgery of some confrontation," since Elise was not only living in sin but was in more basic rebellion against parental authority. So Ben brought out his Jerusalem Bible and read a passage for Sandra intended as a rebuke to Elise. It was Jeremiah 2:19–24, with the rebellious Elise playing the part of the faithless Israel and the prophet's metaphor of harlotry taken literally:

> Your own wickedness is punishing you,
> your own apostasies are rebuking you:
> consider carefully
> how evil and bitter it is for you
> to abandon Yahweh your God
> and not to stand in awe of me
> —it is Yahweh Sabaoth who speaks.

> It is long ago now since you broke your yoke,
> burst your bonds
> and said, "I will not serve!"
> Yet on every high hill
> and under every spreading tree
> you have lain down like a harlot.
> Yet I had planted you, a choice vine,
> a shoot of soundest stock.
> How is it you have become a degenerate plant,
> you bastard Vine?
> Should you launder yourself with potash
> and put in quantities of lye,
> I should still detect the stain of your guilt
> —it is the Lord Yahweh who speaks.
> How dare you say, "I am not defiled,
> I have not run after the Baals?"

> Look at your footprints in the Valley,
> and acknowledge what you have done.
> A frantic she-camel running in all directions
> bolts for the desert,
> snuffing the breeze in desire;
> who can control her when she is on heat?
> Whoever looks for her will have no trouble,
> he will find her with her mate![2]

When Elise heard this, Ben said, she turned white with horror. "If Elise has to suffer now, that doesn't compare to the glory she'll receive later on," he told me.

A self-described fanatic, Ben knew there were those who would say "let's be realistic," and he knew that Eric Underwood was one of them. Only later did he learn that Underwood was at that very time trying to take realistic action. Underwood regarded Curt's self-described prophecy prohibiting the marriage as "a dream or a bout of indigestion," and he joined Matt's mother in an attempt to persuade Sandra to give consent. He discussed the legal aspects of the case (which neither side was eager to invoke) with Ed Kearney, his lawyer friend on the church session. All else failing he gave Matt and Elise his blessings, as he told me one night during the elopement crisis. Six weeks later, while he and I were on our way from the church to the Deli for lunch, Matt and Elise walked by hand in hand. "Hello, folks," Underwood said. "Why don't you come by sometime?" Though he insisted that he did not condone the affair, Underwood had accepted a fait accompli, and Ben Moss later let him know to his face of his displeasure at the minister's action. That Matt's stepfather, on whose land the new couple lived, was reputedly a drug dealer did not make Underwood feel better about the relationship he felt powerless to change. But he did not condemn Elise.

Only once (in my experience) did Underwood attempt to exclude someone from his church. The object of his ire was Jonah Harris, the single most threateningly intense religious person I have ever met, a Mau-Mau among evangelicals, a powerfully built, keenly intelligent man of thirty-four, who felt called to pass prophetic judgment on the shallowness of the religion of the institutional churches. Harris had angered Underwood by abruptly ending a discussion with Underwood's wife by invoking a scriptural excuse that her opinions as a woman did not concern him (probably 1 Timothy 2:11–12). Harris meant what he said, and he was obnoxious again to Vonnie on an occasion two months later. Underwood's reaction was to "excommunicate" Harris (a member of Beacon House, not of the church) by passing the word that he was unwelcome in the church without Underwood's prior permission. Underwood's half-serious action only highlights his general policy: only incivility was unforgivable. Only those intolerant of the church's tolerance were unwelcome.

Neither Redford and his fellowship nor Underwood and his church courted confrontations with deviants. There were many episodes of backsliding I knew of or heard of among younger fellowship and church members during 1976 that never elicited action from either group: the man who had left his wife to play the field; the single woman who had a new "roommate"; the married man who sat at home stoned while his wife went to work. These cases were handled by prayer and default as the deviant would stop coming to meetings while "the walk" was not right. "Darkness doesn't want to be around light," as Larry Redford put it.

Yet the fellowship was, by its nature, a group mobilized for the purpose of social control. It was not always Redford who admonished the backslider; it might be one of his elders, one who was closer to the person involved. The effective principle of confrontation required that there be some personal connection between the deviant and the group, but preventing the spread of bad leaven was more important than simply saving the soul of the sinner. The fellowship was a group collectively responsible for purity.

The church, by contrast, was an educational and sacramental institution serving individuals within a pluralistic society. The theological and moral doctrine preached there by Underwood was closer to Redford's doctrine than to Mark Kimmerly's or Peter Hsu's. It was religiously evangelical and socially traditional. Yet that doctrine was preached more than enforced. If someone living in sin cared to come to worship and risk hearing a sermon extolling the virtues of premarital chastity (along with the virtues of mercy and compassion), that was up to him or her. Individual counseling was available by request, but the church was not organized to provide surveillance of the lives of its members in the secular community.

As Underwood put it, he wanted to "come alongside" the deviant. To Matt's marijuana-dealing stepfather, a church member, he reported saying, "I'm not going to chase you through the woods. You know—the Lord is in you—that what you are doing is wrong." Underwood criticized Redford's more rigorous approach as building dependency in the relationship between himself and the members of his flock. Sue Redford, in her own way, agreed with this analysis. She thought that the fellowship had lost members to the church because Underwood's moral demands were not as stringent as Larry's. Speaking in retrospect about Peggy, Larry said, "We pursued her with love." The objects of such pursuit did not always see it as loving, however. Monty Greene summed up his own comparison of the fellowship's and the church's response to deviance two years after resigning as Antioch elder:

> Christ offers freedom, forgiveness and grace, but Antioch takes that away. That's where Eric is beautiful, that he allows sinners to come to his church. Larry comes across judgmentally. . . . Now I don't want to compare, and Larry has helped lots of people. But if you take the same idea up the ladder, you get Boyle [of Beacon House], Reverend Moon, and Jim Jones. It's the lack of freedom.

(Jim Jones' rural ranch was a two-hour drive eastward in Mendocino County, and the infamous Guyana massacre was a full year in the future when Greene spoke these words.)

Whom To Serve

When Larry Redford brought Eric Underwood to Mendocino Presbyterian, he brought an ideological ally who became an organizational rival. His own evangelical-charismatic social movement found itself in competition with the worldly evangelicalism of an institutional church, and he was losing the battle for the loyalty of constituents. In the three years between Underwood's coming and the bicentennial, thirty-two affiliates of Redford's fellowship became members of the church. Of the twenty-six who were still active in either organization in the middle of 1976, fifteen were still active in both. They were the most faithful of those who were to be seen in charismatic worship in Preston Hall on Friday night and again in the church sanctuary on Sunday morning. But eleven had decided between the two bodies and of those nine had left the fellowship for the church. Meanwhile the church membership had contributed only a handful of sometime visitors—all single women—to the roster of the fellowship. The flow of members would, from Redford's point of view, get worse in the months to come. But already by Bicentennial Day, the church was receiving a massive transfusion of human commitment at the expense of the fellowship.

A woman who deeply desired to maintain both the fellowship and the church as spiritual homes recalled her chagrin at Larry Redford's response to her joining the church late in 1975. She wanted to thank him for bringing her to the Lord and to His church, but his response, she said, was to appear hurt. "But I'm supposed to be your shepherd," she remembers him as saying, and she felt suddenly, unaccountably, disloyal. She too later dropped out of the fellowship altogether.

It was not an easy or obvious thing to do, to cease involvement with a group where one had been reborn, to leave the couple who had been one's spiritual guides, to take up with the engaging man whom they regarded publicly as a weaker exponent of their message and privately as a powerful rival to their ministry. Here I will recount several stories of these deliberations. What we will see in these narratives are the thoughts of those who, in effect, opted for a more worldly form of evangelicalism than that represented by Larry Redford's Antioch Fellowship.

Arturo de Grazia's resignation as elder in the spring of 1975 was the first blow that the church seemed to inflict upon the fellowship. De Grazia, whom Mark Kimmerly had tried to interest in the Presbyterian church as early as 1968, joined Antioch with his wife Anne in 1972. Recognizing his stature (he was the best known as well as the oldest Antioch regular), Redford appointed him one of the five elders early in 1973, and de Grazia brought his personal influence and spiritual gifts into the service of the fellowship. But after Eric Underwood's arrival, he and his wife decided to join the church and he soon felt himself overcommitted at Antioch. He showed me a diary entry dated June, 1974, in which he complained about the amount of time Redford and his elders wasted (he thought) in long deliberations and expressed his desire to spend more of that time in discussions (about culture, politics, or education) with secular friends. Or, as he once put it in a prayer meeting, "I love hanging out."

De Grazia's differences with Redford were several, and he made no secret of his impatience with Redford's indecisiveness. But as a professional artisan whose childhood religious background was Roman Catholic and whose wife's was Episcopalian, he also brought a high-church sensibility to his religion, an orientation that, except for music, was mostly missing at Antioch. He thought Redford's style of leadership too verbal, too literalist, insufficiently aware of the spiritual truths that generations of nonliterate peoples had gleaned from religious art.

The Presbyterian church, though predominantly low-church and reformed in aesthetics, had more room for the work of artists, as Mark Kimmerly and Eric Underwood had both shown him. So he took on the job of elder in charge of worship on the church session at the start of 1976, where he continued to experiment with ideas (such as an outdoor communion) that Kimmerly had encouraged years before.

By the end of 1975, he had ceased attending Antioch functions altogether. Anne, who had become a deacon soon after joining the church, continued involvement in both groups in the summer of 1976, but then she, too, ceased coming to Antioch. Both found their needs for profound religious experience better served by the intense but periodic Cursillo weekends, for which they became ardent proselytizers in the years to come.[3] At the end of 1976, they divided their tithe between Antioch, the Presbyterian Church, and the San Francisco Cursillo Center.

Throughout the 1970s, the de Grazias' pottery business was increasingly prosperous. There were steady orders for cookware—descending dove logo and all—from galleries in Mendocino and from Gump's, the prestigious San Francisco store. There were one-man (and one-couple) shows at galleries and churches. There were special commissions for costly wall-size ceramic murals. There were students at the Mendocino Art Center. And there were regional, national, and then international workshops on pottery as a metaphor in Christian theology. De Grazia's $75 handmade cabin grew to four rooms, then five, then six. He gained legal building status, brought in electricity, and began to enjoy some of the comforts that befit a successful middle-aged man.

Coming out of the counterculture ("I'm eating my goats," he told me in 1976), he felt that he and his Comptche Road neighbors, who were experts at frugal living off the land, nonetheless needed instruction in providing worldly security for a family. What does one do about managing an intermittent income, about life insurance, college for the kids, and medical care? A religious body that disdained to answer these questions was not truly serving the needs of its members.

Looking back from the perspective of 1982, de Grazia recognized that his career had benefited from his church affiliation and he wondered out loud why another talented new charismatic, Ben Moss, had not taken advantage of the church connection to capitalize on his gifts as a teacher. "But Ben," he sighed, "is just too suspicious of institutions."

Jeffrey and Pat Wakefield were spared the trouble of choosing Eric Underwood's church over Larry Redford's fellowship by their summer 1976 departure to England, where Jeffrey took up formal studies for the ministry. But their hearts had already been won by the church. They had converted late in 1972 and had only a few months' intense experience in the fellowship before Underwood came to Mendocino. They were the first Antioch couple to take formal vows in the church. Underwood, immediately recognizing Jeffrey's secular learning, asked him to take the high schoolers' Sunday School class, but Redford's roll of elders had already been filled. When the Albion Chapel opportunity came, Jeffrey took it on with the understanding that he was under the joint authority of Underwood and Redford, but he felt like a pawn in a high-pressure game. His discontent was only increased when Underwood asked him late in 1974 to serve as a church elder, having checked out that request with Redford. He knew Redford wished he would not accept the nomination, but he did so anyway.

For years, the Wakefields had led an exemplary existence first as neoprimitive refugees from Berkeley, later as dedicated new evangelicals. For five years, before moving to the Albion property, they lived in a handmade house built without a county permit and hence lacking an electrical hookup. Prior to their conversions they had, therefore, already been removed from much of the world's influence. The Christian fellowship and, even more, the Presbyterian church were to serve them not as an escape but as an avenue of reentry into the world. When Larry Redford reported a prophecy ("You're a teacher, Jeffrey, but I don't know why I'm saying this.") and Eric Underwood began jovially addressing him as "Rabbi Wakefield," Jeffrey heard a calling.

Jeffrey and Pat both epitomized the Mendocino stereotype "overqualified." They both had University of California master's degrees and had been fellowship students in economics when they'd left graduate school. But the self-congratulatory label overqualified ceded to the discontent of "underemployed" as land values, taxes, and prices rapidly inflated in the 1970s. Pat earned a minuscule salary teaching in the Good Shepherd School, and Jeffrey, having no teaching credential, was a teacher's aide in a public school. Jeffrey began to think of the ministry as a career, hardly lucrative, but worthy of his gifts.

Antioch's informal charismatic worship was still for them the central spiritual event of the week, but the church opened the door to a wider Christian world. The church, Jeffrey explained in retrospect, had more structure. There were more roles to play, including that of elected elder. The church's membership was more diverse than the fellowship's in age, social class, and religious experience. And the Presbyterian church, as a denomination, had a long-standing tradition of respect for education. By contrast, Antioch fellowship had little to offer one who was dissatisfied with the state of his career.

So Jeffrey and Pat searched out a theological seminary that maintained high educational standards and welcomed charismatic gifts, and they found one in England. Both Antioch and the Presbyterian church sent them off with promises of financial aid, but the fellowship had ceased to exist when they returned to the United States for Presbyterian ministerial studies in 1979.

Those aware of the increasing tension between the church and the fellowship in 1976 knew that it created no more agony than that of David and Jeannie Baker, who for years had been the Redfords' neighbors and right hand couple. David and Larry had taken the original Antioch Ranch proposal up the Presbyterian hierarchy back in 1969. David had represented the ranch on the local church session from 1971 through 1973 and had been part of Redford's bloc on the pastor-seeking committee in 1972. Sue and Larry had provided the contacts through which Jeannie and David bought their land next to the ranch, and the Redfords had introduced the Bakers to the baptism of the Holy Spirit. David had been an elder of the ranch fellowship since 1972, and Jeannie had been in charge of taping Eric Underwood's church services since 1974. Both of them preferred the fellowship to be a *collegia pietatis*, a school of piety where religion is experienced more intensely yet more informally than in church. David was especially drawn to the fellowship, where he could serve others unobtrusively and yet be an organic part of spirit-filled worship. Jeannie was attracted to the church, with its frequently stirring choral music and its heterogeneous membership. To have both involvements—Friday night and Sunday morning—was deeply satisfying for both. The rivalry between the groups hurt.

The Bakers were children more of the depression than the baby boom, and their values were plainly rather than newly traditional. They had met in high school in a Baptist church and had naturally become the devoted, deeply religious spouses and parents their ideals would have prescribed. He was a state park ranger; she volunteered in the church and in the public schools. Since their mortgage was soon to be paid off and their tastes were plain, their material needs were modest and each seemed to have no ambition other than to treat each other and their two children with kindness and respect. Their worldliness was humble.

If a choice had to be made between the church and the fellowship—the choice the de Grazias had made and the Wakefields had finessed—David and Jeannie knew what they faced. Eric Underwood, said David, saw his function as refueling the congregation so that they could get through the week. He liked to set things going and then step back out of the way. But Larry, David went on, saw pastoring as a full-time role. He wanted to be involved in everything that his people did. David appreciated both of these models and he felt drawn to both men. Jeannie, who was often the more articulate of the two, knew her husband's thoughts. Throughout 1976, David and Jeannie shared their feelings on what Jeannie always called the impending divorce between the church and the fellowship, but they stayed involved with both. Ultimately the commitment demands of Redford's fellowship proved excessive and the Bakers stayed with the church.

Those who gravitated toward the church and away from the fellowship were not becoming less religious. These three couples were not only still deeply involved in religious activities and private devotions but they also continued to enroll their children in the Good Shepherd School. But they were coming to feel less need for the religion Antioch provided and more for that of the church. They did not want organized religious activity to monopolize all their time, energy, and attention, and most of what they did want a religious body to provide could be found in the church. As a religious social movement, Antioch Fellowship attempted to be an alternative to the secular world, and it therefore had to be everything to its adherents. As a social institution, the church could afford to be many things—learning center, concert hall, career ladder, sacred edifice—to many people, but it presupposed that its constituents had demanding, satisfying, and salient roles elsewhere in the world. It was an unfair competition: the church and the world against the fellowship. The conventional families as well as those who deviated from the moral code felt the pull of the Presbyterian church.[4]

Comparing Antioch the movement with Mendocino Presbyterian the institution did not always favor the latter, and many persons remained firmly committed to the fellowship, including Burt Rogers, who had been one of its earliest recruits, and Steve Hunter, who remained Larry Redford's most loyal elder. Neither of them was inclined to criticize Eric Underwood, but neither had much good to say about his church. Rogers's praise was faint indeed. The church, he said, was light and comfortable, but went only so far, whereas in the fellowship there were deep relationships of genuine commitment. Hunter acknowledged Underwood's contributions as an evangelical preacher but frowned upon the pluralism of the church congregation. Eric, he said, was way ahead of his people. Neither Rogers nor Hunter saw spiritual power in the church.

Ben Moss most forcefully articulated the limitations of the church in comparison to the more radical fellowship. While he admitted having been nurtured in his faith by Underwood and acknowledged personal love for him, he disparaged the ministerial profession Underwood represented. The institutional church by its nature, he said, is caught up in an ethic of realism and expediency in its dealings with the world. He longed for a "fundamental" expression of Christian faith, and he frequently—in testimonies and prayers as well as interviews—spoke of the dangers of sophistication, which he defined as the love of worldly wisdom for its own sake. Insisting that he made no personal claim to perfection, he nonetheless wanted me to know that "there are some fanatics," himself included, who scorned compromise with the world. For Ben and those like him, the movement had greater allure than any mere institution. Ben and Beatrice Moss asked to be released from their vows to the Presbyterian church in March of 1977. The church was not set up for those who turned their backs on the world.

11.

Separate Ways

The group of people within which a nascent state
has arisen tries to introduce a way of life com-
pletely different from everyday customs and institutions. But in doing this, precisely in order to
explore this possibility, it is obliged to assume a
form, to acquire a structure. That is, at a certain
point it must become a concrete and historical project and collide with the contingent concrete and
historical forces, thus becoming, itself, an institution and a part of everyday life.
—Francesco Alberoni, *Movement and Institution*

Let us recall Larry Redford exulting in February 1973 over his
triumph as chair of the pastor-seeking committee. Of Eric he wrote in
his newsletter, "We sense we are on the brink of a new era." Remember that Redford exhorted his flock at the Ranch to check out the really
neat new pastor at the Presbyterian church. Consider that they
heeded his advice, and for that among other reasons Mendocino Presbyterian grew and prospered and witnessed to the evangelicals' faith.
Redford acknowledged to me in 1976 that Underwood had opened
the Presbyterian church to his kind of faith, *yet he never again mentioned
Underwood's name in his newsletter after that one brief note of triumph.*
What happened?
Some said that Eric and Larry got off to a bad start when Larry,
having organized a work party to move the Underwoods' household
into the manse, made a disparaging, perhaps envious, remark about
the relative opulence of Underwood's furniture, a remark that got
back to Eric. Some said that Larry was surprised and disappointed to
find that Eric prepared his sermons in writing. Some said that they
had a personality problem, the one shy but emotionally transparent,
the other extroverted but emotionally guarded. Redford himself came

closest to the truth in an unguarded moment during a conversation with me late in 1976. "Our job would be easier without Eric," he blurted. Even as he said that, he winced, for he usually wanted me to hear how much he respected and admired Underwood, which was also true. The fact is that Underwood, the institutional clergyman, was giving him, the shoestring charismatic, a very hard time.

For his part, Underwood told me in June 1976, shortly after I arrived in Mendocino to begin my fieldwork, that he would expect Antioch Ranch to phase itself out when its work of converting the hippies was done. In three years, he said, there would still be a Mendocino Presbyterian Church but there would be no more Antioch Ranch. Speaking with the casual authority of the town pastor, at his desk in the church office, he implied that the phaseout of Antioch Ranch might already have transpired but for Redford's precarious finances and ego involvement. Underwood knew he was in a protracted struggle with Redford, but he may not have known what it would cost him. In 1982, commenting on a draft of chapters four through seven of this book, Underwood only half joked when he told me that he never would have taken the job in Mendocino had he known then the full story of the tangled relation of the ranch and the church up to 1973.

Thus Redford and Underwood recognized in 1976 that they were locked in struggle. Redford's job *had* been easier with Kimmerly than with Underwood. And Antioch Ranch *would* be gone in three years. Redford complemented Kimmerly's church, but he competed with Underwood's. Redford and Underwood, though ideological allies in the evangelical camp, represented the opposing principles of social movement and social institution. Those who were drawn to evangelicalism in a part-time, pluralistic, worldly context could meet their religious needs in Underwood's church. Redford was left with only those whose evangelicalism was as intense, totalistic, and radical as his own. Since he lacked the personal magnetism to engender that kind of commitment in many others, he could only try to hang on to the followers he had as they gravitated toward Underwood and the institutional church. The fundamental conflict was not over dollars— Redford's operation was better off financially with Underwood than it had been before—but over persons and their loyalties.

In this chapter we will chronicle Redford's attempts to give his fellowship an identity independent of the Presbyterian church, culminating with a short-lived unilateral declaration of independence. We will see Underwood's efforts to frustrate Redford's move—his attempt to keep Antioch fellowship in the position of ecclesiola in ecclesia—and Redford's ultimate defeat.

"We Are a Church"

Larry Redford was in an unenviable position. He was at once dependent upon Eric Underwood and in hot competition with him. Mark Kimmerly did not steal his thunder, but Eric did. How galling that Eric was his own man, younger in age and in Christ than he!

Always emotionally ingenuous, Redford told readers of his newsletter's December 1975 issue that he'd been studying a very exciting book, *The Problem of the Wine Skins,* by the respected Free Methodist leader, Howard Snyder. He wrote that Snyder's chapter six, "Must The Pastor Be A Superstar?" had greatly encouraged him. Here is the opening of that chapter:

> Meet Pastor Jones, Superstar.
>
> He can preach, counsel, evangelize, administrate, conciliate, communicate and sometimes even integrate. He can also raise the budget.
>
> He handles Sunday morning better than any quizmaster on weekday TV. He is better with words than most political candidates. As a scholar he surpasses many seminary professors. No church social function would be complete without him.
>
> His church, of course, Counts Itself Fortunate. Alas, not many churches can boast such talent.
>
> I confess my admiration, perhaps slightly tinged with envy. Not because of the talent, really, the sheer ability. But for the success, the accomplishment. Here is a man who faithfully preaches the Word, sees lives transformed by Christ, sees his church growing. What sincere evangelical minister would not like to be in his shoes? Not to mention his parsonage.
>
> I think of all the struggling, mediocre pastors, looking on with holy envy (if there be such), measuring their own performance by Pastor Jones' success and dropping another notch into discouragement or, perhaps, self-condemnation.[1]

Snyder's point was that the superstar model is both unbiblical and counterproductive, because it tends to stifle the development of lay talent in the church. Redford did occasionally voice that criticism of Underwood's church, and he saw his own fellowship as a more organic body, less a matter of leader-versus-led than the Presbyterian church. Yet how encouraging, indeed, it must have been to read those words from Howard Snyder about Eric Underwood!

To recognize a problem is not, however, to solve it, particularly for one as deliberate, even timid, in decision-making as Larry Redford. He once said of himself, "Sometimes I feel the best way to solve a pressing (but not urgent) problem is to wait. The Lord has a way of bringing things to a head." Nonetheless, for several years Redford nudged his fellowship in two simultaneous directions to give it greater integrity. One direction was to make the fellowship itself into a local church; the other was to incorporate the body within a wider association of like-minded radical charismatic Christians. In the next century, historians may look back to find that a new American denomination was begun by such men as Larry Redford in the 1970s.

We saw the beginning of this two-directional evolution in chapters 5 and 6. On the one side, Redford gave his fellowship internal ecclesiastical structure through the appointment of four other elders and the establishment of small koinonia groups under those elders. On the other side, Sue and Larry Redford made contact with scores of other Jesus movement ministries at the 1973 Leadership Conference in Florida but they had refused to be incorporated into one of those ministries, Jack Boyle's Beacon House. Quite consistently through the years, Larry Redford had wanted to know what his place was in the wider structure of Christ's church.

Yet we know that he was never content with the traditional, flawed, hereditary expressions of Christ's church, the institutional denominations. It was not enough for him to be a mere Presbyterian. Once (Sue Redford thought it was in 1975) he did ask Eric Underwood to "cover" him, to be his spiritual counselor, and Underwood says he once offered to arrange an associate pastor position for Redford in his church. But these were ill-considered gestures of desperation, for the two men operated with opposed concepts of the sacred-secular nexus, the one totalistic, the other pluralistic. Redford did want security for himself and his flock, but not at the price of becoming an organ of the Presbyterian church.

In the previous chapter, I stressed Redford's organizational rivalry with Underwood as a factor in his ever more urgent need to have Antioch Fellowship recognized as a separate entity. Other observers in Mendocino attributed Redford's action to his ego needs. Redford himself, as well as those who stayed with him as his struggle with Underwood grew more intense, stressed the fellowship's need for clear lines of authority. Yet no matter whether personality or social levels of causation are adduced, the effect was the same: an evolution toward clearer boundaries. The issues were organizational, not ideological. Underwood and Redford differed theologically, of course. Underwood was not a charismatic and thus did not, as the jargon went, "preach the baptism of the Holy Spirit." Yet Redford had had far greater differences with Kimmerly and Hsu without having to underline his autonomy from them. Quite simply, he had lost his monopoly on evangelical leadership in Mendocino.

His overtures to other leaders outside Mendocino began in 1973.

There was the Florida conference. There was also a huge week-long evangelical workshop in Oakland run by Bill Gothard on the topic of raising children into adulthood. Among the twelve thousand persons there, Sue and Larry made the acquaintance of a couple from Willits, a mill town in the interior of Mendocino County, who ran a ministry similar to theirs. He was Phil Sinclair, and Redford wrote, "It is likely that the Lord wants that tie strengthened!"

In 1974, some Antioch people participated for the first time in the "Festival of the Son," the annual Jesus movement rally. Thousands of new charismatics—individuals, families, and whole delegations from other parachurch organizations like Antioch Fellowship—spent Memorial Day weekend with teach-ins, small-group discussions, musical performances and dramatic skits, mass baptisms, and healing ceremonies. Jack Boyle's Beacon House and its satellites were prominent in the Festival of the Son, but Redford also met other, less threatening colleagues. The Festival became a yearly event for Antioch people, and I was lucky to arrive in Mendocino to begin fieldwork just four days before the 1976 festival, which, along with the Redfords, Wakefields, de Grazias, Rogerses, Mateos, and Hunters, I attended.

The decisive moment in Redford's turn toward interorganizational articulation came with a leadership conference held in Sacramento under the auspices of the Florida group in the summer of 1975. The featured speaker was Charles Simpson, by reputation a "church architect," meaning that his specialty was providing ideas about structures emerging among previously inchoate Jesus movement groups. Redford recalls that he "came back burdened with the thought that there was no one in my life that I was under." Others corroborated Redford's memory, yet with their own colorations. Monty Greene remembers being "blown away" by the doctrines promulgated at the conference on themes of authority and submission. Eric Underwood, whom Redford invited but who did not attend, remembers asking Larry, "Why can't we stay on the main road, in the institution?" Jeannie Baker remembers Redford's excitement but also recalls that "Larry didn't jump on it right away." Characteristically, Redford took his time.

But that fall Redford did come together with a handful of other Mendocino county movement leaders, including Phil Sinclair, to form what they called a presbytery, using the ancient Greek designation for a collegium of church elders. This group met monthly, and it began to provide an answer for Larry's need for "covering." In November, sixteen men from the Antioch group joined in a weekend retreat with members from the other groups in the "presbytery." Just between the lines in Redford's December 1975 newsletter, one can discern the two directions of the emerging structure:

The Lord granted us our 2 requests [on that weekend]: we needed a
deeper loyalty and oneness between us, and He gave us a desire and
vision for sharing what we have in Christ with our neighboring towns.

Within the new presbytery, Redford was to be the shepherd for
Mendocino and its surrounding area. He would have designated authority and responsibility.

When the 1976 Festival of the Son came around, Redford was eager
for contact with other elders. Every morning of the three-day weekend, over one hundred northern California leaders came together for
discussions and words of advice from Ern Baxter and Bob Mumford of
the Florida group. Not myself being a sheep, let alone a shepherd, I
was not privy to these meetings. I was told later that the Mendocino
delegation discovered that all over northern California ministries
were evolving complex eldership structures in conformity with the
principle that "everyone should know who is over you and who is
under you in the Body." But the doctrines presented in those closed
sessions, if not the details of implementation, were clearly articulated
in the public "teachings" given to the four thousand festivalgoers,
myself among them.

Bob Mumford's speech was a masterly combination of soft sell and
hard doctrine, spiced with self-mockery and rollicking humor. His
message was that we have entered a "new dispensation, that means a
change in the way God keeps house." The antinomianism of the
counterculture had gone too far, and the concern that authority
should not be abused had been overdone. We need now to pay close
attention to our relationship with our leaders. (Mumford stressed this
word by lengthening it, each syllable becoming itself a word: ree LAY
shun ship.) Leaders, himself included, were called to, not hungry for,
the burdens that had been thrust upon them, and they should be
respected for their willingness to bear them. "You say 'he's talking
about *authority*!' " Mumford said, feigning shock. "Well you're right. I
am," he answered in a mock sinister voice. "But you can't have community without authority." Laughter and murmurs and shouts of
approval ("Praise God!") greeted this speech, and Mumford walked
off the stage to a standing ovation.[2]

While new to me, Mumford and his pitch were familiar to Redford
and the Antioch contingent. New to them was a new charismatic
leader from Santa Rosa, Gary Armstrong, whose name vaguely and
whose style of speaking vividly recalled to me the Berkeley student
movement of twelve years earlier. Armstrong's speech was more
overtly demagogic than Mumford's—he shouted himself hoarse as if

he were speaking through a bullhorn to a crowd on Sproul Hall steps rather than through a sophisticated public address system to a crowd comfortably lying about on beach blankets under a starry sky. But his message was the same as Mumford's: the patriarchal family, with its defined relationships and lines of authority, is the basis for the kingdom of God. "God wants safe sheep pens and predictable shepherds," he said. But he made it clear that he did not accept the authority of the established churches. "Satan is fully willing to coexist with the church as the church is now constituted," he said. He called for spiritual warfare to frustrate Satan's design and to vindicate God's purpose of fellowship with man.

Frightening to me in its militancy and its manicheanism, Armstrong's speech was greeted with enthusiasm by the crowd ("Hallelujah!") and by those who were becoming my informants ("incredibly anointed teaching"). More important for our story, Armstrong was leader of a group called New Life Ministries in Santa Rosa, and he was in the process of becoming the northern California bishop, as it were, within the Florida-based organization. Larry Redford, Steve Hunter, and Jeffrey Wakefield met him at the elders' meetings, and they found they had a great deal in common. Redford in particular was encouraged to find so forceful a leader who was not Jack Boyle. Gary Armstrong was to become Larry Redford's shepherd, though he was a full decade younger in Christ than the veteran he was to lead.

Developments internal to Antioch Fellowship itself were parallel, both in their direction and in their sporadic nature, to Redford's groping for external linkages. We have already seen that Redford had developed a doctrine of division of labor in defense of inequality, that he introduced an eldership structure before falling under the sway of Mumford's organization, and that he believed strongly enough in authority to take the step of expelling Peggy from the group. But his fellowship, as we have also seen, was a shifting assembly of new Christians of varying levels of commitment and varying attraction to the beckoning Presbyterian church. Seldom did change within the fellowship occur smoothly.

Signs of structural development are apparent in Redford's newsletter. Returning from Florida at the end of 1973, he spoke of lessons learned there on evangelism, the church, elders, community, authority, and submission. From February 1975 we read:

There is no escaping the fact that authority is a reality in the New Testament Church. We must not return to the heavy power structure we read about in church history. Instead, we must face up to the struggle of finding that authority which does not "Lord it over," but rather comes alongside to lift. We need to find the balance between having an authoritarian hierarchy and having a "just me and Jesus" attitude.

In the March 1975 newsletter, Redford referred to himself as "pastor." In October, he reported that he and Sue were on a "salary" of $750 per month from fellowship income, partly generated by tithes. In November, he was "ordained" as a Christian pastor by seven local ministers, from Presbyterian to Roman Catholic, at an Antioch meeting. By December 1975, he retitled his newsletter the "Antioch Fellowship [instead of 'Ranch'] Newsletter."

Only occasionally did these movements toward independent status impinge on the rank and file. Insiders knew what was happening, and some, like Turo de Grazia and Monty Greene, refused to go along with it. Others, such as Jeannie Baker, watched the evolution with quiet misgivings. Those outside the circle of elders, many of them powerfully drawn to both the intensity of the fellowship and the dignity of the church, were seldom faced with the strain between the two. One event, recounted to me with dismay by several participants, occurred on a Friday night in the fall of 1975 when Redford, inspired by ideas from the Charles Simpson conference and from the Willits presbytery, demanded that Antiochers "submit" to his authority, making a "commitment" to his leadership. That demand was the last straw for some waverers, and for others it was a signal to become more deeply involved with the fellowship. Still others, however, effectively ignored the demand and continued to attend Antioch meetings despite Redford's grumbling about "spectators" in the body. Some thought that Larry had a good reason to want to know who was his. Antioch did organize work parties and make loans and gifts (as it had for the Wakefields), and it was reasonable to ask what were the boundaries of such self-imposed obligations.

The simple idea that finally brought the simmer to a full boil was broached at a meeting of the Willits presbytery in the spring of 1976. Giving a report from Mendocino, Steve Hunter painted a gloomy picture of the status of the fellowship (it was Steve's wont, observed Larry, to emphasize the negative), and one of the other elders asked if Antioch held its meetings on Sunday. Hearing the negative answer, the man shot back, "well that's your problem!"

Larry was fired up with the idea of Sunday-morning meetings and brought it back first to the elders (David Baker, having a full-time job, did not attend the Willits meetings) and then to a recently constituted group of "elder brothers" in the fellowship, an offshoot of the November men's retreat. Discussions within this group, several participants told me, were vigorous. Some were so enthusiastic about the idea of

Sunday meetings that they saw the original suggestion as a "directed prophecy" from the Willits group. Others questioned whether the man whose idea it was knew anything at all about the unique circumstances of the Antioch group. Steve Hunter and Burt Rogers pushed for the idea. Sol Bloom fought it outright. David Baker, knowing what his wife's reaction would be, pleaded for caution. The prayerful considerations continued.

The first mention of the possibility of Sunday meetings to the Fellowship as a whole—and the first mention I heard of the proposal—came an hour into the regular Friday meeting two weeks after the bicentennial weekend. The meeting had been a good one despite the unusually sultry weather. There were songs, prayers of praise and intercession, and muted glossolalia. There were testimonies. Tim Stockton, professional musician and veteran of Beacon House's camp at Therese's Land, shared his conviction that evangelicals' prayers for Godly men to be elected to public office were being answered with the Democratic Party's nomination of Jimmy Carter at its New York convention. Tim's musical partners, Josh and Susan, told a brand-new miracle story about getting a desperately needed car battery from a Christian gas-station attendant late one night when they were broke and stranded on the long road from San Francisco. Sue Redford prayed that athletes at the Montreal Olympics might be spared the terrors visited upon those in Munich four years before. Lucille Rogers asked the group to pray for the Campbell children out in Comptche, whose babysitter had called their parents at the meeting to tell them of their fright at an approaching thunderstorm. (Summer electrical storms are unusual on the northern California coast.)

When Larry got up—Bible in hand, blackboard ready—to give his teaching, he said that he first wanted to share some things that were happening in the fellowship. He mentioned the older brothers' meetings and the Willits presbytery and said that there had been a strong suggestion given in a prophetic way, although whether it had the blessing of the Lord was still undetermined, that Antioch ought to start meeting on Sunday morning. The possibility had been discussed with Eric Underwood, he said, and with Daryl Ritchie (of the Mendocino Baptist Church) and Pastor Mill (of the Foursquare Gospel Church in Caspar).

Sunday morning! I began writing furiously (Sue Redford was also taking notes) and will quote verbatim excerpts from my field notes' paraphrase of the ensuing discussion:

Now, we are a church. We've been a church, but that's the first time we've ever used that word here, although it describes us accurately.

Redford then gave some background:

> Hardly anyone, except the Bakers, has been with us the full eight years. In the beginning, no one, not the Presbyterians nor the Baptists, would have anything to do with us, with a ministry that deals with those who have been hippies. The Bible indicates that there's only one direction that we can go, namely "churchhood." We've shied away from taking that step because we didn't want to be seeming to be engaged in disunity, particularly with the Presbyterian church.

> We've never used that word church until tonight. But we should admit that we're a church, coexistent with others. What we need now is for all the brothers and sisters to pull with us. We want you to pray for the brothers' meetings on Tuesdays as we travel lovingly, boldly, and firmly. We're seeking that people should sense a call to one group or the other, so that we can have a real pastoral relationship. This seems to be a logical progression.

Redford closed by saying that Steve Hunter had especially urged that there be an announcement about these deliberations. Then he asked for questions.

Many of the regulars were there that night—Judy Mateo and several of the sisters from the Land, the Rogerses, Hunters, Wakefields, Blooms, and Bakers—but it was the single persons and newcomers, who were more marginal to the fellowship, that had been left out of the discussions. It was they who spoke up.

> Raul (a bearded man, veteran of the charismatic movement, with a heavy accent): Isn't this a kind of competition?

> Redford: We're not competing. We're not going out to sell something. We're just clearing up the pastoral relationship.

> Mike (a new convert, ex-radical, now a millworker): You're thinking of meeting on Sunday?

> Redford: That's what was in the prophecy. That's what's on the table for decision.

> Mike: I've heard that it's now legal for people in Hungary to worship together once a week, but more than that is illegal. More than once is OK here in the United States, but still I'd rather be illegal. (laughter)

> Bobby (the LIFT regular): You're talking about a Sunday morning meeting? That would be pretty hard for those of us who go to the Presbyterian church. What about unity?

Redford: What we're looking for is a clarification of the relationship of the sheep with each flock.

Steve Hunter (addressing Bobby): Is unity dependent on being in the same building at the same time? Can't we think of ourselves as being in the same body with Pastor Mill, Daryl Ritchie, and Jack Halloran [the Catholic priest]? I have been concerned about the question of unity too, but I don't think it's a matter of being in the same building.

Redford: We're concerned about unity.

Tim Stockton (the musician, a moderating influence in the older brothers' group): We don't want to be a nebulous group or to just withdraw into ourselves.

Redford: Whatever we do, we're going to doubly intensify our relationship with other groups. This will clear up what those relationships are.

Randy (recently born-again, married and a father, but too new in the Lord to be a member of the older brothers' group): I'm bothered about not being invited to these older brothers' meetings. My father is a minister, and I've been around church organizations for a long time, and I've never seen a meeting be closed to members of a congregation like this. So you're asking the sheep to go blindly behind the shepherd. Do you hear what I'm saying?

Redford: I hear what you're saying, but in my understanding of the New Testament, the church is not a democracy.

At this instant, there was a brilliant flash of lightning (I am not making this up), and the power went out all over town. The meeting came to an abrupt halt, and concern turned to the children and their caretakers in the pitchdark basement. (It was plenty dark upstairs where we were.) People went outside to get flashlights and to shine their car headlights into the building. Everyone got out safely, the power came back on the next morning, and nothing was ever said to me of the coincidental thunderbolt except by Simon, a baby Christian whose spiritual immaturity was legendary.

No action was taken that week, but discussions about Sunday meetings continued among the older brothers and the elders through the year and into the next winter. Steve Hunter pushed. David Baker questioned. And Larry Redford temporized. In November, the idea seemed to receive a burial when the Antioch elders brought it before Gary Armstrong and Bob Mumford at a newly organized San Francisco area "presbytery" meeting. Armstrong recounted that his group had decided in 1975 to cease Sunday meetings so that they could be "leaven" in the local churches (as Antioch people were in Mendocino). Mumford cautioned Redford that Sunday meetings would bring out only those people already committed to his fellowship and no others. When I left Mendocino just before Christmas, I thought the issue was closed.

For two years, Eric Underwood fought Redford's drive for independence with every resource he had. He offered inducements, including the free use of Preston Hall during prime time, publicity and institutional cover for fellowship ventures such as the Good Shepherd School and a retail Christian bookstore, and continued use of the fund conduit system.

He flattered Redford, notably in a February 1976 sermon on the miracle of the loaves and the fishes (John 6:1–15):

> How many organizations begin that way, with someone who opens a little bag and says "God, here's what I have. Take it, and use it for your service." A couple arrives on the Mendocino coast, has a vision to reach the people that are here. God miraculously provides them with a small piece of land up on the Comptche Road, they open the sack and the barley loaves and the fish are there, and God stands in the gap and provides. And countless people are blessed through the ministry of Antioch Ranch.

Earlier, he joined with other Mendocino ministers in Redford's "ordination."

He mocked Redford's demand that people choose which flock they were committed to by reading a Dr. Seuss story, "The Sneetches on the Beaches," straight through without comment before giving his sermon on an October Sunday in 1975. The Sneetches came in two kinds, those with stars on their bellies and those without, and a cynical entrepreneur, McBean, made a fortune exploiting their envy of each other by alternately adding, then removing, stars from the bellies of those who were the temporary have-nots. Finally, though, the Sneetches wised up.

> But McBean was quite wrong. I'm quite happy to say
> That the Sneetches got really quite smart on that day,
> The day they decided that Sneetches are Sneetches
> And no kind of Sneetch is best on the beaches.
> That day, all the Sneetches forgot about stars
> And whether they had one, or not, upon thars.[3]

The point, I am told, was lost on some, but not on Redford himself.

Underwood solemnly admonished against Redford's emphasis on

authority in a June 1976 sermon on Jesus' washing of the disciples' feet at the last supper (John 13:1–17). Though Redford was not in church that day and although Underwood did not mention him by name, the preacher looked right at the Antioch contingent:

I have a little problem with the teaching that's going around on "undershepherds" in the church. The *Lord* is our shepherd. Elders in his church are there to *serve* the body of Christ, to *serve* the flock. And something does not ring well when someone says, "will you submit to my eldership?" Our Lord never would have said that. . . . When we are tempted to think of *our* dignity and *our* place and *our* rights, you can be assured that the Devil is thrilled and that he's active and well and vital in your life.

Heavy words, those, and the point was not lost. During the coffee hour afterward, one woman caught in the fellowship-church tension expressed her surprise "that Eric took out after Larry that way."

Underwood scolded Redford face to face. He told him that to set up Sunday meetings would be to break the solemn vows he had made when joining the church a dozen years earlier, as if he were just to walk out on his wife. He likened the impending split to a divorce in which innocent children, those bound to both sides, would be hurt.

Finally Underwood threatened Redford financially. He reminded him that three Presbyterian churches donated $1000 a year each to Antioch. If Antioch pulled out, he said, he would be obliged to write these churches, telling them that although Mendocino Presbyterian was still in the business of having a counterculture ministry, donors should now make out their checks to the Albion Chapel. He added in bitterness that at least Redford's departure would mollify the uptight ladies who would have less reason to give him grief over folk gospel music during Sunday services. Underwood knew he was making it very hard on Redford, but he valued the Antioch group's contribution to his church and did not want to see them go.

Underwood and Redford saw less and less of each other as their conflict intensified. Throughout 1974 and 1975, Eric and Vonnie had had weekly breakfast meetings with Sue and Larry, Monty and Audrey Greene acting as go-betweens. But these meetings had ceased, and the last conversation between the two men in 1976 took place early in June when Larry brought his Sunday meeting idea enthusiastically to Eric only to hear the latter's talk of "divorce." Redford let it be known that he was wounded by that response, as he earlier had been by the "Sneetches" recitation. ("I felt he'd drawn his bow and aimed it at my heart," he said to me.) In turn, Underwood always felt manipulated by Redford. They'd have talked through some difference or some misunderstanding and seemed to have reached an agreement when up would pop yet another manifestation of Redford's duplicity, such as the Sunday meeting idea. He was dumbfounded, he said, when his mother-in-law, an Antioch regular, told him of Redford's "we are a church" declaration, since he'd heard Redford deny to his face that he was moving in that direction.

Both men developed psychological theories to account for their adversaries' actions. Underwood saw Redford as insecure and manipulative. Redford saw Underwood as personally frightened of direct confrontation, having to express himself obliquely in sermons. There was some truth to these characterizations, yet each also knew that there was a systematic source of the conflict between them. As Underwood put it, it was the movement leader's push for purity and the institutional minister's priority of unity, combined, as I have emphasized, with their basic ideological similarity, that made them competitors. By midsummer 1976, it was clear to many that a parting of the ways was inevitable.

Humiliation

The next step in marking off the boundaries of Antioch Fellowship was to move the Friday night body ministry meetings back to the Redfords' ranch. This was done at the end of the summer in 1976. To underline the seriousness of the meetings, Redford gave his teachings at the beginning—at 7:30—instead of at the end. After a few weeks, chronic latecomers began to show up on time lest they encounter a sarcastic remark from Larry the teacher when they straggled in late. Moreover, Redford began a series of academic lessons, with mandatory graded homework assignments, on selected topics: six weeks on Luke's gospel, six weeks on the concept of the church, twenty weeks on the Old Testament. For one reason or another—I thought it had to do with the greater human density of the forty to fifty adults overflowing from couches onto the floor of Larry's twelve-by-thirty-foot living room—the meetings back at the ranch seemed less "spectatorish" than they had been at Preston Hall. As the fall wore on into the damp dark of the northern California winter, those three-hour-long Friday evenings at the Redfords' were filled again with the palpable warmth of which I had before only heard.

They were not intense enough, however, for the older brothers, especially those who were not involved with the Presbyterian church. The fellowship was still caught in an unstable compromise with the church. As the church attracted the partial commitment of those with divided loyalties, the totally committed became more dominant in the fellowship. They finally had their way in the spring, after I had left Mendocino, and Antioch Fellowship began to hold its weekly meetings on Sunday mornings, ten to noon, in May.

I first learned of this development in a letter from Eric Underwood dated May 10, 1977.

> I received a letter from Larry Redford yesterday telling me that they will now be worshiping on Sunday mornings on the Comptche Road grounds. It has been a painful decision for Larry, but one that I am sure he can live with. The timing came as somewhat of a surprise to me. My reaction is philosophical, something like the surprise of a partner in a poor marriage that one day finds a "dissolution" notice in the mail box.

Redford did not announce the action in his newsletter but treated it after the fact as a fait accompli. "Since we changed our meetings from Friday night to Sunday morning we have had a few interesting developments"—that was the first mention his readers heard of it, in the June newsletter. Redford went on to insist that "our change to Sunday was in no way a negative reaction to anything about the Presbyterian Church," presumably a statement intended for readers in the churches that had been sending money.

Redford, disappointed at first that some chose to attend the Presbyterian Church, claimed to find the overall effects salutary. The meetings were more participatory. (Having myself attended only one Sunday Antioch meeting during the following summer, I cannot vouch for that but think it plausible.) The children's program—now a true "Sunday school"—was greatly strengthened, no longer a matter of mere child care. That seems more than plausible to me, and another effect was obvious: "we can linger around afterwards, have lunch together, and enjoy ourselves, whereas before it was 'pick 'em up and move 'em out!' " Yet Redford had to admit that he had lost some families and put others into a very uncomfortable spot, alternating between the church and fellowship week to week or covering both by dividing the spouses.

Underwood did not notice an immediate effect on church attendance, ordinary week-to-week fluctuation being too great for that, but he could not ignore the impact on the church's Sunday school—a score of children were suddenly gone—and he knew of those who were heartbroken with the forced choice. There was less spontaneous singing, too, in the church services. Though he felt the move was inevitable, he was not mollified.

When the Sunday meeting question had first come up in 1976, Underwood had informed the chairman of the church's board of trustees, Robert Gamble, who was also a trusted advisor. Gamble set in motion a session reevaluation of the practice of funneling contributions to Antioch Fellowship through the church treasury, and a policy statement was received from a denominational executive in San Francisco at about the same time that Antioch began its Sunday meetings. In a reversal of what had been taken as approval of the conduit policy eight years before, the session was now told that money laundering was improper: "all funds for tax exempt institutions should be given direct to the respective institution, not through the church." In effect, as Gamble recalls, the message from Synod was "get those people to incorporate." Accordingly, a letter went out to Larry Redford urging him to seek independent tax-exempt status "so that further giving through the church may be discouraged and/or discontinued." Redford was warned that the umbilical cord would soon be cut.

The independence of Antioch Fellowship was short-lived. Redford did incorporate, with the help of Ed Kearney, partly to secure legal tax-exempt status and partly to become a Christian camp, so that he might circumvent restrictions on subdividing property and thus build more dwellings on his Ranch. In mid-1977, Antioch Fellowship seemed on paper to be a growing enterprise. There was the Sunday meeting, the houses in which twenty rent-paying fellowship members resided, the sisters' ministry at the Land, the Good Shepherd School, and the new Christian bookstore in town, "The Upper Room." But the financial and human foundation of these ventures was shaky indeed.

Those who opted for the fellowship as against the church were more likely than their opposite numbers to be economically marginal. Though many had college educations, they were—as part-time lumbermen, fishermen, handymen, and teachers' aides—underemployed in Mendocino and subject to the lure of places offering better jobs and lower costs. Having over a period of several years given up the most economically stable part of his clientele to the church, Redford now found himself losing many of the rest to emigration. There was a virtual exodus in 1977.

The most stable perennial source of income had been the yearly grants from various Presbyterian churches. The end of the conduit system for funds and intra-Synod gossip about Redford's doings at Antioch Ranch caused several of these churches to make direct inquiries, to which Redford responded in detail but without a "we are a church" declaration. He said, "We are responsible for around seventy-five people," "We have a Sunday morning meeting," and "We desire ongoing and increased good relationships with the churches in our area, especially Mendocino Presbyterian." He defended the "unique identity" of the fellowship, but came short of acknowledging the intractability of the conflict between him and Underwood. It was ironic that what Redford acknowledged to me as the most faithful part of his funding came from Presbyterian churches. It was possible for a settled institution to foster a radical movement. Yet the churches were beginning to wonder where the money was going.

The end of Larry Redford's career as a pastor, the shepherd of a flock, came not with his return to the institutional fold, but with the deepening of his commitment to the radical Christian movement. At Christmas, reflecting on the exodus of sheep from his flock, he wrote:

> It must be time to panic. No! We learned that lesson too many times before. The reality is—and it is unseen—that God is turning a page, starting a new chapter for us. And that is exciting!

The new chapter came with "submission" to the ministry of Gary Armstrong.

Armstrong provided the spiritual covering Redford had always desired, the authority to answer to, without demanding title to Redford's property, as had Jack Boyle four years before. Eventually, Armstrong's organization would provide employment as teachers for both Larry and Sue Redford. First of all, though, Armstrong humbled Redford and made him give up aspirations to have his own ministry. He was placed not under Gary himself but under a lieutenant, who was, as was Gary, younger in the Lord than Redford himself. Later, when Redford's fellowship had ceased to exist and he decided to move south to join Armstrong's forces, he was offered a job in one of Armstrong's enterprises as a carpenter's aide, work at which he was highly skilled but which was physically and psychologically arduous for a man of forty-eight. Most of all, Armstrong insisted that Redford resolve his dispute with Eric Underwood, and he was made to swallow a very bitter pill.

Early in 1978, Armstrong called Underwood for an appointment and heard the long story of his dealings with Larry Redford. Underwood thought of Antioch "Ranch" (as he always called it) as an arm of the Presbyterian church, and Redford acted, especially in accepting funds and being a church member himself, as if it were. Yet at the same time Redford was calling himself a pastor, causing anxiety for church families, and holding meetings on Sunday. Was Larry just using the church connection for his own ends? Or, wondered Underwood, is there something in me that gets too easily frustrated by Redford himself?

Underwood and Armstrong agreed to hold a meeting with Redford and with some church elders to have it all out, and it was evident that

Redford was being called on the carpet. Redford recalls that Armstrong told him he had to go into the meeting programmed to lose. "I want you to eat crow," he remembers Armstrong telling him. He recalled that he had warned his own fellowship that the day would come when "we will go beyond the good graces of the community and we'll have to be a doormat." He consoled himself with the words of the apostle:

> Beloved, do not be surprised at the fiery ordeal among you, which comes upon you for your testing, as though some strange thing were happening to you; but to the degree that you share the sufferings of Christ, keep rejoicing (I Pet. 4:12–13, NASV).

The meeting was held on a Sunday evening in March, in the comfortably furnished lounge in Preston Hall. Present were Underwood, Redford and Armstrong; Eleanor Kearney, the current clerk of session, who had served with Redford on the 1972 pastor-search committee; Bob Gamble, chairman of the trustees, who had served on session with Redford under Peter Hsu and Mark Kimmerly; and the eighty-six-year-old Frederick Althorpe, who now walked with great difficulty but who still bore himself with great dignity. In effect, Kearney, Gamble, and Althorpe were there to lend gravity to a classic degradation ceremony, in which a person's self-image is shattered and his every defense is turned around as proof of his corruption. Like a military officer being stripped of his insignia of rank while standing at attention in front of his erstwhile peers, the pastor of Antioch Fellowship was reduced to just poor Larry.[4]

Armstrong took charge, and he charmed the Presbyterian elders with his evident desire to find an amicable resolution. He invited Underwood to state his case, and Underwood chose to focus on Redford's apparent violation of the vows he had made when becoming a member of the Presbyterian church in 1964 and then an elder a year later. He cited the vows pertaining to the ordination of elders—an august ceremony performed each year during the Sunday service following the election of new members of session—as they are prescribed in the Presbyterian *Book of Common Worship:*

> Do you sincerely receive and adopt the Confession of Faith of this Church, as containing the system of doctrine taught in the Holy Scriptures?

> Answer:
> I do so receive it.

Do you approve of the government and discipline of the United Presbyterian Church in the United States of America?

Answer:
I do.

Do you accept the office of Ruling Elder in this congregation, and promise faithfully to perform all the duties thereof?

Answer:
I do.

Do you promise to study the peace, unity and purity of the church?

Answer:
I do.[5]

Those must have been the words you spoke twelve years ago, Larry,
and what now? asked Underwood.

Redford was hoist with his own petard. Faithfulness, duty, and
unity were some of his own themes, after all. Yet, he protested, he
had never intended to pledge total allegiance to the Presbyterian
church. He had thought of himself as a missionary on the north coast
flexible enough to abandon the Baptist cliches of his spiritual youth in
favor of doing things the way they were done in Mendocino. Those
particular vows, especially about accepting the formal Presbyterian
confession of faith as definitive, he never intended literally, and he
remembered being assured by Peter Hsu that he did not need to do
so. (Indeed, Hsu recognized that thousands of Presbyterian ministers
would have trouble with their vows if they were to be construed
literally, so he told me in 1984.) The vows were conveniences, weren't
they?

It seemed, Armstrong observed, that Redford had been flying two
flags, as Presbyterian elder and charismatic pastor. Which were his
true colors? Redford was stung by the accusation of hypocrisy, and he
left the meeting in total defeat. The Presbyterian elders remember
feeling sorry for him, feeling that he really was not as sinister as he'd
been made to look. Redford's struggle to get the church to live up to
his understanding of its Christian identity, his desire to live a life of
total religious commitment in exchange for little more than subsis-
tence for his family, his evolving attempt to provide an intensive
Christian life for a group many of whom deeply desired such involvement—all these profound though flawed efforts wore the retrospec-

tive coloration of crass careerism. All along, it seemed, Redford had been pursuing selfish goals.[6]

In fact, Redford was no more the hypocrite than the public interest lawyer who draws his salary from the government he regularly meets in litigation or the seminary Bible professor who casts doubt on the scriptures that are revered by the rank and file of his denomination. But these analogies were not raised on that March Sunday, and even now they would not appeal to Redford, for whom the religious life is sui generis, not to be illuminated by sociological perspectives.

Redford capitulated. He made a formal request to be released from his vows as a member and as an elder of the Mendocino church. He wrote to each of the churches that had sent aid to explain that "Antioch Ranch is not a Presbyterian organization and our members are not members of the Mendocino Presbyterian Church" (and the trickle of contributions stopped altogether). And he ceased holding Sunday meetings.

Antioch Fellowship was in a shambles, many of its former members having moved away, many having joined the Presbyterian church, a rump keeping a fellowship together on Therese's Land, and a few—Steve and Dianne Hunter, Burt and Lucille Rogers—following Larry and Sue into Gary Armstrong's ministry. The nine years of the Antioch ministry were ended.

Armstrong consoled Redford with the thought that there are pioneers in the church and there are settlers. Larry and Sue, he said, were pioneers, those with the gift to lead the way. The time had come for others, those with what a sociologist would call greater organizational skills, to step in.

In my last interview with Sue and Larry, I shared much of this manuscript with them, including all of chapters four through seven. I also let them know of the great pain I thought Larry had caused Peggy. But I said that, nonetheless, they had for many years been a bridge between ex-counterculture new Christians and the institutional establishment these young people had once scorned. "Yes," Sue Redford said with uncharacteristic bitterness. "But you know what they do to a bridge. They walk on it."

More than any other family, it was David and Jeannie Baker who felt torn asunder by the forced choice between the church and the fellowship. Jeannie picked up Eric Underwood's metaphor of divorce to describe the Antioch Sunday meeting idea. She protested against the necessity of choosing one of her spiritual parents over the other, and she and David refused to undermine the spiritual intimacy of their marriage by each going his or her own way on Sunday morning.

For a while, they did alternate between the two bodies, one of the Bakers always doing the tape recording at the Presbyterian church, the other sharing in the worship at the Ranch, trading places the next week. But Jeannie could not believe Larry when he taught about "unity in the body," and so she and David ceased going to either. "Our decision was to back off from both, so that we didn't have to choose one over the other," Jeannie said.

"Then, one Sunday," she recalled, "Eric just asked us to read the scriptures in church, and that was a hand reaching out for us. It was warm, not grasping. From Eric that was a healing." "So we went back to the Presbyterian church," said David. "That was logical. It was our home."

12.

The Shape of the Vessel

I went down to the potter's house; and there he was, working at the wheel. And whenever the vessel he was making came out wrong, as happens with the clay handled by potters, he would start afresh and work it into another vessel, as potters do. Then this word of Yahweh was addressed to me, "House of Israel, can not I do to you what this potter does?"

—Jeremiah 18:3–6, JB

As long as the Antioch Fellowship was yoked to the church, the movement nourished the institution. But when the yoke was broken, the Fellowship itself soon expired and the church was vulnerable to spiritual starvation. It might have lapsed into lassitude and mediocrity. The growing gap between membership and attendance after 1976 that is visible in figure 17 (see p. 192) does suggest that some of the excitement of the revival days waned, no doubt due to the loss of the Antioch energies. Things did settle down.

Nevertheless, there remained a qualitative difference between the institutionalized evangelicalism of Underwood's pastorate after 1977 and the liberal days before 1972, as is clear from table 6. Even after the rupture of 1977, the church operated at a higher level of mobilization.

The records that I have drawn on to construct this table are flawed,[1] yet the cumulative impression they leave is unmistakable: the church was transformed in 1973. Sunday worship, which brought out nearly everyone in the heady years from 1973 to 1976, dropped back only to two-thirds, not half, of the enrolled membership at the end of the decade. Spending per capita, measured in dollars corrected for the rampant inflation of the period, grew and grew again. In the sixties, the institutional life of the church had first been slack and then became stringent. At the end of the seventies, it was bustling and

Table 6 *Indicators of Commitment, Mendocino Presbyterian Church, 1958–1982*

Years	1958–1962	1962–1966	1967–1972	1973–1976	1977–1979	1980–1982
Pastorate	Higginson	Hsu	Kimmerly		Underwood	
Attendance Average Sunday attendance as percent of membership	50	46	51	90	74	68
Spending per capita in constant (1967) dollars (internal and denominational figures averaged)	$75	$82	$112	$172	$191	$228

Source: See note 1.

increasingly opulent. Measured in these terms, the church was a vehicle for a whole new order of human commitment.

This chapter explores first the sources of that commitment[2] and then the ways the church put it to use.

The Cursillistas

When I first went to visit the potter, Turo de Grazia, it was June 1976, and he was hard at work in his studio. He told me as he worked about the discipline of his craft, but he was especially enthused that day about the Christian encounter movement called *Cursillo* to which he and his wife had recently been initiated. At the time, I did not understand that I was refusing a sacrificial offering when I declined his invitation to sponsor me to my own Cursillo. But over the next several years, I came to see that Cursillo was a way of reshaping the church.

Cursillo de Cristianidad ("short course in Christianity") is a spiritual-renewal movement operating primarily within the Roman Catholic church, which traces its roots to the Spanish island of Mallorca in the late 1940s. It was introduced to Spanish-speaking Catholics in the American southwest in the 1950s and, along with the charismatic renewal movement, began to affect mainstream American Catholicism in the 1960s.[3] The goal of the movement is reportedly to deepen the commitment of influential laypersons to the church by providing them with an emotionally overwhelming model of Christian faith and love.

The means to this goal is a carefully prepared, intense weekend retreat for three dozen novices (men or women only) presided over by a generous and benignly manipulative crew of priests, cooks, and Cursillistas (the initiates who have sponsored the novices).[4] Since a novice must be sponsored and the applicants are screened by the spiritual director to admit only those who are considered mature and emotionally stable, there is a long wait between one's expression of interest and the experience itself. So the Cursillo weekend is eagerly anticipated. When the time arrives, initiates are brought by their sponsors to the Cursillo center, a parochial school gymnasium, and told that they will be picked up on Sunday afternoon. The notion is that the brand-new Cursillistas will be in no condition to drive themselves home. Meanwhile, they will not leave the gymnasium for three days and nights.

The weekend is packed with a schedule of morning chapel, informal lectures (called "rollos"), small group discussions, impromptu skits, hearty meals, and calculated surprises. All the novices' needs are to be taken care of (if you need cigarettes, the cooks will go out and buy them), and one's personal relationships are built up from scratch. (Barracks-style cots, mealtime chairs, and places at the rollos are assigned by the staff, and those previously acquainted are kept separate.) Everything is done to take the novice "out of the world for three days," and the solidarity that emerges is thus based only on the Cursillo experience itself. There are group rituals (breaks in the program are signaled by the director's bell), there is a common culture (depending especially on Spanish jargon), and there are many hours of structured interaction.

The intent is to get every individual emotionally involved, and to that end powerful psychological techniques are used. Each rollo is given by a different individual, who had previously appeared to be merely one of the novices. It turns out that they are plants, veteran Cursillistas, and the novice is led to the paranoid thought that he or she is the only one not in on the conspiracy. The cooks present a continual threat of hilarious chaos (at one Cursillo they baked the frantic director's bell into a pie), but they allow nothing bad to happen. The staff shows a surrealistic movie of a clown, clearly representing Christ, who is about to be crucified when suddenly the movie screen is raised and the lights turned on to reveal a live human clown who wordlessly invites the novices to follow him on a treasure hunt. The hunt ends at a sumptuous table on which each novice has a personalized guest card reading

> Jesus of Nazareth
> requests the honor of your presence
> at a meal to be given
> in His name

and the whole group sits down to a joyful and tipsy communion. The spiritual director's statement that the novice's friends and sponsors are praying for him is taken as a pleasantry until he returns to his cot to find it buried in their "palanca," notes, drawings, flowers, and other symbolic offerings of Christian love. Everyone (it seems) is eventually reduced to a state of helpless gratitude, ready to open himself to the group and to Christ. Men particularly, who in our culture are inhibited from emotional expression, are deeply affected.

The most touching interview I had in 1976 was with a new Mendocino friend whose habitual air of cynicism had been vanquished by his recent Cursillo weekend. Another Mendocinoite told Underwood's LIFT group that Cursillo was "the most moving experience of my life." A woman told me that her Cursillo was more meaningful than her own wedding day. Several persons said that the weekend personalized God for them and made Holy Communion meaningful for the first time. I spoke with very few Cursillistas who did not share this glowing attitude. But one deeply religious woman was outraged by the mockery made of faith by the Cursillo's machinations. One noonday at her Cursillo, the cooks emerged from the kitchen to express dismay at the large crowd that had showed up for lunch, since they had prepared only one bowl of salad and three loaves of bread. They asked everyone to pray with them for a miracle, and then everyone was supposed to enjoy the joke and learn a lesson in faith when the salad bowl turned out to be a wheelbarrow and the loaves to be twelve feet long. My informant did not put it this way, but the cooks' stunt was clearly her idea of blasphemy. But others evidently learned the Cursillo lesson that "faith is not left to chance" and "Christ is counting on you."[5]

Eventually, about seventy-five members of Mendocino Presbyterian made Cursillo, including most of the session, or so I was told by Eric Underwood in 1982. There were former Antioch people like Turo and Anne de Grazia, David and Jeannie Baker, Monty and Audrey Greene, and Jeffrey and Pat Wakefield. There were veterans of the Holy Land: Bobby Houston, Ben Moss, Jerry the stonemason, and Therese herself. There were also many of the straight couples of the church, including Eric and Vonnie Underwood and Ed and Eleanor Kearney.

The organizational principles of Cursillo created new social bonds in the church, bringing together young and old and those from high and low church traditions. The Cursillistas were a special group, for they shared a precious secret. Since the power of the experience depended on surprise, Cursillistas were admonished not to recount details of their experience to others but to sponsor them to their own Cursillos. (It was not Turo de Grazia who gave me the outline I have excerpted above but one of his recruits whom I convinced that I was not a candidate.) The Cursillistas formed a clique within Mendocino Presbyterian, a clique anyone was free to join who would be willing to be implicated in its expanding chain of spiritual obligation. (Ed Kearney said that Monty Greene hounded him for years to make Cursillo. "He camped on my doorstep.") In lieu of Antioch Fellowship, Mendocino Presbyterian had a new agency of evangelism, but one that directed spiritual energies into the church itself.

New Wine

Though filled with evangelical energy and new members, the church in Mendocino was still a familiar institution. The venerable women's association was still a group of mostly elderly widows, who met for lunch every other week and planned for their yearly bazaar and other worthwhile activities. The main effect of the evangelical regime was to bring in more members. The Rotary club still met monthly in Preston Hall, though it, too, had many new members. The session, charged with the spiritual governance of the congregation, and the trustees, responsible for the legal and financial affairs of the corporate face of the church, maintained their respective roles in what institutionally was still the Presbyterian Church of Mendocino. There was always plenty of business to take care of—fire marshall codes to meet, purchases to authorize, salaries to adjust, reports to give, minutes to read, and the chronically inadequate water supply to worry over—and Eric Underwood was dependent on the routine good sense of his officers. The session continued to be a board of directors, as some of its newer, spirit-filled members such as Turo de Grazia complained. The traditional church structure was not abandoned.

What did happen to the structure is that it became the vehicle for the mobilization of new energies. Here are two examples. Daniel Whitman, about thirty, came to Mendocino with his growing family in the early 1970s. Trained as an architect, he started to build his own home (to become, within ten years, a showplace among owner-built dwellings on the north coast), and he decided to try to make his living as an independent designer and builder. Shortly after Eric Underwood began his Mendocino ministry, Whitman, not at the time a religious man, got a job making fire-code alterations in Preston Hall. The two men got acquainted there and, since both were young, professional, family men, became good friends over the next three years, frequently meeting for breakfasts and lunches. Whitman remembers Underwood's friendship as a case of "quiet, sweet evangelism," but he recalled that Underwood once conceded that it was difficult to have a part of life— his faith—that he couldn't share with a friend. Whitman's wife, Lesley, whose ancestral Methodism slept less soundly than her husband's Episcopalianism, got interested in Underwood's church and joined in 1975. She wanted her husband to share her faith, too.

Daniel gave in and joined the church in the fall of 1976, but at the time he thought of the church, he told me later, as a "social club, a service club, and an entertainment center." "My vows were shallow," he recalled. Yet they were sufficiently serious that he set himself to finding out more about what he'd gotten involved in. He became a regular churchgoer, read religious books, began to pray, signed up with Lesley for a year-long couples' koinonia group, and made his Cursillo. He found himself becoming a man of faith. A year after his shallow vows, he said yes to Underwood's plea that he go on session as Missions Chairman. In that capacity, he was instrumental in the church's decision to call an associate pastor for youth (which story is still to come). He formed a committee dedicated to local action on world hunger. (The result was the church's sponsorship of a large refugee family from Vietnam in 1979.) Later, he and his wife became leaders in the antiabortion movement on the north coast. Whitman has had no "road to Damascus" experience but he has become, through involvement in the round of evangelical and ecclesiastical activities, a pillar of the church and a leading Christian layman. "Having faith is having a higher energy level than not having faith," he told me, "and you have to work at keeping it high."

Maile Perrow, a former real-estate broker and wife of a semiretired dentist, moved to Mendocino in 1976. Nominally a Christian Scientist, she had had little religious involvement for years, but she was drawn to the Presbyterian church. So beautiful outside, it must be so on the inside, she thought, and she found inside a core of younger Christians, Dan Whitman included, whose "peace" and sense of values she envied. So she and her husband joined in 1977. Still, as she looked back from 1982, using an evangelical vocabulary she had adopted in the intervening years, "When I got up there and gave my life to Christ, I didn't know what I was doing. I only knew it *felt* good."

Sensing her willingness to become involved and recognizing her business experience, Underwood asked her to take up a trustee slot. She agreed but found she didn't like the job. "I'm not a money person," she told me. She did, however, discover that she enjoyed representing the church to the community (she later called it "witnessing") in fund-raising campaigns. So when the evangelism committee slot on session opened up, she readily agreed to switch her assignment. "I am a real estate broker," she told me. "It doesn't bother me to go into people's homes. I love it." But first she had to learn what evangelism was about, and only then, two years after joining the church, did she come to "know Christ" through koinonia and study groups, Cursillo, and her participation in each new-member class that Underwood offered. She is now a spirit-filled Christian, and her efficient evangelism committee helped continue through 1982 the pattern of membership growth set by Underwood in the mid-1970s.

The Presbyterian church had "magnetism," as they said in Mendocino. Some gathered for the evangelical message that Underwood preached. Others were drawn to Underwood himself. Still others, many of them erstwhile skeptics, found themselves attracted by the diverse body that had gathered around Underwood. In the case of each person, Underwood would try to find a form of participation

Table 7   Approximate Age Distribution of Mendocino Presbyterian Church Membership, 1972 and 1976

		Age Ranges						
		0–20	20–30	30–40	40–50	50–65	65+	Total
September 1972	%	3	8	15	15	31	28	100
(Pastor-seeking								
Committee Report)	N	(4)	(10)	(18)	(18)	(37)	(34)	(121)
June 1976	%	3	11	19	16	21	30	100
(Author's Tally)								
	N	(6)	(20)	(35)	(31)	(39)	(57)	(188)

Source: See note 6.

that would increase his or her religious commitment. It might be as small a thing as reading the scriptures at Sunday worship, or it might be a demanding job on session. Frequently, the performance of these roles by relative unknowns was a disappointment to Underwood and a perplexity to onlookers. ("What did Eric expect from the likes of him?") Yet many enlistees not only carried through on the job but— and this was Underwood's ulterior motive—got themselves more deeply involved in the life of the church. Taking such risks was one practical way Underwood witnessed to his faith.

Step of Faith: The Youth Ministry

By the middle of 1976, Mendocino Presbyterian Church was larger, stronger, and richer than at any time in its history. It was also younger. Compared to four years previously, before the call to Eric Underwood, there were twice as many young adults. (See table 7.)

From a statistician's point of view, table 7 leaves much to be desired.[6] The data are based on observers' knowledge, not questionnaire responses. The age ranges do not tell us where to place someone of exactly twenty, thirty, forty, fifty, or sixty-five years of age. Some of the ages, especially of persons over fifty, are guesswork. Combining two adjacent categories, however, it is clear that the number of persons in the age range of twenty to forty doubled between the informal survey done by the pastor-seeking committee in 1972 and my own tally of those who were members on bicentennial day.

Meeting the spiritual needs of young adults had been one of Larry

Redford's chief goals as chair of the pastor-seeking committee. On the copy of the church information form he annotated for candidate Eric Underwood, he circled the figures eight percent and fifteen percent under the age twenty-to-thirty and thirty-to-forty categories and wrote in the margin: "Eric: Note the obvious gap! This is where my heart is!!" With what unforeseen consequences for Redford and his fellowship this gap in young adults was filled we have seen. But the consequences for the church were just beginning to be felt, for adults between twenty and forty are likely to bear children.

Exactly how many young children were thus attached to the Presbyterian church in 1976 I do not know. Counting just the families I knew, there were over fifty dependent minors among the church families at that time. Birth announcements and infant baptisms had become common church events; appeals for infants' and children's good behavior during worship were frequently heard; and child-care costs were cited by trustees as factors to consider in decisions to hold concerts and other special events. That the church population was getting younger was obvious. Attending to the nurture of these young persons—so that they would bring happiness to their families and themselves lead happy lives; so that their parents' solemn responsibilities might be rightly discharged and they themselves might in due course become members of Christ's church—became Underwood's major unmet goal.

He had plenty of prodding. Shortly after he arrived in Mendocino, his new friends, the Kearneys, complained to him that the church and the community had "nothing for our boys," their three high-school–age sons. (Those sons did eventually have their conversions and join the church.) Jeffrey and Pat Wakefield, who had run a counterculture school before their conversion, told Underwood of the shock it was for their son to attend the public schools after their school folded and to find there, in the fourth grade, the germ of a nihilistic youth culture. The mother of a second grader was dismayed that babysitters coming to work in the afternoon directly from the high school would arrive at her house clearly stoned. Underwood was himself not entirely pleased with what his children picked up in school, once they came of school age. Shirley Grant brought her teenage children to Underwood's Thursday fellowship group out of the lack, it seemed to me, of any more wholesome local entertainment. The Matt and Elise affair could be cited by those who worried about loosely supervised young people growing up too fast. In truth, there were in the early 1970s precious few recreational outlets for Mendocino highschoolers other than those their own imaginations could provide. There was no bowling alley, no movie theater, no skating rink, no ice-cream parlor, no youth center. Many parents feared the kind of work that might be made for such idle hands, especially those who, like the Underwoods, had decided on the public schools over the evangelical alternative in Good Shepherd.

What did finally bear fruit for the youth program of Mendocino Presbyterian was the arrival in town of a couple named Bruce and Sara Douglas in 1976. As we have seen in chapter ten, Eric Underwood was relatively sparing among evangelicals in his acknowledgment of miracles, but he had no hesitation in seeing the hand of the Lord in the advent of Bruce Douglas, a young licensed Presbyterian minister and counseling psychologist, who showed up out of the blue on Underwood's doorstep that winter and announced that he and his family had come to settle in Mendocino County.

Meeting Bruce and Sara at Eric's home one night in the summer of 1976, I felt an immediate affinity with them. They, too, were college-educated (he at Stanford, she at Macalester, both as psychology majors) and cosmopolitan (having grown up in Chicago and served in the Peace Corps in Brazil). Bruce had a graduate divinity degree from the Presbyterian McCormick Seminary, where he had majored in pastoral counseling. Sara was a registered Montessori teacher. After their Peace Corps stint, reluctant to return to the United States, they lived for a while in Mexico. There they met another couple who told them of the inexpensive land available on the unspoiled redwood coast of California. Thus it was that they came to "homestead" a plot of land near Point Arena, forty miles down the tortuous coast highway from Mendocino, and to look for what employment could be found for teachers and psychologists in the county. Bruce had no intention of being a preacher, but he and Sara were told what other migrants to Mendocino had learned. If you wanted to work in Mendocino, you had to bring your own job.

My most immediate sense of camaraderie with Bruce and Sara was a shared amazement at the evangelical culture we had all so recently encountered in Mendocino. The Douglases were knowledgeable in matters of religion, he having a divinity degree and she having a Swiss father who knew his Bible, she said, as well as he knew his Latin. Both were Presbyterians, but it was a new experience for them to hear so many people talking about what the Lord had done in their lives. The man who had installed their phone (and mine, too), a "woman named Therese," and lovable Bobby Houston all bore witness to their faith in front of Bruce and Sara with the unself-conscious assurance of those who expect their message to be received as a matter of fact. Sara was used to hearing formal prayer offered for guidance and growth, but to hear someone pray earnestly that God might grant his family a Doberman pinscher (as she did at Underwood's prayer meeting the night I met her) was astonishing.

For Eric Underwood, the Douglases seemed promising as an answer to his prayers for a youth ministry. Bruce was a "licensed," but not ordained, Presbyterian minister. He had the right ecclesiastical credentials but did not need to be wooed away from another church position. His skills—pastoral counseling and group process—and his background (theologically and politically liberal) would complement Underwood's own. Sara was a teacher in the progressive but rigorous Montessori system, and she had plenty of church and Sunday-school stories from her youth to recount in evangelicals' conversations. The Douglases were both attractive, he in a ruddy, mesomorphic Scots-Irish way, she in a fair and willowy way. They were young, married, and had two children about to enter school. They were talented, at hand, and underemployed. What a godsend!

The timing could not have been better, for the Wakefield family was about to vacate Albion Chapel to pursue Jeffrey's education for the ministry. With their imminent departure, Underwood knew he had a vaguely defined position to fill and a spacious but ramshackle dwelling to offer. After sounding the matter out with a few elders—nobody but a longtime member of the Albion Chapel Committee wanting to bother very much about it—Underwood offered the Douglases the free rent of the chapel. They moved in as soon as the Wakefields left. Without making the matter fully explicit to the session, the Douglases, or even to himself, Underwood thought he might have found a youth pastor-in-training.

Underwood became a patron to the Douglases. He invited them to his Thursday fellowship group so that they might meet people and begin learning the evangelicals' vocabulary. He put in good words for them with prospective employers, and Sara was hired by the (secular) daycare co-op, which rented Preston Hall, while Bruce got a part-time job as a teacher's aide in the public schools. Then Underwood asked Bruce to fill the pulpit, as Jeffrey Wakefield had done on occasion, when he was to be out of town.

For Bruce Douglas to preach a sermon at Mendocino Presbyterian was less a matter of a favor to Eric Underwood—the church had a budget line for "pulpit supply" and candidates were usually at hand—than a challenge to Bruce himself. He would be on trial, for, seminary graduate though he was, he had never preached a sermon or even had a class in homiletics. He had been trained in the antiauthoritarian, the-minister-is-only-a-facilitator wake of the 1960s in a theologically liberal Presbyterian seminary, with counseling, not preaching, as a career goal.[7] The text for his first-ever sermon (in

October 1976) was to be the next installment in the series on Genesis that Underwood had begun in September, the story of Noah. What a fix! A theological liberal had to give his maiden sermon on the topic of Noah's flood in front of a congregation filled with both college graduates and prosaic Biblical literalists![8]

Bruce worked over the service. Underwood gave him the list of the sick to be prayed for, the joyous occasions—a new baby, the progressive dinner—to announce, and the scripture passage to be read, Genesis 6:5–22. He worried over the sermon and on Saturday morning was to be seen with pencil and paper, a Bible, coffee, and cigarettes in a Main Street restaurant. He decided to focus more on the end of the Noah story (Genesis 8:20–9:17, where God gives the sign of the rainbow as a reminder of his promise of a lawful order) and to skim over the building of the ark and the flood itself. He finished writing his sermon late Saturday night.

The service went well enough, although some complained that it was over too soon (11:40) because of Bruce's short sermon. The youth and adult choirs did lively numbers, the hymns were evangelical chestnuts ("Jesus, Savior, Pilot Me" and "Amazing Grace"), and Bruce's prayers and sermon successfully finessed the literalism/liberalism question by focusing on the enduring meaning of flood and rainbow as symbols. For those who listened attentively, Bruce presented a sophisticated, neoorthodox interpretation of the Noah story, but he read his tightly written text too hurriedly. Passages like this one, packed with allusions to Genesis and Galatians, whizzed over many heads:

> In Noah we have the seed of the covenant relationship which is formally established with Abraham: the rudimentary regulations laid down by Yahweh to Noah form the embryo of the Deuteronomic Code of which the Ten Commandments are the nucleus. The universal rainbow pledge of the Lord to preserve life on the planet is the forerunner of the more particular promise to Abraham and his children that "you shall be my people." The rainbow serves to remind us that we are remembered.

Yes, Bruce was nervous, but he did sound like a proper minister. And he also did something that Larry Redford used to do: open himself for public inspection. So just after the dense passage I have quoted, Bruce paused, slowed his pace, and said:

> I was tempted to close here at this historic juncture of reconciliation, when a new covenant is made between God and man, with the rainbow still shimmering overhead. Unfortunately, this isn't the end of the story. In the space of three verses we are back to business as usual. Noah is lying drunk and naked in his tent. How insidious is the temptation to

complacency following a heroic deed! How intoxicating is the self-righteousness which comes from having done a good job! How infinite are the possibilities for rationalizing a minor vice! I must confess to lying right there next to Noah, having used the occasion of writing this sermon to justify buying my first pack of cigarettes in several weeks.

The chuckles that greeted this confession expressed a wry recognition of Bruce's humanity as one who harbors a minor vice and, more to the point, one who lets his feelings of insecurity show.

Bruce Douglas won the affection of the congregation as an educated and open man more than he impressed them as a preacher. No matter. Eric Underwood did not need an assistant or a rival in the pulpit. He wanted a youth minister, and the sophistication and openness that Bruce showed in his first sermon were the ingredients in the success he was soon to enjoy as a group leader. That success, in turn, gave him the inside track for whatever mission Underwood might be able to persuade the session to undertake.

The Douglases first showed their talents in their leadership of a couples' Christian koinonia group beginning in October. For eight weeks, by consensual contract, seven couples met on Monday nights at Albion Chapel for an evening of what one called "techniques of Christian nuts-and-bolts," under the guidance of Bruce and Sara. The meetings had a prayer circle, an occasional communion, a great deal of open discussion, but most of all the freedom and encouragement to share feelings in an atmosphere of trust. Strong bonds were formed in this group along with an air of exclusive privilege, and one member once made a joke at Larry Redford's expense to the effect that the group could meet on Sunday morning and call itself a church. So lasting were those bonds that the group decided to continue on a series of eight-week contracts under a rotating leadership. A year after it began, the group was still meeting on Monday nights. Only one couple had dropped out, and two new ones (including Eric and Vonnie Underwood) had been added. The members of this group became Bruce's special constituency, and the core of it were just those young adults that had been so dear to Larry Redford.

Of the fourteen members, eight were veterans of Antioch Fellowship, including Turo de Grazia and Monty Greene, who had been Larry Redford's elders. All but two men, married to younger women, were in Redford's twenty-to-forty-year-old young-adult range. All had, or were soon to have, children, with ages from infancy to adulthood. Some had been married before. All but one were or were to become members of the Presbyterian church. And all of them would eventually make a Cursillo, sponsored by Turo de Grazia.

They were a culturally liberal, well-educated lot, several with advanced degrees, and most had reasonably high-status or professional careers: teacher, designer-builder, veterinarian, nurse, social worker. Several were recognized, successful artisans. Two couples enjoyed independent wealth. All had moved to Mendocino as adults. They were worldly evangelicals united by their independent yet collectively unanimous decisions to find a space for living in rural northern California, elective parochials, as I have called them. They joined in a fellowship that was deeper than that of the couples' club of the 1950s and yet more worldly than the intense prayer-and-Bible groups of Antioch Fellowship. This was the position that Eric Underwood had staked out between the legacy of the past and the insistent presence of Larry Redford. Bruce Douglas was to solidify it by fostering a vigorous constituency, and he was himself to benefit as members of this group came to champion him as a new youth minister.

To have at hand a qualified but underemployed Assistant Pastor candidate in Bruce Douglas became the keystone of Eric Underwood's strategy for getting such a position authorized by his cautious trustees. As always, Underwood worked "with the given." And—lest this account be burdened with gratuitous suspense—Bruce Douglas did become the new youth pastor. Yet it was nearly three years after arriving on the coast before Douglas received the appointment, and the wait was an agony for him and his family. The procedure of offering a job and choosing a candidate, when an active candidate was at hand giving shape to what the job would be, was no less awkward for the officers of the church. Underwood first persuaded the session in June of 1977 to establish a committee "to study the possible use of Bruce Douglas." That committee recommended in the fall that Douglas be hired on a quarter-time, temporary basis, to begin an otherwise unspecified ministry to junior-high and senior-high youth in Mendocino. The church's resulting financial commitment was only $2000, and Douglas's progress was to be evaluated the next June. Underwood was being more the prophet than the chronicler when, in his annual report to the congregation (January 1978), he called this action "a bold step of faith."

Douglas worked with students he had come to know through the public schools and through church families, and by the next spring he had brought together the nucleus of what came to be called the "Fellowship of the Carpenter." Meanwhile, Underwood was busy showing his "wish list" to one of the church's most committed and wealthy families. As a means of prodding what he saw as excessively conservative trustees and circumventing cumbersome processes, Underwood had regularly drawn up a "pastor's dream list" for the attention of those church supporters who preferred to target their contributions rather than pledge a weekly amount. One such family were the Pennings, the large clan surrounding the builder-architect who had been among Underwood's first recruits. Underwood knew that Andrew Penning's mother had recently died and that a gift in her memory would appeal to her deeply evangelical son. In March of 1978, the Ardis Penning Memorial Youth Fund, a $24,000 endowment providing partial salary support for a youth pastor, was received. This gift would have to be supplemented from other sources to make a full-time pastorate possible, but it was a substantial beginning. Income from the endowment was used to raise Bruce Douglas's employment as youth coordinator to half-time status later in the spring.

With such encouragement, Underwood and his session moved ahead. An ad hoc committee, consisting of the Christian Education, Worship, and Missions Committee elders, two of them veterans of the Douglases' couples' group, was appointed to study the youth ministry question. They, in turn, called a special meeting of the whole session for May 16. The session approved their recommendations and began the call for an assistant pastor. New committees were appointed and more meetings were scheduled. (There were to be fifteen session meetings, instead of the regular eight, between Easter and the end of the year.)

It was an elaborate organizational mobilization, yet it did not manifest the same level of popular involvement as had the period of revival in 1973–1976. Unlike those earlier days, when the church rode on a wave of evangelical enthusiasm generated first by Larry Redford and Jack Boyle and then by Eric Underwood's preaching, this was an unexciting, formal, tedious process of putting together the necessary forms and funds to meet a growing but not urgent need. Moreover, to insure that the Penning family be represented on the committee and that the search procedure be as little embarrassing to Bruce Douglas as possible, an *assistant* pastor-seeking committee was appointed, to be responsible to the session. (An *associate* pastor search would have required a committee elected by and responsible to the congregation.)

The job description was in part based on the activities Douglas had already taken on, working in the public schools, pastoring youth fellowships, and ministering to the Albion community. The fund-raising committee estimated that, counting on the Penning endowment and increased giving to be expected as a consequence of membership growth, the church's current membership would have to increase their pledges by $13,000 per year to meet the additional expenses of a youth pastorate, a substantial sum amounting to an increase of about two dollars per week per family.

The committee reports were ready in August, and the session planned what was frankly called "a public relations effort" to sell the idea to the congregation at large (whose dollars, not votes, were needed). For three weeks running, a "promotional and informative" talk was given during the Sunday worship hour. This campaign was climaxed by a Sunday afternoon congregational meeting and potluck dinner, at which carefully orchestrated speeches were given to dramatize the need for and feasibility of a youth ministry.

There was a certain strain about the potluck meeting—as if the question of "an Assistant Pastor" could be discussed without reference to Bruce Douglas—and the discussion was muted. The only decision made was to sever the long-standing but basically haphazard connection of the youth ministry to Albion Chapel. Albion Chapel would not be the Assistant Pastor's manse. Certainly the Douglases, if the job came to Bruce, would be happy to abandon the drafty old house and its wispy traditions.

Underwood's session forged on. A "stewardship" campaign was launched and an assistant pastor-seeking committee was instructed to begin its deliberations. The stewardship campaign featured a mailing to all church members and supporters. It included a job description, a proposed budget, and a covering letter from the pastor.

"Dear Church Family," Underwood wrote. "Writing this letter is an exciting step of faith for me. I believe it to be the most important communication I have ever written to you. At long last, we're ready to expand our ministry." He mentioned the Penning bequest, prayerful study, and a summer full of meetings as the solid groundwork behind the decision. He went on:

> This is a bold step for us which will involve a substantial increase in our 1979 church budget, but we believe that the current teen generation of this community needs the support of our church. Our call to Christian stewardship will not allow us to ignore their need; to do so would give the Devil carte blanche. . . .

> And now we come to you . . . the people of God, Mendocino Branch. It will not happen with our current level of giving. . . .

> Please prayerfully seek God's guidance in what you can do for the work of Christ in Mendocino this year. . . .

The proposal was well-planned, financially detailed, and filled with a barrage of religious symbols. The results were encouraging to the session. By the end of the year, the number of pledging "units" (families and individuals) was up from 113 to 131, and the amount pledged was up by $18,900, more than sufficient to meet the anticipated budget increment. Even in that year of rapid inflation, the real dollar amount pledged was up thirty percent.

The pastor search was more difficult. A part-time, temporary youth minister being on the scene made the organizational commitment easier because it was more plausible. But his presence made the work of the search committee awkward and frustrating. On the one hand was Bruce Douglas, a real person known to all with considerable qualifications and obvious limitations. On the other hand were, by November, upwards of thirty dossiers of many able-sounding candidates, whose qualifications were emphasized and whose limitations were obscured by the highly refined procedures of formal resumes and polite letters of recommendation.

In churches, as in businesses and universities, those with a job to offer can use their imaginations to conjure up ideal candidates: shrewd but fair administrators, charismatic teachers who are brilliant scholars, dynamic preachers who can relate to shy adolescents. Mendocino's job description committee knew this and concluded its specification of the responsibilities of the assistant pastor with these words: "If the candidate can sing tenor, play a guitar, and walk on water, we would all be very happy." Bruce Douglas could play a guitar, but had a shaky baritone and was insufficiently spirit-filled for some of the evangelicals. He was certainly no street evangelist. As the man on the scene, he had the inside track for the job, but one would not envy his position.

The search committee had several Douglas partisans: the superintendent of schools, who had worked with him; Dan Whitman, alumnus of the couples' group, who resigned the chairmanship of the search committee when it became clear that a genuinely open search would be conducted; and two high-school students, a boy and a girl, who were already members of Douglas's Fellowship of the Carpenter. Three other elders were willing to look at other candidates. Andrew Penning, architect and benefactor, was, along with Eric Underwood, most deeply committed to the youth pastor concept and most willing to use the job opening to go after the very strongest candidate. There were no fundamentalists or veterans of Antioch Ranch or The Land. Douglas had his fingers crossed.

The committee met for four months, into January 1979, before recommending Douglas to the session. There was the matter of getting a new chairman for the committee. There were the many dossiers, some of which needed supplementation by mail. Favorites emerged, and there was by December a short list of three to be seen in person. Interviews and trial sermons were scheduled.

Douglas could claim credit for recruiting and coordinating adult leadership for the new youth group and for directing a "junior church" on Sunday mornings. He had plans to establish separate junior and senior high-school church groups and a drop-in center for community young people. (He called these ideas, respectively, "hard" and "soft" outreach, the former involving prayer and other religious activities, the latter involving only the minimal expectation of civility on the part of young participants.) Unlike some other candidates, he was married, and despite the formal rules the committee knew that, were he to get the job, Sara could be expected to provide Christian education leadership.

Finally, the competition came down to one other candidate. He looked good. He was dynamic, evangelical, and experienced in youth ministry in a way Douglas was not. So the committee set up a trial sermon at a church near Santa Rosa, some members with high expectations and Douglas supporters with foreboding. But the sermon was a bomb—pedantic, fundamentalist, and delivered with a lisp—and Douglas, weak though he was to the evangelicals on preaching and the Bible, was in. The long wait was over when the session voted in February to make him Assistant Pastor. An Easter-size crowd of 273 attended his ordination service in April. A year later, the congregation promoted him to Associate Pastor.

When Douglas reflected for the annual report on his first year as ordained minister, he thought of the passage in Isaiah. "They that wait upon the Lord shall renew their strength, they shall mount up with wings as eagles." Underwood said of Douglas that "his many gifts are being used fully. Sara's added strength in the Church School we didn't count on. As they say on the Ridge, 'What a blessing!' I personally breathe a little easier because of their presence."

Members of the freshman class at Mendocino High School in 1978 could join, for the first time in nearly two decades, a social, discussion, and service club under adult supervision and church sponsorship. That winter, a columnist in the local weekly, herself a Presbyterian Church member and a fervent crusader against teenage drug use, but no evangelical, wrote:

> If I were a parent and had a teenage kid, I would use whatever parental clout I might have to urge him/her to get into the youth group over at the Presbyterian Church. . . . It's not religion, per se, that the people working with youth over at MPC are pushing. They are trying to put

into an attractive context, along with good, clean fun, and the help of religion, the steps by which young people can build toward fruitful, rewarding lives.

Many kids did join the group, though hardly a major percentage of the town's high schoolers. Some were children of church members but most were not. Some went on to confirmation classes and baptism in the Big River. By the spring of 1983, the proportion of church members who were minors had doubled.

Impact Outside the Church

During the 1960s, Peter Hsu had tried to impress on the church session the view that "the church is a servant to the community." "Our church exists for mission," he had said. But Larry Redford, when it came his turn to shape the church, wanted a "New Testament Church." The mission of the church, he said, is the church itself. Hsu and Redford, both radicals in the context of Mendocino, looked in opposite social directions—the one outward, the other inward. In 1973, Mendocino Presbyterian took Redford's direction and became much stronger in numbers, in dollars, and in the mobilization of commitment. To what goals was this new strength directed? Let us look at the church's stewardship of its material wealth, its buildings and its budget, in the years of Underwood's pastorate.

The call to a new, theologically conservative minister was voted on the same day that five new members were elected to session, three women and two men, three Republicans and two Democrats, all of them affluent, well educated, and articulate. Two of them, the men, were elected trustees, and they immediately set about developing a policy statement that would protect the tax-free status of church properties by guaranteeing their specifically religious function. Soon after Underwood's arrival in the spring of 1973, the trustees called a special congregational meeting after church one Sunday to pass an amendment to the bylaws of the corporation. The amendment began with these words: "The property and assets of this corporation are irrevocably dedicated to religious purposes, and the corporation is organized solely for non-profit purposes." It specified procedures to be used in the event of the dissolution of the corporation, and it cited section 501 (c)(3) of the Internal Revenue Code and the Book of Discipline of the United Presbyterian Church in the United States of America. It was a very formal document, manifesting the hand of Edward Kearney, the lawyer newly elected to the trustees. The congregation required all of five minutes to discuss and pass this provision.

Informants who served on session in the years since the opening of Preston Hall gave different assessments of the possibility that the church properties might be taxed. Some related thirdhand accounts of churches that lost property-tax exemptions because of nonreligious activities. Others told of guidelines issued by denominational executives. The formal records of the church tell at best a sketchy, only partly consistent story. Mark Kimmerly was convinced, he told me, that the threat to Preston Hall's tax deduction was real, that the redneck sergeant was ready to take him to court over the use of church properties, and that nonetheless, he, Kimmerly, was ready to defy threats in the name of Christian witness. Eric Underwood, on the other hand, thought the tax threat was spurious and was used by conservatives to deny building use to causes they disliked. But those serving as trustees seem to have passed down year to year the norm that preserving the tax exemption of the properties under their care was their uppermost responsibility.

Thus the formal "not for profit" wording joined the "volatile issue" provision passed five years earlier to provide the Preston Hall committee with official, invocable guidelines for the case-by-case determination of Preston Hall use. Other buildings, including a refurbished barn called Toad Hall on the Comptche Road, were becoming available to the counterculture population for dances and meetings. Meanwhile, the American participation in the Vietnam war had come to an end. For these reasons, among others, *no further disputes over politically controversial uses of Preston Hall are recorded after Underwood's ministry began.* That the hall belonged to the church and that the church could legitimately impose limits on its use became accepted principles. In this way the church reestablished a boundary between itself and the community.

This provision did not always work to the advantage of conservatives. Rock dances and alcohol were disallowed. Benefit concerts and art shows were allowed in general, but no one was supposed to make a profit. One seemingly arbitrary result of this policy was that the Rotary Club's benefit auction of donated local artists' work became a highly successful annual event, but, after a couple of shows, the Mendocino Woodworkers Guild exhibition had to find other quarters. Proceeds from the former event went to a youth campership fund, whereas those from the latter went to the participating individual craftsmen. The backwoods craftsmen were, however, benefited by free use of the hall for a meeting in 1975 to organize a response to the county building department's drive to enforce the building code retroactively against substandard owner-occupied dwellings. But Daniel Whitman, elder and chair of the missions committee, found that he could not screen a prolife, antiabortion movie in Preston Hall without, according to the 1968 policy, a spokesperson for the prochoice side. When none volunteered, the movie was cancelled. Groups considered worthy were favored by rent-free use of the hall. The Citizens Advisory Planning Board, a county-mandated local committee with responsibility to air views on a proposed county plan, was one. Antioch Fellowship itself, when its meetings outgrew the Redford's living room during 1975–1976, was another.

It was use of the sanctuary that sparked controversy and dissension within the congregation as the question of Preston Hall was settled. Mendocino musicians thought of the Presbyterian sanctuary as acoustically the best hall in town, and, beginning in 1976, there were frequent requests to use it for concerts. After an obnoxious performance by a pseudoprophetic gospel-rock singer offended liberals (including me) and some decidedly nonevangelical words of commentary accompanying a performance of Carl Orff's *Carmina Burana* offended conservatives, the session declared a vague, but unmistakably establishmentarian, policy that musical events to be held in the sanctuary should express "the spirit of the Christian church." That decorum more than doctrine was at issue became clear to me when during a Friday visit to the sanctuary in 1982 I happened upon a rehearsal for an elaborate, traditional bar mitzvah to be held there the next day, the small Mendocino Jewish community lacking a synagogue. What was to go on in the sanctuary was to be "religious."

In sum, the church's stewardship of its facilities after 1973 moved away from "political" involvement and back toward the more neutral "religious," "charitable," and "civic" functions that American local churches have carved out for themselves since the nineteenth century. Such activities effectively endorsed rather than upset the extant social order, but the social order of Mendocino and its church in the 1970s was, partly as a result of the leadership of Peter Hsu and Mark Kimmerly, more liberal, more cosmopolitan, more socially inclusive than it had been a decade earlier. If the newly traditional policy were in some sense more conservative than the one it supplanted, it nonetheless did not have the effect of attracting back into the church the reactionaries who, embittered and disgusted, had left it in the 1960s. In my thorough search of church records, I have found that *the only old-line conservatives who welcomed Underwood's regime were those who had toughed out the days of Hsu and Kimmerly.* Those who left did not return. Underwood consolidated even if he did not extend the social changes of the 1960s.

What, finally, did the church do with its money? It is clear that it had a great deal more money. The increased attendance in 1973 and years following brought first a windfall of unpledged contributions to the plate (what church budgets, in seeming despair, call "loose offering"), then more generous gifts from extant members, and finally new members whose pledges could become the basis for greatly expanded but fiscally sound yearly budgeting. It took time for the trustees to adjust to these upward curves, so often had the church been on the financial edge in the past, and they tended for several years to underestimate the forthcoming year's receipts. We have seen how systematically Underwood pushed the assistant pastor commitment in the face of such caution. Earlier, he had persuaded the trustees to update their end-of-year budget planning with a regular midsummer adjustment, so confident he was that income would grow. Indeed, in real dollars, dollars corrected for inflation, the church's budget quadrupled in Underwood's ten-year ministry. In inflated dollars, church receipts were ten times higher in 1982 than in 1972.

As with any organization, most funds are solidly committed well in advance, and room for discretionary allocation is small. In Mark Kimmerly's days, more than three-fourths of church income went for the pastor's and custodian's salaries, insurance, utilities, and taxes. There was very little left over for educational and musical materials and for contributions to Presbyterian judicatories. But as an organization gets wealthier, it lives less of a hand-to-mouth existence and can commit greater resources, both absolutely and relatively, to concerns beyond its own maintenance. Still, a larger organization has higher routine costs. At Mendocino Presbyterian, for example, the financial well-being brought by Underwood's regime made possible the realization of long-standing goals, hiring a secretary and a custodian (both were part-time). Underwood was also paid much better than his predecessors, the skimpiness of whose salaries had occasioned comment at Presbytery, and by 1975 the trustees, under the urging and support of Ed Kearney, made it possible for him to move out of the manse and buy a house of his own. (The "manse allowance" added to his salary was partly financed by renting out the old manse on the local market.) By 1979, the church was strong enough to double its ministerial staff by calling an associate pastor for youth.

Salaries, insurance, utilities, and taxes—as relatively fixed, slowly growing expenditures—still consumed the greater part of the church's budget under Underwood, but that part had dropped from nearly eighty to around fifty-five percent of the budget, thus allowing an absolutely and relatively larger allocation of money to other causes. Most prominent among those causes were the local and world missions

of the church, with greatly increased allocations to higher judicatories—Presbytery, Synod, and General Assembly—of the national
Presbyterian Church.

Table 8 gives details of this story, including dollar figures for total
church spending for years since 1964, derived from internal church
records.[9] For 1964 and 1966 through 1982, it reports, in nominal dollars, real 1967-value dollars, and as a proportion of total spending,
amounts allocated to two budget categories. The first is the "Ministerial Compensation" package, including salary, housing allowances,
pension contribution, health insurance, and other fringe benefits. The
second is "Denominational Support," a sum of funds contributed up
the denominational hierarchy as statutory per-capita dues, discretionary support for judicatory programs, subscriptions to the denominational magazine, and yearly special offerings for the denomination's
"One Great Hour of Sharing" and the ministerial pension fund,
among other extracongregational, denominationally administered programs. (Mendocino church's occasional contributions to nondenominational causes, including evangelical missions, are not included.)
The comparisons are striking. All of the dollar figures, nominal and
real, are much larger under Underwood's evangelical regime. Moreover, the proportion of the budget allocated to denominational support was, on the average, twice as high under Underwood as under
Kimmerly, and even higher than the figures for the two years of Hsu's
ministry for which I have data from the church's own records. Correspondingly, the proportion for ministerial compensation, even after
an assistant pastor was added in 1979, is lower.

Table 9 reports similar but less detailed data derived from denominational records comparing financial commitments for the past five
pastorates at Mendocino Presbyterian.[10] Each figure represents the
total dollar contributions to the denomination as a proportion of the
total dollar receipts of the church treasurer, an "index of fiscal cosmopolitanism." This index is low during the pastorates of Althorpe and
Kimmerly, because of heavy building fund expenses, but higher in
the prosperous 1950s than at the lean end of the sixties. The index is
high for the pastorates of Higginson and Hsu, and highest of all for
Underwood's years. Using these financial reports as an index of
intracongregational or parochial versus extracongregational or cosmopolitan commitment, we reach the ironic but not unpredictable result
that *the parochially inclined evangelical regime of Eric Underwood was four
times as heavily committed to the wider church as Kimmerly's church, and a
third again as much as Hsu's church.* In absolute dollar amounts, the
evangelicals' commitment to the denomination was even greater, so
much larger were their resources.

Table 8 MPC Selected Financial Commitments

Year	Pastorate	Total Spending[a]	Ministerial compensation[b]			Denominational support[c]		
			Amount	1967 $s[d]	% T.S.	Amount	1967 $s[d]	% T.S.
1964	PH	$ 5,987	$ 5,987	$ 6,442	55.9	$ 866	$ 932	8.1
1965	PH	N/A				N/A		
1966	PH	11,939	6,492	6,680	54.4	1,215	1,250	10.2
1967	MK	14,953	6,402	6,402	43.9	846	846	5.8
1968	MK	13,484	6,937	6,660	51.4	674	674	5.0
1969	MK	16,155	7,897	7,194	48.9	931	848	3.3
1970	MK	20,804	8,709	7,490	41.9	741	637	3.6
1971	MK	17,706	9,001	7,417	50.8	769	634	4.3
1972	MK	15,840	8,017	6,406	50.6	801	640	5.1
1973	EU	24,935	N/A			N/A		
1974	EU	38,983	13,374	9,068	34.3	4,656	3,157	11.9
1975	EU	53,134	19,099	11,860	35.6	4,620	2,869	8.7
1976	EU	60,976	23,746	13,939	38.9	7,586	4,453	12.4
1977	EU	70,840	24,816	13,674	35.0	8,957	4,935	12.6
1978	EU	77,875	26,750	13,696	34.3	10,617	5,436	13.6
1979	EU+BD	120,242	44,225	20,388	36.8	13,192	6,082	11.0
1980	EU+BD	147,168	49,264	20,001	33.5	11,855	4,813	8.1
1981	EU+BD	162,244	58,110	21,326	35.8	13,397	4,917	8.3
1982	EU+BD	171,265	64,880	22,578	37.9	16,261	5,659	9.5

a. From session records
b. Salaries, housing and utility allowance, pension, health, travel, etc.
c. Per capita tax, general mission, special offerings
d. Using "Purchasing Power of the Dollar," from *Statistical Abstract of the United States*

Table 9   Index of Fiscal Cosmopolitanism[a]

Years	1955–1957	1958–1961	1962–1966	1967–1972	1973–1981
Pastorate	Althorpe	Higginson	Hsu	Kimmerly	Underwood
Index	.057	.104	.084	.029	.115

[a]Proportion of Total Congregational Receipts allocated to Presbytery, Synod, and General Assembly. From United Presbyterian Church General Assembly statistical report. See note 9.

The point is not that Underwood was a closet liberal, much less that Hsu or Kimmerly and their allies were hypocrites. It is that when we look at deeds as well as sentiments we find that what the church could not afford—*while remaining a church*—in the liberal 1960s, it could afford in the evangelical 1970s: generous support of its liberal parent denomination. Hsu's congregation was generous with its contributions to the denomination. Kimmerly and his congregation had to sacrifice even more to restore the church properties. But Underwood's larger congregation was motivated to give yet more, and causes dearer to Hsu and Kimmerly than to Underwood himself were among the beneficiaries of their largesse.

Reflective church leaders are understandably wary of judging churches solely by their growth rate.[11] A church is not a business firm. Yet, according to James R. Wood, whose study of Indianapolis churches was cited in chapter two, "a church that had most of its resources committed to salaries and building maintenance would have little left to spend on social action even if its members desired such action."[12] Clark Roof and his associates, in a study of over a thousand Presbyterian congregations in 1975, found that "growing churches appear to be achieving other goals a bit better than those that are stable or declining in membership."[13]

The church in Mendocino grew because of the evangelical preaching of its pastor. That growth brought nearer to realization not only evangelical goals of spirit-filled worship and popular biblical literacy. It also made possible a nondoctrinaire ministry to the town's young people, the resettlement in the United States of eleven Chinese refugees from Vietnam, and much-appreciated support of its beleaguered parent denomination. Mendocino's achievement was cited in a commendatory letter received from the Presbytery in 1978. Citing the extraordinary growth in membership and mission contributions, the letter praised Underwood's "enthusiastic Christian leadership" and his congregation's "faithful dedication to mission." "It is hoped that your example will be an inspiration to all other pastors and congregations" in the area.

Both at the local and at the cosmopolitan levels, the tangible social effect of Underwood's evangelical revival was the bolstering of pluralistic institutions. To a very great extent, the church was doing better what both Peter Hsu and Larry Redford wanted it to do, though neither could have been fully pleased with the result.

Conclusion: Of Wine and Wineskins

It follows that resurgence of an authoritative Christian ethic across American society can occur only with the revitalization and growth of congregational if not sectarian organizations. For they carry the sort of powerful ritual experience, affective communal ties, and prophetic leadership such an ethic requires.
—Steven M. Tipton, *Getting Saved From the Sixties*

Mendocino and its people, being real, are unique. I know of no other persons quite like the blithe but dedicated Peter Hsu, the principled but nurturant Mark Kimmerly, the committed but indecisive Larry Redford, or the affable but guarded Eric Underwood. I will never forget thoughtful Jeannie, vital Arturo, fanatic Ben, or bubbly Sol.

Though there are other living museums soaked in history and overrun by newcomers—Leadville, Colorado; Galena, Illinois; Harpers Ferry, West Virginia—I know of no place other than Mendocino where you find the particular combination of sea and mountains and straights and hippies, with a century-old English Gothic church bursting at the seams with new recruits. I know of no other small-town white church whose complacency was challenged by a nonwhite pastor only to have the helm of its leadership grabbed by evangelicals and his dropouts replaced manyfold by their recruits. At a minimum, this book is the story of that singular mixture.

The precise trajectory of Mendocino Presbyterian undoubtedly has no parallel. Yet it is only within the particular that the general resides, and the experience of Mendocino does teach lessons about our society. Demographic factors about which we can generalize—birth, death, and migration rates—played their parts. Nationwide cultural currents—ethnic identification, political protest, drug use, sexual freedom, small-town nostalgia—had their impact. Familiar patterns of social organization—the perquisites of land ownership, education, age, and gender; the exigencies of work and parenthood; the authority of government and formal organization—had their place. Since our interest is understanding Protestant churches, the most important elements in the story are those introduced in chapter two, the concepts of the theological divide between evangelicalism and liberalism and the formal contrast between nascent and institutional religion.

Two Dimensions, Four Types, Twenty Years

We distinguished between evangelicalism and liberalism as two opposed theological parties in American Protestantism and hazarded a few summary characterizations of these two tendencies. Evangelicals differ among themselves on the nature of Biblical authority and on the priority given to evangelism, so the heart of their theological position boils down to their Christology. For the evangelical, Jesus Christ is a living savior whom one must acknowledge publicly. The other party, the liberals, also attempt to spread the message of Christ but think that "naming the name" of Jesus is less important than changing people's worldly circumstances for the better.[1] If for the evangelical Jesus is the savior, for the liberal he is a teacher, a model, a prophet. The liberals' Christ does not insist on being worshipped and would be outraged were he to know of those who use his name in support of narrowness and bigotry.

The liberal-evangelical contrast amounts more to a sociological than a logical contradiction. The one side is united by its theology, the other by its social ethics, and each side recognizes its unity by its use of common symbols. It is possible for an individual to be both liberal and evangelical, as Peter Hsu has told me about himself. Formal theologies and individual beliefs of religious professionals and activist laity do not neatly coincide with the theological party lines, but group affinities within contemporary white American Protestantism do. Thus Mark Kimmerly's deepest theological beliefs were neoorthodox rather than liberal, but his commitments to the social causes of the 1960s, *for which he is remembered in Mendocino*, mark him as a liberal. Peter Hsu's Chinatown Presbyterian upbringing combined salvationism with activism, but it was the latter with which he challenged the Mendocino congregation. The evangelical Eric Underwood differed with the fundamentalist Larry Redford on the issue of Biblical creationism, but they each spoke of Jesus Christ as "personal savior" and were thus recognized as preachers of the same message, a message that differed from that of Hsu and Kimmerly.

Similarly, each party recognizes the other by slogans rather than by full, complex theologies. Mark Kimmerly recognized Eric Underwood's evangelicalism by its "stilted language." Peter Hsu could judge the Mendocino church twenty years after leaving it to be "miles to the right of where it was in the '60s," not because of Bruce Douglas's "soft outreach" to town youth and the church's generous support of its parent denomination, but because of the evangelical language used in its newsletters.[2] Similarly, conservative parishioners objected to Peter Hsu's "changing" religion because he spoke the language of prophecy instead of pastoral care.

Both the liberal and the evangelical strains within American Protestantism have their "institutional" and "nascent" forms, so our second distinction was one of form. Institutional religiosity, the religiosity of the "church," is part of a bargain made with secular society. It can have many ideological tendencies. Richly robed clergymen can express generally liberal or generally conservative sentiments in institutional services, but they know it is risky to be specific. Religion is afforded the autonomy of being a differentiated institution within the whole society in exchange for its recognition of its proper place.[3]

In extraordinary times, however, religion breaks out of its structured boundaries to invade the world or be invaded by it. In such periods, religiosity is "nascent," striving not to accommodate to the society but to compete with it or transform it. Not content to utter stereotyped religious formulae, those in the nascent state take risks with their lives. Peter Hsu took a pastorate in a town not known for its hospitality to Chinese, and Larry Redford quit his tenured teaching job to be a full-time worker for Christ in a "faith ministry." Hsu and Redford and others like them insist that God demands specific actions to be taken.

One controversial point I have made is that the nascent strain in American Protestantism can be theologically conservative. It appeared not only on the side of the left and it contributed not only to the drive for social justice. It also mushroomed on the religious right, and it has contributed to a renewed emphasis on the family and interpersonal relationships. The action in American Protestantism is not the one-dimensional dilemma between "comforting" and "challenging" religion.[4] It is the two-dimensional swing between ideological poles and between institution and movement.

Combining the categories of theological party and religious form gave us our map, or typology, of American Protestant tendencies (see fig. 11), where we used the convenient labels for each of the four types provided by David Roozen and his associates.[5] Though the typology is simplified, it does distill lasting tendencies.

1. Institutional liberalism, the "civic" orientation, is the churchly religion of mainstream American Protestantism. Although traditional Christian symbolism is used in worship, the meaning of this symbolism is "demythologized," subtly in sermons and ritual, overtly in seminaries. Its religious content is primarily a matter of social ethics, though its institutional form allows for considerable attention to be paid also to aesthetics. It is in institutional liberal churches that one regularly hears sermons that use religious symbolism and secular learning to urge greater attention to the welfare of society on the part of the congregation.

The strengths of the civic orientation are several. Its morality appeals to cosmopolitans, and its muted theism is conformable to educated tastes. Its weaknesses are also significant. Those to whom it most strongly appeals are not, in general, strongly drawn to churches. Being identified more by its ethics than its theology, it is vulnerable to those secular radicals who would urge it to live up to its standards. Being ambivalent about its symbolism, it is vulnerable to entropy.[6]

The civic orientation was the dominant Protestant religiosity of the 1950s and thrives in many churches today, but it was put on the defensive by sixties radicals and the backlash against them. In Mendocino, it was the orientation of Frederick Althorpe and later of Mark Kimmerly. A man whose theology put him in the center but whose politics put him on the left, Kimmerly was buffeted by both sides and distinguished his approach from that of the vigorous activist who preceded him only by the greater attention he gave to the congregation's pride in its architectural heritage.

2. Nascent liberalism, the "activist" orientation, was the religion of the prophetic clergy of the 1960s. Activists wanted to take the secularized religious ethic out of the churches and into the world. They felt that there could be no justification for the walls of the sanctuary when the symbols therein had been demythologized, and they knew that Christ made his manifestation in the streets, the lettuce fields, and the rice paddies. They shook up the FBI, the City of Chicago, California agribusinessmen, and local draft boards, and are now giving a hard time to the Immigration and Naturalization Service and corporations investing in South Africa. In Mendocino, Peter Hsu made the Rumford Act and the Vietnam War into local issues, and he openly offered the hand of his friendship to town leftists.[7]

The strengths of nascent liberalism are its manifest courage and its ideological consistency. These people put their money, their feet, their time, and their reputations where their mouths are. But activism suffers an inherent weakness. Ready to see "the Christ" in the unfortunates of society, activists risk disillusionment with a chosen representative.[8] If Black Power, Angela Davis, or the National Liberation Front were eventually perceived (rightly or wrongly) to have feet of clay, the activists could easily be blamed for their shortcomings. In Mendocino, the legitimacy of Peter Hsu's cultural progressivism was shaken by a sexual scandal in 1965. He had no more to do with its occurrence than Eric Underwood did with Elise's love for Matt in 1976, but he was blamed in a way that Underwood was not.

The greatest vulnerability of Christian activism is that it is enmeshed in organizations dedicated to Christian worship. Conservative rhetoric of "God," "salvation," and "faith" has more currency in such places than talk of "human values," "justice," and "service," which occupies the high ground of secular discourse. Thus, in Mendocino, the nascent evangelicals, led by Larry Redford, took the ground of relevance and challenge right out from under the weakened liberals.

3. Nascent evangelicalism, the "evangelist orientation," was what I discovered when I went to Mendocino. Many Americans, and even many commentators on religion, are evidently under the impression that evangelicals live in, or want to live in, another world.[9] This characterization may have been accurate early in this century, but it is not today, and evangelicals can be as "relevant," engaged, and courageous as the liberal new breed of the 1960s. Nascent evangelicals have taken over mainline congregations and have brought new energy to the Catholic church. They have frightened mass-media executives, taken credit for defeating Senatorial candidates, challenged local school boards, and sent chills up the spines of denominational bureaucrats.[10] In Mendocino, they brought the minister of their choice to a vacant pulpit, and they set up an alternative Christian school. They were not "pie in the sky when you die" Christians.

The most obvious strength of nascent evangelicalism is its capacity for popular mobilization under the power of divine sanction. Its religious exercises have the vitality of Woodstock and the teach-ins.

The weaknesses of the evangelist orientation are equally tangible. Existing in a world populated by ordinary humans and dominated by an alien secular culture, nascent evangelicals must withdraw from that culture, in the Old Amish manner; compete on unequal terms against it, as the Redfords did; or finally compromise with it, as did most of the Antioch membership. Americans seem to want the benefits of modern medicine, higher education, and social mobility for their children if not for themselves, and these benefits come at the cost of accepting the secular world's terms. Nonetheless, for all the inevitable compromise middle-class American evangelicals face, there is still a hidden strength in their theology. Rejecting human self-sufficiency and looking to a supernatural deity, they can be insulated from disillusionment with human institutions.

4. If liberal critics have any one tendency in mind when they scorn the religion of "comfort," it is institutional evangelicalism, the "sanctuary orientation," which can be uncharitably called the religion of a God who has been kicked upstairs. The sanctuary orientation is more than that, however. Its worship can unabashedly indulge in both the traditional symbols of Christianity (the nativity, the cross, the resurrection, the conversion of Saul) and in the majesty of churchly trappings. Visiting a sanctuary church during Advent or Holy Week, one encounters a well-orchestrated presentation of the sacred realm, without a hint of the embarrassment one senses in liberal churches. Evangelical sermons can employ the scriptures not only as a repository of wisdom and a goad to action but also as the source of wonderful, half-familiar stories lying at the foundation of Western culture, to be recalled and elaborated in loving detail.

The strengths of the sanctuary orientation are its symbolic consistency and its willingness to meet humble religious needs. Moreover, its spiritual individualism is closer to American civic culture than is the sociologism of the liberal party, so it is useful to those who have a stake in the social status quo.[11] Its institutional state means that it is unlikely, except in extremity, to meddle directly in public affairs, and its evangelicalism means that when it does so it is less likely to rock the distributional boat than to call for moral renewal. Even in the hands of a lifelong Democrat like Eric Underwood, it is frequently conservative by default. I was disappointed that Underwood failed to speak out on behalf of Mendocino's hippie street vendors in 1977 when their livelihood was threatened by local shop owners. I knew that he was reluctant to enter secular disputes, and I imagined that he might have more understanding than I of the reasons the shopkeepers sought restrictive legislation, but I wanted him to side with the obvious underdog on a local matter. So far as I know, he said nothing.

The sanctuary orientation is thus vulnerable to the charge that it is not worthy of the attention of serious people. Under the impression that the United Presbyterian Church has moved toward institutional evangelicalism, John Fry, nascent liberal par excellence, wrote a stinging rebuke:

What the church and women do in their "place" is the trivial, boring, necessary but necessarily *secondary* tasks of nurture and support. To be "feminine" and to be "religious" amount to the same thing; to be banned from anything real and important. . . . The United Presbyterian Church as a corporate entity must be counted *honorary girls* in the American society, thus ending with the worst of both worlds: bemused condescension from the inhabitants of man's world and disgust from the women who are just now waging a momentous fight with male supremacy.[12]

The need for self-respect among middle-class evangelicals is thus a strain pulling them toward engagement with the world. Eric Underwood worked very hard to get his church to finance a youth ministry. Dan Whitman and Jeffrey Wakefield got involved in the world hunger campaign. Some evangelicals have joined the nuclear-freeze movement.

There are other options than these four types, and the four cells themselves are not watertight compartments. The Roman Catholic Church has combined all four types for centuries, since its sacred orders provide a place for those in the nascent state and its celibate priesthood serves the religious dependency needs of the laity while some priests are thus freed to act as prophets in the world. American black Protestantism and leftist fellowships like Sojourners belie the notion that evangelicalism must be politically conservative, and Pat Robertson refutes the idea that it is inevitably politically quiescent.[13] Neoorthodoxy may provide an answer for those who wish to affirm traditional symbols but not withdraw into social conservatism and irrelevance. In Mendocino, the mystical and aesthetic Cursillo movement helped bridge the gap between evangelicals and liberals, allowing the former to embrace the ethics of the latter and the latter to be moved emotionally by the religion of the former.

Yet the strains I have outlined do beset and typify American Protestantism, and this book has shown how they were played out in Mendocino. There is a tension between the church being in harmony with the secular culture (without which it has little resonance for modern persons) and being symbolically distinct (without which it tends to dissipate into the surrounding culture). There is a tension between the church's transcendence of the here and now (without which it courts defeat and disillusionment) and its relevance for everyday life (without which it becomes merely formal and vacuous).

In 1960, Mendocino Presbyterian Church had fairly well embraced the culture; it was the Protestants' place in town. It was not narrow and self-indulgent ("particularistic"), but it was nonetheless a social club, membership in which came more or less automatically ("ascriptively") with Protestant birth. With the call to Peter Hsu and the nearly simultaneous outbreak of the civil-rights movement in California and the south, its latent universalism was mobilized. The church got into competition with secular forces to determine the political direction of the state and the nation, forthrightly under Peter Hsu and more circumspectly under Mark Kimmerly. It was a period of shifting boundaries, and many persons in the church and in the community felt themselves to be living, like Peter Hsu and Pete Mateo, on a peak of existential meaning: radical change, political involvement, harmony with nature, return to the land, community with people, communion with the gods.[14] In this liminal moment, a cadre of dedicated evangelicals staged a coup in the church. They were less concerned to change society than to change persons, but they, too, were on the edge of existence, riding on a wave, as Sue Redford put it. Though their nascent enthusiasm ceded under Eric Underwood to a new differentiation between religion and society, they left to the church a newly invigorated symbolic center and a newly dignified ethical focus on interpersonal relationships. The new ethic tended to the particularistic, concerns being most deeply felt for those whose names or religious identities were known. But it was no longer ascriptive, and it welcomed those who chose rather than bore from birth their identity as Christians. The commitments elicited by the evangelical regime greatly enhanced the capacity of the congregation to meet its goals, including the goals of liberals.

Similar results have been attributed by Douglas McGaw to a charismatic takeover of a Presbyterian church in suburban Connecticut. Mary Jo Neitz's study of a suburban prayer group in Illinois shows how the Catholic charismatic movement, heterodox though it may be, is renewing commitment to Catholic parishes. Clark Roof reluctantly concludes his study of North Carolina Episcopalians with the congruent finding that parochialism is likely to be the cultural backbone of the local mainline church congregation in the foreseeable future.[15]

The Evangelical Ethic and the Spirit of Parochialism

When I crossed the continent in 1976 from Yale University in metropolitan Connecticut to a Presbyterian church in rural California, the most important aspect of my journey was cultural. The distance from secular academia to evangelical Protestantism was immense. Just a few years before, Yale professor Sydney Ahlstrom, dean of American religious historians, had written off conservative Christianity in a widely cited essay on "the radical turn of theology in the '60s."[16] Ahlstrom found orthodox and neoorthodox theologies to be in shambles and thoughtful Protestant, Catholic, and Jewish leaders to have all but abandoned the parish church, religious devotion, and elaborate liturgy. "Traditional forms of evangelism" at home and abroad had been "seriously questioned by all but the most culturally alienated religious groups" such as the "Jehovah's Witnesses, Pentacostalists [sic], and Fundamentalists," leaving only radical, death-of-God theology relevant to a "world come of age." Ahlstrom acknowledged that his impressions were based on his own circle of acquaintances, but the fact is that the vitality of the Southern Baptists, Assemblies of God, and Mormons had evidently escaped his attention. Within a few years, it was radical theology that sounded quaint and alienated and Pentecostalism that had moved to center stage.[17] Why is conservative religion so strong in America and liberal religion so weak despite the predilections of academics?[18]

The answer begins with the tradition of religious "voluntaryism" in American society. It is a fact that the U.S. is the most religious industrial society in the world, judged not only by "belief in God" survey items but also by church participation.[19] Though U.S. religiosity has declined from its 1950s peak, at least one-third of adult Americans are in church each week and two-thirds claim membership. U.S. religiosity is strong because of, not despite, our separation of church and state, and rates of religious participation increased dramatically as the early colonial church-state establishments were abolished and religion became subject to a free market of opinion.[20] The U.S. is a country where men and women on the frontier had to set up their own churches if they were to have any public worship, and where immigrants found that religion was the one part of their traditional cultures that American society would allow them to keep.[21] Consequently, the "congregational" principle of religious organization, the official norm among Baptists and Jews, became the effective principle of popular religious participation for most Americans, regardless of denomination. The laity, men and women alike, have been remarkably free to determine the content of their local religious life and to ignore inconvenient doctrines professed by church officials. That is why denominational labels give one so little information on what to expect on a first visit to a church and why we routinely encounter such seeming anomalies as Baptist baby dedications, Presbyterian altar calls, and Catholic laity speaking in the name of God. For Americans, religion and community autonomy go hand in hand.

The consequences of this organized religious freedom are worrisome for more than church hierarchs. There is a danger that churches will degenerate into what the authors of *Habits of the Heart* call "life-style enclaves," homogeneous associations of persons who share a temporary enthusiasm rather than a common fate.[22] But for our purposes, the consequences for American religion are that the laity have historically had their way; that is why they continue to support their churches. American churches are therefore as diverse as the American people.

But evangelical churches seem particularly strong in America. The experience of Mendocino has shown some reasons why evangelicalism itself conduces to church strength. One is its deliberate lack of sophistication, its relative theological literalism. Though evangelicals are not unanimous about a six-day creation, they profess to believe in a literal resurrection of Jesus, in Jesus' miracles as facts, and in his active love for them today. Evangelicals do not seek demythologized or symbolic interpretations of these ideas, and thus there is little need for a clergy with esoteric learning to provide them. Each person is his or her own priest, and interpretations of religious experience are as often amazingly creative as they are startlingly naive. None of this is to deny the role of the clergy in promoting Biblical knowledge or supplying exegesis of texts, but it is to say that the community of ordinary believers can speak about their faith with confidence, because its formulae mean what they say. In this way is literalism conducive to popular religious involvement and ideological consensus.

Liberalism, correlatively, is likely to be organizationally weak. In the words of Jeffrey Hadden, "when myth and symbol are introduced as the basis for understanding the foundation of a faith, consensus is shattered. What is myth to one is literal to another, and while there may be consensus that a particular passage of scripture may be symbolic, the interpretation may vary."[23] States of pluralistic ignorance and anxiety, rather than consensus and sureness, characterize liberal congregations precisely because liberalism tries to maintain congruence with the wider culture at the same time that it tries to be Christian.[24]

Prosaic literalism, in turn, enhances the capacity of modern evangelicals to appropriate traditional religious symbols. To be sure, the past that evangelicals invoke is not that of the historian. Some evangelicals seem to think that the 1900 years between the composition of the book of Acts and our time are best ignored. In many ways, today's evangelicals are heterodox, expecially in the formerly Calvinistic Presbyterian church. They are certainly heterodox in the Catholic church, even though they see themselves in touch with tradition.[25] But they can better, with alacrity, embrace the very language and imagery of the mainline's theological symbolism—in hymnbooks, ritual confessions, and scriptures—than can the mainline itself, whose leaders may be more rigorous historians. The result is that the evangelicals' rituals can be both more "traditional" and more spontaneous, as was true of Eric Underwood's 1970s services.

So evangelicalism promotes consensus on the group's religious identity and thus promotes solidarity. But what of its actual message? What of walking, joshing, and even drinking with Jesus Christ as one's personal lord and savior? Does this personalism not drive a wedge of spiritual solipsism between people? It does not.

A striking feature of the new evangelical groups is their particularism, their tendency to care most for the near and dear. In Mendocino, Larry Redford spoke of the mission of the church as the church. He had earlier said that the local fellowship was the building project, parallel to the Jewish temple in postexilic days. Eric Underwood taught that prayers should concern "those that we are in relationship to." In Neitz's suburban charismatic group, "there is a sense that the purpose of the group is to attend to the needs of its members."[26] Members are admonished by leaders, by one another, and by their testimonies to pay close attention to neighbors, family members, and especially spouses. "Unity starts with husband and wife," said Bob Mumford at the 1976 Festival of the Son.

Above all, marriage is extolled and invoked as a metaphor to communicate the concept of the group. The church is the "bride of Christ." God is to man as husband is to wife and parent is to child. The Lord was a party to Larry and Sue Redford's betrothal. Dianne Hunter's doubts about her marriage were attributed to Satan, and she stayed with her husband. Lucille Rogers recalled that the Lord told her, "You'll never know me until you are married," and she thanked Him that the husband she found "has a desire for a family stronger than any man I know." Sol Bloom recalled how he and his wife Jane had remained together through a turbulent marriage. "We praise the Lord for that, but when I met Jane I said, 'this is my last relationship. I've had a lot of relationships, but I'm not going to have any more new ones. I'm going to stick with this one whatever it takes,' and I'm really happy I did." Eric Underwood called the breakaway of Larry Redford's Antioch Fellowship a "divorce," a metaphor that appealed to the distressed Jeannie Baker.

Now marriage is the most personal of social relationships in our society, and in that sense it comes closest in the modern world to the idealized values of community, what sociologists since Ferdinand Toennies have called Gemeinschaft. Marriage is a particularistic, diffuse, affective, and collectively-oriented relationship.[27] One cares for and cherishes one specific other person in a total way. But in one crucial respect modern marriage is unlike Gemeinschaft. It is not ascriptive, or determined by birth, but achieved, or chosen on a discretionary basis during one's adulthood. It is that aspect that makes marriage both enormously evocative as a symbol to evangelicals and deeply freighted with personal meaning. One's marriage is itself the most important relationship of one's life (even if one has had more than one marriage) and a highly vulnerable one. It is also a model of one's freely chosen social identity and reflects upon one's social self-image.[28] In Mendocino, I discovered one key to evangelicalism's appeal to a mobile population in its embrace of what social critics mistakenly call "traditional" marriage.

Contrast evangelicals' particularism to the liberals' outward-looking orientation. In 1963, Pastor Hsu told the Mendocino congregation, "Basically, our church exists for mission." The next year he prompted, "We must continue to stand for justice and equality and human values." As Harvey Cox put it, "God wants man to be interested not in Him but in his fellow man." Is this stance not more conducive to social solidarity than the evangelicals' personalism and Christocentrism? It does not seem so.

First of all, the outward-looking message is ambiguous, as the question "who is my neighbor?" attests. The parochial evangelical is inclined to imagine "the Smith family next door," "Fred in the prayer group," or "my husband," moving ever inward. The cosmopolitan liberal is inclined to think of the new family on the block, the people in the projects, Central American peasants, and the South African black majority, moving ever outward. The evangelical's mind moves toward those who are known, even if their needs have not been determined. The liberal's mind moves toward those of whom the only thing known is that they are in need.

And what is to be done for this neighbor? Above all, the evangelical wants to share her or his faith with the neighbor, ultimately to bring the neighbor into fellowship, as Jane Bloom did for a lonely woman stranded in a state park. The liberal scorns what seems to be an ulterior purpose of salesmanship in this approach, and he or she most wants to meet the neighbor's secular needs, rather than somehow to win the neighbor over as a convert. Yet to bring the neighbor into fellowship presumes that the neighbor can be one of us, whereas the sense of obligation to the less fortunate is based on a conviction that they are different. Liberal religion is therefore externally directed; benevolence creates a barrier.[29]

There is an inherent, though implicit, interpersonal bridge in the very nature of the evangelicals' confession of faith, which is the admission of personal spiritual need. In effect, evangelicalism recognizes that it can be as difficult to receive as to give, and its culture is built around a demand for receptivity and a confession of dependence. Evangelicals talk a lot about "spiritual food," and Larry Redford drew an unforgettable analogy between Jesus and the dentist. Catholic charismatics "place a high value on openness, emotional intensity, and childlike characteristics."[30] Contrast this ideal with the sixties liberal ideal expressed by Harvey Cox:

> We speak of God politically whenever we give occasion to our neighbor to become the responsible adult agent, the fully posttown and posttribal man God expects him to be today . . . . We do not speak to him of God by trying to make him religious but, on the contrary, by encouraging him to come fully of age, putting away childish things.[31]

It is the culture of public humbling that is most characteristic of evangelicals in contrast to liberals. When one is willing to acknowledge his or her own religious neediness, the possibility is opened for religious exchange to occur within the fellowship itself, and the fellowship need not search out the needy as recipients of religious benevolence. Hence evangelical groups are parochial; hence they are more likely to be groups. Other things being equal, we should expect to find more vital evangelical than liberal church communities.

Conversely, orientation to the local community promotes evangelicalism. One of the most astute of today's church watchers is the sociologist William H. Swatos, Jr. (a true participant observer, since he is also vicar of a small-town Episcopal church in Illinois). Swatos argues that the essence of historic American religiosity is its localism. The great (now "mainline") denominations grew in the nineteenth century because "they served to fit people into their communities and gave organization to the differences among them." But with the turn-of-the-century split between the parties of the right and the left, the denominations' culture-embracing character caused them to ally with the left and lose sight of their roots. They "developed national staffs, headquarters, programs, and so forth, far beyond the reach of local constituents." The national church, therefore, was experienced by the local congregation as an "invading corporate structure" that could not "recognize the importance of localism" in maintaining the church.[32] Swatos is generalizing, but he might well have in mind the Mendocino search committee's experience with a "farcical" affirmative action exercise.

Swatos observes that the liveliest churches today are the charismatic and evangelical churches, whether local congregations of a mainline denomination, like Mendocino, or independent churches. "The churches experiencing growth are those giving people a sense of place—individual meaning and purpose in a physical and spiritual community. These groups give the appearance—even if the leadership has, in fact, moved in from elsewhere—of having grown from the locality of interest rather than being superimposed upon it."[33] Eric Underwood, a newcomer to Mendocino, sensed his congregation's conviction that "freedom is living in Mendocino." *Liberalism and localism are strangers to each other; evangelicalism and localism are friends.*

Higher education is increasingly important to our society, and I am one of the millions whose careers and identities center on it. Academic culture is meritocratic, organized around work, oriented to cosmopolitan cultural standards, and increasingly dominated by policies of the state. To us, the persistence of conservative religion is an anomaly. But our culture is itself only one American option. There is another culture, one that the political theorist Sheldon Wolin calls "archaic": "there exists a highly flourishing archaic political culture that is democratic, participatory, localist, and, overall, more egalitarian than elitist in ideology. It is negligible as an influence in national politics and yet it occupies the energy, skills, and commitments of thousands of Americans every day."[34]

One index of this "archaic" culture is America's nostalgia for rural life.[35] "The American mind was raised upon a sentimental attachment to rural living," wrote Richard Hofstadter in *The Age of Reform,* and a huge number of Americans say they would rather be living on a farm or in a much smaller town than they actually do. Another index is the perennial popularity of evangelist Billy Graham, who has been named in the Gallup poll as among the ten "most admired men in the world" *for over thirty consecutive years,* far longer than any other individual. Presidents, prime ministers, and popes come and go, live and die, but Graham remains as a symbol of a persistent ideal.

If cosmopolitanism and the universities occupy the cultural center, then parochialism and evangelists hang on the periphery. But the periphery is anything but isolated; it extends throughout the country. The evangelicals have a national network of fellowships, schools, businesses, resorts, and publishing houses as well as churches.[36] They have a language that permits mutual recognition in lieu of formal introduction, much in the way that beards used to function among members of the new left, and living-room magazine displays function among the middle class. Evangelicals' contracosmopolitanism facilitates migrants' locating a new spiritual home, so Americans' geographical mobility does not diminish conservative religion.[37] Evangelicals have an ironic advantage in that their parochialism is not confined to any one locality.

Neither parochialism nor evangelicalism, atavistic though they may seem, is a mere survival of traditional society. Evangelicalism, the Mendocino story shows, can be worldly and optimistic, not a rearguard action. It was not reactionary old-timers in the church who staged a coup against the liberalism of the sixties. It was a group of recent immigrants who infused the church with their evangelical enthusiasm and brought it new vitality. So also localism is not a matter of particular geographic attachments. As Clark Roof shows, localism is a mind-set, not just a personal history. Albert Hunter's work on Chicago neighborhoods shows that community sentiments can emerge, not just survive, in the face of social change.[38]

Not all Americans are churchgoers, let alone conservative Christians. But a huge number are, and they occupy the center of gravity in what is our most important voluntary association. When Americans gather outside the home and off the job, they are far more likely to do so in a church than in any other place. Membership in labor unions, service clubs, the PTA, and professional associations is dwarfed by membership in churches and church-related organizations. The proportion of Americans attending church *weekly* is about the same as that casting ballots *every four years* in congressional elections.[39] Those for whom church involvement is a sporadic thing are as numerous as those who are regulars, but they evidently like knowing that the church will be there when they need it even if they are liberal or agnostic. The people who keep the local church going, meanwhile, are disproportionately likely to be conservatives, including evangelicals.

Of course, there are churches that are not conservative. Living most of my adult life in college towns—Berkeley, New Haven, Palo Alto, and Evanston—I have visited many liberal and radical churches. As a teacher of the sociology of religion, I hear of them all the time from students disgusted with the conservatism of the churches in which they were raised and enthusiastic about the freedoms they experience away from home. My class attended a parish of the Metropolitan Community Church, the gay and lesbian denomination, and we witnessed there an undeniable spiritual vitality. One student observation team recently came back with news of a Wiccans' coven meeting in a local Unitarian church. Around the corner from my home are several "nuclear free zone" churches.

But these instances prove the rule that churches reflect their local cultures. A longer-term view would be required to determine whether these congregations will prove the other part of the rule, that while liberal churches attract recruits, they have difficulty holding on to them.[40]

Political Implications

What does the evangelical resurgence, as represented in Mendocino and elsewhere, portend for American public life? Does it represent a threat to our institutions? Is it, as is often alleged, the herald of a would-be theocracy? Do the evangelicals want a "Christian republic"?

Certainly, the sort of evangelicalism that took over Mendocino Presbyterian Church gives secularists no cause for alarm. It was moderate and dominantly apolitical. In organizing materials for the book, I actually had to highlight political references from my field notes so as to give the reader a sense of the context in which I did the research (the Ford-Carter campaign), thus giving Mendocino's evangelicals a more politicized appearance than they had. To the extent that there was a clear political message at Mendocino Presbyterian, it was the one enunciated by Eric Underwood on bicentennial Sunday. The civic duty of Christians is individually to accept God as master over their passions and collectively to provide a model of voluntary order in their local churches. People looking for right-wing activism would have been bored, not frightened, had they been in my place.[41]

Let me grant, however, that my direct observations come from young evangelicals in a mainline church in 1976, a year when the Democratic candidate carried the evangelical banner, three years before Jerry Falwell founded the Moral Majority organization. Undoubtedly, things are different in the Reagan years. Surely the conservative tide in religion is part of the rightward swing in American culture in the seventies and eighties, and just as surely those committed to conservative politics will use what leverage they can to effect their designs.[42] The impact of politicized evangelicals on the elections of 1980 and 1984 has often been exaggerated, not least by their own spokesmen. Nonetheless, they probably did affect some congressional races and may have enlarged President Reagan's margin of victory.[43]

However, the United States is in no danger of theocratic authoritarianism. Americans, from the pious to the agnostic, are notoriously prickly about religious authority, and American religious leaders have trouble getting their people to follow them, as Peter Hsu and the left discovered to their dismay in the 1960s. Larry Redford on the right fared no better in his attempt to discipline a woman for sexual misconduct in the 1970s, and members of his fellowship could always use their Bibles to dispute his authority. No Pope can stop the vast majority of American Catholic women from using contraception.[44] Whatever the aspirations of religious zealots, religious Americans are not promising material for political mobilization.

Evangelicals in particular, so long on the defensive in American public life, have an apolitical culture. Evangelicals do not seek salvation through politics and do not expect to be told how to vote in their churches. They can agree that homosexual acts and unrestricted abortion are morally wrong, but they offer little support for the idea of a distinctively "Christian" political platform. Social surveys have repeatedly shown that those who have heard of the Moral Majority are more likely to oppose than support it, and the same is true of evangelicals. Those who watch religious television shows, even Jerry Falwell's relatively political *Old Time Gospel Hour*, do so for their religious, not their political messages. Moreover, Falwell's audience share dropped as his programming became more political.[45]

It is also unlikely that evangelicals could use politics to impose their collective will. United as they may be theologically, they are diverse politically. Because of the historic prominence of evangelicalism in the American south, evangelicals tend to be Democrats, thus connected politically to the party of liberals. Because their circumstances in life differ—farmers, businessmen, service workers, homemakers, retired; rich and poor; men and women—their positions differ on issues that differentially affect these statuses. There is no "evangelical line" on the economic issues that perennially sway the American electorate.

It is on such "social issues" as abortion, homosexuality, and prayer versus sex education in the public schools that evangelicals' political voice has caused most concern among secular liberals. It is true that opinions on these issues are strongly correlated with religiosity, but evangelical opinion is neither sectarian nor monolithic. Evangelicals overwhelmingly support a constitutional amendment to permit introduction of "voluntary" prayer in public schools, *but so also does the majority of the American population.* Most evangelicals do not think that abortion should be legally available under all circumstances, *but neither does a majority of the American population.* In terms of social attitudes, as distinguished from theology, voting intentions or policy preferences, more than two-thirds of the American people could be described as fellow travelers with the Moral Majority.[46] To the extent that evangelicals have a program for public life, it is distinguished not by its social conservatism but by its theistic language.

Though their general values tend to be conservative, evangelicals would have a hard time uniting on policy. Take abortion, for example. Depending on the particular survey, the definitions of "evangelical" employed, and the policy options offered, evangelical opinion on abortion is as divided as that of the general public. About one quarter of evangelicals, compared to a third of the population, would grant a right to abortion under *any* circumstances. About one-fifth of evangelicals, compared to a seventh of the population, would ban abortion in *all* circumstances. The median opinion, among evangelicals as among the American public generally, is that abortions should be available in cases of rape, fetal abnormality, or danger to the health of the woman, but no clear policy commands a decisive majority either among evangelicals or among Americans generally. Indeed, one careful study reports that evangelicals are more polarized among themselves than is the population at large.[47] Evangelicals are in no position to tell the rest of us where to draw the line on abortion.

What evangelicals seem to want from the rest of us is not conformity to their rules but respect for their values. Though they mostly agree that abortion is morally wrong, they cannot unite to erect a ban against all abortion. But they are united two-to-one on rejecting *government funding* of abortion for women in poverty. They do not wish to see that of which they disapprove receive the sanction of government support.[48]

To take another example, a study of political activists supporting an evangelical candidate in Virginia in 1978 showed that only ten percent of them were primarily motivated by a desire for legislative action. Most of them wanted to elect their candidate to bring a "Christian" or "moral" *influence* into politics. They wanted to legitimate their family-centered values.[49] More than any other public matter, conservative Christians care about *religion*.

In Mendocino, I sensed that the evangelicals who thought about my presence wanted me to tell their story with sympathy. Many of them also wanted me to share their faith, although only a few—Ben Moss, Jonah Harris, Sol Bloom, and Maile Perrow—made much of a point of evangelism. But *no one* tried to change my behavior, to make me adhere to some "Christian" lifestyle. Larry Redford and his elders disfellowshipped Peggy because she stepped out of line while a member of the group. Ben Moss had to have a relationship to Elise in order to chastise her with the words of Jeremiah. Among the evangelicals I knew, for one person to intervene in another's life first required that the two be in fellowship. But they would not stop witnessing to any and all.

What is new on the public scene is not the evangelicals' social conservatism, but their obtrusive theism. Their language—God, Jesus, the church, and religiously inspired ideals for family life and personal virtues—is what makes them noticeable. Having made a reappearance among us, it is not likely soon to go away. In the words of Richard John Neuhaus:

the activist fundamentalists want us to know that they are not going to go back to the wilderness. Many of them, being typical Americans, also want to be loved. They explain, almost apologetically, that they did not really want to bash in the door to the public square, but it was locked, and nobody had answered their knocking. Anyway, the hinges were rusty and it gave way under pressure that was only a little more than polite. And so the country cousins have shown up in force at the family picnic.[50]

Whether one welcomes the evangelicals' contribution to public discourse or abhors it, it is likely to stay polite. With deep roots in American culture, evangelicalism is not as radical as secular liberals think.[51] America is a society that has successfully combined religion and social participation throughout its history. The rules of American religion are that one does not have to stop enjoying the fellowship of secular society to please God; nor must one stop being religious to be a citizen. Moreover, church congregations tend to be moderate, because their members live in society and their caretakers have worldly concerns like utility bills and the water supply. That is why congregational religion is the bane of ideologues' dreams. In a Connecticut independent fundamentalist congregation studied recently by Nancy Ammerman, the doctrines preached by the popular pastor could not convince the members that adherents of other faiths were damned. In this congregation, many of its members were converts, especially from Roman Catholicism.[52] They could not humanly regard their unconverted family members as beyond God's grace.

The structured locus of religious radicalism—the perennial source of new wine—is organizations dedicated to ideology and relatively free of worldly cares: denominational bureaus and parachurch missions, communes, and theological seminaries.[53] In the United States, people have to go out of their way to become isolated or encapsulated if they wish to be religiously radical. The ideas that issue from seminaries and religious missions can revitalize congregations. They can also affect parishioners' opinions in matters remote from everyday life, such as formal theology and foreign policy. But the potency of ideas is limited when it comes to matters of daily life. The fundamentalists studied by Ammerman affirmed that the proper role of women was to be wives and mothers, and Ammerman found herself accepted among the congregation only when it became apparent that she, the researcher, was pregnant. But *half of all the mothers in the congregation worked outside the home*, evidently so that they could afford to be homeowners.[54]

Even the nascent, radical evangelicals in Mendocino were worldly, astonishingly so. They talked about heaven as the abode of departed loved ones, but not as a refuge from the world. They almost never talked of hell. They assumed God's interest in kids' bicycles, family pets, and the prosperity of fishermen. They put their own money and time into an academically sound school to prepare their children for the future. They were not immune to the joys of sex.

American culture makes religion available. Evangelical ideals propel the faithful into the secular world. Into the world, evangelicals bring their talk of God.

Epilogue: 1986

God moves in a mysterious way
His wonders to perform;
He plants his footsteps in the sea,
And rides upon the storm.
—William Cowper

Eric Underwood pastored Mendocino Presbyterian longer than any other minister, but he and his family finally tired of it, of the pressure, the climate, and the drug culture. He left in October 1983 to accept a call from a conservative southern California church. "We miss the funny folk of Mendocino," he wrote me that Christmas, "but our lives cry out for some normalcy."

Bruce Douglas stayed on at Mendocino for six months and helped set up the search for a new minister before receiving another call himself. He now pastors a new congregation in a Pacific northwest town, where he leads the campaign against a neo-Nazi organization headquartered there.

Larry Redford is the principal and Sue is a teacher at a Christian high school in a fast-growing fringe suburb of San Francisco. The school is attached to Gary Armstrong's ministry, which also includes several churches in California, Hawaii, and Mexico, and construction and tire reprocessing companies.

Burt and Lucille Rogers are members of a Gary Armstrong fellowship in central California.

Steve Hunter works in microcomputers in Silicon Valley, and Dianne has a job with a brokerage firm. They are members of a Presbyterian church.

Sol Bloom works for an encyclopedia company in the Central Valley. He and Jane are members of an Assembly of God congregation. Their sons are college-shopping.

Jeffrey Wakefield was ordained to the Presbyterian ministry in

Mendocino in 1980 and now pastors another old, rural congregation in northern California. Pat is finishing her dissertation in economics and teaches in the Christian high school in their town.

David Baker gave up his state park job rather than move to a new assignment and now works as a handyman in Mendocino. Jeannie gave birth to their fourth child, a boy, in 1984. The older Baker children are now members in their own right of the Presbyterian church, and the oldest is in college.

Turo and Anne de Grazia divide their time between their ceramics studio in Mendocino and workshops they lead at colleges and seminaries in the U.S. and Canada. Their older daughter will soon enter college.

David Baker, Monty Greene, and Turo de Grazia meet Friday mornings for Bible study at the Presbyterian church. Jeffrey Wakefield joins them when he is in town to look after his property on the Comptche Road. But other veterans of Antioch Fellowship have switched over to the Foursquare Gospel church in Caspar.

Therese runs a Christian retreat center under the authority of Jack Boyle. She still lives in the Big House.

Pete and Judy Mateo travel in southern California and Hawaii.

Ben and Beatrice Moss run a gourmet boutique in another rural California tourist town. She and their daughter attend the local Presbyterian church. Ben goes to a Bible fellowship.

Bobby Houston lived for a while in Mexico and is now back in Mendocino, where he attends the Presbyterian church.

Laurie is raising a family in Mendocino, where she is a well-known musician.

Mark Kimmerly has been pastor of the Presbyterian church in Arena, California, for fourteen years. His parishioners came to his side when his marriage broke up and he was left as a single parent of two adolescent children. He earned a Doctor of Ministry degree in 1976 with a thesis on the topic, "The Church as an Extended Family."

Peter Hsu has been a church executive and seminary professor since leaving Mendocino. He recently wrote his former congregation that because of his teaching and writing "the life of the Mendocino Presbyterian Church has enriched the church life of countless others throughout the United States and Canada." He lives and works in New York City.

Pastor emeritus Frederick Althorpe died on October 29, 1980. The former manse, now the site of church offices and the town library, was named in his memory.

I met Anne Heider, the director of the adult choir, on bicentennial Sunday. When she left Mendocino in 1977 to resume graduate studies in music at Stanford, I began to spend summers and weekends away from my Chicago job in Palo Alto. She and I were married in 1979 by Eric Underwood in the Peninsula church where she was choir director. We now live in Evanston, Illinois.

My son, Alan, is doing graduate work at the University of California, Berkeley. He was one of a three-person team that won the 1985 William Lowell Putnam Mathematical Competition, and he donated his share of the prize money to the evangelical high school of which he is an alumnus.

Albion Chapel was decommissioned and sold to a developer in 1979. The building burned to the ground in November 1981.

The Good Shepherd School, now quartered in Albion, entered its twelfth year in 1986.

Mendocino Presbyterian Church observed its 125th anniversary in 1984 with a year-long calendar of events organized by new and longtime elders. It was only in 1985, however, that a new pastor, another alumnus of Fuller Theological Seminary, was installed. The pastor-seeking process was long and arduous.

But that is another story.

Notes

1. A Quarter Century Distilled

1. Data from *Yearbooks*, 1961–1984. In case of denominations with a history of mergers (e.g., the United Methodist and United Presbyterian churches), membership figures total all the later-merged bodies retroactively. For brief discussions of the validity and reliability of church membership statistics, see Greeley, 1972, pp. 86–89; Kelley, 1977, pp. 14–16; and Roozen and Carroll, 1979, pp. 28–32. See also Doyle and Kelly, 1979.

2. Quoted in Herberg, 1960, p. 84. This and the following paragraphs draw heavily on Herberg's analysis.

3. Herberg, 1960, p. 41. Herberg adds: "No suggestion of insincerity is here implied, nor does what I have said preclude the operation of other factors lying closer to the heart of faith. Those who identify themselves religiously and join churches as a way of naming and locating themselves socially are not cynical unbelievers shrewdly manipulating false labels. They mean what they say when they call themselves Protestants, or Catholics, or Jews: it is our problem, as I have suggested, to define just what it is they mean."

4. See chapter four. Mendocino's religious revival of the 1970s was also remote from Calvinism.

5. This and the next paragraph are based on Hadden's analysis and are also informed by Pratt, 1972, and Flowers, 1984.

6. Hadden, 1969, p. 197.

7. These statements are overdrawn, and they are not intended to be overgeneralized—as if laity and clergy did these things everywhere—or reified—as if "laity" and "clergy" acted as corporate bodies.

8. Kelley, 1977. For a hint of the controversy, see Kelley's "Preface to the Paperback Edition" (pp. vii–xiii). The following paragraphs are based on Kelley's book, but it must be acknowledged that Kelley has no data on "conservatism" or "strictness" or any other independent variable hypothesized to be linked to the growth of the Southern Baptists, Mormons, or Assemblies of God. In that respect, his argument is conjectural.

9. Based on data from *Yearbooks*, 1967–1982, multiplied by the year-to-year inflation index in "Purchasing Power of the Dollar," in *Statistical Abstract of the United States*.

10. Johnson, 1960, p. 22; Broom and Selznick, 1968, p. 31. The next two paragraphs draw on the chapters about religion in these two texts.

11. The classic analysis of American denominationalism is Niebuhr, 1929.

12. Broom and Selznick, 1968, pp. 324–325.

13. See Gallup, 1982 and 1984, particularly the commentary by George H. Gallup, Jr., in Gallup, 1982.

14. This analysis draws on Collins, 1975, chapter 6, and on Parsons, 1951, pp. 283–297.

15. Wilson, 1973, p. 7.

16. Wilson, 1973, p. 5.

17. Quebedeaux, 1972.

2. The Action in American Protestantism

1. Marty, 1970, chapter 17.

2. Alberoni, 1984.

3. For the writing of this description, I have drawn on the model provided in Neitz, 1986.

4. Transcribed by Anne Heider from my vocal recitation.

5. Ducey, 1977. See also McGuire, 1974, and, for a more complete theoretical discussion, see Warner, 1985.

6. Alberoni, 1984, pp. 2, 22.

7. Alberoni, 1984, p. 2.

8. Turner, 1977; Ellwood, 1979; Douglas, 1969; Durkheim, 1915; Weber, 1922 and 1968; Troeltsch, 1931; H. R. Niebuhr, 1929; Warner, 1985. "From the social point of view, the talkative, passionate, and sometimes quarrelsome circles that met to read Paul's letters over their evening meal in private houses, or the predawn conclaves of ethical rigorists that alarmed Pliny, were a disconcerting novelty. Without temple, cult statue, or ritual, they lacked the time-honored and reassuring routine of sacrifice that would have been necessary to link them with religion" (Judge, 1980, p. 212).

9. The quotations in this paragraph derive from Alberoni, 1984, pp. 20, 171, and 165, respectively; they are reprinted by permission.

10. Alberoni, 1984, pp. 131–132.

11. Alberoni, 1984, p. 134.

12. Alberoni, 1984, p. 217.

13. Coffin, 1977.

14. Marty, 1970, p. 179.

15. See Quebedeaux, 1978, and Hunter, 1983a, for analyses of what they call, respectively, American evangelicalism's increasing "worldliness" and its "accommodation."

16. Coleman, 1972, chapter 1.

17. Here is how one young clergyman is said to have interpreted the mandate of the Presbyterian board of evangelism: "Therefore, the main task of the church is to work for reconciliation in the world. . . . [R]econciliation can take place without the name of Jesus Christ even being mentioned

and . . . 'naming the name' need not be a goal sought from those who are reconciled." Cited in Goodman, 1968, p. 127.

In Jaroslav Pelikan's history of images of Jesus, we read: "It has almost seemed that in every epoch there were some who were primarily interested in naming the name of Christ, clarifying its doctrinal and theological meaning, and defending that meaning against its enemies—but who named the name without giving the cup of water. Yet it has seemed possible for others to give the cup of water, to provide the healing, and to improve the social lot of the disadvantaged—but to do so without explicitly naming the name of Christ" (Pelikan, 1985, p. 228). The "cup of water" refers to Matthew 10:42 and Mark 9:41.

18. See Parsons, 1951, pp. 58–67.

19. This assertion is controversial. For an elegant theoretical statement, see Iannaccone, forthcoming.

20. See Gallup, 1982 and 1985.

21. Hunter, 1983a, pp. 49, 139–142.

22. Stark and Glock, 1968.

23. Hadden, 1969, pp. 50–54, 113–118.

24. Stark and Glock, 1968, p. 33.

25. Gilkey, 1967, pp. 87–89; Flowers, 1984, p. 3. Johnson (1985) effectively attributes responsibility for the malaise of liberal Protestantism to its leaders' fascination with Neoorthodoxy combined with their inability to generate lay enthusiasm for it.

26. King, 1964, p. 95.

27. For details on these trends, see Hunter, 1983a, and Quebedeaux, 1978.

28. Cox, 1966, pp. 223, 224, 232.

29. Lindsell, 1976.

30. Lindsell, 1979, pp. 256, 332, et passim. For a more moderate conservative polemic, see Norman, 1979: e.g., "western liberalism—whose transient moral enthusiasms are, in characteristic bourgeois manner, represented as eternal verities" (p. 33).

31. For example, Smylie, 1979, pp. 86–89.

32. Fry, 1975, pp. 71–72, 67.

33. Hunter, 1983a, p. 59.

34. Stark and Glock, 1968, p. 215; Hunter, 1983a, p. 67.

35. Roof, 1978, p. 132.

36. Hadden, 1969, p. 219.

37. Hoge, 1976, pp. 148–150.

38. Wood, 1981; see also Berk, 1978.

39. Roozen, McKinney, and Carroll, 1984.

40. For examples, see Ducey, 1977, and Hadden and Longino, 1974.

41. Warner, 1983, compares two suburban churches, one "activist," the other "sanctuary," in these terms; the former is steadily declining, the latter steadily growing.

42. Warner, 1979. "Comfort" and "challenge" was used as a one-dimensional typology by Glock, Ringer, and Babbie, 1967.

43. "Liberalism" and "evangelicalism" as here defined are two theological *parties*, not formal theologies. As such, they are vulgarizations of careful, complex, theological systems. But the vulgarization is a social process in the world of the churches, not an artifact of this discussion. See Weber, 1930, and Zaret, 1985, for analyses of popularization processes.

44. Ladd and Lipset, 1975. See also Snow and Machalek, 1982.

3. Sojourn in the Field

1. Among the theoretical positions to which I was oriented were Berger and Luckmann, 1967; Scheff, 1967; Lipset, 1967; and Parsons, 1969.

2. The extraordinarily valuable ASA seminar was conducted in 1975 by Rosalie and Murray Wax. Published statements of those from whom I learned most about field research include Bettelheim, 1960; Wax, 1971; Lofland, 1971; Becker, 1970; Millman, 1976; Erikson, 1976; Lever, 1981 and 1983; and Rieder, 1985. For a report on field work with evangelicals very different from my own, see Peshkin, 1984.

3. Ebert, 1984, p. 7.

4. See the influential statement in Parsons, 1951, chapter 1.

4. Reorientation: Mendocino Presbyterian, 1959–1970

1. This statement comes from the autobiographical preface to a book of Hsu's published in 1981.

2. Hadden, 1969, p. 120.

3. Hoge, 1976.

4. Quoted from Kimmerly's master of divinity thesis, presented in 1967.

5. From Mission to Parachurch: Antioch Fellowship, 1969–1973

1. Kimmerly's master of divinity thesis draws heavily on sociological studies, including those of Campbell and Pettigrew, 1959; Pope, 1942; and Lenski, 1961.

2. This procedure was, according to a trustee report in September, 1970, approved by the Internal Revenue Service. Subsequently, contributions were channeled through the church treasury under the budgetary category of "Local & World Mission."

3. Schelling, 1963; Becker, 1970, chapter 18; Goffman, 1967.

4. In the analyses of the organization of Antioch Ranch in this chapter and "The Land" in chapter six, I use Talcott Parsons's AGIL scheme as a checklist; see Parsons, 1961.

5. For example, evangelicals are internally divided on the "social" issue agenda of the religious right; see Rothenberg and Newport, 1984.

6. For the relevant sociological theory, see Stark and Bainbridge, 1985, chap. 14.

7. Heirich, 1977; Snow and Machalek, 1984; Richardson, 1985.

8. See Rueschemeyer, 1986.

9. See Quebedeaux, 1976; Neitz, 1986; Gerlach and Hine, 1970; McGuire, 1982.

10. Neitz, 1986.

6. A Hippie Commune Comes to Jesus: The Holy Land, 1969–1974

1. Berger and Hackett, 1974; Berger, 1981, refers to Therese's Land as "Gertrud's Land."

2. See Zablocki, 1971, for a thorough analysis of a modern intentional community; Kanter, 1972, presents an influential theory based on nineteenth-century communes, on which I have drawn for the present chapter.

3. Quoted from Proctor, 1979, p. 61.

4. Richardson, Stewart, and Simmonds (1979) detail the history and inner life of an organization very similar to and contemporary with (but not, despite appearances, identical to) Beacon House.

7. Evangelical Victory in the Church

1. Kimmerly cites Campbell and Pettigrew (1959, p. 111) to this effect in his master of divinity thesis.

2. Because of inflation, the real value of the increased giving was up by only thirty percent, still a healthy figure.

3. Parsons, 1951, pp. 292–297.

8. Church Growth and Decline in Context

1. Gallup, 1985, p. 35; see also Roof and McKinney, 1985, pp. 31–32.

2. See Hill, 1985, pp. 132–141.

3. Gallup, 1985, pp. 40–41. Since 1975, self-reported church members have been seventy-one percent to sixty-seven percent of Gallup's samples of civilian adult Americans eighteen and older, the proportion edging downward. Using the membership figures reported by the churches themselves (in the National Council of Churches' *Yearbooks*) gives the generous figure of seventy-five percent of the United States adult population as church members (the 1986 *Yearbook* total of 141 million church members [for 1984] divided by the U.S. Census estimate of 189 million for the U.S. population fourteen and older in that year.) A conservative estimate is that of the Gallup 1978 study finding that fifty-nine percent of Americans are "churched" (cited in Roof and McKinney, 1985).

4. General Assembly minutes were made available through the courtesy of the Presbytery of Chicago, Mike Troyer, office manager, and Ms. Elvire Hilgert of the Jesuit-Krauss-McCormick library at the Lutheran School of Theology, Chicago.

5. Roozen and Carroll, 1979, p. 39. Quotations in the following paragraph are from pp. 39–40.

6. Gallup, 1985, pp. 16–17.

7. The hymnal chosen was *Hymns for the Living Church* (Hustad, 1974). The previously used hymnal was *The Hymnal*, published by the old PCUSA in 1933. Other available denominational hymnals were *The Worshipbook*, published by the UPCUSA in 1972, and *The Hymnbook*, published by a consortium of five Presbyterian and Reformed denominations in 1955.

8. Fry, 1975, pp. 48–49.

9. See DeJong and Sell, 1977; Long and DeArc, 1980; and Hauser, 1981.

10. See Raphael, 1985.

11. Kelley, 1979, pp. 336–337.

12. See my review of Hoge and Roozen (Warner, 1981).

13. Birthrates are treated ambiguously by Hoge and his colleagues (Hoge and Roozen, 1979, pp. 117–119, 181, 193–194).

14. I am indebted to the Research Committee of the Society for the Scientific Study of Religion, Jeffrey Hadden, 1982 chair. Supplementary funds were provided by the Research Board and the Office of Social Science Research at the University of Illinois at Chicago. My research assistants were Mr. James N. Pasquotto and Mr. Michael D. Matters. Mr. Kwang Park designed the graphs.

15. Roof, Hoge, Dyble, and Hadaway, 1979, pp. 209–211. Our definition of "country" churches differs from their "town and country" category. Our sample included all Presbyterian churches in towns with only one Presbyterian church outside of U.S. Census–defined "metropolitan" counties or outside of "urbanized areas" within "metropolitan" counties. The result is that our sample includes seven large towns with 1980 populations in the 20,000 to 50,000 range.

16. We defined "northern California" according to UPCUSA Presbyteries, to include all counties north and west of and including Monterey, San Benito, Merced, Mariposa, Tuolumne, and Alpine. Within this region, there were, according to 1980 census figures, thirty-two UPCUSA congregations in single-church towns within nonmetropolitan counties. Because California counties tend to be geographically large and topographically rugged, many effectively rural areas are technically defined as metropolitan, falling as they do within counties defined as part of U.S. Census "Standard Metropolitan Statistical Areas," the minimum unit of which is the whole county. Accordingly, we identified twenty-five other UPCUSA churches outside of census-defined "urbanized areas" within SMSAs. The total number of our cases for analysis was therefore fifty-seven. Of these, four were founded during the 1960s and census data for community divisions were unavailable for an additional nine in the 1960 census. The number of cases for the 1960–1970 analysis (Fig. 8-4) is thus forty-four.

The towns (with counties in parentheses, U.S. Census "metropolitan" counties marked with an asterisk) are: Gridley, Oroville (Butte*); Colusa (Colusa); Placerville, S. Lake Tahoe (El Dorado); Orland (Glenn); Arcata, Bayside, Bluelake, Eureka, Fortuna, Garberville, Hoopa, McKinleyville, Miranda, Orick, Scotia, Trinidad (Humboldt); Kelseyville, Lakeport (Lake); Bolinas, Pt. Reyes, Stinson Beach, Tomales (Marin*); Covelo, Ft. Bragg, Leggett, Mendocino, Ukiah (Mendocino); Gustine (Merced); Gonzales (Monterey*); Calistoga, St. Helena (Napa*); Nevada City (Nevada); Walnut Grove (Sacramento*); Hollister (San Benito); Gilroy, San Martin (Santa Clara*); Escalon, Lodi, Tracy (San Joaquin*); Burney (Shasta*); McCloud (Siskiyou); Vacaville (Solano*); Monte Rio, Sonoma (Sonoma*); Newman, Patterson (Stanislaus*); Corning, Red Bluff (Tehama); Columbia (Tuolumne); Davis, Esparto, Weed, Winters, Woodland (Yolo*).

Because of the rapid growth of rural California in the 1970s, three of these counties (Butte, Shasta, and Sutter) became SMSAs in the 1980 census. In the end, only thirty-two of our cases are outside metropolitan areas, due to the paradox that the growth of rural California has made that state second (tied with Rhode Island) to New Jersey in the "urban concentration" of its population.

17. R-squared (the explained variance), population change predicting membership change, is .025 for 1960–1970 and .040 for 1970–1980. Excluding the case of Mendocino yields r-squares of .023 for 1960–1970 and .017 for 1970–1980. Clearly, Mendocino's position as the extreme outlier strongly affects the "explained variance." If we exclude the case the demographic hypothesis is supposed to explain, very little is explained. Another way of saying this is that we must look at other factors than population growth to explain the membership growth of the Mendocino church.

Since the absolute size of a number affects the percentage change of which it is capable, it is relevant to report that the median church size of our sample (on which percent membership change was calculated) was 152 in 1960 and 144 in 1970. Mendocino's size was negligibly smaller (146) in 1960, but significantly smaller (124) in 1970. If Mendocino had been on the median in 1970, the growth of 171 it enjoyed in the 1970s would have yielded a percentage increase of 119% instead of 139%, but the church would still have been the extreme outlier in figure 16, about one-eighth inch below its present position on the scattergram.

18. Technically, this would be an interaction effect between contextual (population) and institutional (local church theology) factors. The hypothesis is that conservative Protestantism appeals especially to the sort of people who are flocking to rural America. We have characterized such persons as "elective parochials."

19. Hadaway (1978, pp. 332–334) found that converts to conservative churches are more likely to participate and contribute than converts to liberal churches. This finding is consistent with the observed changes in Mendocino Presbyterian between the sixties and the seventies.

9. Beachhead for Christ: Mendocino Presbyterian, 1973–1976

1. The tape recordings were begun in 1974, so I have no verbatim record of Underwood's sermons during his first year and a half. It is likely that the parochial part of his appeal developed over time with his increasing familiarity with his congregation. The evangelical aspect was there all along, no doubt.

2. This doctrine was not explicitly stated by Underwood himself, nor had it been formulated at his alma mater, Fuller Theological Seminary, during his student years. By the late 1970s, Richard Quebedeaux, himself a young evangelical of educated tastes and liberal sympathies, was beginning to claim (in *The Worldy Evangelicals*) that Fuller had become "the leading center of neo-orthodox convictions in the world" (1978, p. 100). When I asked him to describe his theology in 1982, Underwood himself used the label "neo-orthodox, in the sense that the meaning of scripture and the nature of its inspiration is to be found in the interaction of the reader and the word, not in the literal sense of the text." In 1976, however, he was still comfortable with the label "evangelical," and in the first years of his ministry he was, as we have just seen, preaching a message of salvation.

3. From a retrospective viewpoint, this can be seen as a practical expression of the neo-orthodox position toward which Underwood was moving during his Mendocino ministry.

4. Merton, 1957; Gouldner, 1957–1958; Roof, 1978.

5. See Howe, 1978; see also Wallace, 1973; Winter, 1974.

6. See Schaeffer, 1970; Sider, 1977.

10. Movement and Institution

1. It was a classic instance of what the sociologist of religion, Joaquim Wach, drawing on his encyclopedic knowledge of church history and citing scores of examples from the past half millenium, called a "collegia pietatis."

> In other words, there is a loosely organized group, limited in numbers and united in a common enthusiasm, peculiar convictions, intense devotion, and rigid discipline. . . . They meet for definite purposes—for prayer, meditation, reading, edification. . . . They consider themselves as the "leaven of the gospel" (1944, pp. 175, 174).

Such groups wish to protect themselves from the compromises made by the environing church, but they disdain to abandon it, for they "aim at the eventual conversion of the entire community."

2. Quoted from *The Jerusalem Bible* by permission of the publisher.

3. For a discussion of "Cursillo," see chapter twelve.

4. Hadaway (1978, p. 335) argues on the basis of national survey data that a combination of doctrinal conservatism and institutionalization conduces to church growth. Sectarian groups like Antioch Fellowship are too unstable to grow as organizations. They may well recruit new members, but they have trouble holding on to those they have.

11. Separate Ways

1. Snyder, 1975, p. 81; used by permission.

2. Mumford's speech is quoted from a tape recording from the 1976 "Festival of the Son," available from Radiance Tapes, Box Z, Eureka, Calif. Quotations from "Armstrong's" (pseud.) speech are from my field notes.

3. Geisel, 1961, p. 24. Used by permission.

4. My sources were interviews with four of the six persons present at the meeting.

5. *Book of Common Worship*, 1946, pp. 246–247.

6. Garfinkel, 1956, pp. 421–422.

12. The Shape of the Vessel

1. The numbers in table 6 are approximate and are presented to provide an impression, not a precise measurement, of the varying levels of commitment in Mendocino Presbyterian Church in a two-decade span.

"Attendance" is average Sunday attendance, not including Easter Sundays or the period between pastorates, divided by the mean enrolled membership for the respective calendar year, then averaged again for the period indicated. Attendance counts date from March 1959 through August 1982.

"Spending per capita" is the total annual receipts or total annual spending reported for the church, multiplied by the U.S. Bureau of Labor Statistics Consumer Price Index (1967=$1.00), and divided by the mean enrolled membership for the respective calendar year, the yearly figures then averaged across the period indicated. Financial figures are for the calendar years 1958 through 1981.

There are two mutually inconsistent sources for the spending figures. One consists of the records of the Mendocino church itself, and the dollar totals represent the reported spending for the year, not including funds channeled to Antioch Ranch or new debt obligations. The internal church records provide a detailed breakdown of categories of spending, but accounting methods changed frequently and considerable study of these records did not resolve all the lacunae and inconsistencies within them. The other source is the annual statistical reports of the denomination, which report "total receipts" of each local church. These figures are much less detailed than the internal ones, but they are more consistent, the same accounting format being used from 1958 through 1972. (Changes in format to provide more detail were made in 1973, 1978, and 1980.) The figures given in table 6 take a weighted arithmetic mean of per-capita spending figures based on these two—internal and denominational—sources.

Except for 1958–1962, the denominational report totals for the Mendocino church are roughly fifteen percent higher than the internal report totals. For the comparison of Higginson's pastorate with Hsu's, this discrepancy poses a problem, since the church under Hsu appears more "committed" if we rely on denominational records, slightly less if we use the internal record. To compare 1958–1972 with 1973–1981, which is the intent of table 6, the discrepancy does not pose a problem. Both sets of figures agree on the qualitative difference between the two periods.

2. One point I cannot clarify is the extent to which the highly skewed distribution of wealth of church members accounts for the greater financial commitment of Underwood's church. First of all, the financial data include

income from all sources—building use "donations" and interest on investments as well as pledges and offerings. Moreover, information on individual contributions was closely guarded by the church treasurer, and I had no access to it. (Underwood told me that even he was not privy to it.) As explained in chapter three, I also had no survey data on individual members' financial worth, some of which was considerable.

It is entirely likely that Underwood's congregation was, on the average, richer than Hsu's or Kimmerly's, although it probably also included more truly poor families (the "voluntary poor" of the counterculture). Yet it is well known among students of church life that poor people tend to give more *because they are more likely to belong to conservative religious bodies that make higher demands on members*. In other words, wealth alone does not account for church contributions, and one has to explain why the wealthy would care to dispose of their worth in this way.

3. See Bord and Faulkner, 1983, pp. 59–67; see also Marcoux, 1982.

4. The description of a cursillo weekend is based partly on the literature but primarily on interviews with members of Mendocino Presbyterian Church who attended cursillos at centers in San Francisco and Santa Rosa between 1976 and 1981.

5. Marcoux, 1982, pp. 93, 97.

6. Source of table 7: 1972 figures given as percentages in 1972 Pastor-seeking Committee "church information form," head count calculated back by author based on N=121 for resident church membership in 1972; data for 1976 compiled by author given his own and his informants' knowledge on 188 persons listed on the church roster as resident members in June 1976, actual count, ages estimated.

7. Kleinman, 1984, provides a picture of a seminary experience similar to Douglas's but at a neighboring seminary.

8. For a vivid fictional account of the dread this dilemma can cause a young minister to a mainline congregation, see Martin Gardner's novel, *The Flight of Peter Fromm* (1973), especially part 3.

9. See chapter twelve, note 1, for cautions regarding church financial data.

10. Source of table 9: based on denominational records (see chapter twelve, note 1). Denominator is total congregational finances or total receipts (accounting format changes). Numerator is total congregational contributions (including both statutory "per capita apportionment" and benevolences) to Presbytery, Synod, and General Assembly (accounting format changes). Totals summed for years indicated before ratio computed.

11. Smylie, 1979; Evans, 1979.

12. Wood, 1981, p. 80.

13. Roof et al., 1979, p. 207.

Conclusion: Of Wine and Wineskins

1. For details of the contrast, see chapter two; a useful guide is Coleman, 1972.

2. The quotations from Kimmerly and Hsu derive from a conversation with the former in 1976 and correspondence with the latter in 1986.

3. Institutional religion has been analyzed most astutely by Talcott Parsons (1978) and Robert Bellah (1970), and its manifestation in the 1950s was most tellingly described by Will Herberg (1960).

4. The reference is to Glock et al., 1967; see also Warner, 1979.

5. Roozen et al., 1984

6. See Roof, 1978, pp. 125–126; Kelley, 1977, pp. 127–128. Peter Berger writes: "A secularized Christianity has to go to considerable exertion to demonstrate that the religious label, as modified in conformity with the spirit of age, has anything special to offer. Why should one buy psychotherapy or racial liberalism in a 'Christian' package, when the same commodities are available under purely secular and for that very reason even more modernistic labels?" (Berger, 1969, pp. 20–21)

7. Hadden, 1969; Quinley, 1974; Wills, 1972. In the United Presbyterian Church, activists secured a $10,000 grant for the Angela Davis Marin County Defense Fund, and, when the predictable conservative reaction inundated them with a 70:1 ratio of unfavorable comment, they defended themselves in typical liberal language.

> The church cannot be bound only by the values and traditions of the majority. The challenge is to the church, in part through the ministry of those the General Assembly has elected to the Council on Church and Race, to continue to "comfort the afflicted and afflict the comfortable," to dare to champion unpopular causes if this is the will of Christ, and to immerse the church in the milieu and experience of despised, neglected and oppressed peoples in order that we may "share his sufferings, becoming like him in his death, that if possible [we] may attain the resurrection from the dead" (Phil. 3:10–11). Faithfulness can mean no less. (Quoted in Fry, 1975, pp. 16–17)

8. See Berger and Neuhaus, 1976, for an articulation of this line of criticism.

9. Among those referring recently to evangelicals as "otherworldly" are Ducey, 1977, p. 41; Quinley, 1974, p. 5; Marty, 1970, p. 227; Roof, 1978, p. 36; Roozen et al., 1984, p. 34.

10. For details, see McGaw, 1980; Neitz, 1986, and Connelly, 1977; Hadden and Swann, 1981; Kelley, 1977.

11. Hoge, 1976, develops this point at length.

12. Fry, 1975, p. 70.

13. Moberg, 1977, argues that the contemporary conservative tenor of evangelicalism is a "great reversal" of the historical American pattern.

14. For a general treatment connecting new left and hip charisma, see Roth, 1975, esp. pp. 154–157.

15. McGaw, 1980; Neitz, 1986; Roof, 1978.

16. Ahlstrom, 1970.

17. Woodward, 1986, writes that liberal Protestants must consider adapting to their status as a minority sect.

18. It should be pointed out that one of the theories that have been developed to account for the weakness of liberal and the strength of evangelical

churches, Dean Kelley's "strictness" theory, has not been supported by the Mendocino findings. Kelley (1977) claims that churches that are strict about membership standards and expect sacrifices from members are more likely to be strong than churches that tolerate doubts and only partial commitment. It is not *what* churches profess, but *how* they profess it, says Kelley, that makes them strong. In the terms of this book, Kelley is talking about a *formal* property like the nascent state. Yet many subsequent studies have cast doubt on Kelley's "strictness" thesis (Hadaway, 1983), and the organizational failure of Larry Redford's behavioral strictness in the face of Eric Underwood's "realism" is more evidence against it. Contrary to Kelley's explicit thesis, I think his data can better be explained under the assumption that there is something about evangelicalism itself that conduces to strength and liberalism weakness, *when we are talking about Christian churches.*

19. See Caplow et al., 1983, chapter 1, for a recent overview of religious statistics in the U.S. See also Gallup, 1985.

20. Mead, 1956; Herberg, 1960, chapters 4 and 6.

21. Based on a study of women's auxiliaries in a frontier Episcopal church in Minnesota, Gundersen (1986, pp. 316, 322) writes: "The major difference between east and west was the local orientation of the western groups in their early stages. Rather than forming to foster outreach to distant areas or others within their community, the women in the frontier towns were the subject of their own activism. They were missionaries on the scene, building for their own families. . . . Even hierarchical denominations such as the Episcopal church were shaped by powerful women's organizations."

Based on his study of the Dutch communities of Chicago, Amry Vandenbosch (1927, p. 24), wrote: "The reason that the Hollander is so conservative in his church and religious life is probably due to the fact that in his economic and social life he is forced to make adjustments to his new environment. He has no choice. Thus it often happens that the second generation is Americanized in all but his church life. His church life he can order as he pleases and here alone his old loyalties can find expression."

Andrew Greeley (1972, p. 105) summarizes: "American religion has strongly insisted on the need for congregational independence and for democratic administration of church affairs."

22. Bellah et al., 1985, pp. 71-75. "When we hear such phrases as 'the gay community' or 'the Japanese-American community,' we need to know a great deal before we can decide the degree to which they are genuine communities and the degree to which they are lifestyle enclaves" (pp. 74–75). Daniel Bell says of the charismatic movement that it relies on "an acting out of feelings in a permissive group setting" (1971, p. 485); see also FitzGerald, 1986.

23. Hadden, 1969, p. 21. It must be emphasized that theological tendencies are discussed here *as they appear in the congregation,* not as they are professed in seminaries. It is to the congregational, not the intellectual, level that the contrast between "lack of sophistication" and "pluralistic ignorance" pertains.

24. Stark and Glock, 1968, p. 213; Roof, 1978, pp. 131–132. Talcott Parsons argued forcefully that religion and the secular order may converge not be-

cause of the capitulation of the former to the latter but because "the secular order may change in the direction of closer approximation of the normative models provided by a religion" (1978, p. 240). From this point of view, American society, especially the educational system, implements Christian values. See also "Christianity" (chapter 9 in Parsons, 1978), and Parsons and Platt, 1973.

25. Neitz, 1986.

26. Neitz, 1986.

27. Parsons and Bales, 1955, chapter 1; see also Goode, 1959; D'Antonio, 1980; Neitz, 1981.

28. The romantic love complex threatens to make marriage itself into a "lifestyle enclave" (Bellah et al., 1985, pp. 73–74). In their study of social mobility, Lipset and Bendix found a greater *ideology of* opportunity in the U.S. than in Europe, though actual rates of mobility were similar. They speculated that "in the United States the modest social origin of a prominent man is a matter of pride to him and a source of inspiration to others, while in Europe it is more likely to be hushed up or conveniently forgotten" (1959, p. 82). Americans' concept of religious careers may have converged on that of their occupational careers. They are proud of their individual achievements.

29. See Simmel, 1965.

30. Neitz, 1986.

31. Cox, 1966, p. 223. According to Max Weber, the doctrine that the faithful were the children of God rather than the instruments of His will "has often driven strong men out of the church" (Weber, 1922, p. 571). It is startling, from this point of view, to see so many manifestly strong men and women staying in churches that preach human dependency on God in the evangelical manner.

In the following theological confession of Jim Wallis, leader of the socially concerned, communitarian evangelical fellowship Sojourners, I take the sociological message to be that the acknowledgment of what I have been calling dependence and humility (as opposed to sufficiency and respectability) is the necessary condition for community.

> In the early days of our community . . . we learned that all our models and schemes for community had to die before God's creative work among us could begin. Our plans and pride over what we could build with our own strength and resources had to be shattered before the spirit had any room to work. And we had to learn that the necessary building materials of Christian community include two characteristics of love: forgiveness and a humble spirit. . . . Learning to forgive one another, and to know our own need for forgiveness, were early lessons that tested the survival of the community. We also had to get over the notion of being perfect people building the perfect community, which could then take on all the big issues of the church and the world. . . . The lesson here is a basic one: The church will never discover what it means to lay down its life for the world until its members begin to lay down their lives for one another (Wallis, 1981, p. 27).

32. Swatos, 1981, pp. 223–226; see also Bossy, 1970; Luidens, 1982; Garrett, 1986. Swatos's argument might be seen as the Protestant analog to the concept of the local congregation's "ethnic" functions, put forward by the

(Roman Catholic) Andrew Greeley, who writes: "The secret of the survival of the organized churches in the United States . . . is their ability to play an ethnic, or at least quasi-ethnic role in American society. By 'ethnic' I mean a phenomenon by which the members of a religious denomination are able to obtain from their religion means of defining who they are and where they stand in a large and complex society" (1972, p. 108). Given the importance attributed in the present study to "achieved" statuses, "ethnic" should be construed broadly.

33. Swatos, 1981, p. 226.

34. Wolin, 1985, p. 16; see also Huntington, 1973; Pekelis, 1973; Calhoun, 1983.

35. The essay by Hulbert (1985) describes some current trends in American culture. The popularity of Garrison Keillor's satirical but affectionate stories from Lake Wobegon (1985) is an index of continuing fascination with small-town life. See also the chronicles of neorural life in Eberle (1982) and Kidder (1985). Hofstadter (1955 and 1963) deals extensively with popular anticosmopolitanism in American culture. Data on American public opinion ("ideal place to live" and "most admired man") are taken from Gallup (1972–1986). In a 1985 Gallup poll, forty-eight percent of the respondents preferred to live in a small town or rural area; of the thirty-eight percent who wished to live in a city (i.e., community of over 50,000 residents), *nearly two-thirds* would prefer to live actually in its suburbs (1986 volume, pp. 64–65).

36. Proctor (1979) is a "how-to-find-it" book for the mobile evangelical.

37. Stump, 1984; Hill, 1985. See also Wuthnow and Christiano (1979), who suggest that migration may self-select for those who are, in terms of the present chapter, cosmopolitan.

38. Roof, 1978, pp. 62–67; Hunter, 1978. Fischer shows how urban Americans choose like-minded friends. Those for whom religion is salient seek out coreligionists. For them, "population concentration supported social involvement in a religious subculture" (1982, p. 213).

39. Church membership data are drawn from *Yearbook*, 1985, and Gallup, 1985. See also chapter eight, note 3. A reasonable estimate is that sixty percent of American adults are *church members*. Other group membership figures can be inferred from General Social Survey items asked repeatedly from 1972 to 1985 (Davis and Smith, 1985, pp. 190–194). According to these data, fifteen percent of Americans belong to labor unions, fourteen percent to professional or academic societies, thirteen percent to school service groups, ten percent to fraternal groups, four percent to political clubs, and twenty-nine percent to no groups at all. But, according to the same surveys, thirty-seven percent belong to church-affiliated groups. (The General Social Survey does not ask about church membership as such.)

Data on church attendance derive from the General Social Survey (Davis and Smith, 1985, p. 124); for the period 1972–1985, 36.1% of the samples (persons eighteen and over) reported attending church "several times a week," "every week," or "nearly every week." Data on voting are taken from *Statistical Abstract of the United States* (U.S. Census, 1986, pp. 238–258); actual votes for the congressional elections of 1974, 1978, and 1982 average 36.3% of the voting-age population (persons eighteen and over) in those years.

40. I have analyzed records from two suburban Presbyterian churches in California, one liberal, the other evangelical, one declining, the other growing (Warner, 1983). Both attracted hundreds of new members during the 1970s, but the evangelical church retained a higher proportion.

41. The authors of the Middletown Ill. study have a different prognosis: "As the relationship between the individual and the polity becomes more encompassing, more uncertain, [and] more antagonistic, the refuge offered by the churches against the insatiable demands of the state seem to become more attractive" (Caplow et al., 1983, p. 301). See also Berger and Neuhaus, 1977.

42. "Conservative" may not be the best word to use in reference to policies some of which are quite radical from the point of view of contemporary practices. Nonetheless, it is a generally understood designation, and no alternative is preferable. For some ambiguities on "conservative" regarding public schools, see Dolbeare and Hammond, 1971, and Vitz, 1986.

43. Rothenberg and Newport, 1984, chapter 1; Wald, 1987, chapter 7.

44. See McNamara (1985, pp. 66–69) on American Catholics. For some indications of successful use of church authority on foreign and defense policy questions, see Rothenberg and Newport, 1984, pp. 50–53, and Tamney and Johnson, 1985. In any discussion of religious authoritarianism, it should be pointed out that Jerry Falwell has scrupulously attempted to keep his activities within constitutional bounds.

45. Shupe and Stacey (1982 and 1983) report data on the public response to the Moral Majority; Moore and Whitt (1986) report on results from a Nebraska survey; Tamney and Johnson (1983) have data from Indiana. Rothenberg and Newport (1984, chapters 6 and 8) report results of a national survey of evangelicals' opinions on a variety of topics, including political-religious leaders; they write: "our data indicate that evangelicals and fundamentalists do not believe that the local church is an appropriate forum for politicking" (p. 150). See also Liebman, 1983, p. 232; Hunter, 1984, p. 374; Wald, 1987, pp. 272–278; Liebman and Wuthnow, 1983; Bromley and Shupe, 1984. In response to the generally negative popular response to the "Moral Majority," Falwell has recently merged it into the "Liberty Federation."

46. Simpson's (1983) analysis of 1977 General Social Survey data indicates that thirty percent of adult Americans take consistently "conservative" positions on four items: the morality of homosexual relations, school prayer, women's role, and abortion rights. Another forty-two percent can be classified as conservative supporters. Only six percent take a consistently "liberal" line on these items. On evangelicals' opinions, see Rothenberg and Newport, 1984, chapter 5; on public opinion regarding abortion and school prayer, see Gallup (1972–1986), 1983 volume, pp. 139–143 and 172–174. The notion that evangelicals are "united theologically" is relative to their disagreements with liberals and modernists.

47. Data on evangelical and general public opinion derive from four

sources. (1) A national survey of evangelicals conducted in 1983 by Stuart Rothenberg and Frank Newport (1984, at pp. 70–76), who used a broad criterion of "evangelical" similar to that developed in chapter two—confession of personal faith in Jesus Christ—and asked Gallup poll questions on abortion. (2) Gallup poll results for 1975–1983, reported in Gallup 1972–1986, 1983 volume, pp. 139–143. (3) General Social Survey data for 1972–1985, marginals reported in Davis and Smith (1985), pp. 215–217. (4) Machine-readable General Social Survey data for 1984, analyzed by the author, using Biblical literalism (BIBLE=1 or BIBLEY=1) as the index of evangelicalism for the purposes at hand. Gallup and Rothenberg and Newport ask whether respondents agree or disagree that abortion should be or should not be legally available in the U.S. The General Social Survey asks respondents' opinions whether a pregnant woman should be able to obtain a legal abortion under a variety of circumstances (rape, serious fetal defect, poverty, etc.). The most stringent criterion has been found to be serious danger to the woman's health; the least, abortion for any reason. Assuming that "no" on GSS item ABHLTH is equivalent to Gallup's "Illegal—all circumstances" and that "yes" on ABANY equals Gallup's "Legal—all circumstances," and attributing all other respondents, including those who "don't know" and did not answer, to "legal—some circumstances," we have the following distributions of opinion (in percentages):

| | General Population | | Evangelicals | |
	Gallup 75–83	GSS 72–85	R–N 1983	GSS 1984
Legal, all	23	36	29	21
Legal, some	58	55	44	64
Illegal, all	19	9	27	15

See also Gallup, 1972–1986, 1984 volume, p. 240. Barna and McKay (1984), pp. 14–16, decry the lack of consensus among evangelicals on abortion. I am indebted to Kristin Luker (Luker, 1984) and Elfriede Wedam for heightening my awareness of the complexity of opinion on abortion.

48. Rothenberg and Newport, 1984, pp. 75–76. Such an attitude, which would seem to countenance abortion as long as it is not publically funded, is often dismissed as "hypocritical," but public adherence to values in spite of "institutionalized evasion" is a long-standing American pattern (Williams, 1970, Chapter 10).

49. Lorentzen, 1980, pp. 152–153.

50. Neuhaus, 1985, p. 46. "The clamor at the gates may not be the sound of hostile wrath. It may be, simply, a plea for admission" (Brinkley, 1986, p. 33). What we see in the public appearance of the religious right is an attempt to resurrect "Biblical language" in American discourse (Tipton, 1982, chapter 2; Bellah et al., 1985, chapter 2; Swidler, 1986; Neuhaus, 1984). Single-issue voting (on right to life or, twenty-five years ago, on right to work) is neither new nor the preserve of the right. What distinguishes the right, then, is less "deflation" of values than a stubborn competition over the terms of debate (cf. Parsons, 1969; Lechner, 1985b).

In this sense there may be some truth to the . . . fundamentalist/evangelical claim that "secular humanism" has gained priority and thus threatens to become *the* superstructure. . . . In addition, the state, in its judicial, executive, and legislative branches, has become more and more involved in areas of life that formerly were within the orbit of religion. Such processes can be seen as threatening secularistic dedifferentiation. If this is so, then a case can be made that while the impulse on the part of fundamentalists is toward dedifferentiation, they may, if their efforts are kept limited, actually contribute to maintaining cultural tension and institutional differentiation [Lechner, 1985a, pp. 256–257].

51. Wood and Hughes, 1984. The danger from the political-religious right wing has been exaggerated by the combined efforts of the right and left. Jerry Falwell has gone out of his way to claim influence over public opinion and public events, and Norman Lear, founder of "People for the American Way," has found it convenient to take Falwell at his word. Falwell returns the favor. According to a recent *Washington Post* story distributed by Lear, PAW raises money "through a time-honored technique: painting the opposition in fearsome colors. . . . Lear, in turn, is a leading character in Falwell's fundraising appeals" (Kurtz, 1986). For an example of overreaction, see Judis, 1986; for a trenchant analysis, see Hunter, 1983b.

52. Ammerman, 1987, chapter 5; see also Caplow et al., 1983, pp. 98–99, 118–121, 127, 316–317, on intermarriage and interfaith civility. Two generations ago, American Catholics were those who, nominally at least, were ecclesiastically exclusive, but American religious accommodation changed that: "Though theologians might protest, the average American Catholic—to the degree that he became an American—could not help but regard American society as intrinsically pluralistic, and his own church as one among several" (Herberg, 1960, p. 151).

53. This is a very summary proposition. On bureaus and missions, see Harrison (1959), Pratt (1972), Berk (1978), Richardson et al. (1979), P. Berger (1981), Hill and Owen (1982); on communes, see Zablocki (1971), Kanter (1972), Harris (1973), B. Berger (1981), Gordon (1984); on seminaries, see Hadden (1969), Wills (1972), Kleinman (1984); on congregations (parishes) as moderating, see Neal (1965), Wood (1981).

54. Ammerman, 1987, chapter 7.

Glossary

altar call:

an appeal by an evangelist at the end of his sermon for worshippers to come forward to signify their decision to commit their lives to Jesus Christ.

Arminianism *(after Jacob Arminius, 1560–1609):*

doctrine opposing Calvinism (q.v.) and maintaining that Christ died for all humans, not only the elect, and that the individual must voluntarily accept the gift of salvation; historically the doctrine of American Methodism.

baptism, infant:

ceremonial sprinkling with water as a token of the child's reception into the "body of Christ," i.e., the church.

baptism, believer's *or* adult:

sprinkling or immersion in water as token of the individual's willed acceptance of the Lordship of Jesus Christ.

baptism, spirit; second; *or* fire:

experience of reception of the Holy Spirit, often in the form of speaking in tongues; frequently referred to by pentecostals as "the Baptism."

Bible translations:

Since the Reformation, there have been two major traditions in English translation of the Bible. The medieval Latin Bible, known as the Vulgate, took form by the seventh century, largely on the basis of work by St. Jerome in the fourth century. When Protestants came to translate the scriptures, they excluded certain books and passages included in the Old Testament by the medieval editors that had not been part of the Hebrew Bible. They called these excluded materials "apocryphal," but the Protestant objections were anathematized by the Roman Catholic Council of Trent in 1546. The main Roman Catholic English version of the Bible, the Rheims-Douai version dating from the sixteenth century and revised in the eighteenth, is a translation of the Vulgate, and therefore contains material that Protestant translations do not. Foremost among English Protestant translations is the King James, or Authorized, Version of 1611, a masterpiece of English literature, for which *KJV* is the abbreviation used in this book. I have cited KJV passages when they seemed the most familiar to modern secular readers. The KJV is held dear by many evangelicals and fundamentalists, some, as Ammerman (1987) shows, regarding it as the only true voice of God. Among the evangelicals I knew in Mendocino, the KJV held a place of special honor, but it was only one of many translations and paraphrases used. *RSV* refers to the Revised Standard Version of 1951, the standard Bible of mainline American Protestantism, the copyright to which is owned by the National Council of Churches. The Bible I carried in Mendocino and still use for reference is the *Oxford Annotated Bible with the Apocrypha*, an RSV Bible with the "apocryphal" material added as an appendix, but few other persons at Mendocino prayer meetings seemed to have an RSV. In the text of the book, I use RSV citations for the sake of modern English intelligibility and ecumenical meaning. *NASV* refers to the New American Standard Version, a modern (1971) revision of the KJV that stays closer to literal Greek and Hebrew than does the RSV. It was preferred by many conservative evangelicals during my period of field work. Today, most of them would be using the *NIV* or New International Version, published in 1978 in the United States by Zondervan of Grand Rapids, Michigan, but that translation was not completed at the time I was doing fieldwork. A surprisingly large number of Mendocino evangelicals used *The Jerusalem Bible* (JB), which is an authorized Catholic Bible (i.e., containing the "Apocrypha" as canonical material), but one based on modern scholarship into ancient manuscripts instead of on the Vulgate. An English version of a French translation dated 1956, the JB was published in the United States by Doubleday in 1966 and is distinguished for its scholarly notes, literary style, typography, binding, and size. It is a physically large and beautiful book.

call *(Presby.):*   the invitation leading to a quasi-contractual relationship between a member of the clergy and a local congregation.

Calvinism
(after John Calvin, 1509–1564):

doctrine stressing the absolute sovereignty of God and, consequently, the eternal predestination of humans either to salvation or damnation, and, as a corollary, the irresistibility of God's grace; historically, the doctrine of the Presbyterian and Reformed churches.

charismatic:

one who has experienced the baptism of the holy spirit; theologically equivalent to *pentecostal* but socially differentiated; used by middle-class pentecostals.

clergy titles
(Presby.):

clergy (who may be male or female) are called "ministers," technically "teaching elders," to signal that they serve, rather than dominate, the laity; they are not to be called "priests," which suggests that an intermediary is needed between humans and God. The minister of a congregation, or chief minister if more than one, is called the "pastor."

deacons *(Presby.):*

a group of specially designated (ordained) laypersons, with traditional responsibiliity for the care of the needy and infirm; distinguished from "elders."

Doxology, the
(Protestant):

the congregational hymn, words by Thomas Ken, melody by Louis Bourgeois, sung typically after the offering, beginning with the words, "Praise God From Whom All Blessings Flow."

elders, ruling
(Presby.):

laypersons elected and ordained by a congregation to serve on its governing board, or "session."

elders, teaching:

see "clergy titles."

elders *(new evangelical):*

persons recognized within a fellowship as having special authority.

evangelist:

one who preaches the gospel; often itinerant.

evangelical:

one who believes in salvation by faith in the atoning death of Jesus Christ, the authority of scripture, and the centrality of preaching as contrasted to ritual (based on Webster's; see also chapter 2).

fulfilled Jew
(new evangelical):

a Jewish convert to evangelical Christianity who stresses the fulfillment of messianic promises in Jesus Christ and thereby maintains the continuity of his or her religious identity.

JB:

see "Bible translations."

KJV:

see "Bible translations."

Koinonia *(from the Greek):*

sharing, deep fellowship, communion; a fashionable concept among Protestant seminarians in the 1950s and 1960s.

liturgy:	prescribed form of public worship.
mainline church:	an imprecise and fluid, but irreplaceable, term designating the Protestant churches that adhere to the norms of American denominationalism, mutual tolerance chief among them; indexed frequently by denominational affiliation with the National Council of Churches, hence including the American Baptist Church, the United Church of Christ, the Episcopal Church, the (new) Evangelical Lutheran Church in America, the United Methodist Church, and the Presbyterian Church; meant to exclude fundamentalist and separatist churches, such as many independent Baptist churches and pentecostal and holiness groups. The status of congregations of the Southern Baptist Convention is ambiguous, those dominant in their community often having a mainline self-concept, despite their denomination's refusal to align with the National Council of Churches. Ambiguous also is the status of such black denominations as the African Methodist Episcopal Church, the AME Zion Church, and the National Baptist Convention, members of the N.C.C. For an even broader use of the term, see Marty, 1976, chap. 3.
NASV:	see "Bible translations."
pentecostal:	see "charismatic."
Presbyterian Church:	denominations historically distinguished by Calvinist theology and representative polity; as historical doctrinal disputes are mooted, distinguished increasingly by organizational form, especially rule by "elders" (Presbyters, from the Greek). For the period of this study, Mendocino Presbyterian Church was a congregation of the United Presbyterian Church in the United States of America (UPCUSA), also known as the "northern" Presbyterian church, which was the product of a 1958 merger between the Presbyterian Church in the United States of America (PCUSA), to which the Mendocino congregation had belonged, and the United Presbyterian Church in North America. In 1983, the UPCUSA merged with the Presbyterian Church in the United States (PCUS) or "southern" Presbyterian church, to form a new Presbyterian Church in the United States of America (PCUSA), thus ending a split going back to pre–Civil War disputes over slavery.
	Presbyterian governance is representative and

multitiered. Lay *elders* (q.v.) are elected by the local congregation to govern its spiritual affairs in the body known as the *Session*, or board of elders, of which the pastor is presiding officer, or "moderator." Lay elders are in theory represented equally with clergy at every level of governance, or "judicatory," above the local congregation. The first judicatory above the congregation is the *Presbytery*, where each congregation is represented by its minister and a lay elder. The minister is, in fact, a member of the Presbytery, not of his own congregation, and answerable to it. The Presbytery meets regularly several times a year, and it actively reviews the records of local congregations. Mendocino Presbyterian is part of the Presbytery of the Redwoods, which encompasses the territory from San Francisco Bay to the Oregon border and from the Pacific Ocean to the Coast Range.

The next level of judicatory is that of the *Synod*, whose meetings are less frequent but principles of representation are similar to those of the Presbytery. In California, Synod boundaries have recently been unstable: prior to 1967, the Presbytery of the Redwoods was part of the Synod of California, comprising California, Nevada, and Utah. From 1968 through 1972, it was in the Synod of the Golden Gate, a much smaller area of coastal California from Monterey County northward. Since 1973, there has been a Synod of the Pacific, incorporating central and northern California, southern Idaho, and Nevada and Oregon. It is important to note that "Synod" does not have for Presbyterians the importance attributed to it for Lutheran denominations.

The highest judicatory, and the authoritative denomination, is the *General Assembly*, which meets annually with equal numbers of lay and clerical delegates. The various boards and agencies of the church, headquartered primarily in New York, are responsible to the General Assembly.

Presbytery: see "Presbyterian Church."

RSV: see "Bible translations."

service, church: is to Protestants what "mass" is to Catholics.

Session *(Presby.):* see "Presbyterian Church."

Synod *(Presby.):* see "Presbyterian Church."

Trustees *(Presby.):*	body of elders (q.v.) responsible for the property and legal affairs of the congregation.
UPCUSA:	see "Presbyterian Church."
walk *(new evangelical):*	behavior, from a religious point of view; "his walk is not right" means that he is misbehaving.
witness:	to testify publicly about one's religious faith.

References

Ahlstrom, Sydney E. 1970. "The Radical Turn in Theology and Ethics: Why It Occurred in the 1960s." *The Annals of the American Academy of Political and Social Science* 387 (January): 1–13.

Alberoni, Francesco. 1984. *Movement and Institution.* Translated by Patricia C. Arden Delmoro. New York: Columbia University Press.

Ammerman, Nancy. 1987. *Bible Believers: Fundamentalists in the Modern World.* New Brunswick, N.J.: Rutgers University Press.

Barna, George, and McKay, William Paul. 1984. *Vital Signs: Emerging Social Trends and the Future of American Christianity.* Westchester, Ill.: Crossway Books.

Basham, Don. 1972. *Deliver Us From Evil.* Grand Rapids, Mich.: Zondervan

BCW. 1946. *The Book of Common Worship.* Philadelphia: Presbyterian Church in the United States of America.

Becker, Howard S. 1970. *Sociological Work: Method and Substance.* Chicago: Aldine.

Bell, Daniel. 1971. "Religion in the 'Sixties." *Social Research* 38 (Autumn): 447–497.

Bellah, Robert N. 1970. *Beyond Belief: Essays on Religion in a Post-Traditional World.* New York: Harper and Row.

Bellah, Robert N.; Madsen, Richard; Sullivan, William M.; Swidler, Ann; and Tipton, Steven M. 1985. *Habits of the Heart: Individualism and Commitment in American Life.* Berkeley, Los Angeles, London: University of California Press.

Bendix, Reinhard, et al., eds. 1973. *State and Society: A Reader in Comparative Political Sociology.* Berkeley, Los Angeles, London: University of California Press.

Berger, Bennett M. 1981. *The Survival of a Counterculture: Ideological Work and Everyday Life Among Rural Communards.* Berkeley, Los Angeles, London: University of California Press.

Berger, Bennett M., and Hackett, Bruce M. 1974. "The Decline of Age Grading in Rural Hippie Communes." *Journal of Social Issues* 30 (2): 163–183.

Berger, Peter L. 1969. *The Sacred Canopy.* Garden City, N.Y.: Doubleday Anchor.

————. 1981. "The Class Struggle in American Religion." *The Christian Century* 98 (February): pp. 194–199.

Berger, Peter L., and Luckmann, Thomas. 1967. *The Social Construction of Reality*. Garden City, N.Y.: Doubleday Anchor.

Berger, Peter L., and Neuhaus, Richard John, eds. 1976. *Against the World For the World: The Hartford Appeal and the Future of American Religion*. New York: The Seabury Press.

————. 1977. *To Empower People: The Role of Mediating Structures in Public Policy*. Washington, D.C.: American Enterprise Institute for Public Policy Research.

Berk, Marc. 1978. "Pluralistic Theory and Church Policy Positions on Racial and Sexual Equality." *Sociological Analysis* 39 (Winter): 338–350

Bettelheim, Bruno. 1960. *The Informed Heart: Autonomy in a Mass Age*. Glencoe, Ill.: The Free Press.

Bonhoeffer, Dietrich. 1954. *Life Together*. San Francisco: Harper and Row.

Bord, Richard J., and Faulkner, Joseph E. 1983. *The Catholic Charismatics: The Anatomy of a Modern Religious Movement*. University Park, Penn.: Pennsylvania State University Press.

Bossy, John. 1970. "The Counter-Reformation and the People of Catholic Europe." *Past and Present* 47 (May): 51–70.

Bradshaw, Ted K., and Blakely, Edward J. 1979. *Rural Communities in Advanced Industrial Society*. New York: Praeger.

Brinkley, Alan. 1986. "The Oral Majority." *The New Republic* 195 (September 29): 28–33.

Bromley, David G., and Shupe, Anson, eds., 1984. *New Christian Politics*. Macon, Ga.: Mercer University Press.

Broom, Leonard, and Selznick, Philip. 1968. *Sociology: A Text with Adapted Readings*. Fourth edition. New York: Harper and Row.

Calhoun, Craig Jackson. 1983. "The Radicalism of Tradition: Community Strength or Venerable Disguise and Borrowed Language." *American Journal of Sociology* 88 (March): 886–914.

Campbell, Ernest Q., and Pettigrew, Thomas F. 1959. *Christians in Racial Crisis: A Study of Little Rock's Ministry*. Washington, D.C.: Public Affairs Press.

Caplow, Theodore; Bahr, Howard M.; and Chadwick, Bruce A. 1983. *All Faithful People: Change and Continuity in Middletown's Religion*. Minneapolis: University of Minnesota Press.

Coffin, William Sloane, Jr. 1977. *Once to Every Man: A Memoir*. New York: Atheneum.

Coleman, Richard J. 1972. *Issues of Theological Warfare: Evangelicals and Liberals*. Grand Rapids, Mich.: Wm. B. Eerdmans.

Collins, Randall. 1975. *Conflict Sociology: Toward an Explanatory Science*. New York: Academic Press.

Connelly, James T. 1977. Neo-Pentecostalism: The Charismatic Revival in the Mainline Protestant and Roman Catholic Churches in the United States, 1960–1971. Ph.D. diss., School of Divinity, University of Chicago.

Cox, Harvey. 1966. *The Secular City: Secularization and Urbanization in Theological Perspective.* Revised ed. New York: Macmillan.

D'Antonio, William V. 1980. "The Family and Religion: Exploring a Changing Relationship." *Journal for the Scientific Study of Religion* 19 (June): 89–104.

Davis, James Allan, and Smith, Tom W. 1985. *General Social Surveys, 1972–1985: Cumulative Codebook.* Chicago: National Opinion Research Center.

DeJong, Gordon F., and Sell, Ralph R. 1977. "Population Redistribution, Migration, and Residential Preferences." *The Annals of the American Academy of Political and Social Science* 429 (January): 130–144.

Dolbeare, Kenneth M., and Hammond, Phillip E. 1971. *The School Prayer Decisions: From Court Policy to Local Practice.* Chicago: University of Chicago Press.

Douglas, Mary. 1969. "Social Preconditions of Enthusiasm and Heterodoxy." Pp. 69–80 in Robert F. Spencer, ed., *Forms of Symbolic Action* (Proceedings of the 1969 Annual Spring Meeting of the American Ethnological Society). Seattle: University of Washington Press.

Doyle, Ruth T., and Kelly, Sheila M. 1979. "Comparison of Trends in Ten Denominations, 1950–1975." Pp. 144–159 and 364–365 in Hoge and Roozen, 1979.

Ducey, Michael H. 1977. *Sunday Morning: Aspects of Urban Ritual.* New York: The Free Press.

Durkheim, Emile. 1915. *The Elementary Forms of the Religious Life.* Trans. Joseph Ward Swain. New York: The Free Press, 1965.

Eberle, Nancy. 1982. *Return to Main Street: A Journey to Another America.* New York: W. W. Norton.

Ebert, Roger. 1984. *A Kiss Is Still a Kiss.* Kansas City: Andrews, McMeel, and Parker.

Ellwood, Robert S., Jr. 1979. *Alternative Altars: Unconventional and Eastern Spirituality in America.* Chicago: University of Chicago Press.

Erikson, Kai T. 1976. *Everything in Its Path.* New York: Simon and Schuster.

Evans, Robert A. 1979. "Recovering the Church's Transforming Middle: Theological Reflections on the Balance Between Faithfulness and Effectiveness." Pp. 288–314 and 372 in Hoge and Roozen, 1979.

Fischer, Claude S. 1982. *To Dwell Among Friends: Personal Networks in Town and City.* Chicago: University of Chicago Press.

FitzGerald, Frances 1986. *Cities on a Hill: A Journey Through Contemporary American Cultures.* New York: Simon and Schuster.

Flowers, Ronald B. 1984. *Religion in Strange Times: The 1960s and 1970s.* Macon, Ga.: Mercer University Press.

Forell, George Wolfgang. 1976. "Reason, Relevance and a Radical Gospel." Pp. 63–77 in Berger and Neuhaus, 1976.

Fry, John R. 1975. *The Trivialization of the United Presbyterian Church.* New York: Harper and Row.

Gallup. 1972–1986 *The Gallup Poll: Public Opinion, 1935–1971.* Three volumes. New York: Random House, 1972.

The Gallup Poll: Public Opinion, 1972–1977. Two volumes. Wilmington, Del.: Scholarly Resources, 1978.

The Gallup Poll: Public Opinion, 1978 [through] *1985*. Annual volumes. Wilmington, Del.: Scholarly Resources, 1979 through 1986.

———. 1982. "Religion in America, 1982." *The Gallup Report* 201–202 (June–July).

———. 1984. "Religion in America, 1984." *The Gallup Report* 222 (March).

———. 1985. "Religion in America, 50 Years: 1935–1985." *The Gallup Report* 236 (May).

Gardner, Martin. 1973. *The Flight of Peter Fromm*. Los Altos, Calif.: William Kaufmann.

Garfinkel, Harold. 1956. "Conditions of Successful Degradation Ceremonies." *American Journal of Sociology* 61 (March): 420–424.

Garrett, William R. 1986. "Religion and Politics in the Constitutional Era: A Reinterpretation of the Localist/Cosmopolitan Orientations in Early American Social Experience." Paper presented at the Annual Meeting of the Society for the Scientific Study of Religion, Washington, D.C.

Geertz, Clifford. 1973. *The Interpretation of Cultures*. New York: Basic Books.

Geisel, Theodor Seuss. 1961. *The Sneetches and Other Stories*. New York: Random House.

Gerlach, Luther P., and Hine, Virginia H. 1970. *People, Power, Change: Movements of Social Transformation*. Indianapolis: Bobbs-Merrill.

Gerstner, John H. 1975. "The Theological Boundaries of Evangelical Faith." Pp. 21–37 in Wells and Woodbridge, 1975.

Gilkey, Langdon. 1967. "Social and Intellectual Sources of Contemporary Protestant Theology in America." *Daedalus* 96 (Winter): 69–98.

Glock, Charles Y.; Ringer, Benjamin B.; and Babbie, Earl R. 1967. *To Comfort and to Challenge: A Dilemma of the Contemporary Church*. Berkeley and Los Angeles: University of California Press.

Goffman, Erving. 1967. *Interaction Ritual*. Garden City, N.Y.: Doubleday Anchor.

Goode, William J. 1959. "The Theoretical Importance of Love." *American Sociological Review* 24 (February): 38–47.

Goodman, Grace Ann. 1968. *Rocking the Ark: Nine Case Studies of Traditional Churches in Process of Change*. New York: Board of National Missions, United Presbyterian Church in the U.S.A.

Gordon, David F. 1984. "The Role of the Local Social Context in Social Movement Accommodation: A Case Study of Two Jesus People Groups." *Journal for the Scientific Study of Religion* 23 (December): 381–395.

Gouldner, Alvin W. 1957–1958. "Cosmopoltians and Locals: Toward an Analysis of Latent Social Roles." *Administrative Science Quarterly* 2 (December and March): 281–306, 444–480.

Greeley, Andrew. 1972. *The Denominational Society: A Sociological Approach to Religion in America*. Glenview, Ill.: Scott, Foresman.

Gunderson, Joan R. 1986. "The Local Parish as a Female Institution: The Experience of All Saints Episcopal Church in Frontier Minnesota." *Church History* 55 (September): 307–322.

Hackett, Bruce M., and Schwartz, Seymour. 1980. "Energy Conservation and Rural Alternative Lifestyles." *Social Problems* 28 (December): 165–178.

Hadaway, Christopher Kirk. 1978. "Denominational Switching and Membership Growth: In Search of a Relationship." *Sociological Analysis* 39 (Winter): 321–337.

———. 1983. "Conservatism and Social Strength in a Liberal Denomination." *Review of Religious Research* 21 (Summer): pp. 302–314.

Hadden, Jeffrey K. 1969. *The Gathering Storm in the Churches.* Garden City, N.Y.: Doubleday.

Hadden, Jeffrey K., and Longino, Charles F., Jr. 1974. *Gideon's Gang: A Case Study of the Church in Social Action.* Philadelphia: Pilgrim Press.

Hadden, Jeffrey K., and Charles E. Swann. 1981. *Prime-Time Preachers: The Rising Power of Televangelism.* Reading, Mass.: Addison-Wesley.

Hammond, Phillip E. 1983. "Another Great Awakening?" Pp. 207–223 in Liebman and Wuthnow, 1983.

Hammond, Phillip E., ed. 1985. *The Sacred in a Secular Age: Toward Revision in the Scientific Study of Religion.* Berkeley, Los Angeles, London: University of California Press.

Harris, W. Russell, III. 1973. Urban Place Fellowship: An Example of a Communitarian Social Structure. Ph.D. diss., College of Education, Michigan State University.

Harrison, Paul M. 1959. *Authority and Power in the Free Church Tradition.* Princeton, N.J.: Princeton University Press.

Hauser, Philip M. 1981. "The Census of 1980." *Scientific American* 245 (November): 53–61.

Heinz, Donald. 1983. "The Struggle to Define America." Pp. 133–148 in Liebman and Wuthnow, 1983.

Heirich, Max. 1977. "Change of Heart: A Test of Some Widely Held Theories About Religious Conversion." *American Journal of Sociology* 83 (November): 653–680.

Herberg, Will. 1960. *Protestant, Catholic, Jew: An Essay in American Religious Sociology.* Second ed. Garden City, N.Y.: Doubleday.

Hill, Samuel S. 1985. "Religion and Region in America." *The Annals of the American Academy of Political and Social Science* 480 (July): 132–141.

Hill, Samuel S., and Owen, Dennis E. 1982. *The New Religious Political Right in America.* Nashville: Abingdon.

Hofstadter, Richard. 1955. *The Age of Reform: From Bryan to F.D.R.* New York: Knopf.

———. 1963. *Anti-Intellectualism in American Life.* New York: Knopf.

Hoge, Dean R. 1976. *Division in the Protestant House: The Basic Reasons Behind Intra-Church Conflicts.* Philadelphia: The Westminster Press.

Hoge, Dean R., and Roozen, David A., eds. 1979. *Understanding Church Growth and Decline, 1950–1978.* New York and Philadelphia: The Pilgrim Press.

Howe, Richard Herbert. 1978. "Max Weber's Elective Affinities: Sociology Within the Bounds of Pure Reason." *American Journal of Sociology* 84 (September): 366–385.

Hulbert, Ann. 1985. "Rural Chic." *The New Republic* 193 (September 2): 25–30.

Hunter, Albert. 1978. "Persistence of Local Sentiments in Mass Society." Pp. 133–162 in David Street and Associates, *Handbook of American Urban Life.* San Francisco: Jossey-Bass.

Hunter, James Davison. 1981. "Operationalizing Evangelicalism: A Review, Critique and Proposal." *Sociological Analysis* 42 (Winter): 363–372.

——. 1983a. *American Evangelicalism: Conservative Religion and the Quandary of Modernity.* New Brunswick, N.J.: Rutgers University Press.

——. 1983b. "The Liberal Reaction." Pp. 149–163 in Liebman and Wuthnow, 1983.

——. 1984. "Religion and Political Civility: the Coming Generation of American Evangelicals." *Journal for the Scientific Study of Religion* 23 (December): 364–380.

——. 1985. "Conservative Protestantism." Pp. 150–166 in Hammond, 1985.

Huntington, Samuel P. 1973. "Political Modernization: America vs. Europe." Pp. 170–200 in Bendix et al., 1973.

Hustad, Donald P., ed. 1974. *Hymns for the Living Church.* Carol Stream, Ill.: Hope Publishing Co.

Iannaconne, Laurence R. forthcoming. "A Formal Model of Church and Sect." *American Journal of Sociology.*

Johnson, Benton. 1985. "Liberal Protestantism: End of the Road?" *The Annals of the American Academy of Political and Social Science* 480 (July): 39–52.

Johnson, Harry M. 1960. *Sociology: A Systematic Introduction.* New York: Harcourt, Brace, and World.

Judge, E. A. 1980. "The Social Identity of the First Christians: A Question of Method in Religious History." *Journal of Religious History* 11 (December): 201–217.

Judis, John B. 1986. "The Charge of the Light Brigade." *The New Republic* 195 (September 29): pp. 16–19.

Kanter, Rosabeth Moss. 1972. *Commitment and Community: Communes and Utopias in Sociological Perspective.* Cambridge: Harvard University Press.

Keillor, Garrison. 1985. *Lake Wobegon Days.* New York: Viking.

Kelley, Dean M. 1977. *Why Conservative Churches Are Growing.* Second ed. San Francisco: Harper and Row.

——. 1979. "Commentary: Is Religion a Dependent Variable?" Pp. 334–343 in Hoge and Roozen, 1979.

Kidder, Tracy. 1985. *House.* Boston: Houghton-Mifflin.

King, Martin Luther, Jr. 1964. "Letter from Birmingham Jail, April 16, 1963." Pp. 77–100 in *Why We Can't Wait.* New York: Harper and Row.

Kleinman, Sherryl. 1984. *Equals Before God: Seminarians as Humanistic Professionals.* Chicago: University of Chicago Press.

Kornhauser, William. 1959. *The Politics of Mass Society.* Glencoe, Ill.: The Free Press.

Kurtz, Howard. 1986. "Norman Lear's Crusade Widens." *Washington Post* (February 3).

Ladd, Everett Carll, Jr., and Lipset, Seymour Martin. 1975. *The Divided Academy: Professors and Politics.* New York: McGraw-Hill.

Lechner, Frank J. 1985a. "Fundamentalism and Sociocultural Revitalization in America: A Sociological Interpretation." *Sociological Analysis* 46 (Fall): 243–259.

———. 1985b. "Modernity and Its Discontents." Pp. 157–176 in Jeffrey C. Alexander, ed., *Neofunctionalism*. Beverly Hills: Sage Publications.

Lenski, Gerhard. 1961. *The Religious Factor*. Garden City, N.Y.: Doubleday.

Lever, Janet. 1981. "Multiple Methods of Data Collection: A Note on Divergence." *Urban Life* 10 (July): 199–213.

———. 1983. *Soccer Madness*. Chicago: University of Chicago Press.

Liebman, Robert C. 1983. "The Making of the New Christian Right." Pp. 227–238 in Liebman and Wuthnow, 1983.

Liebman, Robert C., and Wuthnow, Robert. 1983. *The New Christian Right: Mobilization and Legitimation*. Hawthorne, N.Y.: Aldine Publishing.

Lindsell, Harold. 1976. *The Battle for the Bible*. Grand Rapids, Mich: Zondervan.

———. 1979. *The Bible in the Balance*. Grand Rapids, Mich.: Zondervan.

Lipset, Seymour Martin. 1967. *The First New Nation*. Garden City, N.Y.: Doubleday Anchor.

Lipset, Seymour Martin, and Bendix, Reinard. 1959. *Social Mobility in Industrial Society*. Berkeley and Los Angeles: University of California Press.

Lofland, John. 1971. *Analyzing Social Settings*. Belmont, Calif.: Wadsworth.

Long, Larry H., and DeArc, Diana. 1980. *Migration to Nonmetropolitan Areas: Appraising the Trend and Reasons for Moving*. Special Demographic Analyses, CDS-802. Washington, D.C.: U.S. Bureau of the Census.

Lorentzen, Louise J. 1980. "Evangelical Life Style Concerns Expressed in Political Action." *Sociological Analysis* 41 (Summer): 144–154.

Lowell, James Russell. 1978. *The Poetical Works of James Russell Lowell*. Ed. Marjorie R. Kaufman. Boston: Houghton-Mifflin.

Luidens, Donald A. 1982. "Bureaucratic Control in a Protestant Denomination." *Journal for the Scientific Study of Religion* 21 (June): 163–175.

Luker, Kristin. 1984. *Abortion and the Politics of Motherhood*. Berkeley, Los Angeles, London: University of California Press.

Marcoux, Marcene. 1982. *Cursillo: Anatomy of a Movement*. New York: Lambeth Press.

Marsden, George M. 1980. *Fundamentalism and American Culture: The Shaping of Twentieth Century Evangelicalism, 1870–1925*. New York: Oxford University Press.

Marty, Martin E. 1970. *Righteous Empire. The Protestant Experience in America*. New York: The Dial Press.

———. 1976. *A Nation of Behavers*. Chicago: University of Chicago Press.

McGaw, Douglas B., with Wright, Elliott. 1980. *A Tale of Two Congregations: Commitment and Social Structure in a Charismatic and Mainline Congregation*. Hartford: The Hartford Seminary Foundation.

McGuire, Meredith B. 1974. "An Interpretive Comparison of Elements of the Pentecostal and Underground Church Movements in American Catholicism." *Sociological Analysis* 35 (Spring): 57–65.

———. 1982. *Pentecostal Catholics: Power, Charisma, and Order in a Religious Movement*. Philadelphia: Temple University Press.

McLoughlin, William G. 1967. "Is There a Third Force in Christendom?" *Daedalus* 96 (Winter): 43–68.

———. 1978. *Revivals, Awakenings, and Reform: An Essay on Religion and Social Change in America, 1607–1977*. Chicago: University of Chicago Press.

McNamara, Patrick H. 1985. "American Catholicism in the Mid-Eighties: Pluralism and Conflict in a Changing Church." *The Annals of the American Academy of Political and Social Science* 480 (July): 63–74.

Mead, Sydney. 1956. "From Coercion to Persuasion: Another Look at the Rise of Religious Liberty and the Emergence of Denominationalism." *Church History* 25 (December): 317–337.

Merton, Robert K. 1957. "Patterns of Influence: Local and Cosmopolitan Influentials." Pp. 387–420 in *Social Theory and Social Structure*. Revised edition. Glencoe, Ill.: The Free Press.

Metz, Donald L. 1979. The Dysfunctions of Ritual Innovation. Paper presented at Annual Meeting of the Association for the Sociology of Religion, Boston.

Millman, Marcia. 1976. *The Unkindest Cut: Life in the Backrooms of Medicine*. New York: William Morrow.

Miyakawa, T. Scott. 1964. *Protestants and Pioneers: Individualism and Conformity on the American Frontier*. Chicago: University of Chicago Press.

Moberg, David O. 1977. *The Great Reversal: Evangelism and Social Concern*. Revised ed. Philadelphia: J. B. Lippincott.

Moore, Helen A., and Whitt, Hugh P. 1986. "Multiple Dimensions of the Moral Majority Platform: Shifting Interest Group Coalitions." *Sociological Quarterly* 27 (September): 423–439.

Morgan, Edmund S. 1965. *Visible Saints: The History of a Puritan Idea*. Ithaca, N.Y.: Cornell University Press.

Mouw, Richard J. 1976. "New Alignments: Hartford and the Future of Evangelicalism." Pp. 99–125 in Berger and Neuhaus, 1976.

Neal, Marie Augusta. 1965. *Values and Interests in Social Change*. Englewood Cliffs, N.J.: Prentice-Hall.

Neitz, Mary Jo. 1981. "Family, State, and God: Ideologies of the Right-to-Life Movement." *Sociological Analysis* 42 (Fall): 265–276.

———. 1986. *Charisma and Community: A Study of Religious Commitment Within the Catholic Charismatic Renewal*. New Brunswick, N.J.: Transaction Books.

Nelsen, Hart M., and Potvin, Raymond H. 1977. "The Rural Church and Rural Religion." *The Annals of the American Academy of Political and Social Science* 429 (January): 103–114.

Neuhaus, Richard John. 1984. *The Naked Public Square: Religion and Democracy in America*. Second edition. Grand Rapids, Mich.: Eerdmans.

———. 1985. "What the Fundamentalists Want." *Commentary* 79 (May): 41–46.

Niebuhr, H. Richard. 1929. *The Social Sources of Denominationalism*. New York: Henry Holt.

Niebuhr, Reinhold. 1932. *Moral Man in Immoral Society*. New York: Scribner's.

Norman, Edward. 1979. *Christianity and the World Order*. Oxford: Oxford University Press.

Parsons, Talcott. 1951. *The Social System*. Glencoe, Ill.: The Free Press.

———. 1961. "An Outline of the Social System." Pp. 30–79 in Talcott Parsons, Edward Shils, Kaspar Naegele, and Jesse Pitts, eds., *Theories of Society*. New York: The Free Press.

———. 1969. "On the Concept of Value-Commitments." Pp. 439–472 in *Politics and Social Structure*. New York: The Free Press.

———. 1978. *Action Theory and the Human Condition*. New York: The Free Press.

Parsons, Talcott, and Bales, Robert Freed. 1955. *Family, Socialization, and Interaction Process*. Glencoe, Ill.: The Free Press.

Parsons, Talcott, and Platt, Gerald M. 1973. *The American University*. Cambridge: Harvard University Press.

Pekelis, Alexander. 1973. "Legal Techniques and Political Ideologies: A Comparative Study." Pp. 355–377 in Bendix et al., 1973.

Pelikan, Jaroslav. 1985. *Jesus Through the Centuries: His Place in the History of Culture*. New Haven: Yale University Press.

Peshkin, Alan. 1984. "Odd Man Out: The Participant Observer in an Absolutist Setting." *Sociology of Education* 57 (October): 254–264.

Pope, Liston. 1942. *Millhands and Preachers: A Study of Gastonia*. New Haven: Yale University Press.

Pratt, Henry J. 1972. *The Liberalization of American Protestantism: A Case Study in Complex Organizations*. Detroit: Wayne State University Press.

Proctor, William. 1979. *The Born-Again Christian Catalogue: A Complete Sourcebook for Evangelicals*. New York: M. Evans and Company.

Quebedeaux, Richard. 1972. *The Young Evangelicals: Revolution in Orthodoxy*. New York: Harper and Row.

———. 1976. *The New Charismatics*. Garden City, N.Y.: Doubleday.

———. 1978. *The Worldly Evangelicals*. San Francisco: Harper and Row.

Quinley, Harold E. 1974. "The Dilemma of an Activist Church: Protestant Religion in the Sixties and Seventies." *Journal for the Scientific Study of Religion* 13 (March): 1–21.

Raphael, Ray. 1985. *Cash Crop: An American Dream*. Mendocino, Calif.: The Ridge Times Press.

Richardson, James T. 1985. "The Active vs. Passive Convert: Paradigm Conflict in Conversion/Recruitment Research." *Journal for the Scientific Study of Religion* 24 (June): 163–179.

Richardson, James T.; Stewart, Mary White; and Simmonds, Robert B. 1979. *Organized Miracles: A Study of a Contemporary Youth, Communal, Fundamentalist Organization*. New Brunswick, N.J.: Transaction Books.

Rieder, Jonathan. 1985. *Canarsie: The Jews and Italians of Brooklyn Against Liberalism*. Cambridge: Harvard University Press.

Roof, Wade Clark. 1978. *Community and Commitment: Religious Plausibility in a Liberal Protestant Church*. New York: Elsevier.

————. 1985. "The Study of Social Change in Religion." Pp. 75–89 in Hammond, 1985.

Roof, Wade Clark; Hoge, Dean R.; Dyble, John E.; and Hadaway, C. Kirk. 1979. "Factors Producing Growth or Decline in United Presbyterian Congregations." Pp. 198–223 and 367–369 in Hoge and Roozen, 1979.

Roof, Wade Clark, and McKinney, William. 1985. "Denominational America and the New Religious Pluralism." *The Annals of the American Academy of Political and Social Science* 480 (July): 24–38.

Roozen, David A., and Carroll, Jackson W. 1979. "Recent Trends in Church Membership and Participation: An Introduction." Pp. 21–41 and 358–359 in Hoge and Roozen, 1979.

Roozen, David A.; McKinney, William M.; and Carroll, Jackson W. 1984. *Varieties of Religious Presence: Mission in Public Life.* New York: Pilgrim Press.

Roth, Guenther. 1975. "Socio-Historical Model and Developmental Theory: Charismatic Community, Charisma of Reason and the Counterculture." *American Sociological Review* 40 (April): 148–157.

Rothenberg, Stuart, and Newport, Frank. 1984. *The Evangelical Voter: Religion and Politics in America.* Washington, D.C.: Institute for Government and Politics.

Rueschemeyer, Dietrich. 1986. *Power and the Division of Labor.* Stanford: Stanford University Press.

SAUS. (See U.S. Census, 1986)

Schaeffer, Francis A. 1970. *The Church at the End of the Twentieth Century.* Downers Grove, Ill.: Inter-Varsity Press.

Scheff, Thomas J. 1967. "Toward a Sociological Model of Consensus." *American Sociological Review* 32 (February): 32–46.

Schelling, Thomas C. 1963. *The Strategy of Conflict.* New York: Oxford University Press.

Schneider, Herbert Wallace. 1952. *Religion in Twentieth Century America.* Cambridge: Harvard University Press.

Shupe, Anson, and Stacey, William A. 1982. *Born-Again Politics and the Moral Majority: What Social Surveys Really Show.* New York: Edwin Mellen Press.

————. 1983. "The Moral Majority Constituency." Pp. 103–116 in Liebman and Wuthnow, 1983.

Sider, Ronald J. 1977. *Rich Christians in an Age of Hunger: A Biblical Study.* Downers Grove, Ill.: Inter-Varsity Press.

Simmel, Georg. 1965. "The Poor." *Social Problems* 13 (Fall): 118–140.

Simpson, John H. 1983. "Moral Issues and Status Politics." Pp. 187–205 in Liebman and Wuthnow, 1983.

————. 1985. "Status Inconsistency and Moral Issues." *Journal for the Scientific Study of Religion* 24 (June): 155–162.

Smylie, James H. 1979. "Church Growth and Decline in Historic Perspective: Protestant Quest for Identity, Leadership, and Meaning." Pp. 69–93 in Hoge and Roozen, 1979.

Snow, David A., and Machalek, Richard. 1982. "On the Presumed Fragility of

Unconventional Beliefs." *Journal for the Scientific Study of Religion* 21 (March): 15–26.

———. 1984. "The Sociology of Conversion." *Annual Review of Sociology* 10: 167–190.

Snyder, Howard A. 1975. *The Problem of Wineskins: Church Structure in a Technological Age.* Downers Grove, Ill.: Inter-Varsity Press.

Stark, Rodney, and Glock, Charles Y. 1968. *American Piety: The Nature of Religious Commitment.* Berkeley and Los Angeles: University of California Press.

Stark, Rodney, and Bainbridge, William Sims. 1985. *The Future of Religion: Secularization, Revival, and Cult Formation.* Berkeley, Los Angeles, London: University of California Press.

Stinchcombe, Arthur L. 1968. *Constructing Social Theories.* New York: Harcourt, Brace and World.

Stump, Roger W. 1984. "Regional Migration and Religious Commitment in the United States." *Journal for the Scientific Study of Religion* 23 (September): 292–303.

Swatos, William H., Jr. 1979. *Into Denominationalism: The Anglican Metamorphosis.* Storrs, Conn.: Society for the Scientific Study of Religion.

———. 1981. "Beyond Denominationalism?: Community and Culture in American Religion." *Journal for the Scientific Study of Religion* 20 (September): 217–227.

Swidler, Ann. 1986. "Culture in Social Action: Symbols and Strategies." *American Sociological Review* 51 (April): 273–286.

Tamney, Joseph B., and Johnson, Stephen D. 1983. "The Moral Majority in Middletown." *Journal for the Scientific Study of Religion* 22 (June): 145–157.

———. 1985. "Research Note: Christianity and the Nuclear Issue." *Sociological Analysis* 46 (Fall): 321–327.

Tipton, Steven M. 1982. *Getting Saved From the Sixties.* Berkeley, Los Angeles, London: University of California Press.

Tocqueville, Alexis de. 1945. *Democracy in America.* Two volumes. New York: Knopf.

Troeltsch, Ernst. 1931. *The Social Teaching of the Christian Churches.* New York: Macmillan.

Turner, Victor. 1977. *The Ritual Process: Structure and Anti-Structure.* New edition. Ithaca, N.Y.: Cornell University Press.

UPCUSA. 1960–1982. *Minutes of the General Assembly, Part III* [or] *Part II: The Statistical Tables and Presbytery Rolls* [1959–1981]. Philadelphia [1960–1973] or New York [1974–1982]: United Presbyterian Church in the United States of America.

———. 1980. "Presbyterian Panel Findings: The January, 1980, Questionnaire." United Presbyterian Church in the United States of America, Advisory Council on Discipleship and Worship.

U.S. Census, 1986. *Statistical Abstract of the United States, 1986.* 106th edition. Washington, D.C.: Bureau of the Census.

Vandenbosch, Amry. 1927. *The Dutch Communities of Chicago.* Chicago: The Knickerbocker Society.

Vitz, Paul C. 1986. "Religion and Traditional Values in Public School Textbooks." *The Public Interest* 84 (Summer): 79–90.

Wach, Joaquim. 1944. *Sociology of Religion*. Chicago: University of Chicago Press.

Wald, Kenneth D. 1987. *Religion and Politics in the United States*. New York: St. Martin's Press.

Wallace, Ruth. 1973. "The Secular Ethic and the Spirit of Patriotism." *Sociological Analysis* 34 (Spring): 3–11.

Wallis, Jim. 1981. "Community." *Sojourners* 10 (October): 25–28.

Warner, R. Stephen. 1979. "Theoretical Barriers to the Understanding of Evangelical Christianity." *Sociological Analysis* 40 (Spring): 1–9.

———. 1981a. Review of Hoge and Roozen, 1979. *Sociological Analysis* 42 (Spring): 73–74.

———. 1981b. Review of Hadden and Swann, 1981. *Sociological Analysis* 42 (Winter): 376–378.

———. 1983. "Research Note: Visits to a Growing Evangelical and a Declining Liberal Church in 1978." *Sociological Analysis* 44 (Fall): 243–253.

———. 1985. "Monistic and Dualistic Religion." Rodney Stark, ed., *Religious Movements: Genesis, Exodus, and Numbers*. Pp. 199–200. New York: Paragon House.

Wax, Rosalie. 1971. *Doing Fieldwork: Warnings and Advice*. Chicago: University of Chicago Press.

Weber, Max. 1922. *Economy and Society: Outline of Interpretive Sociology*. Ed. Guenther Roth and Claus Wittich. Totowa, N.J.: The Bedminster Press, 1968.

———. 1930. *The Protestant Ethic and the Spirit of Capitalism*. Translated by Talcott Parsons. New York: Scribner's.

———. 1968. *On Charisma and Institution-Building: Selected Papers*. Ed. S. N. Eisenstadt. Chicago: University of Chicago Press.

———. 1985. "'Churches' and 'Sects' in North America: An Ecclesiastical Sociopolitical Sketch." *Sociological Theory* 3 (Spring): 7–13.

Wells, David F., and Woodbridge, John D. 1975. *The Evangelicals: What They Believe, Who They Are, Where They Are Changing*. Nashville: Abingdon Press.

Wilcox, Clyde. 1986. "Evangelicals and Fundamentalists in the New Christian Right: Religious Differences in the Ohio Moral Majority." *Journal for the Scientific Study of Religion* 25 (September): 355–363.

Williams, Robin M. 1970. *American Society: A Sociological Interpretation*. New York: Knopf.

Wills, Garry. 1972. *Bare Ruined Choirs: Doubt, Prophecy, and Radical Religion*. New York: Delta Books.

Wilson, John. 1973. *Introduction to Social Movements*. New York: Basic Books.

Winter, J. Alan. 1974. "Elective Affinities Between Religious Beliefs and Ideologies of Management in Two Eras." *American Journal of Sociology* 79 (March): 1134–1150.

Wolin, Sheldon S. 1985. Archaism and Modernity. Paper presented to the Annual Meeting of the American Sociological Association, Washington, D.C.

Wood, James R. 1981. *Leadership in Voluntary Organizations: The Controversy Over Social Action in Protestant Churches.* New Brunswick, N.J.: Rutgers University Press.

Wood, Michael, and Hughes, Michael. 1984. "The Moral Basis of Moral Reform: Status Discontent vs. Culture and Socialization as Explanations of Anti-Pornography Social Movement Adherence." *American Sociological Review* 49 (February): 86–99.

Woodward, Kenneth L. 1986. "From Mainline to 'Sideline.'" *Newsweek* 108 (December 22): 54–56.

Wuthnow, Robert. 1983. "The Political Rebirth of American Evangelicals." Pp. 167–185 in Liebman and Wuthnow, 1983.

———. 1985. American Democracy and the Democratization of American Religion. Paper presented to Annual Meeting of the American Sociological Association, Washington, D.C.

Wuthnow, Robert, and Christiano, Kevin. 1979. "The Effects of Residential Migration on Church Attendance in the United States." Pp. 257–276 in Robert Wuthnow, ed., *The Religious Dimension: New Directions in Quantitative Research.* New York: Academic Press.

Yearbooks. 1961–1986.

> *Yearbook of American and Canadian Churches, 1973* [through] *1986.* Ed. by Constant H. Jacquet, Jr. Nashville: Abingdon.
>
> *Yearbook of American Churches, 1972.* Ed. by Constant H. Jacquet, Jr. Nashville: Abingdon.
>
> *Yearbook of American Churches, 1970* [and] *1971.* Ed. by Constant H. Jacquet, Jr. New York: National Council of Churches.
>
> *Yearbook of American Churches, 1969* [and] *1968.* Ed. by Lauris B. Whitman. New York: National Council of Churches.
>
> *Yearbook of American Churches, 1967.* Ed. by Constant H. Jacquet, Jr. New York: National Council of Churches.
>
> *Yearbook of American Churches, 1961* [through] *1966.* Ed. by B. Y. Landis. New York: National Council of Churches.

Zablocki, Benjamin. 1971. *The Joyful Community.* Baltimore: Penguin Books.

Zaret, David. 1985. *The Heavenly Contract: Ideology and Organization in Pre-Revolutionary Puritanism.* Chicago: University of Chicago Press.

Acknowledgments

It is a pleasant but humbling duty to recall the help I received in my work on this book. Though I alone am responsible for its shortcomings, its value has many sources.

My greatest debt is to the people of Mendocino, present and past, living and dead. They opened to me not only their homes but also their lives; some, their hearts. I benefited from their confidences, their hospitality, and their interest. Portions of the manuscript were read by several of them, and I was saved from numerous errors of fact and oversight by their comments. I regret that I cannot thank them by name, but I am delighted to make an exception in the case of Lea Anderson, a member of Mendocino Presbyterian Church, who did the illustrations.

It is fitting that I record my obligation to the scholarly institutions that have fostered my work. I was enjoying a year's leave under a fellowship from the John Simon Guggenheim Memorial Foundation when the project was conceived, with results that neither the foundation nor I anticipated. I deeply appreciate the intellectual freedom made possible by the foundation and the confidence in my work that the fellowship represented. I wish also to thank Yale University for the Junior Faculty Fellowship I was granted for 1974–1975.

The University of Illinois at Chicago facilitated the completion of the project through grants from its Graduate College Research Board and its Office of Social Science Research, through the collections and staff of its Main Library, through the facilities of its Computer Center, and especially through a fellowship awarded by its Institute for the Humanities, which gave me the time, the space, and much of the stimulation to write the most difficult parts of the book in 1984–1985. I am grateful to the officers and fellows of the Institute. The Department of Sociology at UIC, my academic home since 1977, has offered a congenial working environment under the headships of David P.

341

Street, John W. C. Johnstone, and Robert L. Hall. Anthony M. Orum has my best wishes.

The Research Committee of the Society for the Scientific Study of Religion, under the chairmanship of Jeffrey K. Hadden, gave me a grant in 1982 for follow-up field work and some strategic suggestions on ways to spend the money.

The Sociology departments at the University of California, San Diego, Stanford University, and Northwestern University offered me their hospitality during peripatetic summers.

Friends, colleagues, and professional associates came to my aid in a variety of ways. In the earliest stages of the project, I was advised, edified and encouraged by Howard S. Becker, Bennett M. Berger, Jeffrey A. Berlant, Bliss C. Cartwright, Aaron Cicourel, Mary Curran, Fred Davis, Ellen Fine, Bruce M. Hackett, Christine Leigh Heyrman, Luiza Jatoba, Bruce C. Johnson, Bennetta Jules-Rosette, Joyce Ko-zuch, Janet Lever, Marcia Millman, Joanne Millot, Jonathan Rieder, Diane Rizzo, Neil J. Smelser, Susan Spinner, Ronnie Steinberg, Laura Teller and Lenore Weitzman. Without their help, I might have been lost in Mendocino.

When I was new to Chicago and to the sociology of religion, Joy C. Charlton, who was then at work on her study of women seminarians, helped me to understand what I had brought out of Mendocino by asking questions, offering suggestions, and insisting that I write The Story. Later, she took precious time from her schedule at Swarthmore College to read the manuscript front to back (in one long sitting, she claims), and her trenchant comments decisively shaped its final appearance.

My tutoring in qualitative studies of religion was furthered by Mary Jo Neitz, who at the time I met her was doing her dissertation on Catholic charismatics. Mary Jo's deep insights and vivid writing have inspired me for years. Her timely comments on early drafts of each chapter of the book, after she took a job at the University of Missouri, helped me keep on course even as they undoubtedly impeded her in our polite race to publication. (She won nonetheless.)

Others who gave me the benefit of their reactions to drafts of the manuscript in whole or in part are Patricia A. Adler, Peter Adler, Isaac Balbus, Lewis Coser, Kathleen S. Crittenden, Kai Erikson, Arthur W. Frank, Bruce Hackett, Sydney Halpern, Carol Heimer, Christine Heyrman, Benton Johnson, Howard Kerr, Rachael L. E. Kohn, Edward O. Laumann, John M. Mulder, Charlene Pyskoty, Wade Clark Roof, Michael Schudson, Mildred A. Schwartz, Barry Seltser, the late David Street, Michael R. Warner, Norbert Wiley, and Robert Wuthnow. Wuthnow provided especially penetrating comments on the next-to-last draft. Kathy Crittenden and Mildred Schwartz have been exemplary colleagues.

Through their own research in religion, several students provided me with valuable leads: Thekla Caldwell, Michael D. Matters, Daniel V. Olson, Javan B. Ridge, Jr., Richard Lee Rogers, and Elfriede Wedam.

Discussions with Michael Ames, Rosanna Hertz, Michael Lieber, Jonathan Rieder, Michael Schudson, Ronnie Steinberg, and Ann Swidler helped me get oriented to the world of book publishers. I was fortunate that Stan Holwitz was supervising the University of California Press display booth when I stopped by during the 1984 American Sociological Association meetings in San Antonio. His interest in my recitation then was affirmed later by the courtesy and professionalism with which he saw the book through publication. It has been a pleasure to work with Shirley Warren as managing editor.

I have been bemused by the discovery that computer technology is an interpersonal equalizer, as represented in the informal society of the UIC Sociology terminal room, where expertise is, as a rule, an inverse function of age. Leonard M. Greski, Vincent Parker, and Newton Suwe are three cases in point. James N. Pasquotto and Mike Matters provided capable research assistance and valuable perspective. Helen Hicks and Elizabeth Jaworski did most of the word processing, under the supervision of Sue Lopez of the Office of Social Science Research at UIC. The graphs were executed by Kwang Park, also of OSSR.

I hope that my own teachers, Reinhard Bendix, Kenneth Bock, Leo Lowenthal, Guenther Roth, Neil Smelser, Gardner Stout, and Sheldon Wolin, will find something of their own influence to enjoy in this book, for there is no other way I can repay them. My debt to Neil Smelser is particularly profound.

It gives me greatest pleasure to thank members of my family, who have been simply wonderful throughout. My father and stepmother, Robert and Helen Warner, have succored me in many years of vagabondage; they welcomed me for tours of rest and recreation from Mendocino in 1976 and continue to offer me a California abode. My mother, Ethelyn Seeman Warner, did not live to see the beginning of the project, let alone its conclusion, but I like to think that those who knew her will see something of her spirit reflected in the work. Besides, it was she who bequeathed me the battered Datsun in which I roamed the hills of Mendocino. My sister, Karlette Warner, family matriarch since 1972, accompanied me to Mendocino on several occasions as confidante and research assistant. In Palo Alto, she gave me an office in her home for two summers. Her husband, Ward Hoffman, is a voracious reader who always enjoyed discussing the project. My brother, Mike, challenged me with his skepticism of things religious and his passion for lean writing. He gave me quick and pointed feedback on the next-to-last draft. My former wife (called Jane herein) and members of her family have given me far more than their hospitality and advice. Concern for my son's upbringing was the first occasion for my interest in this project, and his story gives me faith in its findings. My parents-in-law, Alene Harrington and the late Joseph Harrington, Jr., have never known me as other than the would-be author of a book on a small-town church, yet their support was unwavering. My stepdaughter, Dove Heider, like me a country kid from California gone to the big city, charmed me with her literary imagination (most of the book's pseudonyms are her invention) and came to enjoy our conveniently late dinners. My fondest obligation is to my wife, Anne Heider, who has been implicated in this book since I met her in Mendocino, first as respondent, then choir director, then confidante and theoretical sounding-board, later as my most faithful reader, discussant, and critic. She read every chapter first in handwritten draft, then midway in the editing, and finally just before the manuscript went to press. Her knowledge of music and love of English have enriched the book (and my life). Her professional involvement in the world of churches complements my own. In such ways she has been my most appreciated colleague. But it is as her partner in life that I feel most blessed. Her hard work, wisdom, and serenity helped make our three-person household into a new family. Her steady confidence in me kept me at work in times of discouragement. Her own scholarship never prevented her from taking delight in the fruits of mine. Her love has been my joy.

Index

Designer:	U.C. Press Staff
Compositor:	Huron Valley Graphics, Inc.
Text:	Palatino 10/12
Display:	Palatino
Printer:	Maple-Vail Book Mfg. Group
Binder:	Maple-Vail Book Mfg. Group